APPEALING TO GOD OR MAN

APPEALING TO GOD OR MAN

Contrasting Barrenness
and Family Death Narratives
in the Hebrew Bible and Ancient Near East

NICHOLAS J. CAMPBELL

WIPF & STOCK · Eugene, Oregon

APPEALING TO GOD OR MAN
Contrasting Barrenness and Family Death Narratives in the Hebrew Bible and Ancient Near East

Copyright © 2025 Nicholas J. Campbell. All rights reserved. Except for brief quotations in critical publications or reviews, no part of this book may be reproduced in any manner without prior written permission from the publisher. Write: Permissions, Wipf and Stock Publishers, 199 W. 8th Ave., Suite 3, Eugene, OR 97401.

Wipf & Stock
An Imprint of Wipf and Stock Publishers
199 W. 8th Ave., Suite 3
Eugene, OR 97401

www.wipfandstock.com

PAPERBACK ISBN: 979-8-3852-3675-6
HARDCOVER ISBN: 979-8-3852-3676-3
EBOOK ISBN: 979-8-3852-3677-0

VERSION NUMBER 03/20/25

To Haloy
For your patience through my obsession

CONTENTS

Abbreviations | xi
Table | xii

CHAPTER 1
INTRODUCTION | 1
   Progeny in the ANE and HB | 2
   Research and Classification | 4
   Methodology | 10
   Outline of Chapters | 14

CHAPTER 2
MALE-CENTRIC FAMILY DEATH NARRATIVES IN THE ANE | 17
   Kirta Epic | 18
   Story of Aqhat | 23
   Babylonian Theodicy | 30
   Conclusion | 34

CHAPTER 3
FEMALE-CENTRIC FAMILY DEATH NARRATIVES IN THE HB | 36
   Lot's Daughters | 36
   Judah and Tamar | 41
   Zelophehad's Daughters | 47
   Conclusion | 51

CHAPTER 4
FEMALE-CENTRIC FAMILY DEATH NARRATIVE IN RUTH | 53
   Background Literature | 55
   Death of the Household in Moab | 58
   Joining the Household in Bethlehem | 69
   Renewed Fertility Through Boaz | 80
   Conclusion | 91

CHAPTER 5
MALE-CENTRIC FAMILY DEATH NARRATIVE IN JOB | 93
- Origin of Deaths | 94
- Loss of Inheritance | 96
- Restoration | 102
- Conclusion | 103

CHAPTER 6
BARRENNESS NARRATIVES IN THE HB AND ANE | 104
- Sarah | 105
- Rebekah | 112
- Rachel | 115
- Manoah's Wife | 121
- Hannah | 125
- Myth of Etana | 130
- Conclusion | 133

CHAPTER 7
COMPARISON OF THE PORTRAYAL OF PROGENY IN BARRENNESS AND FAMILY DEATH NARRATIVES | 134
- Barrenness and Family Death | 135
- Marriage and Barrenness | 136
- Divine and Human Responses: Barrenness and Family Death | 146
- Conclusion | 153

APPENDIX
FOUR NEAR MISSES: THE SHUNAMMITE WOMAN, THE TALE OF APPU, THE OLD MAN AND THE YOUNG GIRL, AND THE DOOMED PRINCE | 155
- The Shunammite Woman | 155
- The Tale of Appu | 159
- The Old Man and the Young Girl | 161
- The Tale of the Doomed Prince | 163

Bibliography | 171
Scripture Index | 223
Subjext Index | 227

ABBREVIATIONS

ANE	Ancient Near East
ANET	J. B. Pritchard, ed., *Ancient Near Eastern Texts Relating to the Old Testament*, 3rd ed. with supplement, Princeton: Princeton University Press, 1969
AoF	*Altorientalische Forschungen*
ATANT	*Abhandlungen zur Theologie des Alten und Neuen Testaments*
BAR	*Biblical Archaeology Review*
BDB	Francis Brown, S. R. Driver, and Charles A Briggs, *The Brown-Driver-Briggs Hebrew and English Lexicon: With an Appendix Containing the Biblical Aramaic*. Peabody, MA: Hendrickson, 2005
BibInt	*Biblical Interpretation*
BT	*The Bible Translator*
HALOT	Ludwig Koehler and Walter Baumgartner. *The Hebrew and Aramaic Lexicon of the Old Testament*, translated by M. E. J. Richardson, New York: Brill, 1994
HB	Hebrew Bible
HUCA	*Hebrew Union College Annual*
IDS	*In die Skriflig*
JBL	*Journal of Biblical Literature*
JHS	*Journal of Hebrew Scriptures*
JSOT	*Journal for the Study of the Old Testament*
OTE	*Old Testament Essays*
SJOT	*Scandinavian Journal of the Old Testament*

| VT | Vetus Testamentum |
| ZAW | Zeitschrift für die alttestamentliche Wissenschaft |

Table

Barrenness and Family Death | 136

CHAPTER 1

INTRODUCTION

THE ORIGIN OF THIS study is an article that I published on progeny in Job.[1] In the midst of this research, I increasingly noticed the similarity between Job and Ruth. Scholars have long noticed that the families die in both stories, but few have treated the progression toward a solution for the empty household in these narratives in depth.

A basic Google search for "Ruth and Job" shows the dearth of literature on the subject.[2] Among the search results related to biblical studies are a self-published book, *Understanding the Books of Ruth and Job: Kindness, Morality, Suffering and Justice*,[3] a bullet pointed, but insightful, blog post, "Ruth vs Job,"[4] and a second blog post, "Job, Naomi and Ruth."[5] Full-length monographs, academic articles, or even pastoral books and articles comparing Ruth and Job are not in the top page of search results, and the

---

1. Campbell, "God and Heirs," 150–62.
2. This was done in July of 2022.
3. This book apparently contrasts Ruth and Job with the understanding that Job was self-righteous and was punished because of his "hypocritical moral posturing," but Ruth shows God's mercy for those showing unceasing kindness. I think his understanding of Job's sinfulness is incorrect but, even still, the focus is upon the morality of the main characters, not their concern for progeny. Moseley, *Understanding the Books of Ruth and Job*.
4. This is essentially a list of similarities and differences between the two books. Some of the comparisons are quite insightful but, since it is in list form, little exploration or detail of these points is offered. Barrett, "Ruth vs Job."
5. This is a short post explaining how Job, Naomi, and Ruth are all characterized by faith, even though Naomi and Job offer deep criticism of God. Vandop, "Job, Naomi and Ruth."

subsequent pages are employment websites (interpreting "Job" as "job").[6] A deeper search of resources, specifically academic ones, results in studies that are concerned primarily with either Ruth or Job and reference the other book only secondarily.

Further research on the similarities between Ruth and Job led me to a much more expansive study. Not only are Ruth and Job similar, but family death narratives in general share similar narrative developments. These family death narratives are often considered barrenness narratives, but a comparison between biological barrenness (e.g., Sarah, Hannah, or Rachel in the HB) and family death narratives (e.g., Lot's daughters, Tamar, or Ruth in the HB) show two streams of plot development.

This book argues that barrenness and family death narratives contain unique elements that separate them into two narrative tropes. Specifically, it is the actions of the women that define the narrative types. In barrenness narratives, women appeal to God, but in family death narratives, women appeal to men. This difference between the two narrative tropes reflects the ANE perception of barrenness as a crisis within the woman's body that the divine alone can resolve, but family death can be resolved through remarriage, which is under the purview of men.

This chapter will provide an overview of the importance of progeny in the HB and ANE as well as current research and classifications of barrenness and family death narratives. I will conclude this chapter with the methodology and outline of the chapters.

Progeny in the ANE and HB

The need for heirs is a common theme in ANE literature. In the HB, the lack of heirs is a cause of distress (Gen 17:18–20; 20:17–18; 25:21; 29:31; 30:1) and even a curse from God (2 Sam 12:11–18; Exod 20:5).[7] However, a large family is seen as a blessing from God (Deut 4:40; 5:29; 7:14; 28:11; Exod 20:6; 23:26; Lev 26:9; Judg 13:2–3; 1 Sam 2:5; Pss 113:9; 115:14; 127:3–5). In these stories, it is not the children themselves that are the focus but progeny.[8] Phrases like "God opened/closed the womb" show that the authors were not

---

6. The primary scholarly text comparing Ruth and Job is an article (in Hebrew): Bazaq, "עולם חסד בנה' - בין מגילת רות לספר איוב' ['A World of Kindness Will Be Built'– Between the Scroll of Ruth and the Book of Job]," 169–75.

7. McKinlay, "Who's/Whose Sarah?," 141.

8. For additional exploration of fertility and barrenness as divine gifts and curses, see Perdue, "Household, Old Testament Theology," 223–58; Cook, "Death, Kinship, and Community," 106–21; Wilcox, *Bitterness of Job*.

viewing God's blessing or curse as the individual children themselves but the ability to produce offspring. Even the traditional blessings given to the patriarchs and the Israelites during the conquest have a multiplication focus ("offspring like sand on the seashore") rather than a focus upon individual children as the final, ultimate blessing.

Within the HB tradition, the father's name exists so long as it is attached to land.⁹ The father's house was the smallest social unit in Israel, and the continuation of the household is only possible through the inheritance of the family property.¹⁰ An example of this concern for the family name and its connection with property is Num 36 where the daughters of Zelophehad ask for an inheritance of land so their father's name is not cut off from among his brothers since he died without sons. The Mosaic remedy for the potential loss of Zelophehad's name is for the daughters to receive an inheritance, but they are then required to marry within the clan. The household name continuing in the inherited property is so valuable that special laws must be created to ensure that the father's household will continue even if there are no sons to inherit the property.¹¹ The value of children is the inheritance and continuation of the family line rather than the individual children themselves.

The importance of family is also echoed in other ANE texts like the Kirta Epic and the Story of Aqhat. The death of the main character's family in these texts causes a crisis that only the gods can remedy. Aqhat begins with Danel sacrificing in order to obtain a son. However, it is not just a child that he is desiring but a legitimate heir.¹² The request is for a son "who sets up the stelae of his ancestral spirits . . . who frees his spirit from the earth . . . drives off [those] who attacks his abode."¹³ Likewise, after Kirta's family

---

9. Milgrom, *Numbers* = במדבר, 231.

10. Ben-Barak, *Inheritance by Daughters*, 4n2. See also Bendor, *Social Structure of Ancient Israel*.

11. The daughters ask for a possession (אחזה Num 27:4) because they are afraid their father's name will be "cut off." They are granted a possession of inheritance by divine decree (אחזה נחלה Num 27:7). The added term has a specific meaning in ancient Israel. This property is more than just an estate owned by the family; it is an inheritance passed down through the generations. It is also important in the levirate marriage laws where a childless widow marries her husband's brother and their children take on the name and inheritance of the deceased (Deut 25:5–10). See also Westbrook, *Property and the Family*.

12. As Koowon Kim notes, "The lack of a legitimate son or a proper heir would be a deplorable state that begs to be rectified." Kim, *Incubation as a Type-Scene*, 100. See also Schloen, *House of the Father*, 48, 350.

13. Ginsberg, "Tale of Aqhat," 149–55. Wyatt, "Story of Aqhat," 246–312, KTU 1.17i:25–30.

dies in a series of tragedies, he asks El in a dream, "grant that I may beget children, that I multiply kinsmen."[14] In both instances, the plea is not for a specific child or the reinstating of one generation. Kirta and Danel are concerned with the eternal continuation of their household and multiplication of their family. They call upon the gods as those who hold the power of progeny and eternal life for mortals through heirs.[15]

Curses in the treaties of the ANE also link barrenness and fertility to divinity by calling down the gods' wrath on the wives and children of offenders.[16] A common phrase with only slight variations in numerous Hittite treaties is "you with your property, your wives and your sons, will have no offspring."[17] This is usually followed by more explicit agricultural imagery where the people are described as being pulled up like a plant. The continued progeny of the offender is destroyed like plants uprooted in a field. Here again, the focus of the curse is the gods' ability to end the family line by withholding heirs.

Research and Classification

In this book, I argue that women appeal to men and men appeal to the divine in the family death narratives, in contrast to the barrenness narratives where women interact with the divine directly. For example, Hannah prays for children in 1 Sam 1, and Sarah laughs when hearing the Lord talk in Gen 18. God hears Rachel (Gen 30), and an angel appears to Manoah's wife and speaks to her in Judg 13. These differences indicate a distinction between family death narratives and barrenness narratives. In this section, I will outline several categorizations that have been proposed by scholars and evaluate their advantages and some of their drawbacks. The categorizations are general barrenness (including family death narratives), the quest for an heir, birth of a hero and annunciation type-scenes, the conflict of the barren wife type-scene, and the trickster motif.

---

14. Ginsberg, "Legend of King Keret," 142–48. Wyatt, "Story of King Keret," 176–241, KTU 1.14ii:5.

15. Van der Toorn, *From Her Cradle to Her Grave*, 77–82; Ashley, "'Epic of AQHT' and the 'RPUM Texts,'" 340.

16. Rooy, "Fertility as Blessing and Infertility as Curse," 225–36; Finkel, "Dream of Kurigalzu," 75–80.

17. Kitchen and Lawrence, *Treaty, Law and Covenant*, 1:379, 397, 401, 417, 425.

Barrenness Category

In most academic literature, family death and barrenness are both categorized under barrenness narratives.[18] Janice De-Whyte utilizes the helpful term "social barrenness" to describe narratives where the women are not physically barren but still without children.[19] For example, Ruth is socially barren because she is without a husband and is following her mother-in-law. However, she is not physically barren because she gives birth to Obed later in the narrative. This definition is helpful when categorizing women of marriageable age without children as "barren." However, it is a sociological category rather than an element within the narrative. The family death narratives do not describe the women as "socially barren," and the women in the family death narratives do not respond to their crisis in the same way as the women in the barrenness narratives. For this reason, the concept of socially barren might be helpful in recognizing that the women experiencing family death are seeking, but not having, children, but it is not helpful in identifying characteristics of the biblical or ANE narratives. Simply labeling them as "barrenness" narratives because the women do not have children, as many scholars do, is unhelpful and uses the term "barren" in an uncommon and overly broad way.

The Quest for an Heir

J. David Schloen claims, "Action stemming from the 'house of the father' can also be found in later biblical narratives; for example, in the patriarchal narratives of the book of Genesis and in the stories about the Israelite kings. Such plot structures include 'the quest for an heir' (with subplots concerning 'the lack/death of an heir' and 'the search for a suitable wife')."[20]

The challenge of this model is that "the quest for an heir" is so broad that it encompasses nearly every household in the ANE and HB. With this plot, narratives almost unrelated to each other are considered similar or subplots of a single plot structure. For example, Jacob charged Isaac with finding a suitable wife and sent him to Paddan-aram (Gen 28). The lack of an heir for Rachel, though not for Jacob, is described in Gen 29:31—30:22.

---

18. Kramer, "Barrenness"; White, "Deconstructing Barrenness in the Texts"; Moss and Baden, *Reconceiving Infertility*; De-Whyte, *Wom(b)an*; Claassens, "Resisting Dehumanization," 659–74; van Wolde, *Ruth and Naomi*; Green, "Plot of the Biblical Story," 55–68; Sutskover, "Themes of Land and Fertility," 283–94; Havrelock, "Myth of Birthing the Hero," 154–78; Grohmann, "Barrenness," 546–47.

19. De-Whyte, *Wom(b)an*, 252.

20. Schloen, *House of the Father*, 48.

These are two subplots of the quest for an heir but have little in common. Isaac and Jacob are the primary actors in Gen 28, Isaac and Laban in Gen 29 with the bridal deception narrative, but the women are the primary characters in the competition for children between the sisters. In addition, one narrative is concerned with births while the other is concerned with endogamy.

With the broad concept of finding a suitable wife, even Gen 2 could fit this category as God made the woman as a "suitable helper" for the man (v. 20).[21] However, this does not appear to be a quest for an heir nor related to barrenness or family death narratives. Therefore, a narrower description of the plot is necessary. As will be demonstrated "the lack/death of an heir" should be split into separate narratives as their plots develop quite differently.

Birth of a Hero and Annunciation Type-Scenes

Robert Alter calls the narratives about barren women the "annunciation type-scene"[22] while others call it "the birth of a hero"[23] narrative. Alter's focus is on the divine interaction with the women in the narratives. God or angels are "announcing" the miraculous birth of a child. The "birth of a hero" classification emphasizes the importance of the child who is born.[24]

---

21. All HB translations are my own unless otherwise noted.

22. Alter, "How Convention Helps Us Read," 119; Knight, "Apparitions and Appellations," 99. Coats agrees with Westermann and claims this is part of the texts about divine annunciation healing a barren wife. Coats, *Genesis*, 137–38; Westermann, *Genesis 12–36*, 275. See also Muñoz Iglesias, "Procedimiento Literario del Anuncio Previo," 58; Tatko, "Vowing Mothers and Avowed Sons," 132–50; Wenham, *Genesis 16–50*, 40; Irvine, "'Is Anything Too Hard for Yahweh?,'" 295–97; Rosenberg, "בעת חיה," 701–20; Williams, "Beautiful and the Barren," 110; Fuchs, "Literary Characterization of Mothers and Sexual Politics," 117–36; Fuchs, *Sexual Politics in the Biblical Narrative*, 49–65.

Scott A. Ashmon claims there is "no single fixed form for the annunciation itself in the HB and ANE." Ashmon, *Birth Annunciations*, 366. Similarly Timothy Finlay offers some reservations on this structural comparison. Finlay, *Birth Report Genre in the Hebrew Bible*, 216–18; Johnson, "Barrenness, Birth, and Biblical Allusions."

23. Birth of the hero or annunciation type-scene has been argued by Athalya Brenner, and she also connects it with conflict between the wives in the narratives. Brenner, "Female Social Behaviour," 257–73. Also Cook, *Hannah's Desire, God's Design*, 10; You, "Historian's Heroines," 181; Willis, "Cultic Elements," 40; Exum, *Fragmented Women*, 120; McAfee, "Patriarch's Longed-for Son."

24. Joan Cook calls this the "barren mother type" while also emphasizing that the children become pivotal leaders. She divides the type-scene into three models, and all of them share the important son feature. Cook, "Hannah's Initiative, God's Fulfillment," 12.

The problem with these classifications is that they lose the central character: the woman.[25] As Lee Young Gil notes:

> What should not be overlooked is that hero studies are typically focused on men rather than women . . . . a *male* child becomes the central character of the subsequent stories. Thus, within research on heroic biographical patterns, the mother characters who are prominent in the HB birth narratives have no place in the discussion. An associated problem connected with this issue is that, most unfortunately, female heroes have largely been ignored in the folklore studies devoted to the heroic pattern.[26]

The children are flat background characters in the barrenness narratives, even if they become heroes later. For example, 1 Sam 1 is focused upon Hannah, not Samuel, because he is not born yet. Likewise, Isaac is promised in Gen 18 but does not become an active character until chapter 24. Also, the divine interactions do not necessarily indicate that the women will have heroic children. Rachel is barren, and all that is indicated is God remembered her, and she was thankful that God took away her reproach (Gen 30:22–23). Hannah asks for a child and promises to dedicate him to the temple in 1 Sam 1:11, the text records that God remembered her, and she conceived (v. 19). However, nothing in Hannah's barrenness narrative, nor Rachel's narrative, indicates that the child will be a hero. This could be assumed because the biblical text portrays significant characters and events rather than the births of average farmers or herders, but barrenness narratives are focused upon the women experiencing the crises not their children. This makes the "birth of a hero" identification problematic.

The annunciation type-scene is also a challenge. First, the women do not always receive an "annunciation" in the sense of a divine oracle from on high. God remembers Rachel, but neither Rachel nor any of the other characters in Gen 30 receive divine announcements. Likewise, the barrenness stories of Rebekah (Gen 25) and Hannah (1 Sam 1) record people praying for children, but they do not record a divine annunciation that the prayer has been answered. Lee critiques this category as well, claiming:

> Although Alter's type-scene—betrothal or annunciation—ultimately sparked much discussion about female/mother characters, it does not fully encompass all of the women in HB birth narratives. Most of all, Alter does not include Hagar in his annunciation type-scene since he regards the motif of barrenness

---

25. See Amit's acknowledgment of the emphasis on Manoah's wife in Amit, "'Manoah Promptly Followed His Wife,'" 146–56.

26. Lee, "From Fertility to Manipulation," 15.

as essential for this type-scene. Hagar is not barren, despite the fact that she clearly receives the birth annunciation.[27]

Second, and more importantly, the narrative focus is upon the human characters not the divine character. This human focus is true throughout the HB and ANE. The Genesis narratives are called the patriarchal narratives with individual narratives referred to by the name of the patriarch involved: Abraham, Isaac, Jacob, one of Jacob's sons, or another significant human character who is driving the plot. They are not called "God's intervention to build a nation" narratives. In the same way, the human judges are the focus of Judges and the human monarchs are the focus of Kings and Chronicles. Even the redaction-critical scholars name the elements of 1–2 Samuel as "the Saul Cycle," "David's Ascension," and "the Succession Narrative." They are not labeled as the "Chronicles of God's Judgment of Royalty" or "God's Choosing the House of David." ANE texts are also named for their leading human characters when they are the primary characters. For example, the texts examined in this book are referred to as the epics of Kirta, Etana, and Aqhat rather than El, Shamash, and Anat, even though the divine figures all have lengthy discourses with the human characters. For some reason, though, when God is interacting with the barren women, the stress falls on divine annunciation rather than women who are appealing for fertility.

This might seem like a minor disagreement over labeling conventions, but the name "barrenness narratives" highlights the main character and crisis in the narratives: the women experiencing barrenness. Focusing upon the heirs or God's intervention does not account for all the features of the barrenness narratives and relegates the main character to a simple conduit for introducing the hero or divine speech.

Conflict of the Barren Wife

Another type-scene that overlaps with the texts included in the barrenness narratives is the "conflict of the barren wife."[28] This conflict narrative is found in the struggles of Sarah and Hagar, Rachel and Leah, and Hannah and Peninnah. The connection between the favor of the husband and barrenness is significant, but it is only found in a selection of the barrenness

27. Lee, "From Fertility to Manipulation," 11.

28. Williams claims the Sarah and Hagar narrative is an example of the "agon (conflict) of the barren wife" type-scene along with the Leah and Rachel narrative. Williams, "Beautiful and the Barren," 109. See also Roskoski, "Isaac and Samson," 198–215; Gaiser, "Sarah, Hagar, Abraham—Hannah, Peninnah, Elkanah," 273–84; Klein, "Hannah," 77–92; Leitch, "Redeeming Peninnah," 280–91; Leshem, "Two Biblical Families," 1–15.

narratives, as many scholars have already noted.[29] Instead of a unique typescene, the conflict of the barren wife appears to be a subset of the barrenness narratives. Some of the barrenness narratives contain the secondary conflict motif, so it is a variation of the larger barrenness trope.

Trickster Motif

Several scholars have categorized the narratives as trickster motifs. For example, Sandra Collins examines Lot's daughters, Tamar, Ruth, and Bathsheba. She describes them as tricksters who use sexuality and guile to resolve their respective issues.[30] She acknowledges that they do not pray to God like Sarah, Rebekah, Rachel, and Hannah but does not explore this in depth. Instead of comparing responses to death in the family by men and women in the HB and ANE, Collins only focuses on the four "trickster" narratives and their place in the HB. Another scholar, Melissa Jackson, compares Tamar with Lot's daughters, and in her later book with Rebekah, Leah, and Rachel, calling all six women "trickster matriarchs."[31]

Though an element of trickery is found within these narratives, the development of the plot is quite different, as are their methods of trickery. For example, Lot's daughters and Bathsheba are encountering different circumstances, and the experiences of an affair with the king (initiated by the king) versus incest with one's father (initiated by the daughters) are hard to relate together. Similarly, Rebekah experiences barrenness, but her tricks are about inheritance division not conception like Tamar and Lot's daughters.

Unlike the trickster analyses, I compare family death narratives to barrenness narratives within conception, or desire for conception, narratives rather than inheritance, extra-marital affairs, or other narratives. I also focus more heavily upon the need for heirs and the responses of the women to the crises than the trickster elements of the female protagonists (though these are noted in the relevant places).

---

29. See Williams, "Beautiful and the Barren," 109; Gaiser, "Sarah, Hagar, Abraham—Hannah, Peninnah, Elkanah."

30. Collins, *Weapons upon Her Body*; Jackson, "Lot's Daughters and Tamar as Tricksters," 29–46; Shields, "'More Righteous than I,'" 31–51; Doniger, *Bedtrick*; Pietersen and Fourie, "Bible, Culture and Ethics," 1–8; Chan, "Ultimate Trickster in the Story of Tamar," 94–95; Mathewson, "Exegetical Study of Genesis 38," 378; Niditch, "Samson as Cultural Hero," 611. See further Adelman, *Female Ruse*; and the collection of essays on trickster narratives in Exum and Van Wijk-Bos, *Reasoning with the Foxes*.

31. Jackson, "Lot's Daughters and Tamar as Tricksters," 44; Jackson, *Comedy and Feminist Interpretation*.

Methodology

In order to analyze the texts in a coherent way, one foundational definition and the two methodological procedures used in this study must be explained. I can then discuss how genre affects my argument and methodology. The foundational consideration is a working definition of type-scene and how these narrative conventions are identified within the text.

In this work, "trope" and "type-scene" are used interchangeably while "elements" refer to the constituent parts of the type-scene (e.g., barrenness or family death) or the sections of a specific narrative (e.g., Judah and Tamar, Ruth, Myth of Etana, etc.). The concept of type-scene is based on Alter's argument, and many other scholars after (see the "Research and Classification" section above), that HB and ANE narratives have literary conventions that can be identified in certain types of narratives.[32] Specifically, plots in barrenness and family death narratives develop in conventional ways that the audience would understand and, to a certain extent, expect when they encountered these types of narratives. My argument builds upon this observation, arguing that these literary conventions reflect human crises and responses in real life. These type-scenes obviously have variations, as will be shown, but they also represent idealized or mythologized responses to crises.

The first methodological procedure is the selection of texts. This is most important in the ANE section but will also be a factor in the discussion of the biblical passages. The selection of family death narratives is threefold: the text must contain the death of the family (whole or partial), the character(s) or narrator must attribute their situation to God, and the text should describe the restoration of the family (whole or partial). Not every text discussed will contain all these elements for a variety of reasons. For example, ANE texts are often damaged or incomplete, so if the ending is missing, restoration may have been in the original text, but it is no longer clear in the extant text. Another consideration is that the divine origin of the deaths might be implicit rather than explicitly stated in the narrative. As noted above, family death and infertility were often considered divine curses, so divine disfavor might be assumed in an unexpected death even though the text does not state the divine origin. Therefore, overly rigid application of these criteria may exclude texts that should be considered. With these considerations, the texts explored in the family death narrative study must have at least two of the three criteria to be included. The purpose of the criteria is to separate the family death narratives from the barrenness

---

32. Alter, "How Convention Helps Us Read," 128; Alter, *Art of Biblical Narrative*, 47–62.

narratives. Using these criteria, the family death narratives are Lot's daughters (Gen 19), Judah and Tamar (Gen 38), Zelophehad's daughters (Num 27), Ruth, and Job in the HB and the Kirta Epic, the Story of Aqhat, and the Babylonian Theodicy in the ANE.

The second group of texts, the barrenness narratives, has similar criteria. The texts must contain barrenness (entire household or an individual in the household), the character(s) or narrator must attribute their situation to God, and the text should describe the restoration of the family (whole or partial). The barrenness aspect should be physical barrenness caused by infertility not death or social isolation (e.g., Lot's daughters) like the family death narratives. Again, each narrative must contain at least two of these criteria to be included in the barrenness category. Utilizing these criteria, the barrenness narratives in this study are Sarah (Gen 18), Rebekah (Gen 25), Rachel (Gen 30), Manoah's wife (Judg 13), and Hannah (1 Sam 1) in the HB and the Myth of Etana in the ANE.

The second methodological procedure is the structure of analysis. The family death narratives will be analyzed according to three aspects: the origin of deaths, discussion of land inheritance, and restoration of the household. These three elements have been selected because they appear to be the most prominent parts of the search for heirs in the lengthiest and most complete family death narratives, Job and Ruth. The goal of analyzing each text according to these three elements is to create a foundation upon which the texts can be assessed equally. A summary of the narrative for every text will be provided, and then the three major narrative elements will be examined to focus upon the shared narrative plot points. For example, in this study very little space will be devoted to the siege of Udum in the Kirta Epic, but the description of Kirta's son, Yasib, as "the heir" will be given special attention because it is part of household restoration and especially the fulfillment of the search for an inheritor. The siege of Udum is also part of this fulfillment as Kirta was attempting to obtain a wife by force, but the description of the siege is less important for this study than the marital purpose of the siege.

The barrenness narratives have a similar analysis structure. The framework is again threefold: description of barrenness, interaction with the divine, and restoration. The first and last elements are similar to the family death narratives, but the second is different. Inheritance is significant in the family death narratives and the barrenness narratives. However, it is more prominent in the family death narratives, as the family has an heir or a family capable of producing an heir but then the heir or family member dies. In the barrenness narratives, the need for an inheritor is less prominent as the women appear to be unable to bear any children, sons or daughters. The theme throughout the barrenness narratives is (female) infertility rather than the desire for a specific inheritor. In addition, the barrenness narratives and family death narratives are separated based upon the women's appeal to the divine in barrenness narratives, unlike their appeal to men in the family death narratives. Therefore, the second element in this framework shows how women, sometimes with men, interact directly with the divine.[33]

Preliminary Remarks About Genre

Genre must be considered when applying these narrative elements to the texts. The identification of a text's genre can sometimes be clear, law codes versus narrative, but often it is quite murky. Genre classifications are descriptors but frequently rely upon the reader to interpret the text in a certain way to find the appropriate elements of the genre. For example, the identification of Ruth as an idyll relies upon a generally positive reading of the text.[34] However, recently, post-colonial and feminist readings have questioned how idyllic the book truly is when it narrates the story of an impoverished foreigner whose mother-in-law forces her to sexually entrap a wealthy man in the middle of the night in order to provide financial security for her and her daughter-in-law.[35] As Wyatt observes, "Not only is one man's myth another man's history, but 'epic,' 'legend,' 'saga,' and 'folktale' can all be (or if they cannot, or should not be, they *are*) used to denote the same texts. Some scholars even use two or three of these terms for the same composition in the same discussion."[36]

For this study, finer categorizations of genre for each text do not need to be resolved definitively. However, the texts must contain a storyline. Law codes about land redemption and levirate marriage are relevant to Ruth and the Tamar and Judah narrative. In the same way, inheritance laws, especially for daughters, help readers understand the ending of Job. Law codes, though, do not contain narrative elements. So, they may assist in identifying

---

33. Implied in these methodological criteria is the exclusion of metaphorical descriptions of barrenness. For the purposes of this study, they lack the experience of the individual(s) and are often found in prophecies rather than narrative. In addition, scholars have noted that the imagery of barren nations or cities is different from barrenness experienced by individuals in the description of the experience and the terminology. See Blessing, "Desolate Jerusalem and Barren Matriarch," 47–69.

34. Gunkel, "Rut," 2180–82; Würthwein, *Fünf Megilloth*; Zakovitch, *Buch Rut*; Myers, *Linguistic and Literary Form of Ruth*.

35. Fischer, "Book of Ruth as Exegetical Literature," 140–49; Zenger, *Buch Ruth*; Levinson, *Legal Revision and Religious Renewal*.

36. Wyatt, "Epic in Ugaritic Literature," 246, italics original.

the background in which the events of a narrative are happening, but they do not contain the specific elements of death and restoration of the family (though they may have laws regulating how to deal with these situations). Therefore, law codes will be discussed in the final chapter where they provide necessary information for understanding the narratival categories suggested in this study, but neither ANE nor HB laws will be the focus of the study.

Though narratives are the ideal type of text, much of Job and some of the ANE texts contain lengthy dialogues. For example, the Babylonian Theodicy is an acrostic poem made up of speeches from two friends. This is obviously not narrating a sequence of events but recording a discussion about justice and divine order, much like the dialogues in Job. However, though the events do not progress the way they would in a narrative, the sufferer's description of the tragedies befalling his family illustrate that narrative elements are a necessary part of the discussion. In other words, though the death of the family and issues of land inheritance are not presented sequentially, as they would be in a narrative, they are still present. Even more importantly, the speakers attribute these events to divinity or sin and present what they believe to be the correct course of action to resolve the problem. Though the dialogues present the crises in argumentative speech, one of the characters typically claims the events happened in their life so there is an assumed narrative setting behind the speeches, even if it is not explicitly described, unlike Job, whose narrative setting is presented in the prologue and epilogue.

Another genre that presents interpretive issues is the epic. The challenge for comparing Ruth, and to a lesser extent Job, to ANE texts is that some of the ANE texts, specifically Kirta, Aqhat, and Etana, are epics.[37] The minimalist definition of epics is a "heroic and ideological narrative, generally poetic in form, which seeks to promote the identity, values, and concerns of a culture."[38] The ANE epics especially describe heroes and gods speaking and performing super-human feats.[39] Ruth, as noted by scholars using terms like "idyll" and "novella," does not contain obviously super-human acts nor conversations between humans and the divine. Job contains a few scenes with the divine, in the prologue and epilogue, but humans only speak

37. Gibson calls Kirta and Aqhat "folk-tales" but this distinction is based more upon his particular definition of the term than a substantial difference in the genre-indicative elements. Gibson, "Myth, Legend and Folk-Lore," 60–68.

38. Wyatt, "Epic in Ugaritic Literature," 246–47.

39. Wendy Doniger claims, "Epics, too, so closely related to myths, have as their central theme the interaction of the two planes, the human and the divine, as the gods constantly intervene in human conflicts." Doniger, *Implied Spider*, 29.

with God in the epilogue. By contrast, an epic like the Story of Aqhat has gods giving speeches at a feast and presenting a special bow to Aqhat as well as a goddess promising him immortality if he gives the bow to her. The description of death and birth as coming from the divine is much more detailed in epics, and this is partially due to their genre. Besides the interaction with divinity, epics typically center around a king or other socially powerful individual, whereas HB narratives like Ruth or Manoah's wife describe impoverished and oppressed individuals.

These features of epics will be noted in the sections where epics are treated, and some of the differences in the narratives can, and will, be attributed to the style of the genre. However, noting locations where people interact with the divine even though they are not royalty or reading texts where sufferers appeal to God even though there is no epic-style divine scene (e.g., HB barrenness narratives or the Babylonian Theodicy) can offset the genre-specific narrative elements.[40] Since other texts which are not considered to be epics contain the narratival features that I am addressing, the presence of these features in epics may not be entirely due to their epic genre.

In addition, as noted in the definition above, epics display cultural values, concerns, and morals.[41] This interest in upholding cultural values spans many genres of literature. Therefore, the interactions with deities may make epics appear different from the less mythological stories, but the problems of and solutions to moral and cultural dilemmas are still pertinent. Kirta may have lengthy interactions with El, but his appeal to the divine when his family dies reflects the cultural concerns and responses to that crisis.

These introductory remarks about genre will be further explored in the discussions of the specific texts. The intention of this discussion is to justify the use of texts from different genres and set a foundation for the more detailed discussions about how genre affects the family death and barrenness narrative features that will take place in later chapters.

Outline of Chapters

The next chapter of this work is entitled "Male-Centric Family Death Narratives in the ANE." In this chapter, I will discuss the Kirta Epic, the Story

---

40. It should be noted that "epic" can be used for a wide range of texts, and, in fact, the patriarchal narratives of Genesis have been called "royal epics," though this designation makes similarities between Genesis and Ugaritic royal epics appear stronger than they truly are. For this argument see Rummel, "Narrative Structures in the Ugaritic Texts," 291–92.

41. Wyatt, "Epic in Ugaritic Literature," 252.

of Aqhat, and the Babylonian Theodicy. These are organized by genre and clarity of the three narrative elements: the origin of deaths (divine or unknown), discussion of land inheritance, and restoration of the household. So, the Kirta Epic and the Story of Aqhat are epic narratives with death, land inheritance, and restoration within the texts (though the elements are clearer in the Kirta Epic). The nature of narratival elements in the dialogue, the Babylonian Theodicy, will be the last text discussed. The sufferer and his friend's conversation about the origin of family deaths, inheritance, and a plea for restoration (though lacking a clear statement that the sufferer experiences restoration) will be explored.

The third chapter is "Female-Centric Family Death Narratives in the HB." The texts discussed in this chapter are Lot and his daughters in Gen 19, Judah and Tamar in Gen 38, and Zelophehad's daughters in Num 27. These will be discussed in canonical order and analyzed according to the narratival elements: the description of barrenness, interaction with the divine, and restoration. Unlike the works examined in the previous chapter, these texts are all narratives, though Zelophehad's daughters are a narrative about judicial precedent rather than narrating the actual death of Zelophehad. Therefore, the influence of genre will be emphasized less in this chapter compared to the discussion of the Babylonian Theodicy in the previous chapter.

The following two chapters, 4 and 5, are "Female-Centric Family Death Narrative in Ruth" and "Male-Centric Family Death Narrative in Job." These two books receive their own chapters because they are the lengthiest death and restoration narratives. They also show both the male and female responses to death and their actions toward restoration. The same framework of origin of deaths, discussion of land inheritance, and explicit restoration of the household will be used to examine these two books.

Chapter 6, "Barrenness Narratives in the HB and ANE," discusses the involvement of women in the interactions with God in the HB and ANE barrenness narratives. The framework for analyzing these narratives is description of barrenness, interaction with the divine, and restoration. The HB narratives that will be discussed are Sarah in Gen 18, Rebekah in Gen 25, Rachel in Gen 30, Manoah's wife in Judg 13, and Hannah in 1 Sam 1. In each of these texts, the wives are involved in the conversation with the divine, but the husbands are only occasionally involved. Even in the texts where husbands appeal to the divine, the wives also directly interact with God, unlike the family death narratives. The ANE text used in this chapter is the Myth of Etana. Though the husband is more central in this narrative than in the HB narratives, Etana's wife interacts with the gods and receives a divine dream, unlike the women in the family death narratives. The mythic elements of the Etana narrative will be addressed as well as the difference in the centrality of the husband compared to the HB narratives.

The final chapter, 7, is "Comparison of the Portrayal of Progeny in Barrenness and Family Death Narratives." In this chapter, the observations from the preceding chapters will be synthesized. The unique role of men and women in family death narratives will be compared with the barrenness narratives. It will be shown that texts containing the death of the family are resolved differently from the barrenness narratives. In the family death narratives, women appeal to men, and men appeal to God. This will be shown most clearly in Job and Ruth, as they are the lengthiest narratives from each perspective (male and female), but will also be demonstrated in the other HB and ANE family death narratives. However, in the HB and ANE barrenness narratives, women appeal to God directly (and God responds directly to the women) even when the husbands are appealing to God as well. This observation will incorporate gender roles in marriage practices and fertility in the HB and ANE. In addition, women's roles in cultic practices (formal and domestic) will be discussed in relation to their interactions with the divine in the barrenness narratives.

An appendix has been added to address four texts that scholars have categorized as barrenness narratives: the Hurrian-Hittite Tale of Appu, the Egyptian Tale of the Doomed Prince, and the biblical story of the Shunammite woman. I will show that each of these texts lack essential features of barrenness narratives and, in the narratives of Appu and the Doomed Prince, likely do not contain a description of barrenness at all.

CHAPTER 2

MALE-CENTRIC FAMILY DEATH NARRATIVES IN THE ANE

IN ORDER FOR AN ANE text to be considered as part of the family death genre, it must contain at least two of three themes: the death of the family (either whole or partial), attribution of their situation to God, and a restoration of the family (either whole or partial). Many texts without these themes have been compared to HB family death narratives, typically Ruth or Job, or at least described as having a relationship to them in some way.[1] However, in this chapter I will only focus upon texts that contain at least two of the features of family death and restoration. I want to consider texts that deal with the specific issue of the household being destroyed before fertility is restored in order to show how women appeal to men, but men appeal to God in family death narratives.

The texts that will be discussed in this chapter are the Kirta Epic, the Story of Aqhat, and the Babylonian Theodicy. This discussion will focus upon the texts' portrayal of the significant narrative elements for the death and restoration of the household: the origin of deaths, land inheritance, and restoration of the household. These texts have been arranged from most closely related to family death narratives (i.e., narratives with all three features) to least related (non-narrative texts with only two features). The intention in this chapter is to provide background information for the deeper

---

1. For a lengthy list of "comparable" texts that do not contain family death within the narrative, see Moore, "Ruth 2," 1685–99; Hartley, "Job 2," 871–906; Fensham, "Obliteration of the Family as Motif," 191–99; Foster, *Before the Muses*, 1:410.

comparison of gender and the restoration of fertility in family death and barrenness narratives in chapter 7.

Kirta Epic[2]

The most commonly cited text in relationship to HB family death narratives, specifically Job, is the Kirta Epic (also written Keret or Kirtu).[3] The narrative begins with the death of King Kirta's family in great detail followed by a lengthy description of his weeping (KTU 1.14i).[4] Most scholars claim that the description of Kirta's weeping is an incubation technique to induce an encounter with the divine after his family's death.[5] The incubation apparently works, and Kirta has a vision where he speaks with the god El, claiming that he wants sons rather than wealth (KTU 1.14ii). El's instructions to Kirta are to offer sacrifices and then besiege Udum and demand King Pabil hand over Hurriy for marriage, which Kirta subsequently does (KTU 1.14iii–vi). The siege of Udum is a lengthy passage with significant dialogue and interplay between King Kirta and King Pabil. This heightens

---

2. Stephanie Budin claims, "This same scribe Ilimilku is also responsible for the Ugaritic texts of the *Epic of Kirta* (*CAT* 1.14–16) and *The Baal Cycle* (*CAT* 1.1–6), of which the latter is dated in its colophon to the reign of Niqmaddu, probably Niqmaddu II of Ugarit, who reigned ca. 1380–1346 B.C.E. Our version of Aqhat, then, was probably redacted in the second quarter of the 14th century, when Ugarit was under considerable Hittite and Hurrian influence." Budin, "Gender in the Tale of Aqhat," 51. McAfee claims it "is dated to the mid-14th century BCE by the presence of the name of the scribe Ilimilku in its colophon (CTA, PI. XXX)." McAfee, "Patriarch's Longed-for Son," 60. See also Dressler, "Problems in the Collation of the Aqht-Text," 45n5; Margalit, *Ugaritic Poem of AQHT*, 3, 475–77; Virolleaud, *Légende Phénicienne de Danel*, 85; Parker, *Pre-Biblical Narrative Tradition*, 99.

3. For discussions of the spelling of Keret, Kirtu, or Kirta, see the comments on the spelling of the name in Wyatt, *Religious Texts from Ugarit*, 179n5.

4. Several numbering methods are used for the Ugaritic texts. I follow the method used by Wyatt, *Religious Texts from Ugarit*, 177.

5. Gnuse, *Dreams and Dream Reports*, 55; Mullen, *Divine Council*, 248; Jeffers, *Magic and Divination*, 128n21; Gordon, *Ugarit and Minoan Crete*, 100; del Olmo Lete, *Mitos y Leyendas de Canaan*, 44, 248; Cross, *Canaanite Myth and Hebrew Epic*, 40, 153; Greenfield, "Studies in Aramaic Lexicography I," 296n62; Greenfield, "Some Glosses on the Keret Epic," 62; Greenfield, "Aspects of Aramean Religion," 67–78; Greenfield, "Keret's Dream," 87, 90; Gray, "Canaanite Kingship in Theory and Practice," 205; Engnell, *Studies in Divine Kingship*, 152; Robinson, "Dreams in the Old Testament," 123; Ackerman, "Deception of Isaac," 110; Obermann, *How Daniel Was Blessed*, 10n13; Ehrlich, *Traum im Alten Testament*, 42; Coogan, *Stories from Ancient Canaan*, 52; Mendelsohn, "Dream," 868; Selms, *Marriage and Family Life*, 15; Greenstein, "Kirta," 10; Kim, *Incubation as a Type-Scene*, 168.

However, Dietrich and Loretz are skeptical of this incubation interpretation. Dietrich and Loretz, "Keret-Epos," 1218n33.

the narrative tension and displays many significant details about the two kings and the value of heirs.[6] Once Kirta receives Hurriy as a wife, he returns home, has many sons and daughters through Hurriy, and holds feasts for the gods (KTU 1.15).[7] However, the cycle of trouble begins again and Kirta becomes ill, then drought and famine afflict the land (KTU 1.15-16).[8] Kirta appears to be healed through religious rites, which apparently summon El to create a deity out of clay to take Kirta's sickness.[9] However, Kirta's son Yasib attempts to usurp the throne, and the text ends with Kirta cursing his son for the attempted usurpation.[10]

Death

Death, betrayal, and loss surround Kirta and his family. As Eugene McAfee notes, "Kirta's family troubles do not end with the deaths of his brothers; they follow him into the next stage of his life, his marriage . . . Kirta finds himself without a wife, whether through death, divorce, or repudiation . . . the enumeration of Kirta's loss . . . with his biological relatives (i.e., siblings or children)."[11] The deaths of Kirta's family are attributed to many causes. Some are destroyed while others died of pestilence, disease, drowning, and battle. The emphasis is on the totality of the destruction (KTU 1.14i7-11; 1.14i24-25).[12] Some translators believe that the reference to pestilence and

---

6. See further in Greenstein, "Role of the Reader in Ugaritic Narrative," 145-46. For a discussion of the interpretation of Kirta's appeal to Pabil in this section, see Hillers, "Proposal for a Difficult Line," 222-24; Gregory, "Narrative Time in the Keret Epic," 61-63.

7. For the significance of the feast for indicating the social roles of kings and deities in Kirta and Aqhat, see Belnap, *Fillets of Fatling and Goblets of Gold*, 127-66.

8. Parker claims that the family death and restoration originally stood on its own, and the illness narrative was later attached to it. Parker, "Historical Composition of KRT," 167.

9. For a discussion of the creation out of clay and the identity of the being that was created, see Lewis, "Identity and Function of Ugaritic Sha'tiqatu," 1-28; Lewis, "Sha'tiqatu Narrative from the Ugaritic Story," 188-211; Saliba, "Cure for King Keret (IIK, Col. vi, 1-13)," 107-10.

10. Eissfeldt, "Sohnespflichten im Alten Orient," 39-47; Virolleaud, "Roi Kêret et Son Fils (II K)," 105-36.

11. McAfee, "Patriarch's Longed-for Son," 134-37.

12. Kim, *Incubation as a Type-Scene*, 168-72. For a discussion of the fractions in the number of those who died, see Finkel, "Mathematical Conundrum," 109-49; Braber and Wesselius, "Unity of Joshua 1-8," 262.

the sea are references to the god of pestilence, Reshef, and the god of the sea, Yam.[13]

Scholars are divided over which family members are dying at the beginning of the narrative, mostly due to the fragmentary nature of the text. Many scholars believe that Kirta's children are the ones being killed.[14] However, other scholars claim it is Kirta's wives who died.[15] The latter option seems more likely for two reasons. First, Kirta is sent by El to find a wife rather than an heir, so it would make sense for him to lose his legitimate wives at the beginning of the narrative. Second, Kirta could conceive an heir if his children died but he still had living wives. If his wives died, though, he would be unable to replace his lost children, which leads to his appeal to El and search for a legitimate wife. However, the message that Kirta's household is empty and he is without heir is present in both interpretations. Kirta is entirely alone. Using the second interpretation, he had no children and now he has no wives either.

Regardless of whether it is his children or wives who died, the deaths do not appear to be the result of sins by the family or Kirta. Even when El addresses Kirta, he does not claim that Kirta sinned, or his family died because of guilt (KTU 1.14i38–iii49).[16] Nothing in the text indicates the

---

13. Wyatt, *Religious Texts from Ugarit*, 181nn17–18; Tsevat, "Canaanite God Šälaḫ," 49; del Olmo Lete and Sanmartín, *Dictionary of the Ugaritic Language*, 816; Kim, *Incubation as a Type-Scene*, 252; de Moor and Spronk, "Problematical Passages in the Legend," 153–71. Gary Knoppers claims, "The aftermath of Kirta's ruin reveals that he has (or acquires) a close relationship to El, who becomes intimately involved in Kirta's quest for a new family; the gods deprived King Kirta of wives and children, but he paradoxically relies upon one of their number to find a new wife and children (KTU 1.14.1.51–II.5)." Knoppers, "Dissonance and Disaster," 575.

14. O'Connor, "Keret Legend and the Prologue-Epilogue of Job," 1; Tsumura and Mikasa, "Problem of Childlessness," 11–20; Greenstein, "Kirta," 42n3; Verreet, "Keret-Prolog," 328–29; Dietrich and Loretz, "Prolog Des KRT-Epos (CTA 14 I 1–35)," 32; Wyatt, *Religious Texts from Ugarit*, 181n19; Finkel, "Mathematical Conundrum," 109–49; Sasson, "Numeric Progression in Keret I: 15–20," 181–88; Caquot et al., *Textes Ougaritiques*, 505nK; Ginsberg, *Legend of King Keret*, 33; Jirku, *Kanaanäische Mythen und Epen aus Ras Schamra-Ugarit*, 85; Coogan, *Stories from Ancient Canaan*, 58; del Olmo Lete, *Mitos y Leyendas de Canaan*, 290; Fensham, "Remarks on Certain Difficult Passages," 19; Gray, *Krt Text in the Literature of Ras Shamra*, 27; Fensham, "Obliteration of the Family as Motif," 195.

15. Kim, *Incubation as a Type-Scene*, 172–74; Cassuto, "Seven Wives of King Keret," 18–20. See also Pardee, "Kirta Epic," 333n8; Tropper, "Sieben Frauen des Königs Keret," 531; Margalit, "Studia Ugaritica II," 144; de Moor, *Anthology of Religious Texts from Ugarit*, 192; de Moor, "Contributions to the Ugaritic Lexicon," 643–44; de Moor and Spronk, "Problematical Passages in the Legend," 156; Aistleitner, *Mythologischen und kultischen Texte aus Ras Schamra*, 87.

16. It has been noted that the text does not record a prayer or vow to the gods before the divine encounter. However, the weeping might have included prayer, and the

deaths were the consequences of wrongdoing. This is unlike Kirta's illness later in the text, which appears to come from his failure to fulfill his vow to Athirat (KTU 1.15iii26–30).[17] The text shows that one affliction (Kirta's illness) is the result of wrongdoing, but the other affliction (family death) is not the result of any wrongdoing, but divine control over life and death appears to be in the background of both.

Inheritance

The second element, land inheritance, is more subtle. Providing land to Kirta's children or passing down ancestral land is not explicitly discussed in the narrative. However, Kirta's status as king makes the discussion of ancestral land inheritance different from the average landowner.[18] Kirta's desire for an heir and the later description of Yasib as his heir show that passing down inheritance is in view (KTU 1.15ii26).[19] In addition, when "Yasib the heir" attempts to take the throne in the final scene, he clearly views himself as inheriting the kingdom (KTU 1.16vi39–53). The blessing by the god El, "their last one (i.e., the youngest child) I shall treat as the firstborn," indicates that Kirta's wealth was sufficient to provide a substantial inheritance to all his children.[20] So, Yasib, or any of Kirta's other children, is not inheriting a piece of ancestral farmland or a household but the wealth and rulership of the kingdom that Kirta ruled over. The concept of continuing the name and inheritance of Kirta is present even though, as a ruler, the inherited land is a kingdom rather than an individually owned property.[21]

---

interaction with the divine indicates that he is responding to Kirta's sorrow regardless of whether prayer is explicitly mentioned. That is to say, this is still an appeal to the divine in response to the crisis even if the exact words and cultic rituals are not described. Kim, *Incubation as a Type-Scene*, 189–90. The words for dream also indicate visions and manifestations of the divine. Greenfield, "Keret's Dream."

17. Kim, *Incubation as a Type-Scene*, 253; O'Connor, "Keret Legend and the Prologue-Epilogue of Job," 241.

18. Rowe, "King's Men in Ugarit and Society," 1–19; Rowe, *Royal Deeds of Ugarit*, 62–65; Thomas, "Reconceiving the House of the Father."

19. Kim, *Incubation as a Type-Scene*, 202–3; Parker, "Ugaritic Literature and the Bible," 230; Meek, "Abishag Episode," 8–9.

20. Gray and Wyatt see this also as an anticipation of the curse upon Yasib later in the narrative. See Wyatt, *Religious Texts from Ugarit*, 212n157; Gray, *Krt Text in the Literature of Ras Shamra*, 19. For a comparison of this blessing with the end of Ruth, see Rummel, "Narrative Structures in the Ugaritic Texts," 321.

21. Wyatt, "Word of Tree and Whisper of Stone," 489, 506.

Restoration

The restoration of Kirta's household is described in a series just like the death of his household.²² El promises Kirta, "she will bear you seven sons, indeed eight sons . . . and she will bear you daughters" (KTU 1.15ii24–25; 1.15iii5).²³ The daughters are then listed individually, though their name or number are broken off in the text.²⁴ As Koowon Ķim argues, "Although most of 'Ilu's blessing concerns the enumeration of the sons and the daughters that will be born of Kirta's new marriage, 'Ilu decides to go extra miles to add some details about the firstborn and the last born children."²⁵ The text claims that this is fulfilled "as had been promised," likely referring to the conversation with El earlier (KTU 1.15iii24–25). So, the total restoration of Kirta's household completes the first cycle of the epic. This restoration comes from divine intervention and Kirta's adherence to the divine instructions.²⁶

Kirta is the protagonist in the restoration of his family. He communicates with El and acts in accordance with El's commands. The women in the narrative, namely Hurriy and Pabil's wife, are passive characters. Hurriy's activity, besides marrying Kirta, is preparing a feast for the gods, but this is at the command of Kirta rather than her own appeal to the gods.

---

22. Cyrus Gordon claims, "In Keret, however, the hero's personal mortality is compensated by the immortality of his line through securing god-granted progeny." Gordon, "Notes on the Legend of Keret," 212.

23. Kristin Saxegaard makes a comparison to Ruth being worth more than seven sons (Ruth 4:15), claiming, "In Ugarit's story about king Keret, we find a similar statement where it is said that his woman will give him 'seven, yes, eight sons' (KRT B ii20)." Saxegaard, "'More Than Seven Sons,'" 272n38.

24. For a discussion of the remaining text and possibilities for the missing names, see Pardee, "Kirta Epic," 338n51.

25. Kim, *Incubation as a Type-Scene*, 250; Virolleaud, "Mariage du Roi Kéret (III K)," 137–72.

26. Parker, "Historical Composition of KRT," 165, 173–74; Fensham, "Obliteration of the Family as Motif," 196. Theodore Lewis argues, "We read in our tale about how the senior god 'Ilu comes to the king's rescue time and time again." Lewis, "Sha'tiqatu Narrative from the Ugaritic Story," 188. See also Wyatt, "Word of Tree and Whisper of Stone," 495; Parker, *Pre-Biblical Narrative Tradition*, 211–15; Knoppers, "Dissonance and Disaster," 574.

Story of Aqhat[27]

The Story of Aqhat, also from Ugarit, has many similarities to the Kirta Epic.[28] Unfortunately, the beginning and end of the text is broken off, which affects the understanding of the destruction and restoration of Danel's family. Not only are several preceding lines are broken off, but some scholars have also supposed that an entire preceding tablet is missing.[29] This missing portion leaves the reader unsure if Danel's children died initially, though the text records his son Aqhat dying later in the narrative. Some have posited parallels to Kirta, which would imply that some sort of family death occurred in the missing text at the beginning of the Story of Aqhat.[30]

The narrative, as it currently stands, begins with Danel performing rituals for the gods in order to receive a son. The identity of Danel has been discussed many times by scholars. Some have claimed he was divine or semi-divine, but the text portrays him as performing human cultic rituals and interacting with deities more like a mythic hero than a god.[31] Though his divine or semi-divine status does not have a direct impact on the family death aspects of the text, this study regards him as a human hero appealing to the gods to intervene on his behalf throughout the epic.

In any event, after Danel performs all the rituals, Baal speaks to El on his behalf and El responds by blessing Danel and promising him a son. This

---

27. Budin, "Gender in the Tale of Aqhat." The version of the text discovered by Claude Schaeffer in the 1930–31 campaigns at Ras Shamra is dated to the mid-fourteenth century BCE because of the name of the scribe Ilimilku in its colophon. Dressler, "Problems in the Collation of the Aqht-Text," 45n5; Margalit, *Ugaritic Poem of AQHT*, 475–77. The text was discovered in a room in the high priest's house, which was located between the two temples on the city acropolis according to Virolleaud, *Légende Phénicienne de Danel*, 85; Margalit, *Ugaritic Poem of AQHT*, 3; Parker, *Pre-Biblical Narrative Tradition*, 99. Charles Virolleaud estimates that only a quarter of the entire epic is preserved. Virolleaud, *Légende Phénicienne de Danel*, 85. See also McAfee, "Patriarch's Longed-for Son," 60.

28. Wyatt, *Religious Texts from Ugarit*, 247; Koch, "Sohnesverheißung an den ugaritischen Daniel," 211–21; Mrozek, "Ugarycka idea boskiego gniewu," 129–52.

29. Wyatt, *Religious Texts from Ugarit*, 250n3; Margalit, *Ugaritic Poem of AQHT*, 250–51.

30. Aitken, "Structure and Theme in the Aqhat Narrative," 145. In a later work, Aitken states, "A certain Dan'el is saddened at the prospect of being without a male heir (or has been brought to grief because of the death of his issue recounted in a lost part of the tale; see Kirta, 1.14.1.7–25)." Aitken, *Aqhat Narrative*, 82. See also McAfee, "Patriarch's Longed-for Son," 62.

31. See discussions in Barton, "Danel, a Pre-Israelite Hero," 223; Day, "Daniel of Ugarit and Ezekiel," 174–84; Dressler, "Identification of the Ugaritic Dnil," 152–61; Dressler, "Evidence of the Ugaritic Tablet CTA 19," 216–21; Margalit, "John Day and the 'Kinnereth Hypothesis,'" 373–75.

divine response lends credence to the view that Danel's actions are incubation intended to elicit a divine revelation, much like the weeping scene in the Kirta Epic.[32] Danel then holds a feast for the goddesses to celebrate the gift of a son.[33] Another lacuna is found here, and the narrative picks up with Danel judging cases at the city gate.[34]

Suddenly Kothar, another Ugaritic deity, brings Danel a bow[35] which, though the text is fragmentary, appears to be special in some way, and Danel gives it to his son Aqhat.[36] After another lacuna, Aqhat, the son of Danel, appears to be at a feast with the goddess Anat. She desires his bow, but Aqhat refuses to give it to her even though she promises him eternal life in exchange.[37]

After Aqhat's refusal, Anat goes to El. She complains about Aqhat and threatens El that she will smite him if she cannot destroy Aqhat. El

---

32. Dietrich and Loretz see the rituals as mourning rites indicating Danel lost a son. Dietrich and Loretz, "Aqhat-Epos," 1258n13.

However, the performance of the rituals is most commonly seen as incubation. See Obermann, *How Daniel Was Blessed*; Gaster, *Thespis*, 330–32; Aitken, "Structure and Theme in the Aqhat Narrative," 139; Aitken, *Aqhat Narrative*, 81; Ashley, "'Epic of AQHT' and the 'RPUM Texts,'" 340–50; McDonnell, "Will Womankind Now Go Hunting?," 45; Kim, *Incubation as a Type-Scene*; Pope, "Cult of the Dead at Ugarit," 159; Gibson, *Canaanite Myths and Legends*, 24; Cazelles, "Book Review: Canaanite Myths and Legends by G. R. Driver," 428; Gordon, *Ugarit and Minoan Crete*, 120; Coogan, *Stories from Ancient Canaan*, 27–28; Sasson, "Literary Criticism, Folklore Scholarship," 96; del Olmo Lete, *Mitos y leyendas de Canaan*, 332–34; Gray, *Legacy of Canaan*, 108; Parker, *Pre-Biblical Narrative Tradition*, 100; Pardee, "Emendation in the Ugaritic Aqht Text," 54; Parker, "Death and Devotion," 72.

Several detractors claim that the narrative does not contain enough of the standard elements to be considered an incubation sequence. Margalit, *Ugaritic Poem of AQHT*, 260–66; Husser, *Songe et la Parole*, 29–62; Husser, *Dreams and Dream Narratives*, 46–58, 69–71, 172–75; Husser, "Birth of a Hero," 85–98; Wright, *Ritual in Narrative*, 29n39; Wyatt, *Religious Texts from Ugarit*, 253n12.

33. For the gendered interplay of the male gods promising fertility and the female goddesses in the birth, see Budin, "Gender in the Tale of Aqhat."

34. This indicates his royal status according to most scholars. Wyatt, *Religious Texts from Ugarit*, 267.

35. For a discussion of Danel's hospitality to the deity for which he received the bow, see Xella, "L'episode de Dnil et Kothar," 483–88.

36. For the importance and composition of the bow see Watson, "Puzzling Passages in the Tale of Aqhat," 372–73; Dressler, "Is the Bow of Aqhat a Symbol of Virility?," 217–25; Hillers, "Bow of Aqhat," 207–21; Margalit, *Ugaritic Poem of AQHT*; Budin, "Gender in the Tale of Aqhat," 51–72; Hendel, *Epic of the Patriarch*, 73–81.

37. For a discussion of a study of the aggressive female deity threatening, and perhaps trying to seduce, a male hero, see Brison, "Aggressive Goddesses, Abusive Men," 67–74; Ginsberg, "North-Canaanite Myth of Anath and Aqhat," 3–10; Hillers, "Bow of Aqhat."

then tells her to "seize what is in your mind, take what is in your heart" (KTU 1.18.i.17–18).[38] Anat recruits Yatipan to take the form of a falcon and devour Aqhat. However, the bow falls into the water and breaks and Anat laments her actions.

Danel and his daughter, Pughat, notice a crop failure, which leads them to question where Aqhat has gone. Two messengers tell Danel of Anat's actions and Danel curses the falcons who devoured his son. As he curses them, they fall out of the sky, and, when they hit the ground, he tears open their stomachs searching for his son. After several attempts, Danel finally curses Sumul, the mother of the falcons, and finds his son's body in her stomach. He then buries his son, curses the villages who witnessed the murder, and mourns Aqhat for seven years.[39]

Finally, Pughat, Danel's daughter, receives a blessing from her father to avenge her brother. She dresses like a warrior and meets Yatipan in order to strike him down for killing Aqhat.[40] At this point, the narrative breaks off, so the outcome of Pughat's mission is unknown.

It should be noted that some scholars claim that KTU 1.20–1.22 are the continuation of the narrative.[41] There are mentions of children in these texts, but they are quite fragmentary and the connection between them and the main narrative is unclear. They might be part of the narrative but, in their current state, they do not add any discernible sequence of events.

Death

The death of Danel's family by the hand of the gods is difficult to discern at the beginning of the text because of missing lines. However, Aqhat is later killed by Anat out of jealousy. This does not appear to be caused by a moral failing on the part of Aqhat, though he offends the goddess by refusing her request. Anat accuses Aqhat of impiety before El and states something negative about Aqhat's speech, though the text is fragmentary at this point (KTU 1.17.vi50–55). However, in the argument between Aqhat and Anat, it

---

38. Wyatt, *Religious Texts from Ugarit*, 278.

39. For the challenge of understanding the final Ugaritic word in the line about Aqhat's burial, see Pitard, "Reading of KTU 1.19:III:41," 31–38.

40. For the significance of the warrior's outfit, see Watson, "Puzzling Passages in the Tale of Aqhat," 375–76; Hoffner, "Symbols for Masculinity and Femininity," 326–34; Natan-Yulzary, "Contrast and Meaning in the 'Aqhat Story," 441–43. For the text's positive portrayal of the revenge killing, see Sun, *Ethics of Violence*, 155–88.

41. However, Wyatt and Hillers do not think that these are connected to the Aqhat narrative. Wyatt, *Religious Texts from Ugarit*, 312n282; Hillers, "Bow of Aqhat," 207n1; McAfee, "Patriarch's Longed-for Son," 35n20.

is unclear if Aqhat is insulting Anat or if Anat is attempting to deceive Aqhat (KTU 1.17.vi 15–45). For example, Aqhat suggests that Anat give gifts to Kothar in order to receive her own bow, but she responds by offering eternal life to Aqhat. His response is that she cannot give eternal life. It is unclear whose statements are true or which character is showing the appropriate respect in their response to the other character, though Anat clearly leaves embittered against Aqhat.

Based upon the interactions of Aqhat and Anat and the interaction of Anat and El, the reason for his death is unclear. By Anat's claim, it is because of Aqhat's wickedness. However, according to Aqhat's speech and El's response to Anat, it may also be Anat's vengeance against Aqhat because he would not fall for her deception and give her the bow. In addition, Aqhat mocks Anat by claiming women cannot hunt so he will not give her the bow. This may not be immoral but, based upon Anat's response, it likely sealed his fate.[42] This mocking of the goddess could also be seen as upsetting the hierarchy of divinity over humanity, which would likely also turn the gods against him.[43] These interpretations are somewhat speculative, though, because each of the characters appears to relate a different version of events and it is unclear whose is correct.

This moral ambiguity concerning the death of Aqhat is quite unlike other texts to which the text is frequently compared. Job's moral righteousness is asserted by God and the narrator (Job 1:1, 8). Though the Kirta Epic does not state the reason for the deaths of Kirta's family, it does not attribute them to a negative interaction between Kirta or his family and a divine figure (though his illness is clearly negative). Aqhat's death is not universally depicted as the result of a moral failing, but at least one character appears to make this claim. He offended Anat, unlike Kirta, but his offense is not clearly portrayed as a wicked action in the text. So, the origin is divine but the morality or immorality of the human character's actions that leads to his death is unclear.

---

42. Ashley, "'Epic of AQHT' and the 'RPUM Texts,'" 332. For a discussion of the wisdom in and construction of Aqhat's replies, see Greenstein, "Wisdom in Ugaritic," 73–74; Budin, "Gender in the Tale of Aqhat," 61; McDonnell, "Will Womankind Now Go Hunting?," 50–51; Natan-Yulzary, "Use of Resumptive Repetition," 384; Parker, "Aqhat," 49–50; McAfee, "Patriarch's Longed-for Son," 89; Husser, "Mort d'Aqhat," 323–45.

43. Kim, *Incubation as a Type-Scene*, 121.

Inheritance

The theme of inheritance is never directly addressed by the narrator or the characters. However, the theme is not entirely absent. In fact, the request for a son rather than a daughter is, on some level, a request for an heir. Kim argues more strongly, "But it is not just the lack of a son, it is the lack of a legitimate heir. This is indicated by the four-fold repetition of the list enumerating various duties expected of an ideal son/heir. Whether Dānīʾilu is a territorial king or not, the lack of a legitimate son or a proper heir would be a deplorable state that begs to be rectified."[44] The complaint is not that Danel does not have a child but that he does not have a "son like his brothers, nor scion like his kinsmen" (KTU 1.17i.18–21).[45]

In addition to the request for a son, Baal and Danel describe the six duties of the son, which include taking care of Danel in his old age (and after death) and taking care of the household and the worship of the gods.[46] Though none of these duties concern ruling the land or administering control, they mention plastering the father's roof on a muddy day, raising up monuments to the ancestral god, and driving away enemies (KTU 1.17ii.15–25). These are indicative of inheriting the administrative and cultic duties of the father, who is a royal, and honoring his father in his old age and after his death.[47]

Danel's request for Aqhat to harvest the fields and his choice of burial place for Aqhat also show his view of Aqhat as his heir. Danel wished that he would harvest the fields before all the crops withered (not knowing that Aqhat had already died; KTU 1.19.ii10–25). The king and his heir are typically seen as the origin of fruitfulness in agriculture, so Danel asking for Aqhat to begin the harvest is requesting that he perform an administrative and royal function for the kingdom.[48] The burial of Aqhat in the tomb for chthonian gods also indicates that Danel envisioned him as a king, or at least the heir to the throne, since this was the burial place of dead and

---

44. Kim, *Incubation as a Type-Scene*, 100.

45. Wyatt, *Religious Texts from Ugarit*, 254.

46. Wyatt, *Religious Texts from Ugarit*, 255n23, 258n37, 263–64. For a discussion of the filial duties as an independent unit, and an interpretation of the difficult vocabulary, see Avishur, "'Duties of the Son,'" 49–60; Greenstein, "Wisdom in Ugaritic," 76; Wright, *Ritual in Narrative*, 69; Healey, "Pietas of an Ideal Son," 356.

Contra McDonnell, who considers this integral to the narrative and the duties are fulfilled by Pughat and Anat rather than the son, Aqhat. McDonnell, "Will Womankind Now Go Hunting?" Similarly, Vayntrub, "Transmission and Mortal Anxiety," 73–90.

47. Ashley, "'Epic of AQHT' and the 'RPUM Texts,'" 327–28; McAfee, "Patriarch's Longed-for Son," 69–74.

48. Wyatt, *Religious Texts from Ugarit*, 299n216.

deified kings.[49] So, the expected duties of Aqhat and even his burial place indicate that he is envisioned as heir to the throne and administrator of agricultural functions in the kingdom, which also reflects that he was the fulfillment of the request for an heir at the beginning of the narrative.

Restoration

The nature of the texts makes the full restoration of the household unclear, much like the initial death of the household. Much of the Aqhat narrative is concerned with restoring (or replacing) Aqhat after his death. The text details the rituals and burial process that must be done properly in order to please the gods and restore Danel's family.[50] It appears that the rituals were done properly, and so the family would be restored but, unfortunately, the final resolution is missing from the text.

Beyond the rituals and burial, Danel takes revenge on the falcons and then gives his blessing to his daughter Pughat to avenge Aqhat's death against Yatipan. Again, though, the text breaks off, leaving it unknown whether Danel's household is restored with a new heir or the outcome of Pughat's revenge. In the current state of the tablets, Danel's household was restored initially, but whether it was restored again after Aqhat's death is unknown. However, many scholars have claimed that Aqhat was either resurrected or replaced with a new son in the original text.[51] The important point for this study is that after Aqhat's death, Danel is the primary actor and appeals to the divine. Pughat appears to go to the divine realm, but this is after asking for Danel's blessing to go (KTU 1.19 iv 35–40). David Wright claims, "Dani'il blesses his daughter [to avenge her brother] by his life and virtue, not by the gods or their power."[52] Julie Parker adds, "Pughat, as a mortal, dwells ensconced in the realm of patriarchy. She begins her military exploit with subservience.... Only after receiving her father's approval does Pughat proceed."[53] With an even more Danel-centered interpretation, Kim claims, "Thus one may say that Pūġatu addresses her 'prayer' to Dānī'ilu.

---

49. Aqhat was placed in a hole for chthonian gods. Wyatt, *Religious Texts from Ugarit*, 304. Pardee identifies these with the dead and deified kings. Pardee, "'Aqhatu Legend (1.103)," 353n109.

50. Ashley, "'Epic of AQHT' and the 'RPUM Texts,'" 328–29.

51. See Gordon, *Ugaritic Literature*, 85; Driver, *Canaanite Myths and Legends*, 3:8; Gaster, *Thespis*, 320. Gibson more cautiously speaks of "the resurrection (or the replacement) of Aqhat." Gibson, *Canaanite Myths and Legends*, 27. Day, "Daniel of Ugarit and Ezekiel," 179–80.

52. Wright, *Ritual in Narrative*, 228.

53. Parker, "Women Warriors and Devoted Daughters," 565–66.

The motif of prayer alluded to in this scene would become more explicit, if one considers the structural similarity between Pūġatu's petition here and Ba'lu's petition in the theophany motif (KTU 1.17 I:20–23)."[54]

Regarding the interactions of the human characters in the broader narrative of the Story of Aqhat, Elana Ashley summarizes:

> Danel relates to his wife and daughter in very traditional ways. As head of the family, Danel expects them to cater to his needs and carry out his wishes. He summons them to act and they respond obediently and without question. Thus, according to propriety, Lady Danatay hearkens to her husband and prepares a lamb for the visit of Kothar-w-Hasis. Like her mother, Pughat respectfully ministers to her father's wishes and prepares Danel for travel.[55]

Overall, the three primary narrative elements, death of the household, land inheritance, and household restoration, are found within the Story of Aqhat. However, the missing parts of the text, especially at the beginning and end, make parts of the narrative arc unclear. So, though Aqhat's death appears in the text, it does not begin the narrative in the way that it does in the Kirta Epic (or even Job and Ruth). The restoration of the household begins the text, but the original problem that caused the household crisis is broken off. Again, though the household is restored at the beginning of the story, it is unknown if it is restored again after the death of Aqhat because the conclusion of the narrative is missing. Finally, inheritance is not addressed directly in the text, but the search for a son and the description of his expected actions show that he is supposed to fulfill the role of heir for Danel. However, the household does not appear to be restored immediately after Aqhat's death, so Pughat appeals to Danel to avenge Aqhat's death rather than directly to the gods.[56] So, even in the fragmentary state of the

---

54. Kim, *Incubation as a Type-Scene*, 160.

55. Ashley, "'Epic of AQHT' and the 'RPUM Texts,'" 327.

56. Even Pughat's name simply means "girl" and so is indicative of her gender rather than social attributes or her fulfillment of the role of heir. See McDonnell, "Will Womankind Now Go Hunting?" 50–51; McAfee, "Patriarch's Longed-for Son," 105; Walls, *Goddess Anat in Ugaritic Myth*, 79–80, with a discussion of Ttmnt in Kirta and Anat in the Ba'al story. Wright explains, "This blessing has already been compared to the one that Il gives to Dani'il at the beginning of the story (1.17 I 34–47; see pp. 72–73 above). As in that blessing, a request for a blessing precedes this one. After the request, the blessing begins with an oath, wishing life on the one blessed." Wright, *Ritual in Narrative*, 203–4.

text, women appeal to men to receive justice in the family death narrative, a daughter to a father in this case.[57]

Babylonian Theodicy[58]

The Babylonian Theodicy is an acrostic poem[59] that records a dialogue[60] between a sufferer and a friend on the divine order of the world.[61] Connections are often made between this work and the dialogue portion of Job.[62]

---

57. It should be noted that Danel's wife, Danatay, is mentioned once in the narrative and only as preparing a feast for the gods at the command of Danel. As Ashley comments, "The relationship between husband and wife is that of command and fulfillment. After hearing Danel's request that she prepare a lamb for Kothar-w-Hasis, Lady Danatay immediately obeys and offers the god food and drink. The same relationship exists between King Kret and Lady Hurray when he asks her to make a feast for his friends." Ashley, "'Epic of AQHT' and the 'RPUM Texts,'" 334. McDonnell claims, "Her role is passive, taking instruction from Danel, and her duties are relegated to the home. Indeed, her name, Danatiya, seems derived from Danel's own name. Hardly a character in her own right, she is rather an extension of Danel's agency." McDonnell, "Will Womankind Now Go Hunting?," 52.

58. Oshima argues for the composition in the late second millennium BCE in Oshima, *Babylonian Poems of Pious Sufferers*. Elsewhere, Oshima explains, "Modern scholars normally identify Esagil-kīnī-ubba and Esagil-kīnī-ubbalu with our Saggil-kīnam-ubbib. If that be so, it is very likely that the Urukean thinkers of the second century BCE believed that the author of the Babylonian Theodicy had served as counselor to Nebuchadnezzar I (regnal years: 1126–1105) and Adad-apla-iddina (regnal years: 1069–1048)." Oshima, "Babylonian Theodicy," 484. See also Foster, *Akkadian Literature of the Late Period*, 34; Uehlinger, "Hiob-Buch Im Kontext der Altorientalischen Literatur," 147; Beaulieu, "Social and Intellectual Setting," 14. Dating to the twelfth–tenth centuries BCE according to Krüger, "Morality and Religion," 182–88; "Written around 1000 BCE" according to Keefer, "Meaning of Life in Ecclesiastes," 452; "1200–1100 BCE" according to Berlejung, "Sin and Punishment," 276; about 1000 BC in Lambert, *Babylonian Wisdom Literature*, 63; Denning-Bolle, *Wisdom in Akkadian Literature*, 136; Clarke, "Misery Loves Company," 79.

59. For a discussion of the verse structure see Nurullin et al., "Most Ancient Verse in the World," 173–82.

60. For a discussion of the interplay between dialogue and narrative and the ability to compare the two genres, see Dickman and Spann, "Dialogue or Narrative?," 1–13.

61. Though the text does not name the two individuals, these are the common terms used to identify them by scholars. Oshima, *Babylonian Theodicy*, xi; Lambert, *Babylonian Wisdom Literature*, 63. However, Mattingly and Oshima have argued for "skeptic" instead of "sufferer." Mattingly, "Pious Sufferer," 325; Oshima, "Babylonian Theodicy," 483.

62. Holm, "Ancient Near Eastern Literature," 283; Hoffman, "Ancient Near Eastern Literary Conventions," 399–411; Mattingly, "Pious Sufferer," 305–48; Clarke, "Misery Loves Company"; Gray, "Book of Job in the Context," 251–69; Weinfeld, "Job and Its Mesopotamian Parallels," 217–26; Albertson, "Job and Ancient Near Eastern Wisdom

The sufferer complains that, though he pays tribute to the gods, he is punished.[63] He argues that the gods promote the wicked and the righteous are allowed to suffer.[64] The friend responds by claiming that he is blaspheming the gods and the divine order is difficult for humans to comprehend. However, the narrative ends with the sufferer claiming that the rich are liars and cheats who defraud the poor. The friend responds that this is true, but it is part of the way that god designed human nature.[65]

Death

The sufferer's complaint begins with the death of his family. Oshima claims that this is not literal because an orphan would not become a scribe or scholar, but he might have been sent away to be trained as a scribe, so that might be his abandonment by his family.[66] However, this conflates the character in the dialogue with the scribe who recorded the dialogue. For a theodicy, a situation that questions the gods' morality is the focus, not whether the problematic situation is the lived experience of the author or some other real person that the author knows.

Whether the events are hypothetical or real, unlike Kirta, the sufferer's mother and father left him an orphan,[67] it is not his wives or children who have died (I:9–11).[68] The friend's response is that this is simply the way of all humans and, if the sufferer is pious, he will have a protective angel and accumulate wealth (II:16, 21–22).[69] The friend later suggests that the sufferer's responses are impious, but he does not claim that the deaths are the result of his or his family's impiety.[70] The sufferer claims that he should not have to

---

Literature," 210–30; Müller, "Keilschriftliche Parallelen zum biblischen Hiobbuch Möglichkeit," 360–75; Newsom, *Book of Job*, 92; Carroll, "Tragedy and Theodicy"; Roberts, "Job and the Israelite Religious Tradition," 107–14.

63. For the cultic overtones of the sufferer's speech about fearing the goddess (stanza 7), see Barré, "'Fear of God' and the World View," 41–43.

64. For a deeper discussion of this phrasing, see Gruber, "Akkadian *labān appi*," 81.

65. Lambert, *Babylonian Wisdom Literature*, 65; Hurowitz, "^{d}Narru and ^{d}Zulumaar in the Babylonian Theodicy," 777–78.

66. Oshima, *Babylonian Theodicy*, 27; Oshima, "Babylonian Theodicy," 485.

67. Paul, "Psalm Xxvii 10 and the Babylonian Theodicy," 489–92.

68. Line numbering conventions follow Lambert, *Babylonian Wisdom Literature*, 71–91.

69. Foster, *From Distant Days*, 316–19; Ellerby, "May the Grass Grow Long," 3; Keefer, "Meaning of Life in Ecclesiastes," 452–53; Oshima, *Babylonian Theodicy*, 28; Lambert, *Babylonian Wisdom Literature*, 64.

70. Clarke, "Misery Loves Company," 88.

suffer these deaths because he is a pious person (V:54–55),[71] and the friend does not dispute his assessment.[72] However, he adds that death happens for everyone but those who are committing crimes die sooner so he should continue to seek the reward of the gods (VI:63–66). The friend does not attribute the deaths of the sufferer's parents to sin but simply to the natural course of life. The friend believes that wickedness will lead to premature death and suffering, but this is a warning for the sufferer's current (impious) statements rather than an accusation for the sufferer's status as an orphan. As Oshima claims:

> At closer look, one sees that the friend never really acknowledged the sufferer's innocence; on the contrary, he attributes both the sufferer's refusal to accept his sinfulness and his doubts about the divine order to the lies and deceit innate in human nature. And rightly so, the criminal intentions and impious thoughts expressed by the sufferer on multiple occasions in the poem show that he was hardly as righteous as he claimed to be. Thus, it is not the sufferer who wins the argument, but rather the friend who convinces the sufferer of his guilt.[73]

So, the sufferer's family dying is not necessarily a result of his sinfulness, but his continued doubts throughout the poem are impious. The friend does not claim his sinfulness is the cause of his parents' deaths, but if he continues to question the divine order, he will be guilty and more calamities will come.

Inheritance

Inheritance is also an important aspect of the dispute but not in the same way as Kirta or Aqhat. Unfortunately, several lines in the sufferer's speeches begin with inheritance language but they are broken off. For example, "I will abandon my home . . ." (XIII:133), "I will desire no property . . ." (XIII:134), and "Should I seek a son and daughter" (XV:164).[74] In the remaining portions of the text, instead of searching for an heir, the

---

Contra Cohen and Wasserman's claim that "the poem ends with the sufferer acknowledging that his situation is the result of his former sinful behavior." Cohen and Wasserman, "Mesopotamian Wisdom Literature," 131.

71. Oshima, "Babylonian Theodicy," 485.

72. Bricker, "Innocent Suffering in Mesopotamia," 207; Feder, "Morality Without Gods?," 258; Oshima, *Babylonian Poems of Pious Sufferers*, 76.

73. Oshima, "Babylonian Theodicy," 487.

74. See Lambert, *Babylonian Wisdom Literature*, 77, 79.

sufferer complains that he is the youngest child and firstborn sons get all the privileges (I:9; XXIII). The sufferer goes even further and asserts that younger sons, like himself, bow before god and give food to the destitute while the firstborn is lazy and harsh. Yet, the firstborn receives wealth while the younger sons suffer. The friend's response is, "in the case of a cow, the first calf is lowly / the later offspring is twice as big / a first child is born a weakling / but the second is called an heroic warrior" (XXIV:260–63).[75] Surprisingly, this wisdom is accepted by the sufferer or at least uncontested in the text. However, this does not answer the question why the younger son, specifically the sufferer, is impoverished. His apparent biological fitness does diminish the force of his complaint that the firstborn has undeserved wealth while he has undeserved poverty. Perhaps the answer is in the response of the friend just before this interchange, where he claims that the sufferer should "seek the kindly wind of the god, what you have lost over a year you will make up in a moment" (XXII:241–42).[76] The friend does not directly address the inheritance complaint, but his description of the ability of the gods to make the righteous wealthy and destroy the wicked (or make the firstborn weak and the second-born strong) could be interpreted as negating this perceived unjust situation.[77]

Restoration

The restoration of the household is not present in the text, though several sections of the poem are missing; the concluding stanza appears to portray the sufferer still in the midst of his grief.[78] He continues to say that he has not seen help and ends the poem with "may the god who has thrown me off give help / may the goddess who has [abandoned me] show mercy / for the shepherd Šamaš guides the peoples like a god" (XXVII:295–97).[79] Unlike the Kirta Epic, the gods never enter the conversation. Thomas Krüger notes, "It remains open at the end of the poem whether the gods or the king responded to the petition of the sufferer."[80] The two friends debate the order of the world and the divine plan, but the gods never respond to the complaints or intervene to restore the fortunes of the sufferer, even though

---

75. Lambert, *Babylonian Wisdom Literature*, 87.
76. Lambert, *Babylonian Wisdom Literature*, 85.
77. Krüger, "Morality and Religion," 185–86; Berlejung, "Sin and Punishment," 277.
78. Bricker, "Innocent Suffering in Mesopotamia," 208; Oshima, *Babylonian Theodicy*, 26.
79. Lambert, *Babylonian Wisdom Literature*, 89.
80. Krüger, "Morality and Religion," 187; Clarke, "Misery Loves Company," 82.

the friend routinely encourages the sufferer that the gods will restore him if he acts piously.

The Babylonian Theodicy begins with the death of the sufferer's family. This is explained by the friend as the fate of humans, and the cause of sufferer's family death is not attributed to divine punishment, though some deaths are divine punishment. Inheritance is a theme in the dialogue, but it centers upon the poverty of the sufferer and his position as the youngest child rather than his ability to pass inheritance to his children. Whether the sufferer is ever restored in family or wealth is unknown. The friend's primary refrain is that the ways of god are beyond human comprehension. When the sufferer asks about the deaths of his parents or the disparity between firstborn and second-born sons, the ultimate answer is that the divine mind is too remote for human understanding.

Conclusion

At least two of the family death narrative elements, death of the household, concern for inheritance, and restoration of the household, are represented in the texts discussed in this chapter.

The Kirta Epic and Story of Aqhat fit the family death narrative typescene most closely. These are both narrative texts with heroes interacting with and even challenging divine beings, unlike the biblical family death narratives. However, they both attribute the deaths of their children to the gods and appeal to the gods for the restoration of their households. Both texts focus upon a royal figure, so the inheritance element focuses on an heir to rule the kingdom rather than ancestral land inheritance like one would expect in a rural, agricultural narrative setting. Finally, the birth of children, and thereby the restoration of the household, is attributed to the gods directly in both texts and the gods have recorded speeches blessing the heroes with children.

The Babylonian Theodicy is a dialogue and so resembles the dialogues of Job, though without the narrative prologue and epilogue portions that bookend Job. The sufferer describes the death of his family and claims that the gods are treating him unfairly, but the friend claims this is simply the normal course of human life. So, the divine origin of the deaths is debated. The sufferer is also concerned with inheritance and how it passes through the family, though it is his poverty that is the primary concern not his lack of children. Like Kirta and Job, the sufferer appeals to the gods for restoration but, unlike those texts, the poem breaks off without an explicit restoration.

Despite the genre differences in these texts, the type-scene of family death in male-centric narratives is evident. Two texts are about men with significant landholding and specifically royals (Kirta and Aqhat). One text has a conversation between two males but the sufferer, who experienced family death, is without inheritance, or at least a significant inheritance (the Babylonian Theodicy). All three male figures appeal directly to the gods. Even more, the sufferer in the Babylonian Theodicy attributes poverty and unfairness to the gods. He appeals to the gods to restore his fortunes but also asks his friend to behold his grief and struggles (XXVII 287–94).[81]

The HB texts examined in the next chapter will demonstrate the shared literary movements of female-centric family death narratives. These texts, in addition to chapters 4 and 5, will be used to support the argument for male-centric and female-centric family death type-scenes.

81. Lambert, *Babylonian Wisdom Literature*, 89.

CHAPTER 3

FEMALE-CENTRIC FAMILY DEATH NARRATIVES IN THE HB

MANY OF THE HB family death narratives are female-centric. The female-centric family death type-scene is different from the male-centric pattern shown in the ANE narratives. This chapter will discuss female-centric family death narratives in the HB, and the male-centric HB family death narrative, Job, will be discussed in chapter 5. Female-centric and male-centric family death narratives will be compared in chapter 7. The HB female-centric family death passages discussed in this chapter share three elements. First, they contain the death of the family (either whole or partial). Second, the characters or narrator attribute their situation to God. Third, they contain a restoration of the family (either whole or partial).

The three HB narratives that I will discuss in this chapter are Lot's daughters (Gen 19), Judah and Tamar (Gen 38), and Zelophehad's daughters (Num 27). This discussion will focus upon their portrayal of the significant narrative elements for this study on the female-centric family death narratives: origin of deaths, discussion of land inheritance, and restoration of the household in the text.

Lot's Daughters

The narrative of Lot and his daughters is often interpreted as a political tool for denigrating the traditional enemies of Israel.[1] The basic storyline is that

---

1. Mathews, *Genesis 11:27–50:26*, 245; O'Connor, *Genesis 1–25A*, 281; Brenner, *Israelite Woman*, 109–11. See also Frymer-Kensky, *Reading the Women of the Bible*, 258–63;

Lot and his family were led out of Sodom by angels because God was going to destroy the city. Lot's wife was turned to salt in the process of fleeing, but Lot and his daughters managed to make it to the mountains. However, while in the mountains, his daughters believe that no men are left to have children with, most likely because they just watched fire rain down upon the valley (Gen 19:31).

The solution proposed by the daughters is to make their father inebriated so that they can sleep with him, and eventually both become impregnated by him. Randall Bailey and Ilona Rashkow believe that this story places the blame on the women, but it should be on the father because it is more common that incest is initiated by the parent.[2] Similarly, other scholars see this as a "seductive daughter" trope or an exoneration of Lot's guilt by his claim to not know what happened (Gen 19:33, 35).[3] These critiques might be true, but they are speculative. The narrative, as it is written, does not provide motivations for blaming sexual impropriety on the women. The narrative simply claims it is the daughters' initiative and ends with the two daughters giving birth to the patriarchs, and etymological namesakes, of Moab and Ammon (vv. 37–38).[4]

Sabo, "Blurred Boundaries in the Lot Story," 433–44; Graybill and Sabo, "Caves of the Hebrew Bible," 8.

2. Rashkow, *Taboo or Not Taboo*, 104–11. Also Bailey, "Why Do Readers Believe Lot?," 544.

3. Seifert, *Tochter und Vater im Alten Testament*, 82–86; Fischer, "On the Significance of the 'Women Texts,'" 273–74. For seeing the narrative as an example of the image of "the seductive daughter," see Herman, *Father-Daughter Incest*, 36–49. For a summary of some of these views, see Stiebert, *Fathers and Daughters in the Hebrew Bible*, 130–44; Scholz, *Sacred Witness*, 169–73.

For readings that interpret Lot's cave scene as a distorted version of the father's repressed desire, see Sutskover, "Lot and His Daughters," 2–11; Exum, "Desire Distorted and Exhibited," 83–108; Rashkow, "Daddy-Dearest and the 'Invisible Spirit of Wine,'" 82–107. For these interpreters, the repeated reminder that Lot did not "know" that he was sleeping with his daughters does not so much highlight the poverty of his character as it attempts to exonerate him from guilt. See also Miller, "Sexual Offences in Genesis," 41–53.

Iosif J. Zhakevich argues that the author of Pseudo-Jonathan believed that Lot did know of his daughters' actions based upon ambiguity in the Hebrew text. So, when the Targum translates it that he knew, the author was trying to be faithful to his reading of the Hebrew text. Zhakevich, "Converse Translation," 184–211.

4. Grossman identifies subtle changes in wording that indicate the younger daughter may have backed out the first night and needed convincing to follow through the second night. Therefore, she may have been more hesitant to rape her father than the older daughter. Grossman, "'Associative Meanings' in the Character Evaluation," 40–57. For a similar argument that the elder daughter is portrayed as more responsible for the actions, see Sutskover, "Lot and His Daughters."

Death

Though the narrative is clearly about a family on the brink of extinction and their unorthodox method for continuing the family line, the divine origin of the family deaths is portrayed as a form of punishment. The people of the valley die because of God's judgment, and the decision of the sons-in-law to stay in the city caused them to be included in the punishment. Even Lot's wife turns into a pillar of salt because she disobeyed the angelic command not to look back (Gen 19:17, 26).[5] Alison Stone agrees that Lot's wife dies by divine punishment but then states, "Despite that, we can see the text as specifying that Lot's wife must be killed for her daughters to become mothers themselves and take up their own places in culture."[6] Reading from the end of the narrative, the actions by the daughters being contingent upon Lot's wife's death seems obvious, but in the process of the narrative, her death does not seem at all necessary for the continuation of Lot's line. Whether necessary or not, the deaths as divine punishment is not only obvious to the reader but is also told directly to the main characters (19:12–15).

Inheritance

Land inheritance is not mentioned in the text. Undoubtedly, Moab and Ammon had territory as national entities but neither Lot nor his daughters appear to have any land holdings (in fact, they are living in a cave; Gen 19:30).[7] Therefore, the exclusion of land inheritance is likely situational. The daughters are concerned about continuing the name of their father (as noted by their choice of names), and so inheritance and lineage are in the background of the narrative even though Lot has no property to pass to his children (or grandchildren).

Restoration

The restoration of fertility comes through a negative action: incest. However, the incestuous union of the daughters with Lot results in one child for each of them.[8] The text does not record the daughters continuing the

---

5. Rozmarin, "Staying Alive," 248–49.

6. Stone, "Stealing Lot's Wife and Daughters," 255.

7. Mathews notes that Lot lost his possessions and his legacy was tarnished. Mathews, *Genesis 11:27–50:26*, 246.

8. Robert Letellier notes this is a dark counterpart to Abraham's search for a son in Gen 18. Letellier, *Day in Mamre, Night in Sodom*. See also Rosenblatt and Horwitz,

sexual relationship with their father or marrying another man and having additional children. This restoration of fertility, then, is only partial. They have one child from an illicit union, but nothing is mentioned about the possibility for additional children for the two women.[9] However, each of these children become national entities. Mathews notes that "she named him" in vv. 37 and 38 is a popular formula for naming a son who is the eponymous ancestor of a group (Gen 29:32, 33; 30:8, 18; 35:18).[10] However, it should be noted that the sons are named for their relationship to the father so, in some ways, they are not their mothers' children but the children of Lot.[11] So, the narrative shows continued fertility for the family line even if it does not record additional children for the two daughters.

The actions of the main characters, Lot and his daughters, are incestuous, which is obviously negative within the context of the Pentateuch.[12] In fact, Brian Peterson notes, "Lot's daughters' actions toward their father were not only incest but also a form of rape."[13] Miri Rozmarin claims when the daughters "break one of the harshest social taboos . . . the daughters embody the victory of life over any law inscribed in the figure of the father."[14] This interpretation acknowledges that the narrator and cultural norms portray this as a negative action but maintains a tension between the positive aspect of fertility and the negative action of incest.

Wrestling with Angels, 183.

9. Cobb, "'Look at What They've Turned Us Into,'" 209; Claassens, *Writing and Reading to Survive*, 46.

10. Mathews, *Genesis 11:27–50:26*, 245.

11. Low, "Sexual Abuse of Lot's Daughters," 48–49; Rashkow, *Taboo or Not Taboo*, 108.

12. Robert Alter claims that Moabites and Ammonites "will be somehow trapped in their own inward circuit, a curse and not a blessing to the nations of the earth, in consonance with their first begetting." Alter, "Sodom as Nexus," 154. See also Sabo, "Moabite Women, Transjordanian Women," 95. Stone claims that the daughters try, though perhaps unsuccessfully, to recreate their father's family line which their mother is no longer able to do. Stone, "Stealing Lot's Wife and Daughters." See also Mathews, *Genesis 11:27–50:26*, 245; Turner, "Lot as Jekyll and Hyde," 95–96; Fisch, "Ruth and the Structure," 430.

Graybill claims that the cave is a place where illicit activities and taboo unions can occur. Even the narrative has wordplays that indicate this illicit sexuality. Graybill and Sabo, "Caves of the Hebrew Bible," 6. See also Exum, "Desire Distorted and Exhibited," 96; Rashkow, "Daddy-Dearest and the 'Invisible Spirit of Wine,'" 102; Nohrnberg, "Keeping of Nahor," 165.

13. Peterson, "Sin of Sodom Revisited," 24n43; Hendel, *Remembering Abraham*, 11; Polhemus, *Lot's Daughters*, 3.

14. Rozmarin, "Staying Alive," 250. For the tension in the narrative between the positive aspect of reproduction and negative aspect of incest, see also Polhemus, *Lot's Daughters*, 10; Mathias, *Paternity, Progeny, and Perpetuation*, 192.

Other scholars have argued that the daughters' actions are heroic or acts of love because, believing the world has ended, they are continuing humankind the only way possible (since they believe there are no other men alive).[15] However, this interpretation is from the daughters' perspective only and even then it does not follow the text. The family was in Zoar before the cave and the angels explicitly told Lot and his family that Zoar would be saved from destruction (Gen 19:20-23, 30). The disconnect between the daughters' seeming ignorance of other living men (v. 31) has been explained as "trauma-induced amnesia."[16] Alternatively, Madipoane Masenya suggests that "in that context, it was not a matter of offspring in general, but with a kinsman."[17] So, the eldest daughter does not believe that no men are left alive, but no men who they view as eligible for marriage. Both interpretations attempt to mitigate the incest taboo violation. The psychological trauma of the deaths of their city, husbands, and mother afflicting the women is not addressed in the text, though undoubtedly it would affect them, and so any amnesia claims are beyond what is described in the text. Also, the quality of their marriage prospects is possible, but it implies that incest was preferred to exogamous marriage, which seems unlikely.

Finally, if the daughters are seen as heroic, it is because Lot is passive and incompetent.[18] Sonia Waters believes that the narrative shows Lot is an incompetent patriarch and that after the daughters are offered to the crowd in Sodom and their mother died, "the daughters may not have much respect left for their father."[19] Even more critically, Michael Carden, among others, has suggested that the daughters are enacting revenge upon their father for offering them to the townspeople in Sodom.[20] So, even if the daughters'

---

15. Brenner, *Israelite Woman*, 109; Westermann, *Genesis 12-36*, 313; Frymer-Kensky, *Reading the Women of the Bible*, 263; Tsoffar, "Trauma of Otherness and Hunger," 8.

16. Cobb, "'Look at What They've Turned Us Into,'" 214.

17. Masenya, "Kgarebe (Virgin) and Carnal Knowledge," 4-5. See also Russaw, *Daughters in the Hebrew Bible*, 74.

18. Sabo claims that Lot's passivity in the interaction places him in the feminine role and the daughters in the masculine role. Sabo, "Moabite Women, Transjordanian Women," 95. See also Matskevich, *Construction of Gender and Identity*, 129.

19. Waters, "Reading Sodom Through Sexual Violence," 283; Korpman, "Can Anything Good Come from Sodom?," 334-42; Berman, *Midrash Tanhuma-Yelammedenu*, Vayera 12, pp. 132-33; Hamilton, *Book of Genesis*, 52; Delitzsch, *New Commentary on Genesis*, 2:64. See also the argument for the daughters' actions being less negative than typically understood in Warner, "Finding Lot's Daughters," 49-58.

20. Carden, "Genesis," 39; Fields, *Sodom and Gomorrah*, 124. In a slightly different interpretation, Cobb has called this a traumatic reenactment. Cobb, "'Look at What They've Turned Us Into,'" 215-16; Coats, *Genesis*, 147; Coats, "Lot," 126; Low, "Sexual Abuse of Lot's Daughters," 40.

actions can be excused, explained, or possibly justified, Lot's passivity and his, at least claimed, ignorance of the daughters' actions are still negative.[21] The daughters are likely not considered entirely innocent by the author/editor of the text, regardless of the scholarly attempts to exonerate them, but Lot is also portrayed negatively. As Grossman noted, when commenting on scholars arguing for an original positive etiological narrative, "even if the original purpose of the narrative was to praise the daughters, reading it as an appendix to the destruction of Sodom sheds new light on the story as a critical view of Lot and his daughters."[22]

The broader narrative and the social taboo of incest make the methods for returning to fertility clearly negative from the narrator's point of view.[23] Though father-daughter relationships are not explicitly condemned in the HB, this is against ANE customs.[24] However, even within this negative portrayal, the women, Lot's daughters, look to a man, Lot, to solve their loss of family rather than appealing to God.

Judah and Tamar

The Judah and Tamar narrative is often compared with Ruth.[25] This is partly because the people blessing Ruth state that her house should be like

---

21. Contra those who say that the text makes no comment on the morality of the actions: Coats, *Genesis*, 147; Exum, "Mothers of Israel," 60–67; Bruckner, *Implied Law in the Abraham Narrative*, 83. Paul Tonson took this one step further and asserted that the moral assessment is not addressed in the narrative and diverts the discussion from its main purpose. Tonson, "Mercy Without Covenant," 95–116.

22. Grossman, "'Associative Meanings' in the Character Evaluation," 48. See also von Rad, *Genesis*, 218.

23. Kalmanofsky, *Dangerous Sisters of the Hebrew Bible*, 83–84.

24. As Graybill and Sabo claim, "it should be noted that nowhere in the Hebrew Bible is father-daughter incest explicitly condemned. This absence is most notable in the laws surrounding incest in Leviticus 18–20 (as well as Deut. 27:20–23), in which virtually every other female kinship term (mother, sister, aunt, cousin, sister-in-law, niece, daughter-in-law, granddaughter, and so on) is regarded as off limits—except for daughters." Graybill and Sabo, "Caves of the Hebrew Bible," 7n13. See also Rashkow, *Phallacy of Genesis*, 70–71; Porter, "Daughters of Lot," 128. Grossman even hypothesizes that "the absence in Leviticus 18 of a prohibition against having relations with one's daughter raises the possibility that there was a time when such relations were not prohibited." Grossman, "'Associative Meanings' in the Character Evaluation," 44n16.

25. Coats, "Widow's Rights," 465; Adelman, "Seduction and Recognition," 87–109; Adelman, *Female Ruse*, ch. 4; Frymer-Kensky, *Reading the Women of the Bible*, 238–77; Trible, *God and the Rhetoric of Sexuality*, 166–99; Bal, *Lethal Love*, 68–88, 89–103; Doniger, *Bedtrick*. For further discussions see Niditch, "Wronged Woman Righted," 143–49; Van Wijk-Bos, "Out of the Shadows," 37–67; van Wolde, "Texts in Dialogue

"the household of Perez whom Tamar bore to Judah" (Ruth 4:12). It is also because questions about levirate marriage, the protection of widows, and Davidic genealogy are raised in both narratives.[26] The narrative of Judah and Tamar is decidedly different from Ruth, but Tamar's appeal to Judah rather than God shows that it is in line with the family death narratives. In addition, both narratives, but especially Tamar, are concerned primarily with progeny.[27] The narrative of Tamar and Judah begins with Judah having three sons and choosing Tamar to be the wife of his oldest son.[28] However, the oldest son was wicked, so God took his life (Gen 38:7). Tamar was then given to the second son, following the levirate practice, but the second son refused to have a child with Tamar and God took his life as well (v. 10). Judah then returned Tamar to her family's house and left her there. It appears that Judah was never intending to unite Tamar and his youngest son Shelah, but the text does not state this explicitly (though 38:11 hints at it).[29] After some time passed, Tamar decided to trick Judah into sleeping with her by posing as a sex worker (vv. 14–15). Phyllis Bird notes, "The language is deliberately opaque and suggestive. The narrator does not say that Tamar dressed as harlot. That is the inference that Judah makes—and is intended to make—but the narrator leaves it to Judah to draw the conclusion."[30] Though Tamar might not have explicitly claimed to be a sex worker, she was presenting herself as sexually available in some way, and Judah picked up on the signals.

---

with Texts," 1–28; Mathias, *Paternity, Progeny, and Perpetuation*, 206.

26. See Abasili, "Genesis 38," 276–88.

27. O'Callaghan, "Structure and Meaning of Gen 38," 74; Kim, "Structure of Genesis 38," 554; Sharon, "Some Results of a Structural Semiotic Analysis," 298–302; Stahlberg, "Sex and the Singular Girl," 198.

28. Wénin claims that the structure of the narrative is shown by four temporal markers: "The exposition begins with the words 'in that time' (v. 1) which situates the action at the time of Jacob's mourning following the disappearance of Joseph. This action becomes more complicated when 'the days are multiplied' after Tamar is sent back to her father's house (v. 12). It rushes to its denouement when the pregnancy betrays the woman 'about three months' later (v. 24). It finally finds its epilogue 'at the time of the birth' of the two sons (v. 27)." Wénin, "Ruse de Tamar (Gn 38)," 266.

29. See also Zucker and Reiss, "Righting and Rewriting Genesis 38," 196.

30. Bird, "Harlot as Heroine" (1999), 102. According to Sébastien Doane, a veil is not a biblical description of a harlot's dress. Doane, "Ass in a Lion's Skin," 244. See also Shields, "'More Righteous than I,'" 42; Westenholz, "Tamar, *Qĕdēšā, Qadištu*," 247.

Mark Leuchter claims, "The term קדשה does not therefore refer to a category of sexual-cultic functionary but informs the audience that Tamar's efforts to reverse this injustice and secure progeny are an enterprise of sacred proportions." Leuchter, "Genesis 38 in Social and Historical Perspective," 222.

Three months later Tamar was found pregnant, and Judah wanted to kill her (Gen 38:24). Interestingly, Susan Niditch notes that it is Judah, not her father, who wants to kill her because she technically joined his household even though she now resides in her biological household.[31] This indicates that the levirate marriage was still expected to happen and Tamar was still Judah's daughter-in-law, according to the accepted custom, but Judah had not followed the standard practice. Before Judah was able to kill Tamar, she provided his staff and signet ring to show that he was the father of her twins (v. 25). At this, Judah conceded that Tamar is more righteous than he (v. 26).[32] Tamar gave birth to twins, Perez and Zerah, but Judah did not sleep with her again (v. 26).[33] It is unclear if she was married to Judah's youngest son after this, but it appears that she joined Judah's house in some way because her children (and grandchildren) are listed as Judah's children in the migration to Egypt (Gen 46:12).[34]

Death

Many narrative elements overlap with the narrative of Lot and his daughters.[35] The deaths of Judah's two sons are because of their wickedness.[36] Though it appears that Judah did not recognize that they died because of their own actions, the reader is informed of this by the narrator (Gen 38:7, 10). Judah's action of sending Tamar away likely indicates that he considered her to be the cause of his sons' deaths (Gen 38:11), but the narrator states

---

31. Niditch, "Wronged Woman Righted," 146–47. See also Reiss and Zucker, "Co-Opting the Secondary Matriarchs," 312.

32. For a discussion of historical interpretations of Judah's confession, see Hayes, "Midrashic Career of the Confession," 62–81. For a broader survey of interpretations of the Judah and Tamar story, see Wassén, "Story of Judah and Tamar," 354–66. For a discussion of the composition and structure, see Weimar, "'Und er nannte seinen Namen Perez,'" 193–215.

33. According to Mathews, this shows that Judah had repented of his behavior. Mathews, *Genesis 11:27–50:26*, 723.

34. In their final dialogue, Tamar speaks to Judah as a member of the family, but Judah dismisses this appeal and treats her as a lord and judge. See Petersen, *Reading Women's Stories*, 144–45.

35. For a further comparison between Judah and Tamar and Lot's daughters, see Noble, "Esau, Tamar, and Joseph," 230–32.

36. David Volgger claims that levirate marriage in Ruth 4, Deut 25:5–10, and here are all responses to family death. However, Ruth 4 is a questionable instance of levirate practice as will be shown in the following chapter. Volgger, "Tamar, Rut und Dtn 25,5–10," 235–50.

that Tamar is not the origin of the deaths.[37] Just like the narrative of Lot's daughters, the sinful deaths are not caused by human violence but an act of God, in this case God striking each son down in response to the son's actions.[38] In addition to the causes of the deaths being sin, the actions of the primary characters are negative, if not outright sinful, as will be shown in the restoration section.

Inheritance

The Judah and Tamar narrative lacks explicit description of the sons' inheritance; that is, whether it was land, livestock, or another form of wealth. Onan's refusal to have children with Tamar might be related to inheritance, but this is not stated explicitly. Onan does not want to raise offspring for his brother or have sons that are not his own (Gen 38:9). Mathews claims that Onan "did not want to reduce his share of the family inheritance. He stood first in line after the death of Er, and producing a son by his brother's widow would mean the loss of his new status as heir."[39] It is likely that Judah and his family are semi-nomadic because livestock is mentioned but not land or permanent dwellings (vv. 12–13, 17).[40] This nomadic background provides a different setting from later HB narratives and the ANE narratives because they focus upon heirs for land inheritance, which naturally take place among people with sedentary lifestyles. Naomi Steinberg argues, "Despite the initial impression of landlessness created by the emphasis on promise in Genesis, a closer reading of the texts reveals that property and even conflict caused by excessive wealth are major concerns in the narratives."[41]

One important aspect of the deaths in the narrative is that Onan avoids providing heirs for his older brother, which indicates that the children for the brother would inherit his property regardless of whether this inheritance includes land. Therefore, Onan is concerned with maintaining the firstborn son's inheritance in his family line.[42] Judah and Tamar are also likely concerned with Judah's inheritance as shown in his refusal to give his

---

37. See also Mathews, *Genesis 11:27–50:26*, 717; van Wolde, "Texts in Dialogue with Texts," 14; Claassens, "Resisting Dehumanization," 663n12; Cook, "Four Marginalized Foils," 117; Mwandayi and Chirongoma, "'Suspected Killer,'" 1–10; O'Callaghan, "Structure and Meaning of Gen 38," 78; Ska, "Ironie de Tamar (Gen 38)," 261–63.

38. Jeremiah, "Reclaiming 'Her' Right," 149.

39. Mathews, *Genesis 11:27–50:26*, 716–17; Arnold, *Genesis*, 327; Abasili, "Genesis 38," 281; Wildavsky, "Survival Must Not Be Gained," 39.

40. Stager, "Archaeology of the Family," 1–28.

41. Steinberg, *Kinship and Marriage in Genesis*, 24.

42. Coats, "Widow's Rights," 461–66; Davies, "Judah, Tamar, and the Law," 111–22.

youngest son, and sole remaining heir, to Tamar, but she tricks Judah into providing an heir himself.[43]

Restoration

Johanna Van Wijk-Bos claims that Tamar, like Ruth and Naomi, takes the lead in advancing the promises of God rather than allowing men to take that role.[44] Menn and Abasili argue that the primary concern of the narrative is the search for progeny or an heir.[45] More specifically, as Phyllis Bird notes, Tamar's actions show she is working to have an heir for Judah rather than a husband and she wants intercourse rather than a new husband.[46] The unsatisfying part of the Judah and Tamar narrative is that it resolves with an incomplete restoration of fertility much like Lot's daughters. However, unlike the narrative of Lot's daughters, which leaves the option of further children open (though perhaps unlikely given the incest issue), Gen 38 explicitly states that Judah does not have relations with Tamar again (v. 26).[47] It also appears that she is not given to his youngest son.[48] So, not only is the household not restored to a standard family unit, but the text states that Judah and Tamar do not have any additional children. Chaya Greenberger explains:

> The birth of the two sons, Peretz and Zerah, are a new beginning for Judah—hope for the future, a replacement so to speak, for Er and Onen. There is, however, no full closure and "happily ever after" ending to the story. Judah does not marry Tamar, whom he comes to admire and who is truly a noble *isha*, perhaps because he considers it an incestuous relationship. This is tragic for the two of them and also for the children.[49]

---

43. Chan, "Ultimate Trickster in the Story of Tamar," 94–95; Mathewson, "Exegetical Study of Genesis 38," 378.

44. Van Wijk-Bos, "Out of the Shadows," 37–67; Kruschwitz, "Tamar Among the Matriarchs," 545.

45. Abasili, "Genesis 38," 276–88; Menn, *Judah and Tamar (Genesis 38)*, 15–28.

46. Bird, "Harlot as Heroine" (1999), 102.

47. Adelman, "Seduction and Recognition," 95; Adelman, *Female Ruse*, ch. 4.

48. Also, if she was, that would be breaking the Old Testament law about sleeping with the same woman as one's father (Lev 20:11). Fuchs, *Sexual Politics in the Biblical Narrative*, 72–73; Mathias, *Paternity, Progeny, and Perpetuation*, 210; Jeansonne, *Women of Genesis*, 105–6.

49. Greenberger, "Judah and Tamar," 31.

The two sons have lineages, and Perez is even listed as the ancestor of David, but the potential of the household fertility is limited.[50] Unlike Zelophehad's daughters or even Lot's daughters, if Tamar's sons die, she has no husband or male partner to recreate the family or continue the household name. Tamar gave birth to two sons, but her household cannot produce any additional children because Judah does not marry her or give her to his son.

Judah recognizes his unrighteousness when confronted by Tamar (v. 26), but her actions of disguising herself as a prostitute[51] and sleeping with her father-in-law have incestuous overtones just like Lot and his daughters.[52] Though Tamar is not condemned in the text for this action, it is clearly not the ideal situation as embarrassment and secrecy run throughout the enactment and resolution of Tamar's seduction and pregnancy (vv. 14, 19–23, 26).[53] M. E. Andrew explains:

> The reaction when Tamar is shown to be pregnant shows that Israelites did not normally regard it as right for a widow to act as she had. Judah's judgement, however, is determined by the criterion of levirate marriage which he places above Tamar's sexual act as such. Tamar has been more "righteous" in her relationship to her dead husband, to herself, to Judah himself, and above all to posterity than Judah had been. The continuance of life takes precedence over one particular piece of conduct not usually regarded as right.[54]

Therefore, fertility is restored in this narrative but in a less than ideal and incomplete way. Tamar's actions are more righteous than Judah's in

---

50. Andrew, "Moving from Death to Life," 268.

51. Arbeitman argues that the name Tamar was originally a title, taken from a shared root in Hittite, Cilician, and Etruscan, meaning "cult prostitute/priestess," but eventually that meaning was lost and it was interpreted as her name. Arbeitman, "Tamar's Name or Is It?," 341–55. This is an interesting suggestion and changes the interpretation of her "deception" of Judah in the (hypothetical) original narrative. However, as the Hebrew text stands, Tamar is clearly a given name. See also Leuchter, "Genesis 38 in Social and Historical Perspective," 222–23.

52. This transgresses sexual prohibitions from later Levitical law (Lev 18:15; 20:12). Mathews, *Genesis 11:27–50:26*, 719; Wright, "Positioning of Genesis 38," 524. Mathews argues that Judah's response shows that he was circumventing levirate custom but not that Tamar's actions were approved (723).

53. For the shared incestuous overtones in Lot's daughters and Judah and Tamar, see Smith, "Challenged by the Text," 114; Kim, "From Lot's Daughters to Bathsheba," 49–53.

54. Andrew, "Moving from Death to Life," 267.

restoring fertility but, like Lot's daughters, it is an act of desperation that results in children but not a new household unit.[55]

Zelophehad's Daughters

The final female-centric HB family death narrative that will be discussed in this chapter is Zelophehad's daughters. This narrative is significantly different from the previous ones. In Num 27, the death of Zelophehad has already occurred (v. 3). So, the narrative is not recounting the death of the father but the legal appeal by his daughters to receive an inheritance in the land of Israel. The goal of this text is to set a legal precedent for inheritance by daughters in Israel, which was later revised in Num 36 to include the restriction that the female inheritor marries within the tribe so that the inheritance passes through the family instead of moving to another family or tribe.[56]

Death

Like the previous two narratives, Zelophehad died in sin as part of the generation that died in the wilderness because of their unfaithfulness (Num 27:3).[57] Nothing in this description indicates that he died young or unexpectedly but simply that he died without sons and before the people of Israel entered the promised land, unlike the sudden and divinely ordained deaths of the people of Sodom and Judah's sons. However, it is still a negative portrayal that he died in his own sins, though not as negative as if he had been part of Korah's rebellion (v. 3).[58] Dean Ulrich explains:

> In the presence of Moses, Eleazar, and the priests, they argued that their father had done nothing that would cause his family to be cut off from community life. Zelophehad may have been a

---

55. Doniger, *Bedtrick*, 1; Doniger, *Implied Spider*, 112; Adelman, "Seduction and Recognition," 89; Adelman, *Female Ruse*, 90–125; Black, "Ruth in the Dark," 20; Joo, "Literary Inner Logic of Genesis 38," 119.

56. Aaron, "Ruse of Zelophehad's Daughters," 1–38; Levine, *Numbers 21–36*, 345; Milgrom, *Numbers* = במדבר, xxxv; Noth, *Numbers*, 210; Litke, "Daughters of Zelophehad," 209; Weingreen, "Case of the Daughters of Zelophehad," 518–22.

57. Ahiamadu, "Functional Equivalence Translation of the Zelophehad Narrative," 294.

58. For a discussion of the importance of his dying in his sins but not as part of Korah's rebellion, see Kislev, "What Happened to the Sons of Korah?," 497–511; Litke, "Daughters of Zelophehad," 213.

member of the first generation, but he was not a rebel like Korah, Dathan and Abiram, whose families were condemned with them (Num 16:27, 32).... If Zelophehad had not been dishonorably cut off from the covenant community, then the God of the covenant was still the God of his family. They remained heirs of the covenantal promises. Zelophehad's daughters expressed their faith in God's promise to keep his covenant, and they had every right to hold him to it. If Zelophehad's name disappeared, then God had not preserved the covenantal relationship and the daughters had no part in the covenantal community.[59]

Emmanuel Nwaoru and Funlola Olojede claim that it is likely Zelophehad's wife also died since she is not mentioned in the legal proceeding and levirate marriage for her is not suggested.[60] This is not stated in the text, but the daughters do not mention their mother or a relationship to their mother's family or the family of a new husband that she may have taken after Zelophehad's death.

Also, diverging from the previous narratives, the daughters of Zelophehad do not act in an illicit manner or engage in deception to resolve their situation.[61] However, the death of Zelophehad in sin is similar to the deaths described in the story of Lot in Sodom and Judah's sons, though he apparently did not partake in a particularly egregious sin like those two examples.

Inheritance

Since the narrative is a legal appeal for land inheritance by daughters in the absence of sons, Num 27 is distinct from the two previous narratives.[62] Neither Judah and Tamar nor Lot's daughters address land inheritance. This is due in part to the cultural difference between the patriarchal narratives and the apportioning of the land by Moses. The patriarchs are portrayed as livestock herders and sojourners, but the book of Numbers is preparing the people for a sedentary existence in the promised land.

59. Ulrich, "Framing Function of the Narratives," 535.

60. Nwaoru, "Case of the Daughters of Zelophehad," 51. See also Olojede, "Numbered with the Transgressors," 11–19.

61. Some have even argued that the daughters are heroically standing up for their rights in a patriarchal system. Camp, "Daughters, Priests, and Patrilineage," 177–94; Claassens, "'Give Us a Portion,'" 319–37.

62. For a discussion of the daughters' claim to land ownership compared with the theological understanding of divine ownership of the land of Israel, see Resane, "Daughters of Zelophehad," 1–8.

FEMALE-CENTRIC FAMILY DEATH NARRATIVES IN THE HB   49

This narrative of land inheritance by the daughters of Zelophehad is often cited as related to Ruth and Job by scholars, but there are some significant differences.[63] Job concludes with his daughters receiving inheritances, but not because of a lack of sons. This is a sign of his immense wealth. He is able to provide an inheritance for both his sons and daughters (Job 42:15). Ruth also shows women in control of property, but it is Naomi, the widow of Elimelech, who appears to have a claim over the ancestral land rather than a daughter (Ruth 4:3). So, neither of the texts precisely utilizes the legal precedent of daughters inheriting land in the absence of sons, though they provide examples of related inheritance issues.

Zelophehad's daughters inherit land because they have no brothers. The words for "property" and "inheritance" in Num 27 have been discussed by scholars. Jelle Verburg explains the lexical interchange as:

> Perhaps that is the nuance Numbers 27 expresses: if a male heir inherits, the law consistently calls the property a *naḥᵃlâ* in 27:9–10, but if a daughter inherits, the law considers it "an acquisition of an inheritance" in 27:7. The daughters of Zelophehad themselves never asked for a *naḥᵃlâ* proper, but requested a mere *ᵃḥuzzâ* in 27:4, perhaps in an effort to mitigate the tone of their request . . . . When the ruling does refer to the daughters' property as a *naḥᵃlâ* in 27:7–8, it is not "given" (*ntn*) to the daughters, as in the case of sons, but "passed on, transferred" (*'br*) to them.[64]

However, whether the daughters obtain an inheritance through a different process than sons, the purpose of the inheritance is not for the daughters themselves. The text indicates that the goal is to maintain the father's name among his family (27:4). Moses's initial decree, based upon the appeal of Zelophehad's daughters, is that a man who dies without sons passes his land to his daughters (27:8). After a second appeal, this time by the sons of Gilead, the marriage of the daughters is restricted. If a daughter inherits land from her father, she must marry within the tribe so that the land does not pass to another tribe (Num 36:6). These legal declarations are based upon the death of a landowner with no male heirs. Using the case of Zelophehad's daughters, Moses determined that they should be allowed to inherit their dead father's property, and, in a further declaration, they must

---

63. N. H. Snaith also notes this difference. Snaith, "Daughters of Zelophehad," 125. See also Shemesh, "Gender Perspective on the Daughters of Zelophehad," 89; Nwaoru, "Case of the Daughters of Zelophehad," 53; Sabo, "Moabite Women, Transjordanian Women," 93–110.

64. Verburg, "Women's Property Rights," 599.

marry within their tribe to ensure the succeeding generations of landholders are part of the tribe of the original landowner (their father).

Restoration

The restoration of Zelophehad's daughters to fertility is unstated in the text. The purpose of the restoration would be to continue the name of Zelophehad, not the daughters' names.[65] So, in a sense, household expansion is limited because the father has died. However, through the daughters, the household line can continue into the next generation even if Zelophehad can no longer produce additional offspring. The text, though, is not concerned about the daughters' restoration but the restoration of Zelophehad's household, so it does not address the daughters' progeny.

Though Lot's daughters each have a child and Tamar has twins, the daughters of Zelophehad are not said to have children. The silence of the text on this point highlights the intention as legal precedent for continuing the father's household rather than a narrative about the daughters themselves.[66] M. L. Case argues, more cynically, that the texts focus upon land ownership more than the women because they are concerned with women upending the social order by not having a father or husband over them.[67] In any case, the fertility aspect focuses on inheritance laws to continue Zelophehad's name not the continuation of Zelophehad's daughters.

The narrative crisis appears to be resolved by Moses in both legal cases. First, when the daughters appeal to Moses, he decides, by consulting God, that the daughters' concern is valid, and they should inherit in the land (Num 27:8). Jonathan Grossman notes that the resolution of this issue comes from human initiative as opposed to the census, which was divine initiative. The daughters took it upon themselves to plead their case.[68] After the daughters' appeal and the initial settlement, because of a complaint from the tribe, Moses revises the inheritance law to state that they must marry within the tribe if they are inheriting land so that the property remains within the tribe (Num 36:5–9).[69] Katharine Sakenfeld claims the

---

65. Mathias, *Paternity, Progeny, and Perpetuation*, 232; Shemesh, "Gender Perspective on the Daughters of Zelophehad," 83; Sakenfeld, "Feminist Biblical Interpretation," 157; Ben-Barak, *Inheritance by Daughters*, 163. For a discussion of the argument about keeping the landholding and father's name intact, see Gevaryahu, "Root G-R-A in the Bible," 107–12.

66. Carmichael, "Inheritance in Biblical Sources," 232–33.

67. Case, "Inheritance Injunction of Numbers 36," 194–216.

68. Grossman, "Divine Command and Human Initiative," 63–64.

69. Case, "Inheritance Injunction of Numbers 36," 195; Kislev, "Numbers 36,1–12,"

two narratives address different problems: "These are, on the one hand, the question of preservation of the father's name (chap. 27) and, on the other, the question of property rights (chap. 36)."[70] Even so, the issue of property rights is built upon the endangerment of the father's household. In addition, the daughters play a pivotal role in both narratives as the daughters restore the household in Num 36:11–12, which states, "the daughters of Zelophehad married their uncles' sons. They married from the families of the sons of Manasseh the son of Joseph, and their inheritance remained with the tribe of the family of their father." Though this does not state that they had children, the recognition that the inheritance continued within the family of their father implies that they had children to inherit their property.

In a sense, then, fertility is not explicitly restored, nor are any children named, but it is assumed. Moses's description of inheritance rights and marriage restrictions assumes progeny in order for the land claim to pass from the daughters who inherited the land, and their husbands who are from the same tribe, to the next generation. Mathias claims that this narrative shows the concern for the symbolic capital of "property-progeny-name" that is passed down through continuation of the patrilineal descent.[71] So, the resolution to the narrative indicates that they married and their inheritance stayed in the family, likely through their children.

Conclusion

Using the criteria outlined at the beginning of this chapter, the three narratives, Lot's daughters, Judah and Tamar, and Zelophehad's daughters, fit

---

249–59.

70. Sakenfeld, "Zelophehad's Daughters," 40. Ulrike Bechmann explains, "In particular, with Num 36, the final editors ensure that the land remains within the land allocations determined by drawing lots. So far there has never been any mention of a marriage, now the text states with threefold emphasis (vv.10-12) that the women proved to be godly and married someone from the tribe of Manasseh. The daughters of Zelophehad, the women of Judah, are strictly required not to jeopardize their family's economic base, even if they have the right to land inheritance. The request of the sons of Gilead is not fully fulfilled. Your attempt to reverse this right of inheritance fails. The women could prevent this. But as a compromise, their choice of marriage is limited in terms of preserving land for a tribe. Up to v. 10 in Num. 36 (unlike in Num. 27 and Josh. 17) they are not the subject but the object of discussion. Only in vv.10–12 do they become a subject again. According to the understanding of the entire second generation, the daughters of Zelophehad also behave godly. The continuity of the promised land for all tribes is thus reaffirmed. The federal commitment remains—even in economic and social emergencies." Bechmann, "Prophetische Frauen am Zweiten Tempel?," 61 (my translation).

71. Mathias, *Paternity, Progeny, and Perpetuation*, 242.

within the category of family death narratives, specifically the female-centric narratives. Two of the narratives, Lot's daughters and Judah and Tamar, portray the circumstances of the deaths as sinful, and even the actions of the primary characters to restore fertility are not entirely positive. Zelophehad's daughters find themselves in a situation that results from their father "dying in his own sins" (Num 27:3) but their actions are deemed righteous, and their proposition of inheritance finds God's favor through Moses (v. 7).

Inheritance issues are not addressed in the narratives of Lot's daughters or Judah and Tamar. However, they are the primary topic addressed in the narrative of Zelophehad's daughters, but the issue of fertility is less explicit. Lot's daughters each have a child and Tamar has twins, but there are no recorded children in the narrative of Zelophehad's daughters.

One unifying theme in the narratives of this chapter is that women appeal to men rather than to God. Tamar and Lot's daughters appeal to the head of the household, though perhaps in a deceitful way, while Zelophehad's daughters appeal to a national leader. This is markedly different from the ANE male-centric family death narratives because those men interact directly with the divine. The women's lack of prayer or cultic rituals is striking. They utilize men to restore the household with no appeal to divine favor whereas the male-centric narratives only appeal to God, and even the people nearby direct them to the divine as the only one who they can call upon (e.g., the Babylonian Theodicy).

With these general observations, Ruth and Job will be compared to these family death narrative texts. In the next two chapters, Ruth and Job will be described individually since they are lengthy narratives, with much scholarly work done on their fertility themes, and because they more fully encapsulate the narratival elements discussed in these chapters.

CHAPTER 4

FEMALE-CENTRIC FAMILY DEATH NARRATIVE IN RUTH

Much work has been done on the theme of barrenness in Ruth as well as the implications of a foreign woman being the ancestor of David (often compared with the foreign women crises in Ezra–Nehemiah).[1] The practice of levirate marriage and theme of faithfulness (חסד) in this book have also been discussed.[2] Most of these studies focus on the person of Ruth, though some touch on the character of Naomi or Boaz. However, few scholars have thoroughly explored the theme of household and progeny in the book, though many have noted these themes in passing or examined them in connection with land fertility imagery.

In this chapter, I will explore how the household of Elimelech (and Naomi) nearly dies out but is given new life at the end of the book through Ruth becoming part of the household and bearing a child to continue the household of Naomi and Elimelech. My argument that Ruth joins Naomi's household is meant on a personal level rather than a sociological one. That is to say, Ruth is increasingly portrayed as the daughter of Naomi and relative of Boaz. The debate about whether Ruth is assimilated, integrated, or

---

1. Mangrum, "Bringing 'Fullness' to Naomi," 62–81; Embry, "'Redemption-Acquisition,'" 257–73; Zevit, "Dating Ruth," 574–600; LaCocque, "Date et Milieu du Livre de Ruth," 583–93. George Glanzman uses a comparison with Ezra–Nehemiah to date Ruth's composition to the post-exilic period. Glanzman, "Origin and Date of the Book of Ruth," 201–7.

2. Greenstein, "Reading Strategies and the Story of Ruth," 213–14; Schipper, *Ruth*, 29–35; Thompson and Thompson, "Some Legal Problems," 79–99; Lau and Goswell, *Unceasing Kindness*; Masenya, "Stuck Between the Waiting Room," 163–76.

absorbed into Judahite culture is beyond the scope of this argument. My focus is on the interaction between Ruth and the household of Naomi within the text rather than how Ruth or any other character interprets her place within Moabite or Israelite culture in a broad sense.[3] The goal of this study is to show that the narrative of Ruth is less focused upon security for Ruth or care for widows generally, than the restoration of the household of Naomi by Ruth through the replacement of the deceased sons and the birth of Obed. In addition, Naomi takes on the role of head of household in the narrative as she speaks of her household being empty (1:21), owns the ancestral land (4:5), and is praised by the women for having a son even though it is Ruth's child (4:17).[4] Ruth, on the other hand, moves from a foreign daughter-in-law (ch. 1) to a member of the Bethlehemite community (2:11) to a member of Naomi's household (2:20), finally culminating in her actions as a son reviving the household (4:15). Glover argues that Ruth does not become part of the people of Israel until chapter 4 but admits that Ruth is portrayed as part of the household of Naomi and Elimelech throughout the book because the book prizes the concerns of the father's house over the ethnic group.[5] I will be dealing with Ruth joining the household of Naomi, but I am less concerned with precisely how Ruth is viewed as a Bethlehemite or Israelite, though I do interpret Boaz's speech in 2:11 as indicating she has joined the community in some way.

After a summary of scholarly work on Ruth, the chapter will follow the pattern of the previous two chapters. The narrative will be divided into three sections: origin of deaths, discussion of inheritance through joining Naomi's household, and the return to fertility and restoration of the household. As noted at the end of the previous chapter, the book of Ruth contains these elements in more detail than the texts discussed previously, so the discussion in this chapter will clarify the argument of the previous two chapters.

---

3. For a discussion of sociological models, and an argument for ethnic translation in Ruth, see Southwood, "Will Naomi's Nation Be Ruth's Nation?," 102–31.

4. Caspi and Havrelock note that in chapter 1, "Naomi rises as the family head and claims her independence." Caspi and Havrelock, *Women on the Biblical Road*, 140.

5. See Glover, "Your People, My People," 305, 309.

Background Literature

Recent treatments of Ruth can be separated into four primary categories: feminist,[6] post-colonial,[7] canonical/historical (e.g., comparisons with Ezra–Nehemiah or placement within the canon order),[8] and literary/the-

---

6. For discussion of widows with stigmatization and exploitation, specifically Tamar, Ruth, and Naomi, see De-Whyte, *Wom(b)an*, 242–69. De-Whyte places this book "within the barrenness tradition" as it describes social barrenness and claims that the story is primarily resolving Naomi's childlessness using Ruth as a surrogate (242, 252). See also Sharp, "Is This Naomi?," 149–62; Brenner, *Ruth and Esther*; Brenner, *Feminist Companion to Ruth*; Aschkenasy, "Book of Ruth as Comedy," 31–45.

Fewell and Gunn argue, "Is there not something just a touch bizarre about this model of loyalty, to a 'family' which seems to consist, in essence, of so many dead men? To provide an heir for Naomi is Ruth's redemptive purpose—another male, that is, for the word 'heir' masks 'son.' Naomi wants a son. What price, we may wonder (and the women at the gate echo our thought, 4:15), what price a daughter-in-law? And what about economic security within the structure of the system of levirate marriage? 'Economic security' masks, of course, the fundamental condition of this system, namely 'female economic dependence.' Another term for it is patriarchy; and it creates the conditions for this story. It is why both Ruth and Naomi find themselves destitute in the first place." Fewell and Gunn, *Compromising Redemption*, 12. Esther Fuchs claims, "Ruth, on the other hand, is a means in the process of restoring man's name to the world; that of Mahlon, her husband, and of Elimelech, her father-in-law. Her battle is not for monotheism [like Abraham's] but for the continuity of patriarchy." Fuchs, "Status and Role of Female Heroines," 78. See also Trible, *God and the Rhetoric of Sexuality*, 173.

7. Koosed, *Gleaning Ruth*, 38–47. See also Donaldson, "Sign of Orpah," 130–44; Dube, "Unpublished Letters of Orpah to Ruth," 145–50; McKinlay, "Son Is Born to Naomi," 151–57; Brenner, "Ruth as a Foreign Worker," 158–62.

8. Claus Westermann, as well as several others, parallels Ruth with Tamar in Gen 38: "The two together comprise a group (though a very small one) of narratives about daring and self-confident undertakings of women. Now only these two stories remain, though once there would have been more. We can draw this conclusion because the two stories in question present two clear stages in the history of such a group. This explains also the similarities in the two narratives." Westermann, "Structure and Intention," 290. However, these seem to have very different messages. Who is doing the socially wrong action like Judah does to Tamar? Who is not fulfilling their marital vows like Onan? In my opinion, these are not parallel at all. See also van Wolde, "Intertextuality," 426–51; van Wolde, "Texts in Dialogue with Texts," 1–28. Gerda de Villiers explains, "The death of the two sons vaguely recalls a similar episode in Genesis 38 and the death of Judah's two sons, first Er (v. 7), and then his brother Onan (v. 10). However, both Er and Onan did something that was displeasing YHWH, thus, there were probably reasons why they died. In the case of Mahlon and Chilion, no explanations are given." De Villiers, "Ecodomy," 38. De Villiers also sees Boaz's actions as reversing the Moabite curse (bringing water and bread) and a return from exile. Timothy Stone makes a similar argument about the Moabite curse. Stone, "Six Measures of Barley," 192.

Jonathan Grossman identifies a different connection: "The book of Ruth's objective, therefore, can be defined as a bridge suspended between the book of Judges and the book of Samuel." Grossman, *Ruth*, 19. Gregory Goswell argues, "My aim is to show that the Ruth narrative can he read in relation to the house of David, namely that its

matic treatments.⁹ Beyond these broad methodologies, two narrower lines of inquiry are immediately relevant to this study: the relationship between fertility and plant imagery and studies on Ruth's portrayal as a son.

Many scholars have noted the connection between fertility in the land and the household in Ruth.¹⁰ These connections are important to the

---

main point is the providential preservation of the family that produced King David and the implications for the Judean royal house. My arguments are as follows: none of the canonical positions assigned to the book of Ruth suggest that ancient readers understood it as a critique of restrictive views of intermarriage, whereas two of them assume a connection between the book and David; the genealogy in Ruth 4:18–22 is not easily removed from the book and forges an explicit link between the family history of the book of Ruth and David; the link with David is more than an endorsement of the message of the book that does not as such relate to David; the theme of God's control of events and that of his 'kindness' toward the ancestors of David prefigure God's dealings with David and his house; lastly, scenes that depict turning-points in the plot in chapters 1 and 3 (Ruth's refusal to part from Naomi, and Ruth's appeal to Boaz) find later parallels in the life of David." Goswell, "Book of Ruth and the House of David," 116. See a similar argument in Lau and Goswell, *Unceasing Kindness*, ch. 3.

9. Jacob Myers claims that thirty-three verses are poetic and so this might be the earlier stage of the book, perhaps a nursery tale. Myers, *Linguistic and Literary Form of Ruth*, 42–43. However, Segert Stanislav raised objections to this method of dividing the text. Stanislav, "Vorarbeiten zur hebräischen Metrik, III," 190–200. George Glanzman adds to Myers's work by hypothesizing an intermediate stage when the poetic tale was turned into prose and brought up to date with the law and custom of the time. He also gives dates for the stages. Glanzman, "Origin and Date of the Book of Ruth," 201–7. Nazarov uses a focalization literary analysis to understand the stages of the text. Nazarov, "Focalization in the Old Testament Narratives."

Campbell claims that tracing "the themes of various stages of the story's development has proved to be rather a blind alley in Ruth research." Campbell, *Ruth*, 8. Instead, he examines themes in the current form like activity of God, *hesed*-living, covenant and law, complaint and celebration (28–32). He also traces the structure of the text following the analysis of Stephen Bertman (15–16). Bertman, "Symmetrical Design in Ruth," 165–68. See also LaCocque, "Subverting the Biblical World," 20–30.

Athalya Brenner argues that the book of Ruth has been put together from two independent folk stories: a Naomi story and a Ruth story. Brenner, "Naomi and Ruth" (1993), 70–84.

Other scholars claim that the narrative shows God's involvement in everyday affairs and through one family. Childs, *Introduction to the Old Testament*, 565; Hubbard, *Book of Ruth*, 1–2; Block, *Ruth*, 48–55.

10. Stone, "Six Measures of Barley," 189–99; Naicker, "Food, Sex and Text"; James, "Land and Community in Ruth," 29–39. Sutskover claims, "Different scholars have recognized the analogies in the book of Ruth between the fertile state of the land and of the women, and here I wish to substantiate it at the lexical/semantic level, besides stressing the function of these fields as central elements in the design of the plot and theme of the book." Sutskover, "Themes of Land and Fertility," 284. See also Rauber, "Book of Ruth," 166; Green, "Study of Field and Seed Symbolism"; Greenstein, "Reading Strategies and the Story of Ruth," 211–31; Koosed, *Gleaning Ruth*, 17–27. Rauber highlights the barrenness of the women and the land, claiming, "This controlling pattern can be stated

development of the narrative as famine drives the family to Moab, then death and a restoration of land fertility in Bethlehem brings Naomi and Ruth back. The events also take place within the fields and the threshing floor, which highlight the fertility connection between the land and the people. Many of the studies explore specific imagery in certain scenes or provocative wording that show these connections. However, in this study, I am less interested in connecting fertility than the restoration of the household of Naomi. For this reason, I will reference the agricultural imagery when it adds to the interpretation of the status of Naomi's household, but I will not explore every instance of agricultural fertility language or imagery in the text.

Jon Berquist argues for role dedifferentiation throughout the book and describes how Naomi, Ruth, and Boaz add roles to cope with the crisis of the husband and sons dying.[11] His argument is helpful in describing how each character is portrayed in a different way throughout the text while also acknowledging that they do not lose their previous roles.

So, for example, Berquist claims that Ruth adds the roles of husband and son to Naomi but still maintains the role of daughter-in-law.[12] The characters accumulate roles based upon the needs of the situation rather than a coherent or directional character development. So, the role of husband is added when Ruth "clings" to Naomi (1:14) and the role of a son when Ruth acknowledges that Boaz is a relative of "ours" (2:20). However, these roles do not clearly build upon each other. Berquist notes, "Once Naomi sees Ruth taking the husband role of clinging, Naomi accepts Ruth as kin, in the form of a son."[13] These roles are chronologically related and, in this case, both change the relationship between Naomi and Ruth, but one is not the direct development of the other. He does not claim that Ruth moves from Naomi's son to her firstborn son or from Naomi's husband to the father of her children, but rather that she takes on two somewhat unrelated male roles (and holds them simultaneously).

Kristin Saxegaard builds upon Berquist's work but focuses specifically on Ruth's role as a son to Naomi. Instead of interpreting Ruth as adding roles, she reads the text as portraying Ruth as a son almost from her introduction

---

abstractly as emptiness-fullness." Rauber, "Literary Values in the Bible," 29. See also Saxegaard, *Character Complexity in Ruth*, 32–34. Alicia Ostriker writes, "God's presence in the book of Ruth is uniquely tied up with fertility—and is represented chiefly through invocation, as if God were made real through human discourse, through the fertility of the heart." Ostriker, "Book of Ruth and the Love of the Land," 345.

11. Berquist, "Role Dedifferentiation in the Book of Ruth," 24.
12. Berquist, "Role Dedifferentiation in the Book of Ruth," 27.
13. Berquist, "Role Dedifferentiation in the Book of Ruth," 28.

in the text. For example, in Ruth 1:14, where Berquist understands Ruth's "clinging" as a husband role, Saxegaard claims, "I would prefer to stress the role of the son. We have numerous examples in the Old Testament that sons 'stay with' and take care of their parents as long as they live."[14] This emphasis on Ruth as a son flattens the text in some ways because the relationship between Ruth and Naomi only marginally develops throughout the narrative. In other ways, though, the character development is more cohesive because Ruth is acting as a son rather than accumulating multiple unrelated roles.

In this chapter, I follow the lead of Saxegaard and Berquist, though with some significant interpretive differences. My method and many conclusions are also similar to Peter H. W. Lau's study, *Identity and Ethics in the Book of Ruth: A Social Identity Approach*.[15] However, I analyze the narrative as it progresses through the book of Ruth rather than treating the development of each major character individually. I focus upon Ruth's portrayal as Naomi's son, but with an emphasis on development. Instead of interpreting Ruth as Naomi's son consistently throughout the text, I see a gradual development from foreign daughter-in-law to community member (though perhaps still an outsider interacting within the community) and then to Naomi's son. I would not consider Ruth as a household member of Naomi until Ruth 2:20, and she does not act as a son until chapter 3.

In addition, whereas Saxegaard focused specifically on Ruth, I will also describe Naomi's increasing role as head of the household. Ruth is not just acting as a son to a mother but as a son to a father because, when she gives birth, the son is reckoned to Naomi (4:17) as though she is the head of the household that is being restored.

Death of the Household in Moab

Ruth 1 describes the death of the family and the divine cause behind the destruction of Naomi's household. The first part of the chapter describes the progressive shrinking of Naomi's household, and the second part is a response and explanation of the events by Naomi in recorded speech. Within this second part is the commitment speech by Ruth that shows her intention of joining Naomi's household, even though the offer does not appear to be accepted at this point in the narrative.

---

14. Saxegaard, "'More Than Seven Sons,'" 262.
15. Lau, *Identity and Ethics*.

Progressive Shrinking of the Household

The book of Ruth begins with a short introduction to the setting of the narrative. A couple with their two sons went to Moab because of a famine and remained there (1:1–2). However, the narrative quickly turns into a tragedy. First, the husband and father, Elimelech, dies (v. 3). Ellen Davis notes a subtle change in the wording indicating that "the storyteller underscores Naomi's desolation, the loss of the 'pleasantness' that her very name implies: 'His' sons (vv. 1, 2) are now 'hers' alone."[16] After Elimelech, the two sons die (v. 5) and finally Naomi requests that her daughters-in-law return to their mothers' houses so that they may remarry. One of them, Orpah, returns, but the other, Ruth, remains with Naomi (vv. 8–15).[17]

Within the introductory narrative, the marriage of the sons takes place after the death of Naomi's husband Elimelech (1:4). Carlos Bovell argues, "The opening six verses of Ruth reveal a chiasm; the symmetry centers on the parallel lines: 'The name of the one was Orpah/the name of the second was Ruth.'" This chiasm, with the focus on verse 4b, shows the author's concern for a restoration of the Davidic monarchy and his descent from a "capable woman" in the style of Prov 31 and Song of Songs.[18] Focusing upon the fertility of the household, this presents a hope for progeny for Naomi.[19] Marjo Korpel claims, "The deadening silence between v. 4a and v. 4b may escape a modern ear, but certainly did not escape an audience in ancient

---

16. Davis, *Who Are You, My Daughter?*, 9. Yitzhak Berger claims, "LaCocque, I believe, is circling very near the target. Following Linafelt, I am inclined to see Elimelech's name as representing the concept of God-as-king the realization of which dies with the character in a manner befitting 'the temporality of the book.' It is no accident, however, that Elimelech is the individual who signifies this concept. Abandoning both reliance on God and responsibility to his people, Elimelech, seeking financial security, 'defects' to a nation that carries with it associations that, for Israel, are almost entirely unfavorable. His death, in turn, punctuates not only the demise of the ideal of exclusive divine kingship but also the Israelites' spiritual and social deterioration—exemplified by events in the latter portion of the book of Judges—which spawned the undoing of that very ideal. When My-God-is-King of the House-of-Bread of Judah abandons his countrymen to seek food in Moab, what follows is the death of the man, together with the very concept that he represents." Berger, "Ruth and Inner-Biblical Allusion," 271.

17. Michael argues that Orpah was kind to Naomi by not bringing the additional burden of caring for her and shows that she cares for her own people. He argues that Orpah is sidelined because the narrative only wants to address the royal lineage and Orpah is not a part of this lineage. Michael, "Orpah and Her Interpreters," 390–413.

18. Bovell, "Symmetry, Ruth and Canon," 178.

19. Trible, *God and the Rhetoric of Sexuality*, 167. Campbell claims that this space is not for progeny but "her two sons surely guarantee that she would be cared for." Campbell, *Ruth*, 58.

Israel. Ten years—and two childless couples."[20] Though her husband died, and thereby her ability to bear more children, her sons may continue the family lineage through their subsequent marriages. However, the possibility of a future for Naomi's house only lasts for a single verse, and the sons die in verse 5.[21] It is noteworthy that her sons die before they are able to bear children.[22] So, Naomi has no husband to bear more children with and her sons have died before they could bear children. By verse 5, all the options for continuing the family line have been successively removed.[23] Juliana Claassens notes the dire straits this puts Naomi in: "in a society structured around women's ability to bear children, such 'enforced' barrenness affects their position in society adversely, catapulting these women into a liminal situation with little social status. Enforced barrenness also compels them to resort to humiliating and degrading measures in order to survive in a situation of limited resources."[24]

Significantly, the narrative does not focus upon the individuals that died but upon the shrinking of the household of Naomi. After Elimelech dies, the narrator states, "she was left with her two sons," and then after Mahlon and Chilion die, "the woman remained from her two sons and husband" (1:2, 5).[25] In this way, the text counts down the remaining liv-

20. Korpel, *Structure of Ruth*, 70. See also de Villiers, "Ecodomy," 38.

21. The verse indicates ten years. However, it is unclear whether this was the entire length of the sojourn or the time between the sons' marriages and their deaths. See Campbell, *Ruth*, 58. In any event, the text skips over this span of time quickly (in just four words in the Hebrew). So, the emphasis appears to be on the marriages and deaths rather than the number of years that elapsed. Ellen Davis suggests that the author intentionally leaves multiple interpretations open to the reader. Davis, *Who Are You, My Daughter?*, 11.

22. As noted by Campbell, this is the only place in the Hebrew Bible where ילד is used to designate explicitly married men, and previous to this verse they were called sons (בן). Campbell believes this forms an inclusion with Ruth 4:16 where Naomi holds the child. Campbell, *Ruth*, 56; Nielsen, *Ruth*, 44; LaCocque, *Ruth*, 43; Hubbard, *Book of Ruth*, 96n20; Bovell, "Symmetry, Ruth and Canon," 182n17. James McKeown claims the use of ילד "helps to convey Naomi's loss since, even though they were married, Mahlon and Kilion were still her boys—her children." McKeown, *Ruth*, 18.

23. De Villiers notes, "Three childless widows are left behind. In the ancient Near East this was the deepest tragedy imaginable." De Villiers, "Ecodomy," 39; Fischer, *Rut*, 126; Frevel, *Buch Rut*, 49; Köhlmoos, *Ruth*, 8; LaCocque, *Ruth*, 43; Zenger, *Buch Ruth*, 35, 122.

24. Claassens, "Resisting Dehumanization," 662.

25. Sutskover argues that "Mahlon has been considered a derivative from the Hebrew root חלה ('to be sick'), though Campbell prefers to see it as the derivation of the Arabic *mahala*, meaning either barrenness or craftiness. According to *Ruth R.* 2.5 the name Mahlon is connected by sound resemblance to the root מחה ('annihilate'): 'blotted out from the world.' In any case, the connection with sickness or barrenness

ing members of the household. The causes of the deaths are unstated, but the number of survivors is clearly stated with only Naomi remaining after her husband and sons have died.[26] Hayyim Angel discusses multiple ways in which the deaths could be interpreted: punishment from God,[27] simply death (as background information for the narrative),[28] a parallel to Job, or

---

implies the general idea of death, which is antonymous to the notion of fertility. Kilyon is derived from the root כלה ('perish'), also implying death. Hence, the death of Maḥlon and Kilyon, and the derivations of their names, connect them to the field of Fertility." Sutskover, "Themes of Land and Fertility," 285. James McKeown claims that names mean "Weakening and Pining." McKeown, *Ruth*, 15; also Koosed, *Gleaning Ruth*, 36. Alter claims that the two sons' names "are manifestly schematic names pointing to the fate of their bearers and would not have been used in reality." He claims the same is true of Orpah. Alter, *Strong as Death Is Love*, 80.

Daniel Hawk claims Chilion may be related to Ugaritic for "perfect" or "complete" but claims that any connections with Mahlon are linguistically dubious. However, he admits that they sound like the Hebrew for "weak" and "sick" and so the original hearers might not know the linguistic background and only make the rhyming connection. Hawk, *Ruth*, 55–56.

Campbell claims that Mahlon might imply "little vessel" and Chilion "to be sweet" in addition to the negative connotations. Campbell, *Ruth*, 53. Saxegaard considers these possibilities because it makes them more than caricatures, that is these could be the sons' actual names. Saxegaard, *Character Complexity in Ruth*, 66.

26. E. John Hamlin claims, "Naomi as the last remaining remnant of Elimelech's family." Hamlin, *Surely There Is a Future*, 10. See also Rauber, "Literary Values in the Bible," 29; Trible, "Two Women in a Man's World," 253.

De Villiers claims this "emphasises Naomi's loss of identity—in ancient patriarchal societies women were identified in terms of men, husband or sons. When Naomi loses her husband as well as her two sons, it is more than a deep human tragedy of agonising distress. She also loses her identity. She is no one's wife, no one's mother. She stands there with empty hands." De Villiers, "Ecodomy," 39; so also Frevel, *Buch Rut*, 50. However, this seems to take it too far. Clearly, she lost her household, but the text does not describe her losing her identity or having an identity found only in the male counterparts of the household.

27. Baylis believes that this should be read as a punishment from God for leaving the land and marrying foreign wives, especially when the text is read alongside the Mosaic covenant. Baylis, "Naomi in the Book of Ruth," 420–22; Hawk, *Ruth*, 59. Yee and Moyo conclude that it is punishment for marrying foreign wives based upon the Jewish Targum on Ruth. Yee, "Ruth," 353; Moyo, "'Traffic Violations,'" 89n19.

28. Lau and Goswell argue, "Although, in the book of Ruth, marriage to a non-Yahweh-fearing foreigner can lead to punishment (if the deaths of Mahlon and Chilion are interpreted in this way [1:4–5]), marriage to a Yahweh-fearing foreigner *is* permitted." Lau and Goswell, *Unceasing Kindness*, 8. However, elsewhere (8n12), they claim that "the Ruth narrative itself is silent about whether the deaths were an act of divine judgment, and their deaths remain an unexplained tragedy." McKeown and Koosed agree that the text is silent about the punishment aspect of their deaths. McKeown, *Ruth*, 18; Koosed, *Gleaning Ruth*, 30–32.

a narrative of sin/punishment then hesed/reward.[29] He argues that these multiple possibilities indicate the narrative is intentionally ambiguous.[30]

Within this narrative of household death, the subjects shift. First, Elimelech went with "his wife" and "his sons" in verses 1–2 but then Elimelech is "Naomi's husband" and she is bereft of "her two sons and her husband" (vv. 3, 5).[31] Saxegaard notes that "identifying a man by his wife's name is exceptional."[32] So, even within the first few verses, Naomi begins to be presented as the head of the household, and the family members are reckoned by their relationship to her rather than to their father, Elimelech.

The focus of the text changes after the death of the sons, and the daughters-in-law are again presented but now at a distance from the household of Naomi. Villiers claims, "In Ruth's case, although she seems to have had a very good relationship with her mother-in-law until now, Naomi is not part of her group, Ruth and Naomi belong to different groups of people. Ruth chooses to show her solidarity with someone who is not of her own kind."[33] Naomi's request that they return to their mothers' houses indicates that she no longer considers them a part of her house, or at least that they do not have an obligation to remain in her house (1:8–9).[34] Davis argues

---

29. LaCocque claims that fertility is found in the land of Judah, but sterility and death are in Moab and a sign of divine disfavor. LaCocque, *Ruth*, 42. Hubbard summarizes, "To begin, we consider the emergence and role of the go'el in Ruth. Chapter 1 confronts us with the book's main problem, the lack of an heir. Pointedly, v 5 stresses that only Naomi survived her family's sojourn in Moab. Her bitter outcry (vv 11–13) drops a painful hint: what this story needs is a husband to produce a child (cf. also vv 20–21)." Hubbard, "Go'el in Ancient Israel," 14.

30. Angel, "Midrashic View of Ruth," 92–93.

31. Trible, *God and the Rhetoric of Sexuality*, 167, 167n4. Several scholars have noted this focus upon Naomi and her household continues throughout the book. Lau and Goswell, *Unceasing Kindness*, 25; Berlin, *Poetics and Interpretation*, 83–84; Saxegaard, *Character Complexity in Ruth*, 31, 63; Linafelt and Beal, *Ruth and Esther*, 6.

32. Saxegaard, *Character Complexity in Ruth*, 63. See also McKeown, *Ruth*, 97; Caspi and Havrelock, *Women on the Biblical Road*, 136.

33. De Villiers, "Ecodomy," 40.

34. For a discussion of this and some varying views on the phrase "mother's house," see Campbell, *Ruth*, 64. His view is that this is an unknown custom related to marriage with the phrase "mother's house" in Gen 24:28. Trible claims that it makes a contrast between mother and mother-in-law. Trible, *God and the Rhetoric of Sexuality*, 169. Davis claims that all three places where "mother's house" is used, rather than "father's house," in the Old Testament, have marriage arrangement connotations. Davis, *Who Are You, My Daughter?*, 17. Carol Meyers claims "mother's house" allows us to hear the voice of the female experience. Meyers, "Returning Home," 85–114. Caspi and Havrelock believe that the mother's house is indicated because the mother knows best how to comfort the daughter. Caspi and Havrelock, *Women on the Biblical Road*, 143. De-Whyte argues that this is a matrilineal current within a patriarchal society. De-Whyte,

that the mismatch of masculine pronouns to feminine antecedents in this passage shows Naomi's despondency and:

> When we look at the particular significance of using masculine suffixes to refer to Ruth and Orpah, we should consider the possibility that Naomi is addressing them as the sons she had lost just a few verses prior. Virtually all commentators regard Ruth and Orpah as the antecedents of the suffixes, but if we take literally Naomi's use of the masculine, then her deceased sons (and, perhaps, husband) seem the most likely antecedents.... Rather than being signs of Naomi's deepening love for her daughters-in-law, they are signs of her preoccupation with the sons she has lost, and in this way the discordant suffixes subtly hint at the ambivalence toward Ruth and Orpah that Naomi displays elsewhere in the chapter.[35]

This aligns with the earlier assessment that Naomi is the sole survivor of her household (v. 5). From Naomi's perspective, she is the sole survivor of her household, and the daughters-in-law will return to their maternal households so that they may marry again.[36]

Diane Jacobson notes, "Naomi is left alone with her two Moabite daughters-in-law. This hardly qualifies as a legal family unit, either then or now ... she compassionately tells them to go back to the houses of their own mothers as the surest way for them to find husbands and security (Ruth 1:8–9). In her mind, she is not their family and cannot be their surrogate mother."[37] However, noting that Naomi is increasingly portrayed as the head of the household, Saxegaard claims, "as head of the family, it is her task to find her daughters-in-law new husbands able to support them whilst at the

---

Wom(b)an, 255n54.

35. Davis, "Literary Effect of Gender Discord," 501–2, 503. Myers believes that the gender confusion may have been an early dialectical peculiarity that was "submerged by the later spread of standard grammatical forms." Myers, *Linguistic and Literary Form*, 20.

36. De-Whyte claims, "Customarily when a woman's husband died, and his brothers were also dead, she could not be held to levirate marriage but must return to her own father's house." De-Whyte, *Wom(b)an*, 256. See also Staples, "Book of Ruth," 154; Schipper, *Ruth*, 47. This, then, is the standard way that the family would adapt with the women being separated from the household of their dead husbands and rejoining their fathers' households. Just as Orpah and Ruth are no longer connected to Elimelech's household, Naomi is no longer connected to the daughters-in-law; as Berquist notes, "She is left without affiliation and with little connection to the larger institutions of society (1.21). She severs her remaining connections to her adopted country (1.6–7) and to her daughters-in-law (1.8–9, 11–12)." Berquist, "Role Dedifferentiation in the Book of Ruth," 26.

37. Jacobson, "Redefining Family in Ruth," 6–7.

same time guaranteeing that the names of her sons will go on. When Naomi asks the daughters-in-law to return home, she consequently also asks them to exempt her from this duty."[38] Whether Naomi had a duty to the daughters-in-law or not is unclear, but her portrayal as the head of the household indicates that she is able to make marriage choices for the women so long as they remain in her house, as her suggestion of Boaz to Ruth later in the narrative indicates (Ruth 3).

Next, Naomi speaks directly to Orpah and Ruth about progeny and fertility.[39] She explains how she is too old to bear children and even if she was able to bear sons, the women would be too old to marry the sons once they come of age (vv. 11–13).[40] Her prayer for Orpah and Ruth is that they will find rest in the house of their husbands and that God would deal kindly with them.[41] Naomi's description of her situation as more difficult than the daughters-in-law is likely a reference to age and fertility (v. 13).[42] Orpah

38. Saxegaard, "'More Than Seven Sons,'" 260.

39. Savran claims that this shows a tension between Ruth's view of women's independent lives and Naomi's traditional patriarchal views. It is clear that Naomi and Ruth have different focuses, but patriarchal restrictions or women's autonomy is not the focus of this study. Savran, "Time of Her Life," 7–23. Bovell comments that the speech is about the possibility of having children: "A major part of the ensuing plot is the fact that none of the women have husbands (and, therefore, none of the women [can] have sons). The theme of marriage occupies the rest of the story. Naomi's words in 1.7–15 address the women's prospect of marrying and bearing children. The author uses Naomi's speeches to relegate her (Naomi) to an ancillary role, replacing her with Ruth. The story begs the questions, 'Will Ruth marry?' and 'Will she bear a son?' I realize that this may not agree with certain contemporary sensibilities, yet it is hard to deny that marriage (and, hence, childbearing) becomes the primary motif of the story." Bovell, "Symmetry, Ruth and Canon," 181–82.

40. For the interpretation of "cling and leave" as symbolic for marriage, from Gen 2:24, see Peleg, "Why Didn't Ruth the Moabitess Raise Her Child?," 289; Pardes, *Countertraditions in the Bible*, 102. Exum suggests that Ruth's speech is a symbolic marriage to Naomi that was made in the absence of men and later is shared with a legally recognized marriage with the introduction of Boaz. Exum, *Plotted, Shot, and Painted*, 129–74. Davis claims that this term may relate to Gen 2:24 but it is intending to show that "Ruth is quietly making a bold statement of love in sticking by a woman whom others would see as God-forsaken." Davis, *Who Are You, My Daughter?*, 23.

41. Timothy Decker reads this narrative as suggesting three ways that exiles could return to Judah: "Ruth 1:6–22 demonstrates the possibility of returning from exile in three different ways: backwards in apostasy (Orpah), blessed in covenant (Ruth), or bitter in emptiness (Naomi). Of course, the pragmatics of the text encourages the second of the three." Decker, "Contrastive Characterization in Ruth 1:6–22," 910–11.

42. De-Whyte notes that the text is more concerned with Naomi's womb than Ruth's or Orpah's and her barrenness is not biological but circumstantial. The death of her husband and sons has made her infertile, not necessarily age or biological factors. De-Whyte, *Wom(b)an*, 255. See also Sutskover, "Themes of Land and Fertility," 290. Michael claims that this hypothetical argument is a method of persuading the

and Ruth are still marrying age, able to bear children, and so continue the household of whoever they marry.[43] Therefore, at this point Naomi does not consider the daughters to be part of her household.[44] They belong to their maternal households and, hopefully, the household of their future husbands where they may have children and return to fertility.

Ruth's Promise

In Ruth 1:16–17, Ruth responds to Naomi's dismissal by committing herself to Naomi.[45] Not only does Ruth claim that she will stay with Naomi, but she will become a part of Naomi's people, worship Naomi's God, and stay with Naomi until they die.[46] Charles Baylis notes that Ruth responds to each of Naomi's points by refusing "to go" to her own people, lodge with her own family, worship her family's gods, and accepts the possibility that nothing but death awaits her if she follows Naomi.[47] Grace Park reads Ruth's final statement as a rhetorical question with an implied negative response, "Will death separate me from you?" Whether it is a statement or a question, the promise that Ruth will remain with Naomi permanently is clear.[48]

---

daughters to do what she wants by showing the absurdity of the scenario. Michael, "Art of Persuasion," 153–54.

43. For the argument that יבמתך "your sister-in-law" (v. 15) and Ugaritic *ybmt limm* is possibly a technical term meaning "fertile woman, marriageable woman," see Campbell, *Ruth*, 72–73.

44. LaCocque claims, "On the other hand, the literal obedience of Orpah to Naomi's orders has incalculable consequence of future deprivation for Chilion's family line. Because Orpah has missed the turning point of history in chapter 1 of the narrative, Chilion's death is a double death." LaCocque, *Ruth*, 35. Eryl Davies continues, "Such a fate would have meant the extinction of his family and his own annihilation (cf. 2 Sam. xviii 18; Amos viii 10)." Davies, "Inheritance Rights and the Hebrew Levirate Marriage," 140.

45. Matthews reads this conversation as a play for dominance. Orpah submits to Naomi's dominance and departs, but Ruth asserts her dominance and forces Naomi to submit. This is an interesting interpretation, but the remaining narrative appears to show Naomi in a position of dominance over Ruth, as she frequently obeys the commands of her mother-in-law. Matthews, "Determination of Social Identity," 50.

46. Michael notes that this is the only oath formula in the book of Ruth. Michael, "Art of Persuasion," 158. Linafelt notes that these verses and 1:21–22 are poetic and so should be read differently from the rest of the narrative. Specifically, these give insight into the inner world of Ruth and Naomi that is otherwise missing from the narrative. Linafelt, "Narrative and Poetic Art," 118–29.

47. Baylis, "Naomi in the Book of Ruth," 424–25.

48. Park, "Rhetorical Question in Ruth 1:17b," 87–103.

Some scholars have noted that this has marriage overtones, specifically in the term for "cling" in verse 14 ("but Ruth clung to her").[49] As Jon Berquist summarizes, "Furthermore, דבק refers to the male role in initiating marriage. Outside of Ruth, the term 'cling' never describes a woman's act. This makes Ruth 1.14 all the more striking. When Ruth clings to Naomi, Ruth takes the male role in initiating a relationship of formal commitment, similar to marriage."[50] However, within the narrative of Ruth, this is more likely language about becoming a child in Naomi's household.[51] As Berquist himself states, it is a "formal commitment, similar to marriage" not a proposal of marriage or romantic connection, but a formal commitment to Naomi's household.

Ruth is making a covenant with Naomi and solidifying family ties but, based upon the remainder of the book, she does not appear to be offering to marry Naomi. Mark Smith summarizes:

> Here I point out that it is not covenant that is the lofty concept brought down to routine village life in the book of Ruth, as Campbell understands the situation; instead, family relations are being expressed by Ruth, and it is the model of family extended across family lines that is being expressed in treaty and covenant language . . . . This conclusion of the study confirms what I think many modern readers intuitively grasp: with her words Ruth establishes a family relationship with Naomi that transcends the death of the male who had connected them, and in fact this relationship represents a family tie closer than that expressed by the formal status of former in-laws.[52]

---

49. Peleg, "Why Didn't Ruth the Moabitess Raise Her Child?," 289; Pardes, *Countertraditions in the Bible*, 102; Exum, *Plotted, Shot, and Painted*, 129–74.

50. Berquist, "Role Dedifferentiation in the Book of Ruth," 27. Similarly, LaCocque, *Ruth*, 50.

Other options have been proposed but they are generally not well received. First, Jewish tradition is that this is conversion, but this is rejected by most scholars. Smith, "'Your People Shall Be My People,'" 243–44. Second, this is read as a protest against Ezra–Nehemiah and shows the need for foreigners to convert. Smith, "'Your People Shall Be My People,'" 244. However, the claims of protest against Ezra–Nehemiah stand more firmly on dating the origin of Ruth rather than indications in the text itself. A third option is cementing bonds or pledging labor. Sasson, *Ruth*, 29; Brenner, "Ruth as a Foreign Worker," 159–62. Some of these elements are definitely present, but the text seems to indicate that Ruth is doing more than just offering herself as a foreign laborer.

51. Alter comments on Ruth 2:11, "Ruth is conceived by the author as a kind of matriarch by adoption." Alter, *Art of Biblical Narrative*, 71. See also Hawk, *Ruth*, 48.

52. Smith, "'Your People Shall Be My People,'" 247.

In this process of joining Naomi's family, Ruth's first commitment subsumes her people and God under Naomi's. In other words, Ruth does not offer any of her items to Naomi but only takes Naomi's people and God for herself.[53] So, this is not a mutual covenant where Naomi's people/God are Ruth's people/God and Ruth's people/God are Naomi's people/God. This joining of two families would be expected for a marriage contract or alliance, but Ruth is offering only to relinquish her identity and assume Naomi's household identity.[54] As Saxegaard argues, Ruth is not acting like a conventional daughter-in-law but asks to remain a part of Naomi's household even though her husband is dead because "Ruth does not need an intermediary to stay with Naomi. Instead, she speaks of herself as if she were Naomi's offspring. Therefore, she argues, she must stay with, and take care of, her mother as long as she lives."[55] Saxegaard goes on to claim that the image of Ruth is not as a daughter but as a son. This is because sons stay with the father's household and care for the parents much like Ruth is offering to do for Naomi.[56] I agree that the sonship element is clear in Ruth 4, but I am not convinced that it is clearly present in the text at this point. The focus, it seems, is upon Ruth continuing the household name and inheritance of Naomi, which is typically the task of a son but not exclusively so (see the daughters of Zelophehad in Num 36). Therefore, I opt for more gender-ambiguous terminology like child or heir for Ruth's relationship to Naomi in the first three chapters of Ruth.

A second way that Ruth becomes the daughter of Naomi is the term Naomi uses for Ruth throughout the book. As Smith notes, "at the time of the death of Ruth's husband, Naomi calls Ruth and Orpah 'my daughters' (1:11, 12, 13), and after Naomi and Ruth travel together to Bethlehem, Naomi continues to call Ruth 'her daughter' (3:18). As far as the text reveals, Naomi regards Ruth as family, specifically as her daughter."[57] Jeremy Schipper argues that the language of "going with" also indicates that Ruth is in a familial subordinate position to Naomi (and later to Boaz): "Thus, *'m* may have a technical sense when used to describe asymmetrical relationships among family members in 1:7, 11, 22; 2:6; 2:19 (2x)."[58] So, by Naomi's own words, she understands their relationship as mother and daughter or

---

53. Smith, "'Your People Shall Be My People,'" 257.
54. Smith, "'Your People Shall Be My People,'" 257.
55. Saxegaard, "'More Than Seven Sons,'" 261.
56. Saxegaard, "'More Than Seven Sons,'" 262.
57. Smith, "'Your People Shall Be My People,'" 258.
58. Schipper, "Translating the Preposition '*m*,'" 665.

daughter-in-law, which aligns with the offer of Ruth to relinquish her people and God and join Naomi's people and God.

This description of Ruth joining the people and religion of Naomi is reiterated by Boaz in 2:11, and the interpretation of Ruth as a child to Naomi is confirmed in the events of chapter 4. However, though Ruth offers to join Naomi's household, Naomi continually tries to distance Ruth from her household in chapter 1. Naomi called Ruth "daughter" earlier (1:11), but now she meets Ruth's commitment with silence (1:18) and continues to describe her household as empty when they arrive in Bethlehem, and even the narrator describes Boaz as only Naomi's relative at the beginning of chapter 2.

Description of the Situation by Naomi

As noted, the assessment of Naomi is that she is too old to marry or bear children so the daughters should return to their own households (1:11–12). However, Naomi continues to describe the situation when she and Ruth arrive in Bethlehem. She claims, "I went out full but the Lord has brought me back empty" (v. 21). Timothy Stone explains, "This 'empty' state refers to the loss of her husband and two sons, a state which, from Naomi's perspective, Ruth's loyalty does not remedy."[59] Again, the focus does not appear to be on the individuals who have died nor on her status as a widow, but on the household being decimated.[60] The blessing of the Lord would be a full house and many children that would carry on the household name into the future. However, Naomi has been deprived of this ideal situation and remains as the sole member of her household.

Many scholars have noted the negative implications for Ruth in this statement as well. Saxegaard argues, "Naomi considers Ruth as unimportant when telling her story to the women of the city. She does not mention Ruth with a word."[61] Danna Fewell and David Gunn go even further, claiming, "She went away full, was returned empty. She sees herself alone, apart from

---

59. Stone, "Six Measures of Barley," 191.

60. For the wordplay and possible multiple meanings of the phrase "Yahweh has testified against/afflicted me," see Moore, "Two Textual Anomalies in Ruth," 234–43. De-Whyte claims, "An Akan phrase exists that may be used to describe Naomi's predicament at the beginning of the narrative, *N'ase ahye* (her loins are burnt)," which describes "women who are childless and it means that her bloodline has ended." De-Whyte, *Wom(b)an*, 257.

61. Saxegaard, "'More Than Seven Sons,'" 264.

a vengeful God. The implication for Ruth is devastating. Ruth is nothing. Naomi speaks as though the loyal companion at her side were invisible."[62]

Naomi's final assessment is that the loss of her household is from God. She repeatedly claims that the Lord has harmed her, stating that the Lord has gone forth against her (v. 13), dealt bitterly with her (v. 20), brought her back empty (v. 21), and afflicted her (v. 21).[63] In each of these statements the claim is not that the Lord has killed her husband or sons. The claim is that the Lord has afflicted Naomi. This reinforces the interpretation that the text is focused upon the future of Naomi's household not on the individuals who died.[64] The Lord stripped Naomi of her household and the ability to continue the family name and, therefore, Naomi claims that he brought *her* back empty and afflicted *her*.[65]

Joining the Household in Bethlehem

Chapters 2 and 3 of Ruth do not explicitly mention offspring. However, they contribute to the development of the continuation of Naomi's household by increasingly identifying Ruth as part of Naomi's house.[66] This reverses the complaint of an empty household by Naomi (Ruth 1:21) and sets a foundation for the discussion of restoring the household and inheritance of

---

62. Fewell and Gunn, *Compromising Redemption*, 75. See also Fewell and Gunn, "'Son Is Born to Naomi!'" (1988), 101; Fewell and Gunn, "'Son Is Born to Naomi!'" (1999), 234; Kluger, *Psychological Interpretation of Ruth*, 37.

63. De Villiers, "Ecodomy," 39; McKeown, *Ruth*, 35–36.

Nehama Aschkenasy claims that this complaint empowers Naomi because it places her in the tradition of men challenging God in the Old Testament. Aschkenasy, "Language as Female Empowerment," 111–24.

The name Shaddai, used here in Ruth, is used often in Job as God having immense and hostile power that should be feared by people. Davis also suggests that Shaddai might also be related to an ancient Semitic term for "mountain" (*shadu* in Old Babylonian). However, the word might also be interpreted as "breasts," and so Naomi might be talking about an emptying of her body and "her own breasts, which once nurtured sons who are no more." Davis, *Who Are You, My Daughter?*, 35.

64. Campbell makes the link between God making her house empty and Boaz not sending Ruth to Naomi empty. Campbell, *Ruth*, 29.

65. Panthakan Phanon claims that the book of Ruth shows God's kindness to Naomi and Ruth, which runs contrary to Naomi's statement in this passage by providing not only for those in the promised land but returnees and foreigners as well. Phanon, "Double Ḥesed of God," 20–39.

66. The question of identity and the relationship between Ruth and Naomi is central to the story of Ruth according to Kalmanofsky, *Dangerous Sisters of the Hebrew Bible*, 157–74.

Elimelech/Mahlon in chapter 4.[67] The descriptions of Ruth's relationship to Boaz by the narrator, Naomi, and Boaz show an increasing identification of Ruth with the household of Naomi.[68]

Ruth Unrelated to Boaz

Ruth 2 begins by describing Boaz as a man of Elimelech's family (v. 1). However, the terminology is important in this verse. Naomi is fronted in the passage, so it is "to Naomi, there was a relative of her husband."[69] This verse contains no mention of Ruth, and even in the next verse Ruth asks to glean from the fields but does not explicitly mention whose field she is gleaning in.

This relationship is reiterated in verse 3, but this time only the second part of verse 1 is stated: "he was from the family of Elimelech." In this case the relationship between Boaz and Naomi is unstated. So, the close relative of Naomi and Elimelech is now described as a close relative of Elimelech.

When Boaz first sees Ruth, he inquires about who she is or, more specifically, to whom she belongs (2:5). The question "whose woman is this?" is vague, and Ellen Davis posits several interpretations including who hired her, what is her ethnic origin, and is she single and available for marriage.[70] The response of Boaz's servant is, "she is the young Moabite woman who returned with Naomi from the land of Moab" (v. 6).[71] Several scholars have noted hesitance in the servant's response, for example:

67. Greg A. King explains the impending extinction of the household at this stage. King, "Ruth 2:1–13," 182.

68. The parallel literary structure of these two chapters also indicates that they should be read together. Erich Zenger claims, "Kap. 2 und 3 sind parallel gebaut. Sie beginnen und enden mit einem Gesprach zwischen Noomi und Rut. Dazwischen findet jeweils eine Begegnung zwischen Rut und Boas statt . . . Beide Male bringt Rut der Noomi vort dieser Begegnung als Gabe des Boas 'Brot' mit. Auch die Abfolge der Schauplatze ist analog: Stadt-Feld-Stadt (2. Akt) sowie Stadt-Tenne-Stadt (3. Akt)." Zenger, "Buch Rut," 224. See also Hawk, *Ruth*, 28.

69. Campbell has a discussion on the meaning and spelling of מודע/מידע, but his conclusions are unconvincing. See Campbell, *Ruth*, 88–90.

70. Davis, *Who Are You, My Daughter?*, 45.

71. For an argument that the speech indicates reservation on the part of the supervisor, see Grossman, who concludes, "In summary, the key to resolving the difficulty in interpreting Ruth 2:7 lies in the changing frames of reference in the chapter. This verse reflects the perspective of the supervising boy, who has reservations regarding Ruth and her behavior in the field." Grossman, "'Gleaning Among the Ears,'" 716. McKeown also believes his description highlights that she does not belong. McKeown, *Ruth*, 43.

However, other scholars translate the verse differently to resolve the problem, as Alter explains, "'gather from among the sheaves.' She would not be picking up sheaves but

Though the reader may presume the field, the last line (2.7b) forces a re-reading, especially as the next scene starts (2.8–13). Suddenly, Boaz's house seems the location! The narrative brings the scene into shocking clarity. Boaz entered his property and passed by the fieldworkers on the way to his house, where a surprise awaited him: his field supervisor with a foreign girl. With apt suspicion, Boaz challenged the supervisor, "Who is this girl?" The supervisor's infelicitous speech betrayed the nervousness of his defense, insisting that Ruth intended gleaning and had hardly been inside long enough to do anything improper. In the context of Ruth's announced intentions to seduce some man (2.2), this scene seems clearly to be evoked: during a morning's gleaning, Ruth located the ranking man present and began her seduction. Now an even higher-ranking man catches her and uncovers her plot.[72]

Whether Ruth's intention to seduce the servant or Boaz is accepted, the servant's response clearly distances her from Naomi ("returned with Naomi" rather than "Naomi's daughter/daughter-in-law") and, even more significantly, places Ruth outside of the people of Israel. So, answering Boaz's question, the servant claims she does not belong to Naomi nor even to the people of Israel, but to the people of Moab.

Boaz's Description

The first shift in identity for Ruth happens in Ruth 2:10–12 where she moves from a member of Moab to a member of, or at least resident in, Israel (at least according to Boaz). Ruth asks about the kindness of Boaz while describing herself as a foreigner.[73] E. John Hamlin notes, "A 'foreign woman' was not subject to the protection of laws regarding 'aliens' (*ger*). More than that, the word *nokriya* was ambiguous. From popular proverbs we learn that it could carry connotations of immorality. The same word may be translated 'loose woman' (Prov. 2:16) or 'adulteress.'"[74] However, Boaz's response indicates a shift in the identity of Ruth. He claims that she left her father and mother and the land of her birth to join a people she did not know.

---

rather ears of grain that had fallen from the sheaves." Alter, *Strong as Death Is Love*, 87.

72. Berquist, "Role Dedifferentiation in the Book of Ruth," 29.

73. For a deeper discussion of the Hebrew terminology for "foreigner and stranger" and the changing identity of Ruth in this passage, see de Villiers, "Ecodomy," 41–42; Siquans, "Foreignness and Poverty," 443–52.

74. Hamlin also cites Prov 5:20; 6:24, 26; 7:5. Hamlin, *Surely There Is a Future*, 31–32.

André LaCocque claims the marriage language of Gen 2:24 is present here.[75] However, claiming that Naomi and Ruth are "becoming one flesh" would be a strange statement from the character of Boaz, especially in light of his marriage to Ruth at the end of the book. I think it is more likely that he is describing the totality of her migration: family level to ethnic to religious. Regardless, the perception of Ruth's relationship to Israel is shifting.[76] She perceives herself as a foreigner and even the narrator consistently refers to her as "Ruth the Moabitess" (2:2, 21),[77] but Boaz describes her as seeking refuge from the God of Israel and leaving her people to join the people of Israel (2:11–12). Boaz inviting Ruth to participate in the meal (2:14) likely also indicates that he is viewing her as a community member. Some scholars believe that Boaz is upending multiple social norms by having the owner of the field eating with lower class workers and men eating with women. Therefore, it is difficult to interpret this as solely indicating Ruth's incorporation into the household of Naomi when Boaz does not appear to be following multiple social norms.[78] However, incorporating her into the meal

---

75. LaCocque, *Ruth*, 71.

76. Contra Rauber who claims, "He shows first that he understands what it means to be a stranger.... But this is also a deliberate echoing of something even deeper in the Hebraic past than the exodus; it brings Abraham and the patriarchs to mind." Rauber, "Literary Values in the Bible," 32. This echo with Abraham is true, but Boaz appears to do more than just sympathize with Ruth's status as a stranger.

77. Lau claims that this was a negative appellation for the Israelite readers. Lau, *Identity and Ethics*, 91–92.

78. Stone explains that "by inviting Ruth to share a meal, the story symbolically indicates her inclusion within the community and, quite possibly, Boaz's family or clan in contrast to Deut. 23.4–5's exclusion of Moabites." Stone, "Six Measures of Barley," 192. See also Hawk, *Ruth*, 83; LaCocque, *Ruth*, 74.

Magnus Ottosson expands upon the significance of meals in the HB: "Eating gives life and strengthens the 'soul.' When eating involves some form of fellowship—with one's family, relatives, or covenant partners—it produces divine power which strengthens the unity. Meals establish harmony, which is the prerequisite for all communal life. It was a serious crime to disrupt such a fellowship (Ps. 41:10[9]). It was unthinkable for someone to eat with his enemies." Ottosson, "אָכַל 'ākhal," 241.

Westermann interprets this historically: "The invitation to the meal follows as a confirmation of the agreement that has been reached (v. 14): Boaz invites Ruth to eat with him, and Ruth accepts. The occurrence resembles treaty-making in the ancestral period, which was also confirmed in a meal (e.g., Jacob and Laban in Genesis 31). Boaz's gift for Naomi, given through Ruth, should be seen in the same light (vv. 15–17)." Westermann, "Structure and Intention," 296.

De Villiers claims that "all social boundaries in the Ancient World are transgressed and turned upside down. Firstly, the difference in social status between Boaz and his workers should be kept in mind. In the Ancient World, it was unusual that a landowner would mix freely with his workers and even share a meal with them. Secondly, and even more radically, the gender roles in ancient communities were sharply defined. Men and

likely indicates at least that Boaz believes she is part of the community in some way, or perhaps even that she is a potential marital partner, according to Robert Alter.[79]

This also parallels the promise that Ruth made to Naomi in 1:16–17. Ruth had told Naomi that she would join Naomi's people and her God (1:16). Boaz, though, states that Ruth left her father and mother and the land of her birth (2:11).[80] The parallel in Boaz's speech between "all you have done for your mother-in-law" and "you left your father and your mother" indicates the relationship between Ruth and Naomi.[81] Boaz's description is similar to Ruth's promise but stops just short of the familial language that Ruth uses. Ruth claims to go where Naomi goes even to the point of death (1:16–17). However, Boaz states that Ruth has joined a people and God that she did not know (2:11–12). This description places Ruth within the people of Israel, or Bethlehem, but not necessarily a full member of Naomi's household. However, the interaction between Boaz and Ruth in chapter 3 will move from Ruth acting as someone joining Naomi's people to Ruth as part of Naomi's household (3:9–10).

Ruth a Relative of Boaz

In the next description of the familial relationship with Boaz, Ruth becomes part of Naomi's household (2:20). Davis claims, "It is noteworthy that at the same time Naomi claims kinship with Boaz, she also claims Ruth more fully. Once she told Ruth to go back to her own family (1:8); now Boaz is 'kin to us.'"[82] Saxegaard notes that Ruth bringing back the gleaned grain also shows

---

women seldom ate together." De Villiers, "Ecodomy," 44.

79. Alter claims, "The meal after the arrival of a stranger at a well in a foreign land is still another motif of the betrothal type-scene." Alter, *Strong as Death Is Love*, 88.

80. Prinsloo claims that this is the focal point of this chapter. Prinsloo, "Theology of the Book of Ruth," 334.

For a discussion of gossip as the means by which Boaz knew of Ruth's actions and a catalyst for the plot of the story, see Esler, "'All That You Have Done,'" 645–66.

81. See Matthews, "Determination of Social Identity," 52–53.

82. Davis, *Who Are You, My Daughter?*, 61; Fewell and Gunn, *Compromising Redemption*, 77. Berquist claims, "Ruth's second chapter begins with a notice that Naomi has a relative (2.1). By the end of ch. 2, Naomi exclaims, 'The man is close to us; he is one of our redeemers (מגאלנו)!' (2.20). Thus, family connections provide an important set of roles, including the role of redeemer that would provide a possible solution to the crisis." Berquist, "Role Dedifferentiation in the Book of Ruth," 27. See also Trible, *God and the Rhetoric of Sexuality*, 179. Hawk argues, "The merging of kin and in-law language in the concluding speech accentuates Ruth's new status as insider-yet-outsider." Hawk, *Ruth*, 85.

a familial relationship because Ruth is taking care of Naomi as a child would a parent: "Ruth's speech (1,16–17) and care (2,18) express the fact that Ruth no longer thinks of herself as Naomi's daughter-in-law. She has entered into a closer relationship, as Naomi's child. Naomi confirms this by calling Ruth 'daughter' (2,2.22). The narrator also shows us that Ruth's role as a daughter-in-law is no longer relevant."[83] In Ruth 2:20, Naomi tells Ruth, "This man is a close relative (redeemer) of ours." This, strictly speaking, is untrue since he is a relative of Naomi's husband (2:1) and Ruth is not even an Israelite.[84] However, it reflects a shift that has taken place within the text.[85] Ruth has become part of Naomi's household and Naomi has begun to assume the position of the head of household.[86]

The shift from "a close relative to Naomi's husband" to "a relative of ours (Ruth and Naomi)" continues in chapter 3. In Ruth 3:1 the term מָנוֹחַ

---

83. Saxegaard, "'More Than Seven Sons,'" 265.

Fewell and Gunn claim, "Such nuances suggest the image of Ruth as 'husband' to Naomi and indeed, for much of the story, Ruth replaces husband and son as Naomi's caretaker." Fewell and Gunn, *Compromising Redemption*, 97. This caretaker aspect is found even in the women's claim that Ruth is better to Naomi than seven sons, so it is likely that Ruth is acting as a caretaker son more than husband.

Masenya posits that part of this identity is because the dead husbands are still controlling the lives of the women and a wife is still expected to live as a member of the household of her husband even if he is dead. This may read too deeply into a subject that the text is silent about but, regardless of the state of the dead men, Ruth is clearly considered part of Elimelech's household by Naomi. Masenya, "Who Calls the Shots in Naomi's Life?," 84–96.

Hamlin claims that the not forsaking the living and the dead phrase "meant that somehow the interests of the dead continue with the living, and that the unresolved problem following the deaths of her husband and her two sons would find its resolution in the living matrix of succeeding generations of children's children. This continuity is part of God's plan in choosing and calling a people whose vitality must be preserved from generation to generation." Hamlin, *Surely There Is a Future*, 37.

84. According to Hubbard, "Most scholars believe that go'el anticipates the eventual provision of an heir. In my view, however, her primary concern is with the happy prospect of a marriage for Ruth (cf. 3:1–2)." Hubbard, "Go'el in Ancient Israel," 14n53.

85. Timothy H. Lim argues that Ruth's misquote of Boaz in 2:21 is an indication by the narrator that Ruth is foreign and perhaps not completely fluent in Hebrew. Lim, "How Good Was Ruth's Hebrew?," 101–15. Regardless, Naomi's recorded speech shows an increasing familiarity with Ruth rather than perceived foreignness.

86. Westermann describes, "The day ends as it began with a conversation between Ruth and Naomi (vv. 17–23). In the midst of this conversation, Naomi pronounces a blessing on Boaz, 'Blessed be he by the Lord, whose kindness has not forsaken the living or the dead!' Naomi has reflected and understood. She had complained that the Lord had withdrawn his favor from her, but now she discovers that this is no longer true. So she thinks back on her husband and her sons: God has included even the dead. The family is saved!" Westermann, "Structure and Intention," 296.

is often translated as "security" but in fact it is "rest."[87] George Coats claims that this word is used for sexual relations, not marriage, and cites Deut 28:65, Lam 1:3, and Isa 34:14.[88] However, he does not discuss the relationship with the use of the term in the first chapter of Ruth, which seems to clearly connect it with marriage and should inform the meaning in this text more than uses in other books. This is the term that Naomi used in 1:9, though in a feminine form מְנוּחָה, in connection with Ruth and Orpah joining the household of their new husbands.[89] With this shared terminology, Naomi is likely suggesting marriage for Ruth in the same way that she did for both daughters-in-law in 1:9, which focused upon progeny. Berquist notes Naomi's subtle change in roles when she makes a marriage suggestion for Ruth in 3:1, claiming, "In ancient Israel, fathers arranged marriages for their children. Naomi's matchmaking is a male role. Once more, dedifferentiation sets the narrative into motion. When Naomi oversteps the roles acceptable for women, work toward the permanent solution restarts."[90]

Within Naomi's speech in chapter 1, the focus is not necessarily on the material security of Ruth and Orpah. After Naomi suggests that they find rest in the house of their husband, the women protest. Naomi insists that the women leave her because she is too old to bear sons and, even if she did, they would have to wait too long for the sons to grow up (1:11–12). Naomi's speech focuses upon the women fulfilling the role of wife and mother, which they are unable to do so long as they remain with Naomi. Instead of seeking Ruth's security in Ruth 3:1, Naomi is seeking Ruth's rest in the household of a new husband and, hopefully, bearing children. Charles Halton claims that Naomi is trying to sexually entrap Ruth, but Ruth changes the plan at the last moment. He argues that the preparation, location, and night-time setting indicate that Naomi was prostituting Ruth or planning that her pregnancy would force Boaz to financially support the women.[91] These elements

87. See Preuss, "נוּחַ ;מְנוּחָה," 283–85.
88. Coats, "Widow's Rights," 464–65.
89. Davis, *Who Are You, My Daughter?*, 69.
90. Berquist, "Role Dedifferentiation in the Book of Ruth," 31.
91. Halton, "Indecent Proposal," 30–43.

Baylis argues that the wording and timing of Naomi's charge show that she did not envision marriage according to Mosaic law or levirate custom, though Ruth and Boaz's exchange does follow Mosaic law and undermines Naomi's evil intentions. Baylis, "Naomi in the Book of Ruth," 428–30.

Sakenfeld argues, "It seems probable to me that Naomi is choosing and Ruth is accepting the one possibility realistically available to them, and thus that the village girls in India got it right what Ruth was doing was not appropriate behaviour in her culture any more than it would have been in modern rural India." Sakenfeld, "At the Threshing Floor," 166. McKeown agrees that Naomi's plan is dangerous and wrong. McKeown,

of the proposal might seem suspicious or dangerous, but the statement that she desires security for Ruth, in the same way that she had stated previously in reference to finding a new husband in Moab, raises doubts about how clearly this prostitution element is expressed in the narrative. Naomi seems to be returning to the point that she made while they were still in Moab.

However, this speech has a significant departure from chapter 1. In the first chapter, Naomi tells the women to return to the house of their mother. However, in this passage Naomi desires for Ruth to marry their close relative (3:2). She no longer asks Ruth to depart from her household but intends for Ruth to revitalize it. The statement that he is "our relative" indicates Naomi now views Ruth as part of her household and so she is responsible for continuing the family name (3:2).[92]

The connection between Ruth and the family of Naomi/Boaz continues to strengthen throughout the chapter. When Ruth lays at the feet of Boaz and he asks who she is, her response is "Ruth your maid" (3:9).[93] Claus Westermann claims, "In vv. 9–13 Ruth proposes marriage to Boaz and he accepts. This had been anticipated in the conversation in 2:10–13; it is now confirmed. In Ruth's very brief proposal, she says, 'Spread your cloak over your servant, for you are the גֹּאֵל."[94] Even more significantly, as

---

Ruth, 106.

Fewell and Gunn explain, "Why should Naomi set up such an arrangement? The literary allusions suggest that entrapment is the goal. Sexual intercourse, if not pregnancy, will enforce either marriage or a pay-off. The man, remember, is a 'man of substance' (a 'man of property', we might say, or a 'man of worth' *ish gibbor hayil* [2.1]). He is also a relative (at least by marriage); all the more reason for him to wish to avoid a public scandal." Fewell and Gunn, "'Son Is Born to Naomi!'" (1999), 238.

92. Several verbs with *kethib/qere* are present in Ruth 3:3–4, and most scholars follow the *qere* reading them as second person feminine singular verbs (commands from Naomi to Ruth) or archaic forms of the second person feminine (with an attached *yod*). However, an interesting proposal by Irwin is that a scribe intentionally changed the verbs to first person singular in order to avoid the impropriety of a Jewish man lying with a Moabite woman. The text would read, in this case according to Brian Irwin, "Dress, anoint yourself and put on your cloak. *I will go down* to the threshing floor. Do not make yourself known to the man until he has finished eating and drinking. Then, when he lies down, take note of where he lies down and go up and uncover his feet. Then *I will lie down*. He will tell you what you should do." Irwin, "Removing Ruth," 337, italics original. However, it should be noted that Irwin understands this as a theologically driven emendation that exploits ambiguities in the text, not the original reading of the text. For this reason, I understand the text to refer to Ruth rather than Naomi lying with Boaz.

93. Contra Sakenfeld who claims that it is just about familial and economic security and Ruth is not thinking about offspring. Sakenfeld, *Ruth*, 60–61.

94. For discussions of various interpretations of "spread your covering": as a euphemism for marriage, see De-Whyte, *Wom(b)an*, 261; Westermann, "Structure and Intention," 297; Köhlmoos, *Ruth*, 61–62; Nielsen, *Ruth*, 73; de Villiers, "Ecodomy,"

several scholars have noted, "Ruth does not follow Naomi's instruction to do whatever Boaz says, but rather she takes the initiative, speaking words that are in effect a marriage proposal."[95] This shows a growing connection since Ruth stated in the previous chapter, "You have spoken kindly to your maidservant, though I am not like one of your maidservants" (2:13). The terms for "servant" in 2:13 and 3:9 are different, and Reuter claims, "In Ruth 2:13 she is asking a favor and therefore refers to herself submissively as šipḥâ; in 3:9 she is more demanding and therefore calls herself 'āmâ." However, Reuter notes that the relationship between these two words is obscure and at times they appear to be used interchangeably.[96] Davis claims more strongly that the first term was for a servant and the term in chapter 3 is for a household member of a more elevated standing, so she is presenting herself as a marriage prospect.[97] In any event, she is no longer qualifying her relationship to Boaz or distancing herself from the people of Israel. She also boldly addresses Boaz at this point rather than allowing him to guide the

---

48; McKeown, *Ruth*, 57. As implying a sexual relationship (or emphasizing the sexual aspect of the marriage proposal) see Braulik, "Deuteronomium Und Die Bücher Ijob, Sprichwörter, Rut," 119; Braulik, "Book of Ruth as Intra-Biblical Critique," 15; Sakenfeld, *Ruth*, 58; Fischer, *Rut*, 211; Frevel, *Buch Rut*, 101; Halton, "Indecent Proposal," 35; Zenger, *Buch Ruth*, 71.

95. Sakenfeld, "At the Threshing Floor," 167. See also Coleson, "Peasant Woman and the Fugitive Prophet," 35.

Bernstein claims that the narrative, especially chapter 4, necessitates that Boaz and Ruth did not consummate their relationship in chapter 3, but the wording of the text has sexual overtones that makes the events intentionally unclear. Bernstein, "Two Multivalent Readings," 16–20. For a discussion of the phrases in this chapter and their possible sexual undertones (with a warning about using these supposed sexual undertones as a hermeneutical key), see Keita and Dyk, "Scene at the Threshing Floor," 17–32.

Finlay argues the emphasis on marriage and sex in 4:13 stresses that "Obed's conception occurred after a legal ceremony regarding Elimelech's estate and after Boaz's marriage to Ruth rather than in the night meeting between the couple in Ruth 3." Finlay, *Birth Report Genre in the Hebrew Bible*, 211.

96. Reuter, "שִׁפְחָה Šipḥâ," 409. Also, the Septuagint translates both terms with the same group of Greek words in the same frequency (406–7).

97. Davis, *Who Are You, My Daughter?*, 79. See also Hamlin, *Surely There Is a Future*, 44–45.

De Villiers claims, "The term which she applied to herself in Ruth 2:13, also translated as 'maidservant' was שִׁפְחָה [sic]. According to several scholars, these two terms are not simply synonymous: שִׁפְחָה [sic] suggests a slave girl who worked outside on the fields, while אָמָה pertains to someone who worked inside the house, and could be taken for a second wife if the first wife of a man happened to be barren. It is almost as if Ruth wants Boaz to understand that she is not the slave girl mentioned in chapter 2, but that she has now come into his house and that he should take notice of the change." De Villiers, "Ecodomy," 47. See similar observations in Sakenfeld, *Ruth*, 58; Fischer, *Rut*, 210; Frevel, *Buch Rut*, 100; Köhlmoos, *Ruth*, 61; Zenger, *Buch Ruth*, 71.

conversation like she did in the previous chapter. Boaz responds by calling her daughter twice (vv. 10, 11) unlike his identification of Naomi as her mother-in-law in Ruth 2:11.[98] This again increases the familial connection between Boaz and Ruth from Boaz's perspective.

In addition to the changes in wording, Boaz recognizes the relationship between Ruth and himself in his statement of a nearer relative (3:12).[99] Consistent with the description of Boaz as a near relative of Naomi and Ruth in Naomi's speeches (2:20; 3:2), Boaz claims that he is a close relative but there is a closer one than him (3:12). He does not distinguish between his relationship to Naomi or Elimelech and his relationship to Ruth the Moabitess (unlike the distinctions in 2:1, 3). In the same spirit that Boaz addresses Ruth as daughter and she claims that she is his maid, Boaz identifies his familial relationship with Ruth the way that the narrator did with Naomi and Elimelech in the previous chapter.

The increasing connection between Boaz and Ruth shows that Boaz and Naomi consider her a part of Naomi's household by the end of chapter 2 and throughout chapter 3. This not only changes Ruth from a foreigner to a member of an Israelite household, but it also shows that Naomi is seen as the head of Elimelech's household. In chapter 2, Boaz is described as a relative of Elimelech, but by the end of chapter 2 and throughout chapter 3, Boaz is described as a relative of Naomi and Ruth. This structure of Ruth as

---

98. Robin Branch observes, "When Boaz calls Ruth 'my daughter,' (Rt 2:8–9) he publicly displays a kindness to her befitting his seniority in age and social status." Branch, "Handling a Crisis," 5. See also Loader, "David and the Matriarch," 28. Hawk also believes this could be used from a position of power. Hawk, *Ruth*, 78.

W. F. Stinespring argues that Boaz "did not mean 'my daughter,' ... but something like 'my sweet young thing' or 'my dear.'" Stinespring, "No Daughter of Zion," 134. However, Michael Floyd disagrees with Stinespring, claiming, "Here, however, as well as in 3:10–11, where Ruth's kinsman also addresses Ruth as בתי, Boaz is drawing a contrast between himself and the 'young men' (נערים and בחורים, respectively) with respect to age and status. In the former instance such direct address emphasizes the difference between his protective intentions and their potentially abusive behavior. In the latter instance it emphasizes Boaz's sense of surprise that Ruth has chosen him over one of them. It is more probable that Boaz is being—quite literally—paternalistic." Floyd, "Welcome Back, Daughter of Zion!," 489. Similarly, Hubbard, *Book of Ruth*, 154. BDB and HALOT cite other texts like Ps 45:10 where it appears to be a kind address and can refer to a bride, but Floyd says these are ambiguous and could be taken as paternalistic too. Brown et al., "בַּת," 123; Koehler and Baumgartner, "בַּת," 166; Floyd, "Welcome Back, Daughter of Zion!," 489.

99. Trible considers the possibility that this nearer relative is the reason why Boaz did not assist Naomi and Ruth earlier (they have been in Bethlehem for the barley and wheat harvest; 2:23). Perhaps it was the responsibility of the nearer relative to redeem or provide for them more substantially and he was respecting the customary order. Trible, *God and the Rhetoric of Sexuality*, 185.

part of Naomi's household sets the foundation for the marriage and childbirth in chapter 4.

Ruth's Kindness as Familial Relation

In addition to the descriptions of Boaz as a relative of Ruth, Boaz's claim that Ruth's second kindness was better than her first also shows an acknowledgment of familial relations on behalf of both Ruth and Boaz. As Timothy Stone notes:

> From her many options, Ruth asks Boaz to marry her because he, as a close relative, can raise up the name of Mahlon, continuing Naomi's family line, as Boaz explicitly says in Ruth 4.10. This clarifies Boaz's veiled reference to Ruth's first and last kindness in Ruth 3.10. For this reason, Ruth's last kindness is greater than her first—probably referring to her decision to return from Moab and care for Naomi—of which Boaz is well aware (Ruth 2.11–12) . . . . Ruth's actions are not motivated by a concern for her own security or by some romantic attraction to Boaz, but her faithful commitment to Naomi. It is a greater kindness precisely because it extends beyond Ruth's earlier commitment to Naomi by seeking an heir for her.[100]

So, Ruth was apparently able to marry whomever she chose but went after a relative of Naomi. In chapter 2, Boaz commends Ruth for seeking shelter under the wings of God (v. 12), but this only indicates that Ruth has joined the Bethlehemite community.[101] Even his description of Ruth leaving father and mother and coming to a people she does not know falls just short of joining a new household (2:11). Boaz does not claim she came to Naomi's household but that she left her old household and joined Naomi's people generally (i.e., the Israelites).

---

100. Stone, "Six Measures of Barley," 195–96. Similar conclusions in McKeown, *Ruth*, 58; Hubbard, *Book of Ruth*, 215. For additional discussions on Ruth's freedom to marry outside of Naomi's family, see Green, "Plot of the Biblical Story of Ruth," 63; Robertson, "Plot of the Book of Ruth," 218; Sasson, "Issue of Ge'ullah in Ruth," 55–56.

101. As noted earlier, the nature of Ruth's connection to the community is not my primary focus. Whether Boaz is claiming that she is only part of the community by geographic proximity or believes her to be a full-fledged member does not change my interpretation. Either way, she is no longer a total stranger but involved in the community at some level, even if she is still viewed somewhat as an outsider. For a deeper discussion of Ruth's connection to the Bethlehem community, see Glover, "Your People, My People," 293–313.

When Ruth asks for Boaz to spread his wing (or covering) over her in 3:9, his response is that this kindness is greater than her first kindness.[102] She could have supported Naomi and joined the people of Israel by marrying any Israelite man. However, this greater kindness is moving beyond leaving her family and homeland; it is joining Naomi's household and providing an heir for her. This is a development in Ruth's relationship to Naomi's household. She first was *with* Naomi interacting with the people of Bethlehem and their God. However, now she is no longer just with Naomi but working as part of Naomi's household to inherit the land and provide an heir. Her proposition of marriage is not just to an Israelite man, which would fulfill joining the people she did not know (2:11), but to a relative of Naomi, which is an even greater kindness to her mother-in-law because she is acting as part of her household and attempting to reinvigorate Naomi's household and reclaim the ancestral property.

Renewed Fertility Through Boaz

Chapter 4 concludes the narrative with a raising of the name of Elimelech/Mahlon and a return to fertility for the household of Naomi through Ruth. The first part of the chapter is concerned with raising the name and redeeming the inheritance of Elimelech and his sons. The second half of the chapter focuses upon Ruth restoring the household to fertility and the relationship of Obed to God and Naomi's household.

Raising the Name

In the final chapter of Ruth, an emphasis is placed on raising the name of Elimelech/Mahlon. McKeown argues that even the name of the nearer relative, which he translates as "So-and-So," contrasts with building the name of Elimelech and Boaz: "Therefore, the anonymity is probably significant in the story and provides a contrast between Boaz and Mr. So-and-So (so NJPS), who lacked the vision, commitment, and compassion of Boaz. Whereas Boaz's name became well known, the other potential redeemer remained anonymous."[103]

Much has been published about the practice of levirate marriage and the concern for Ruth and Naomi's security. Many scholars have questioned

---

102. Many have argued the "wings" statements in 2:12 and 3:9 are parallel structures. See Hawk, *Ruth*, 93.

103. McKeown, *Ruth*, 61.

whether the practice in Ruth is levirate marriage because Ruth is not marrying her husband's brother, but even if this is not strictly levirate marriage, it is at least related to a levirate-type practice.[104] Regardless of how strictly this narrative follows the biblical levirate practice, the goal of levirate marriage, and Ruth's marriage, is to continue the family line of the dead husband, rather than the security of the widow. The emphasis on the continuation of the household of the deceased brother is displayed in the apparent discomfort of men in the HB who are supposed to be acting as the levirate contrasted with the women's willingness to participate.[105] This focus on the continuation of the household of the deceased in levirate marriages generally does not mean that Ruth and Naomi were uninterested in their own self-preservation. The text emphasizes the continuation of the household (likely for literary and political reasons with genealogy of David), but self-interest may also be part of the motivation and is hinted at in certain points in the text.[106] Even though the events in Ruth 4 do not follow the levirate practice precisely, Boaz's statement to the nearer relative emphasizes this focus on the family line and the relative's response also reflects this issue. As Milda de Vaal-Stanton explains, "What is the main aim of the marriage which is to take place? The text supplies the 'answer': 'to maintain the name of the dead unto his inheritance.' The fringe benefit for Ruth to get married would be that she will be looked after now. Boaz does not take responsibility for her in respect of any duties as *levir*, but in accordance with his responsibilities as married man."[107]

In a meeting at the city gate, Boaz tells the relative that he must "acquire Ruth the Moabite in order to raise up the name of the deceased on his inheritance" (4:5).[108] This comes immediately after the proposal for the

104. For a discussion of whether it was levirate or not, see Bush, *Ruth–Esther*, 221–27; Bronner, "Thematic Approach to Ruth," 165–67; Stone, "Six Measures of Barley," 191. De-Whyte challenges whether this was levirate marriage or widow-inheritance. Based upon the lack of shame for the relative refusing the marriage and the levirate marriage being specifically confined to brothers, De-Whyte believes that this is more connected to land-redemption law in Lev 25 even though there are some levirate-type responsibilities. De-Whyte, *Wom(b)an*, 263–64. Campbell and Hubbard argue that levirate marriage occurs in Ruth. Campbell, *Ruth*, 132–37; Hubbard, *Book of Ruth*, 212–13. For a succinct summary of the view that argues that neither land nor an heir is in view, see Sakenfeld, *Ruth*, 60–61. See also Eskenazi and Frymer-Kensky, *Ruth* = רות, xxxvi–xxxvii. Tod Linafelt lists several more options and cites scholars defending each approach. Linafelt, "Narrative and Poetic Art," 118–29.

105. See Weisberg, "Widow of Our Discontent," 403–29.

106. See Williams, "Contracts and Care of Oneself," 14–46.

107. De Vaal-Stanton, "Meaning and Implications of Ruth 4:5," 689. For a fuller discussion of levirate and redemption laws in relation to Ruth, see McKeown, *Ruth*, 86–95.

108. The *kethib* is "I (Boaz) will acquire Ruth" (קָנִיתִי) but the *qere* is "you will

relative to redeem Elimelech's field (v. 3). Boaz is connecting Ruth with the land and Elimelech's household. A key component of this verse is the owner of the land, specifically how a widow could inherit according to Old Testament laws. De Vaal-Stanton claims, "In Ruth 4:5 the core action pivots around the sale of 'a piece of land' or 'a share in respect of land' (Ruth 4:3) by the widow of a deceased landowner contradictory to the prescription in Deut 21:15–17 which makes it clear that women did not inherit from their husbands." However, "Naomi (as well as Ruth) did not sell land but a usufruct in respect of that land, to which they both are (legally and customary) entitled. Now the object of the sale provided in Ruth 4:3 will eventually also make sense: חלקת השדה. They are not disposing of ownership to land, but of a lesser right: a 'share (*Anteil*)' or 'interest.'"[109]

Another issue is that it appears Boaz, or the nearer relative, is able and expected to acquire both the widow and the land at the same time. Talia Sutskover summarizes:

> Biblical commentators have been puzzled by the redeeming of both land and woman in this one act, whereas the biblical law acknowledges only the redemption of land (Lev. 25.25), and quite separately the commandment to marry the wife of a dead brother (the levirate law, Deut. 25.5–10). The latter is considered the basis for Boaz marrying his dead kinsman's wife, but even

---

acquire Ruth" (קָנִיתָה). The *kethib* clarifies that the nearest kinsman is concerned about his inheritance because he will farm the land but then lose control of it once Ruth has a son. De-Whyte, *Wom(b)an*, 262; Beattie, "Kethibh and Qere in Ruth 4:5," 493; Eskenazi and Frymer-Kensky, *Ruth = רות*, 77–78; McKeown, *Ruth*, 64; Nielsen, *Ruth*, 84. Fewell and Gunn prefer the *kethib* because they believe that Boaz claiming Ruth as his wife explains the surprise and reversal by the redeemer more clearly. If Ruth has the potential to bring a male heir for Mahlon, through Boaz, then the redeemer may potentially lose a substantial amount of money. Fewell and Gunn, *Compromising Redemption*, 91. See a similar argument in Fewell and Gunn, "Boaz, Pillar of Society," 52. However, this same concern could also extend to the *qere* because Ruth's son would still take ownership of the land. Even more concerning if the relative does not currently have a son (the text does not indicate whether he has children), Ruth's son could be a firstborn son to the redeemer and thereby have a claim to his property as well as Elimelech's property. See further Matthews, *Judges and Ruth*, 240. Hawk uses the *qere* but has a similar discussion: Hawk, *Ruth*, 120. Davis lists three possible translations and claims that the ambiguity might be intentional to make the reader pause at this passage. The translations are "your acquiring the field from the hand of Naomi and Ruth the Moabite, wife of the dead, you acquire . . .," "your acquiring the field from the hand of Naomi and Ruth the Moabite, wife of the dead, I acquire . . .," "your acquiring the field from the hand of Naomi and from Ruth the Moabite, wife of the dead, you acquire . . ." Davis, *Who Are You, My Daughter?*, 100–101.

109. De Vaal-Stanton, "Meaning and Implications of Ruth 4:5," 682, 687. See also Davies, "Inheritance Rights and the Hebrew Levirate Marriage," 138–44.

this law does not include buying land and woman in the same transaction, as in Ruth 4. Hence the execution of the two transactions in one is unique to the book of Ruth, and is in keeping with its two dominant lexical fields.[110]

Though the ability of a widow to inherit property and the redeemer's ability to redeem both the woman and the land are important questions, they lie outside of the argument here. The point is that Naomi has claim over the property of Elimelech in some way according to the text.[111] Boaz's intention for the marriage to Ruth is not to protect her or provide for Naomi. It is to continue the line of Elimelech so that his descendants can inherit his land. As Fewell and Gunn state:

> All this is in the interests of establishing the name (fame and honor!) of the dead man over his inheritance (and notice that these *are* the terms in which the matter is put—and precisely *not* in terms of helping the poor and needy, especially the widow,

---

110. Sutskover, "Themes of Land and Fertility," 292–93.

111. Hawk, *Ruth*, 123–24. For a discussion of how Naomi, as a widow, can own property, see Osgood, "Women and the Inheritance of Land," 51; Bauckham, "Book of Ruth," 34; Sakenfeld, *Ruth*, 70; van Wolde, *Aan de Hand van Ruth*, 7.

Tim van Aarde argues, "The book of Ruth employs the term גָּאַל in the context of Boaz's action as kinsman-redeemer (Ruth 4:4–5:8). Elimelech had sold the usufruct in a time of economic hardship and Naomi did not have the right of redemption of the land which placed her in a precarious position." Van Aarde, "Semantic Relationship Between נַחֲלָה and יְרֻשָּׁה," 630.

Beattie summarizes traditional Jewish views: "The tenth century Qaraite commentator Salmon ben Yeroham suggested three possible answers to this question. First, he asserted that it was customary for the mother to inherit from her sons if they died without issue; commenting on the phrase 'Naomi has sold' (Ruth iv 3), he said 'Naomi inherited from her sons, for the mother inherits from the sons if they do not themselves leave sons. Thus, when Elimelech died, his sons, namely Mahlon and Chilyon, inherited the field, and when Mahlon and Chilion died childless Naomi inherited the field, and when she was in need of sustenance she sold it for it is said "If your brother becomes poor and sells part of his holding" etc.' To this Salmon added the alternative view that 'the mother does not inherit (from her sons) but it (i.e. the field) was Naomi's dowry and the dowry could not be included with other property and she sold the field to recover the dowry,' and also the third possibility that '(the ownership of) the field remained suspended until it should be seen what would become of Ruth, whether a child would be born to her who would inherit the property of Mahlon and Chilon or not.'" Salmon and Ibn Ezra apparently preferred the third view. Beattie, "Book of Ruth as Evidence," 254. Beattie traces this back to ancient Israel, claiming that it shows "(a) that widows could and did inherit the estate of their husbands, and that it was probably the case that childless widows would take precedence, in inheritance, over lateral male relatives of their husbands; and (b) that redemption was not equivalent to purchase, but the original owner was entitled, in certain circumstances, to have his property returned to him or his heirs by his kinsman who had redeemed it" (266).

which is what many critics are so anxious to see here). The patriarchy loves it. What nobler end could one strive for, make sacrifice for? All hail to Boaz! All hail to the man who for sake of his brothers, living and dead, would marry a Moabite woman![112]

The response of the relative also focuses upon descendants and inheritance. He responds to Boaz that he cannot redeem them for himself because it would jeopardize his inheritance (4:6). His reluctance is not because of a difficulty in materially supporting Ruth or even supporting Naomi and Ruth. He is concerned with the inheritance that he will pass through his household.[113] It is unclear what part of this is jeopardizing the inheritance. It could be that the relative felt as though a child from Ruth could make a claim to his property (perhaps he did not have a child/son at the time?) or that he could not absorb the cost of farming the field only to return it to Ruth's children when they come of age. Alter proposes an ethnic concern on the part of the kinsman:

> He leaves unstated why this should be the case. Many commentators conclude that he does not want to contaminate his family by introducing a Moabite woman. The Midrash Ruth Rabba proposes that he fears he will suffer the fate of Mahlon and Chilion, who died after marrying Ruth and Orpah. In any case, if he begets a son with Ruth, the estate will stand in the name of her dead husband, not of the kinsman, as is indeed the aim of the levirate law.[114]

In any event, progeny and inheritance are at the forefront of the conversation.

The same language of raising up the name of the deceased and maintaining the ancestral inheritance in his household is continued in Boaz's promise before the court. Boaz claims, "I have acquired Ruth the Moabite, the widow of Mahlon, to be my wife in order to raise up the name of the dead on his inheritance, so that the name of the dead will not be cut off from his brothers" (4:10). In this way, neither Ruth nor Naomi is the focus of Boaz's statement.[115] He is concerned with progeny. The two purpose clauses

---

112. Fewell and Gunn, *Compromising Redemption*, 92, italics original.
113. Bush, *Ruth–Esther*, 229–33.
114. Alter, *Strong as Death Is Love*, 99.

115. Embry argues that the focus is upon inheritance in the land and that Ruth inherited the property in a similar way to Zelophehad's daughters, so marriage was necessary to provide a male heir to inherit the property. Embry, "Legalities in the Book of Ruth," 31–44.

Fewell and Gunn note a distinction between Boaz's actions in chapters 2 and 3, as

are "raise up the name of the dead on his inheritance" and "so the name of the dead will not be cut off." Therefore, the purpose of Boaz's marriage to Ruth is not to provide for Ruth or Naomi but to continue the household of Elimelech and his son Mahlon.

The people at the gate then respond to Elimelech's marriage claim. Their speech again emphasizes her fertility.[116] First, the people state that she should be like Rachel and Leah who built the house of Israel (4:11).[117] According to Moshe Bernstein, this was likely a standard formula for fertility in marriage ceremonies.[118] Then they proclaim that Elimelech will have strength and a name in Ephrathah and Bethlehem. Finally, they claim that his house should be like the house of Perez through the seed of the woman (v. 12). Besides the obvious claims to fertility in the comparison with Rachel, Leah, and Perez, the references to calling a name and becoming strengthened are references to building a household.[119] Therefore, the people are rejoicing over the marriage, not because it provides security for Ruth or Naomi, but because they now have the possibility of returning to fertility, building a household, and reclaiming the inheritance of ancestral land.

This statement is similar to the blessing of Sarah by God in Gen 17:16: "I will bless her, and indeed I will give you a son by her. Then I will bless her, and she shall be a mother of nations, kings of people will come from her." It is also similar to the blessing of Rebekah by the people in Gen 24:60: "May you, our sister, become thousands of ten thousands, and may your

---

well as his final action, and his speech before the people: "In the public light of the following day, Boaz's talk is all of redeeming land and continuing male lineage and property. But as the story draws to a close, the narrator allows Boaz's final action to speak for itself. For all his piety and generosity, for all his acclaimed responsible behavior, his desire for Ruth cannot be cloaked. His last, and most telling, move is to have sexual intercourse with 'his woman' (4.13)." Fewell and Gunn, "Boaz, Pillar of Society," 48.

116. Loader, "David and the Matriarch," 32–33; Trible, *God and the Rhetoric of Sexuality*, 191.

117. As Pardes notes, בנה can refer to both building and bearing children. Pardes, *Countertraditions in the Bible*, 98n1.

Noting the masculine ending for the same verb referring to Naomi and Ruth in 1:19 and Leah and Rachel in 4:11, Davis claims, "The reuse of שתיהם in 4:11 may be a canny acknowledgment by the author that, despite their common struggle and cooperation, Naomi and Ruth cannot be considered full partners any more than Rachel and Leah can. On the one hand, the discordant form calls to mind how both pairs of women work together, compensating for a lack of male support by assuming more active roles in their predicament, but, on the other hand, the disagreement between the two parts of שתיהם conveys a certain discord between the women themselves." Davis, "Literary Effect of Gender Discord," 512.

118. Bernstein, "Two Multivalent Readings," 23.

119. McKeown, *Ruth*, 65–66; Kluger, *Psychological Interpretation of Ruth*, 91–92.

descendants possess the gate of those who hate them." Each of these speeches shows that the focus of the blessing is not the security of the woman, or widow, but their fertility and the continuation of the name of the household.

Restoration to Fertility

Immediately after the gate scene, Ruth becomes pregnant. Not only does she become pregnant, but the Lord gives her the child (Ruth 4:13). Timothy Finlay notes that in other places in the Hebrew Bible, God opens the woman's womb, remembers her, or does some other action, but this is the only place where Yahweh gives conception to someone.[120] This was a common understanding of conception in the HB and the ANE, but the reference is stark in this text.[121] Ellen Davis notes, "This stands out as one of only two direct statements from the narrator about God's action (cf. 1:6). Thus it underscores the fact that the child's birth is a providential event, the blessed result of both extraordinary human actions and the common but never less-than-miraculous action of God in making the womb fruitful."[122] The deaths at the beginning of the book of Ruth are not described in detail but are clearly explained by Naomi as the work of the Lord (1:20–21). So, the Lord destroys the household of Naomi but then provides a child to Ruth.

This connection between the divine deaths and divine pregnancy is made stronger when the people say a blessing to Naomi rather than Ruth in the following verse (4:14).[123] The phrase is similar to the speech of the people in the city gate (vv. 11–12). They proclaim that the child's name should be called in Israel and that he should restore life to Naomi (vv. 14–15).[124] Though calling a child a "redeemer" seems strange, most scholars believe that the son is Naomi's redeemer since the women are speaking on the occasion of the child's birth and stating that the Lord has not left her without a redeemer "today."[125] The day the son was born, Naomi was given a

---

120. Finlay, *Birth Report Genre in the Hebrew Bible*, 212.

121. McKeown, *Ruth*, 67. Conception by God is probably even more significant here because Ruth was married for ten years without children at the beginning of the narrative.

122. Davis, *Who Are You, My Daughter?*, 113.

123. Fischer claims that Ruth 4 is the only place where a baby was born "for a woman" (Naomi) and not "for a man." Fischer, "Book of Ruth," 32. See also de Vaal-Stanton, "Meaning and Implications of Ruth 4:5," 687.

124. Eugene Roop claims that the "return" (life) participle is an important term for chapter 1 and Naomi's return to Israel. Roop, *Ruth, Jonah, Esther*, 83.

125. Roop, *Ruth, Jonah, Esther*; Gladson, *Critical and Exegetical Commentary on Ruth*; Block, *Ruth*, 235; Finlay, *Birth Report Genre in the Hebrew Bible*, 212.

redeemer. De-Whyte claims that Ruth is acting as a surrogate for Naomi and that the kinsmen may have been brothers to Elimelech so Naomi should have been in the levirate marriage. However, for some reason, Naomi chose not to enter the levirate marriage and has Ruth enter it in her place. This is shown in the blessing of the son as Naomi's redeemer and son but not as an heir of Elimelech or his sons.[126] However, a different explanation for this is that Naomi is acting as the final member of the household (Ruth 1:1–5, 21). She has assumed the duties of Elimelech including owning the land (4:3). So, Ruth is raising up the name of the deceased in the words of Boaz, but the child is reckoned to the household Naomi, who is the surviving matriarch and new head of household. After Naomi receives a redeemer, the text continues using common phrases for increasing descendants: restoring life and building a name.[127] Therefore, the son, Obed, is building a name and continuing the life, or household, of Naomi that was destroyed in chapter 1. Richard Bauckham notes a slight difference between the women celebrating the son and Boaz's marriage declaration:

> From the women's perspective, what has happened is not that Boaz has acquired an heir for Elimelech, but that Ruth's devotion to Naomi has secured a son to be Naomi's support in her old age. From both perspectives the continuity of life into a third generation is secured, and from both perspectives the biological links also serve non-biological connexions, but the concern for patrilineal descent, biological or legal, which dominates one perspective is wholly absent from the other.[128]

126. De-Whyte, *Wom(b)an*, 264–65. Fewell and Gunn also see Ruth as a surrogate but say that it makes Naomi's resolution in the narrative bittersweet. Fewell and Gunn, *Compromising Redemption*, 81.
Brenner claims, "When Ruth finally marries, after much planning and manipulative action initiated by Naomi, she actually relinquishes her maternal status in favour of her mother-in-law (ch. iv). For all intents and purposes the biological mother, in contradistinction to previous behaviour patterns, in fact gives in to the adoptive mother (iv 17)—and willingly so. The reason given by the text for Ruth's generosity is her love for Naomi, which makes her more valuable for Naomi than any number of male sons (iv 14–15)." Brenner, "Female Social Behaviour," 267.

127. Contra Block, who claims, "Unlike the men in the gate, these women expressed no concern for the restoration of hereditary property to the clan of Elimelech or even raising up a name for Mahlon. Their focus was the personal well-being of the older widow." Block, *Ruth*, 235.

128. Bauckham, "Book of Ruth," 36.
Block discusses that "his name" could refer to Yahweh but since the *go'el* is the nearer antecedent, it is more likely the child. He notes that this phrase "means to 'keep the name/fame alive,' even after his death, and to perceive the person as living on in his descendants in the place named." Block, *Ruth*, 235.
Melcher claims, "The blessing in Ruth 4:11 reflects the complex cultural meaning

The final part of the blessing is that Ruth has been better to Naomi than seven sons. This is an ideal number that signifies fullness of the household.[129] However, the relationship between Naomi and Ruth is also important and contrasts the normal role of a daughter-in-law with the role of a son.[130] As a daughter-in-law who has been widowed, but whose husband had no surviving brothers, she would be expected to go back to her family and marry again, as shown by Orpah.[131] In this way, the widow would build the household of her new husband. However, a son would build the household of his own family, and seven sons would be a guarantee of many children to carry on the household name. E. John Hamlin argues, "For Naomi as a woman 'too old' (1:12) for any hope of replacing her dead sons by others, Ruth took the place of her sons in helping solve her problems."[132] Instead of returning to her family, Ruth takes on the role of a son and carries on the name of Naomi and Elimelech's household after the two biological sons died.

The final scene in the book of Ruth is Naomi with the child on her lap and the people proclaiming that "a son has been born to Naomi" (Ruth 4:16–17). Fulata Moyo claims:

> Honig (and Brenner) interprets Ruth's invisibility after Obed's birth as affirming Ruth's lingering foreignness . . . . Naomi's nursing of the baby through whom David's ancestry is traced assures that the baby will grow up as a true Israelite worshiping the "true" God. Thus, even Ruth's marriage to Boaz and

---

attached to the concept of 'name': 'May the LORD make the woman who is coming into your house like Rachel and Leah, who together built up the house of Israel. May you produce children in Ephrathah and bestow a name in Bethlehem.' In the previous verse (10), Boaz states the purpose of his marriage to Ruth: 'I have also acquired Ruth the Moabite, the wife of Mahlon, to be my wife, to maintain the dead man's name on his inheritance, in order that the name of the dead may not be cut off from his kindred and from the gate of his native place; today you are witnesses.' In this instance, the connection of 'name' with progeny is hinted at, while the importance of perpetuating a name upon the family inherited land is stressed." Melcher, "Tale of Two Eunuchs," 121.

129. Block, *Ruth*, 238; Saxegaard, *Character Complexity in Ruth*, 119; Moore, "Ruth the Moabite," 221.

130. Saxegaard views this also as a critique of Naomi's biological sons who died without heirs, but I think this goes beyond the intention of the text. Saxegaard, "'More Than Seven Sons,'" 270.

131. Campbell, *Ruth*, 82.

132. Hamlin, *Surely There Is a Future*, 72.

De-Whyte claims that this fulfills the promise to Abraham in Gen 12:1–3 because the land inheritance is preserved, the promise of descendants is realized, and the promise to be a blessing to all nations is shown through the ingrafting of the Moabite woman into Israel. De-Whyte, *Wom(b)an*, 266–68.

motherhood to Obed ends up benefiting Naomi the trafficker rather than Ruth. Ruth can be absorbed but not integrated into the Bethlehem community.[133]

This scene definitely appears at odds with the narrative, but interpreting Naomi as the head of the household eases the tension. LaCocque clarifies, "Because everything that belongs to Elimelek rightfully belongs to Naomi. It is not necessary to see in this choral proclamation a displacement of Ruth. She remains the mother of Obed, as Ephraim and Manasseh remained the sons of Joseph (the Josephites) after their adoption by their grandfather Jacob (Gen 48:12)."[134] A similar explanation is provided by Davis: "The fact that Ruth is now not named may simply indicate how fully she has been assimilated, in the public mind, into Naomi's Israelite family, whose story is now unfolding in a new generation."[135]

In Ruth 1:11, Naomi positions herself as the last remaining member of her household, which she claims is now empty. In Ruth 4:3, 5, Naomi is the holder of the ancestral land. This is unique because the HB does not indicate that widows normally inherit property.[136] Daughters could inherit if there were no male heirs (Num 27) and it appears that widows could manage the land if the sons were too young to inherit it (2 Kgs 8), but Naomi did not inherit it from her father nor did she have a male heir for whom she was managing the estate. Finally, the description of Ruth as better than seven sons to Naomi appears to indicate that Ruth was carrying on the line of Naomi in the way that sons would carry on the household of their father.[137]

---

133. Moyo, "'Traffic Violations,'" 89–90; Honig, "Ruth, the Model Emigrée," 55–56; Brenner, "Ruth as a Foreign Worker," 162.

McKeown claims that "the invisibility at the end of the book is compensated for by the title of the work, which does not allow us to forget that this is Ruth's story." McKeown, *Ruth*, 101. However, this argument is unconvincing.

Finlay also notes that this is the only place in the HB where a group of women name the son. Finlay, *Birth Report Genre in the Hebrew Bible*, 215. See also Bush, "Ruth 4:17," 3–14. For a discussion of the social role of the women in this interaction, see Meyers, "'Women of the Neighborhood' (Ruth 4.17)," 110–27.

134. LaCocque, *Ruth*, 144.

135. Davis, *Who Are You, My Daughter?*, 117.

136. See Block, *Ruth*, 209. However, as Campbell notes, we do not know what rights they might have had. Campbell, *Ruth*, 158.

137. Brenner claims that "the emphasis is on the child as Ruth's biological son and Naomi's adopted son. The end of ch. 4 signifies that Naomi benefits the most from the child's birth." Brenner, "Naomi and Ruth: Further Reflections," 140. See also Van Dijk-Hemmes, "Ruth," 134–39.

If Naomi is the head of the household, presumably Elimelech's household, the son born to Naomi is a statement of a child in Naomi's house.[138] Therefore, Naomi is not adopting the child as a mother but recognizing the progeny that will carry on the family line (cf. the blessing by Jacob on his grandsons Ephraim and Manasseh in Gen 48).[139] This emphasis on continued generations concludes the book with a genealogy that stretches from Perez to David.[140]

The importance of the child to Naomi's household can also be viewed from the perspective of resolving the narrative. As Green notes:

---

138. Block, *Ruth*, 240. Stone makes an interesting observation: "The pattern of interchange of food between Boaz, Ruth, and Naomi is repeated in ch. 3 and foreshadows the pattern of their relationship regarding Obed's birth in Ruth 4." That is, Obed from Boaz is given to Naomi by Ruth. Stone, "Six Measures of Barley," 193.

139. Block claims it is not an adoption ritual, though he notes some dissenting opinions. Block, *Ruth*, 239. Finlay likewise claims it is tenderness not adoption. Finlay, *Birth Report Genre in the Hebrew Bible*, 212.

Peleg argues that holding a child to the bosom is an ANE way of adopting a child. Peleg, "Why Didn't Ruth the Moabitess Raise Her Child?," 294n30. Similar arguments for an adoption ritual are made in Köhler, "Adoptionsform von Rt 4," 312–14. Donald Leggett claims that this is not a formal adoption (contra Köhler) but Naomi is showing that the child belongs to her in some way. Leggett, *Levirate and Goel Institutions*, 260–63.

Alter rejects the adoption interpretation but suggests some kind of adoption with Obed being a replacement for Naomi's sons: "To cuddle the child and become a caregiver for him is, of course, a natural expression of a grandmother's love, but it also strongly suggests how the child has become a vivid replacement for the two sons Naomi has lost. It is by no means necessary to see this act, as some interpreters have done, as a formal ceremony of adoption, and it would be both odd and unnerving for a grandmother to adopt her grandchild while his mother was alive." Alter, *Strong as Death Is Love*, 101.

140. Obed is the son of Boaz in this genealogy and Campbell is right in viewing the levirate paternity as dual. In certain places, he is referred to as a son of Boaz and in others he is the son of Naomi/Elimelech. Campbell, *Ruth*, 161. In any event, the focus upon progeny is clear because the book is concluding with a genealogy.

Hubbard claims, "In 3:18, Naomi again lauds Boaz, this time for his conscientious follow-through. He promised Ruth redemption (3:13), and he will not relax until she has it. In addition, the closing genealogy lists Boaz seventh in the list, a position of honor second only to that of the tenth place. In sum, according to the book, by serving as *goʾel*, Boaz performs an act of *ḥesed* worthy of honor." Hubbard, "Goʾel in Ancient Israel," 16. So also Sasson, "Generation, Seventh," 354–56; Sasson, "Genealogical 'Convention' in Biblical Chronography," 171–85.

Zvi Ron argues for a symbolic reading of this genealogy. According to Ron, this is not meant to portray history but preserve a seven/ten structure with the most important figures occupying these numerically significant positions in the list. Ron, "Genealogical List in the Book of Ruth," 85–92.

The marriage, conception and birth of a son are related in 4:13. The remaining verses indicate how the child resolves the various problems with which the story has dealt. He is first of all proof that the barrenness of Ruth and the emptiness of Naomi have ended. The blessing of 4:11–12 is accomplished, as the foreign woman builds the house of Israel once again. The second point that is clear is that the birth of the boy furthers the line which will produce the king.[141]

So, several strands of the plot are resolved through the birth of the child. The most significant one, for this study, is the emptiness of Naomi's household. Lau and Goswell claim, "Although they can never be fully replaced, the sons (*yelādîm*; 1:5) she lost have been replaced by this son (*yeled*; 4:17)."[142] The barrenness of Ruth is a narrative crisis (more implied by the text than explicitly stated, unlike Naomi's explicit claim of emptiness) within this emptiness crisis since Ruth is part of Naomi's household and unable to "fill" the household through providing progeny.[143]

---

141. Green, "Plot of the Biblical Story of Ruth," 60.

Lau and Goswell observe, "In addition, as suggested by Hubbard, the importance of the birth of Obed is more than just signifying the survival and future of the threatened family, for Yahweh's intervention strongly implies that the child has a special destiny (cf. Samson and Samuel in the surrounding books). This is supported by the fact that 4:13 is the only time in the book of Ruth that *the narrator* describes God as active in events ('the LORD gave her [Ruth] conception, and she bore a son')." Lau and Goswell, *Unceasing Kindness*, 29.

142. Lau and Goswell, *Unceasing Kindness*, 118. This terminological parallel is interesting, and perhaps points to an indirect connection between the grandson and the sons, but the thrust of the narrative points to Ruth directly replacing the sons and providing a grandson that Naomi's dead sons are unable to provide.

143. Jacobson explains, "First, the child's primary relationship is with his grandmother, Naomi. Her need, her journey from death to life sets the pattern for the story. When the women bless the Lord for the birth of the child, they address the blessing to Naomi: 'Then the women said to Naomi, "Blessed be the LORD, who has not left you this day without next-of-kin (gōʾēl); and may his name be renowned in Israel!"' (4:14). The child becomes Naomi's gōʾēl; she is not left bereft. Next, the women declare that the child will be for her 'a restorer of life and a nourisher of your old age' (4:15), but the reason for the child being described in this way is again remarkable. He will restore and nourish Naomi because Ruth, her daughter-in-law 'who is more to you than seven sons, has borne him!' (4:15). Ruth is not made worthy by the birth of a son; she is already worthy (3:11). Rather the child is made worthy, is of benefit to Naomi, because of the devoted affection of his mother for his grandmother." Jacobson, "Redefining Family in Ruth," 10.

Conclusion

Throughout the book of Ruth, the household roles of Ruth and Naomi develop. What begins as a story of a mother and daughter-in-law ends with a portrayal of them as the head of the household and a son. Naomi develops into the head of the household early in the narrative as family members are reckoned to her rather than her husband in chapter 1, and this continues until the end of the narrative where she is said to own the ancestral land and Ruth's son is said to be born to her. Ruth's development into a son is hinted at in her promise to stay with Naomi until death in chapter 1 but develops slowly over the remainder of the narrative. In chapter 2, she transitions from a foreigner who returned with Naomi to a member of Naomi's household. Chapter 3 confirms her ability to restore the household name through the dialogue with Boaz, and in chapter 4 she acts as a son continuing the name of her in-laws and providing an heir for Naomi.

Like the female-centric narratives of the preceding chapter, Ruth appeals to Boaz rather than to God. Naomi promotes this appeal to men in the first chapter, though she encourages the women to marry men in Moab, and in the third chapter when she encourages Ruth to appeal to Boaz as a near relative. Therefore, the trend that women appeal to men in family death narratives is found in all the female-centric family death narratives of the HB.

CHAPTER 5

MALE-CENTRIC FAMILY DEATH NARRATIVE IN JOB

IN A DISSERTATION ON death and the retribution principle in Job, Varunaj Churnai claims that the death of Job's children is not integral to the story, even within the prologue narrative.[1] This sentiment is echoed by other scholars who claim that the prologue is concerned with Job's wealth and family, while the poetic section is focused upon Job's illness and the certainty of the retribution principle.[2] However, the death of Job's children is a recurring theme throughout the book and is a frequent tool of the friends to try to explain God's control over the lives of the wicked and the righteous.

This chapter will focus upon the portrayal of the significant narrative elements for this study on the death and restoration of the household: origin of deaths, discussion of land inheritance, and explicit restoration of the household in the text. I will use the narrative frame and Job's friends' references to the destruction of his family in the dialogues to demonstrate these narratival elements. The narrative frame of the book attributes the death and restoration to God, and within the dialogues Job appeals to God for restoration and his friends recommend this course of action as well.

---

1. Churnai, "Beyond Justice," 50–51.

2. Wiley writes, "The replacement sons and daughters are all but tokens tossed in at the end of the list of Job's reimbursement." Wiley, "They Save Themselves Alone," 127. Mathewson claims that death runs throughout the book as part of the conversation about divine justice. However, these conversations are about *the concepts* of death and are not directly tied to Job's experience with his family. Mathewson, *Death and Survival in Job*, 39, 84. Schipper, "Healing and Silence in the Epilogue," 17–18; Fleming, "Job," 469; Crenshaw, *Old Testament Wisdom*, 97; Spiegel, "Noah, Danel, and Job," 333–34.

Origin of Deaths

Blessing of God Turned to Death

The story of Job begins with his idyllic life. He is recognized as the greatest man in the East with a large number of animals and the perfect number of children, seven sons and three daughters (1:1–3).[3] Not only is Job wealthy in children and animals, but he has a great deal of property as well. His children have their own houses, rather than living in the house of their father, and they have a regular feast cycle at their houses (1:4–5).[4]

Job's piety and his concern for his children are shown in verse 5 when he offers sacrifices for them in case they have sinned during their feasting. His spiritual preventative measures for his children are unexpectedly undermined by their destruction later in the chapter. Job does not appear to be involved in the feasting, and the narrator does not mention Job sacrificing for himself.[5] The emphasis in the text is Job's care for the purity of his children before God. Though his children have their own homes and are involved in their own activities, Job is still watching over his descendants. His sacrificing is not explicitly performed to prevent divine wrath from destroying his progeny but, in the context of the narrative and in comparative literature, this seems likely.[6]

Job 1:13–19 disrupts the idyllic life. From Job's point of view, this is a sudden and unexpected turn of events. The destruction sequence begins and ends with Job's children. The narrator starts with the children feasting (1:13) but suddenly shifts to a messenger coming to Job with news of destruction (1:14).[7] It is not immediately clear how the children feasting in the oldest brother's house is related to Job and the messenger in the following verse. However, this highlights the sudden shift to a four-stage narrative progression that builds in intensity and foreshadows the final calamity. In

---

3. Mathewson, *Death and Survival in Job*, 40.

4. Some have claimed Job is a king and this activity shows that he is in the upper echelon of society. De Moor, "Ugarit and the Origin of Job," 225–57; Caquot, "Traits Royaux dans le Personnage de Job," 32–45.

5. It may be assumed that Job sacrificed for himself also, but this is not stated in the text. See Cho, "Integrity of Job 1," 234.

6. See also the physical retribution for Kirta when he forgets to offer a sacrifice to the goddess (KTU 1.16) and the warnings against cursing God in the HB (Exod 22:28; Lev 24:15). Mathewson, *Death and Survival in Job*, 48.

7. For the trope of the lone survivor bringing news of destruction, see Andersen, *Job*, 90.

each stage, Job's servants are killed and his property is destroyed or taken, but the means by which they are destroyed are different. The first and third messengers tell Job that the animals are taken by human agents (oxen and donkeys by the Sabeans and then camels by the Chaldeans). The second and fourth events are acts of God (the fire of God killed the sheep and then a great wind killed the children).[8]

The fourth event is the climax of the progression and ties back to the introductory sentence. All the children are killed in one event because they are all feasting together. The feasting does not appear to have a negative connotation and was described as part of Job's prosperity at the beginning of the chapter. However, death by a great wind knocking the house down is significant. They were not victims of human agents like the livestock in the tragedies, but of an unavoidable act of God.[9]

The conversation between God and Satan makes the divine nature of these events clear. Job has children because God placed a hedge around him and his house and blessed him (1:10). The removal of these blessings also comes from the hand of God by his permission for Satan to attack Job (1:11). The divine scene does not add information about Job's family or the nature of his loss but only makes explicit what is already implicit in the story: Job was blessed by God with progeny and wealth but, though he walked blameless before God, God destroyed them.

Inability to Restore Family

After the rapid destruction of his family and wealth, Job responds with mourning and a hymn to God, "Naked I came from my mother's womb, and naked I will return there. The Lord gave and the Lord has taken away. Blessed be the name of the Lord" (1:21). Though this is clearly a statement of mourning, it also shows Job's helplessness. God can bestow or take away Job's progeny. Job does not seek to enlarge his family on his own in this chapter or throughout the rest of the book. When the children are taken away, Job has no option but to mourn the destruction by God and pray for a reprieve.

---

8. For more interpretations of the divisions in the narrative, see Amit, "Progression as a Rhetorical Device," 3–32; Mathewson, *Death and Survival in Job*, 50–52.

9. Clines, *Job 1–20*, 33; Alden, *Job*, 60; Balentine, *Job*, 56.

Loss of Inheritance

Each of Job's friends connects the fate of the household with the father's own righteousness or wickedness. Within each passage discussed, divine control over the family of the father will be shown as well as the application of the retribution principle to the fate of the family and inheritance. In addition, the subtle, or not so subtle, attacks upon Job's own experience will be shown both in the similarities of the friends' descriptions to the events in the prologue and in Job's responses to the accusations. The descriptions will be divided into four foci: children died for their own transgressions, children receive the father's punishment, the wicked are forgotten, and the righteous have heirs and a secure house.

Children Died for Their Own Transgressions

The most direct attack upon Job's family comes from Bildad's first speech. In an attempt to maintain God's justice, he states, "If your sons sinned against him, then he delivered them into the hand of their transgression" (8:4). Bildad apparently believes that Job is also wicked because he claims that Job must ask for God's mercy and, if he is upright, he will be restored even greater than before (8:5–7). The description of the situation by Bildad points to chapter 1 but conflicts with the narrator's description. In Bildad's view, Job is a bad father because his children are wicked. This, then, is an attack on Job by showing the obvious wickedness of his children and his inability to raise righteous progeny.

It is also important to note that within this chapter, obtaining individual children is not the primary focus. Though Bildad starts by indicting Job's children, he quickly moves to the short lifespan of the wicked person's household (8:15–22). The curse or blessing of God is not centered upon the destruction of one generation or a specific child. The curse is that the household will become empty. Much like the ANE literature, it is not just that Job's children died but that all his future descendants, and thereby his name and inheritance, will cease forever.

Children Receive the Father's Punishment

Eliphaz: Chapter 5

Job's friends frequently claim that children receive the punishment of their father. They draw a direct line between the father sinning and the household collapsing. In Eliphaz's first speech, he claims, "I have seen the foolish taking root and I cursed his habitation immediately. His sons are far from safety, they are even crushed in the gate, and there is no deliverer" (5:3-4).

In this claim, the relationship between a father and his children is clear. Children are the extension of their father, so the punishment for his wickedness falls upon them. Eliphaz is not only explaining divine retribution falling upon the heirs of the wicked generally, but he appears to be pointing to Job's children.[10] The lack of a deliverer implies that it is an act of God, and the sons being crushed (דכא) echoes the house falling upon the children of Job. Andersen sees an even stronger connection between Eliphaz's speech and Job's children, suggesting that instead of gate (שַׁעַר), it should be read tempest (שַׂעַר).[11] Whether this emendation to the text is valid or not, the children being crushed by an act of God is reminiscent of Job's situation.

This description of the crushed children is followed by an agricultural metaphor, just like Bildad's indictment of Job. The location of trouble is not the earth, but it is what people are born into (5:7). God watches over the seasons and takes care of the poor but destroys the unrighteous (5:9-16). In this setting, Eliphaz is describing the world working according to divine justice. Though much of his description is broad and even metaphorical, he singles out the crushing of the wicked man's children. In Job 5:2-16, the death of children is the direct connection with Job. In the midst of theological platitudes, Eliphaz suggests that Job is at least in danger of being unrighteous, if not already in need of repentance, by claiming the wicked man's sons meet the same fate as Job's children.[12]

Just like Bildad's metaphor of the wicked thriving before the sun but their roots grasping at stones, the short-lived nature of the wicked is emphasized here (8:16-18). Eliphaz does not curse the children of the wicked but the habitation of the wicked (5:3). The wicked take root but they are still destined for trouble and God will thwart their plans. Just like Bildad, Eliphaz does not claim that God is striking down specific children but, rather, that the entire household will cease to exist. The wicked taking root implies fertility and future fruitfulness. When the wicked are deprived of

---

10. Indirect reference to Job's family death has been noted by Driver and Gray, *Critical and Exegetical Commentary on Job*, 50; Hartley, *Book of Job*, 118; Alden, *Job*, 91; Habel, *Book of Job*, 131; Longman, *Job*, 123; Balentine, *Job*, 112; Seow, *Job 1-21*, 416. Contra Clines who sees no reference to Job's family here and claims it is not intentionally cruel though insensitive. Clines, *Job 1-20*, 141.

11. Andersen, *Job*, 127.

12. As Pyeon notes, "According to Eliphaz, it is Job who has brought about his current plight. Though this is not explicitly expressed, it is hinted at in several passages . . . . Eliphaz requests Job to take his advice to heart and come back to his former piety." Pyeon, *You Have Not Spoken*, 101.

their fruitfulness, the products of their fertility and the vehicles for future fruitfulness (i.e., children) are in danger.

Eliphaz: Chapter 15

Eliphaz again claims divine retribution for the wicked comes in the destruction of their household in Job 15:34. He claims, "The congregation of the godless is barren, and fire consumes the tents of the corrupt." The destruction of the wicked man's entire household and the divine cause is described as barrenness and a consuming fire.[13] The reason for the wicked man's downfall is his attack against God and his arrogant actions in the face of the Almighty (15:25-26).

Like Eliphaz's earlier reference, there appears to be an echo of the tragedies in Job's family, the second of which was the fire of God (1:16-18).[14] The term for company (עֵדָה) only occurs twice in the book of Job: 15:34, "the company of the godless is barren," and 16:7 where Job complains that God "laid waste all my company." Job starting his speech with language reflective of Eliphaz shows that he is interpreting this as a description of his situation. The conceptual overlap of the destruction of the tent by fire and the lexical overlap with Job's description of his situation in his reply suggest that Eliphaz is reflecting upon Job's situation.[15] Job appears to agree with the assessment that God has made his household barren but rejects the implication that it is because he is godless later in his speech (16:17-19). This emphasis on barrenness and the destruction of the entire household fits well with the comparative literature and the previous statements of the friends. Eliphaz views progeny and continuation of the household as the blessing of God, and Job's loss of heirs shows that he has brought about God's wrath.

---

13. Barrenness should be understood as the curse. The house of the wicked is unable to conceive children and so it dies out. Barrenness as indicative of divine displeasure is also seen throughout the HB (e.g., Gen 16:2; 20:18; 30:2; Hos 9:11). See also Clines, *Job 1-20*, 364; Alden, *Job*, 181.

14. Andersen, *Job*, 194; Driver and Gray, *Critical and Exegetical Commentary on Job*, 141; Longman, *Job*, 230; Alden, *Job*, 180. Contra Clines, who claims that it is not about Job because Eliphaz is on Job's side in his other speeches. Clines, *Job 1-20*, 364-65.

15. Longman, *Job*, 230; Alden, *Job*, 180-81; Andersen, *Job*, 194; Driver and Gray, *Critical and Exegetical Commentary on Job*, 141. Contra Clines, *Job 1-20*, 365.

Zophar

In Job 20:26, Zophar provides Job with another description of the wicked man's household: "Total darkness is reserved for his treasures, an unfanned flame will consume him and devour the survivor in his tent."[16] The first clause appears to be referencing earthly treasures but, as Driver and Hartley have pointed out, monetary wealth would normally be hidden in darkness so that thieves cannot find it.[17] The second and third clauses also inform the reading of "treasures" as more than monetary wealth. The unfanned flame consuming him and the remnant of his tent being devoured show that human casualties are in view.[18]

Just like Eliphaz in 15:34, Zophar claims that the destruction of the wicked man's household is an act of God. The divine element of this fire is even more clear here because Zophar claims it is "not fanned." Zophar also claims this is the inheritance that the wicked man receives from God (20:29). A number of scholars believe that this is a reference to lightning, and some claim this is the same interpretation for the second tragedy in Job 1:16.[19]

---

16. The parallel speech in Job 27:13–15 will not be addressed separately for two reasons. First, it mirrors Zophar's speech in 20:26–29 without adding any further narrative or theological information. In fact, the language is almost identical: 27:13, "this is the portion of a wicked man (זֶה חֵלֶק־אָדָם רָשָׁע) from God and the inheritance (וְנַחֲלַת) that oppressors receive from the Almighty," and 20:29, "this is the portion of a wicked man (זֶה חֵלֶק־אָדָם רָשָׁע) from God and the inheritance (וְנַחֲלַת) appointed to him by God." They also both refer to the last survivor (שָׂרִיד) of the wicked being destroyed (20:26; 27:15). The thematic and lexical repetition has led many scholars to question whether it is Job or one of the friends. If it is Job, it is heavily ironic. If it is one of the friends, most believe Zophar, then it is misplaced in the text. Either way, it is using an almost identical formula as the Zophar speech and so adds little to the development of the use of children in the speeches. For more arguments about the parallels with Zophar's speech and the speaker: Bildad speech, see Hartley, *Book of Job*, 355. Zophar speech, see Driver and Gray, *Critical and Exegetical Commentary on Job*, 228; Pope, *Job*, 172; Clines, *Job 21–37*, 651; Reyburn, *Handbook on the Book of Job*, 490; Habel, *Book of Job*, 385. Job speech, see Longman, *Job*, 319; Konkel, *Job*, 167–70; Wilson, *Job*, 292–98; Alden, *Job*; Andersen, *Job*, 238.

17. Hartley, *Book of Job*, 308n40; Driver and Gray, *Critical and Exegetical Commentary on Job*, 181.

18. It is also possible that these could be building on each other. Wealth is destroyed, then the individual, then his household. The second and third clauses are most important in this study, so whether the first is a reference to physical wealth or family is helpful in the comparison but not essential.

19. See Driver and Gray, *Critical and Exegetical Commentary on Job*, 181; Pope, *Job*, 140; Longman, *Job*, 270; Hartley, *Book of Job*, 308; Balentine, *Job*, 316–19. Seow does not believe this is lightning nor connected to 1:16 but, rather, God's wrath connected to 15:34. Seow, *Job 1–21*, 845. Seow does not mention any connection to Job's family in

If the destruction of the wicked man's household by divine fire is an opaque reference to Job's situation, Zophar's appropriation of Job's divine courtroom terminology bolsters this interpretation. In Job 16:18-19, Job appeals to heaven and earth to bear witness to his pain. He asks the earth not to cover his blood and the heavens to bear witness to his plight. He uses divine courtroom imagery to claim his innocence and call for justice. Zophar picks up this imagery in Job 20:27 and claims that the heavens will uncover his iniquity and the earth will rise up against him. He turns Job's requests for uncovering and bearing witness from supporting Job to condemning him.[20] This twisting of Job's speech indicates that Zophar is not just making a philosophical claim about the fate of the wicked man's household but intentionally describing Job.[21] Instead of a short reference to the prologue narrative, Zophar reinterprets Job's complaints about his situation in verses 24-29. Though he does not mention Job's children directly, unlike Bildad in chapter 8, his extended reworking of Job's complaints indicates that Job's life and family are the focus of Zophar's description.

Just like the previous speeches, Zophar focuses upon the destruction of descendants rather than specific children. The wicked, in Zophar's speech, will perish forever and his wealth, or inheritance, will not endure (20:7, 21). The destruction of children, then, is not the curse of God but the way in which God's curse over the continuation of the house of the wicked is displayed.

Wicked Are Forgotten

Bildad claims that the wicked are cut off by God, their tent is brimstone, and they are forgotten among the living (18:14-21). The name of the wicked perishing follows from their lack of descendants and the utter destruction of their household. The destruction of the house in brimstone and barrenness is reminiscent of the curse of barrenness and destruction by fire described by Eliphaz in 15:34.

Connecting his description of the wicked to Job's situation, Bildad mentions skin disease just before the household destruction (18:13). Job's response in the next chapter also shows that he understands this household destruction is directed at him. Job begins by asking how long the friends

---

15:34 but see the discussion of this passage above.

20. This imagery inversion has been noted by Andersen, *Job*, 212; Driver and Gray, *Critical and Exegetical Commentary on Job*, 181; Hartley, *Book of Job*, 309; Holbert, "'Skies Will Uncover His Iniquity,'" 171-79.

21. Contra Clines, *Job 1-20*, 501.

will insult him (19:3), then moves to the fate of his household (19:12–19), and ends with a description of his painful skin disease (19:20–22).[22] In addition to this broad structural overlap, his language parallels Bildad's speech. Bildad describes the wicked as having "roots dried up and branches cut off," while Job claims his "hope is uprooted like a tree" (18:16; 19:10). Job also claims that everyone in his household has forgotten him, just like Bildad claims for the wicked (18:17–19; 19:13–16). Job then finishes his description of himself as being abhorrent to his own family, while Bildad describes the wicked as appalling and a horror (18:19–20; 19:17–19).[23]

Job claims that his situation is a curse from God like Bildad appears to do in 18:21. However, while Bildad claims this is the fate of those who do not know God, Job turns the divine destruction of his household into a question for his friends: "Why do you persecute me like God (19:22)?"

Righteous Have Heirs and a Secure House

After claiming that children are crushed because of the wickedness of their father at the beginning of chapter 5, Eliphaz tells Job about the blessings that will come if he turns to righteousness. He claims, "You will know your tent is secure, for you will visit your abode and fear no loss. You will know also that your descendants are many, and your offspring as the grass of the earth" (Job 5:24–25). This chapter frames the presence or absence of children within the retribution principle. Within chapter 5, Eliphaz uses children for both the negative description, the deaths of Job's children, and a positive possibility, the multitude of future descendants, to make the retribution principle personal. Though he includes general statements like "man is born for trouble" (5:7) and "from six troubles he will deliver you" (5:19), the references to children reflect Job's situation. Eliphaz weaves together general wisdom with hints at Job's life: first, by claiming the children of the wicked are crushed by an act of God and, second, by switching to second person pronouns and telling Job directly that if he is righteous, he will have many descendants in contrast to his current state with no progeny.[24]

---

22. Seow notes the similarity of the two thematically and notes the same word "tearing" (נתק) from his tent and security in verse 14 is used in Job's description of himself in 17:11. Seow, *Job 1–21*, 776.

23. Hartley, *Book of Job*, 284; Habel, *Book of Job*, 300; Alden, *Job*, 200.

24. For the connection with the number seven between this passage, Job's children, and even Eden, see Balentine, *Job*, 118; Seow, *Job 1–21*, 426; Longman, *Job*, 130. Clines and Wilson see cruelty in the reference to children since Job's children have died, while Habel and Hartley draw comparisons between the plant metaphors here and Job's tree metaphor in chapter 14. Clines, *Job 1–20*, 153; Wilson, *Job*, 54; Habel, *Book of Job*, 136;

Restoration

In Job 8:4, Bildad tells Job that his children died because of their transgressions. However, if Job earnestly seeks God and asks for his compassion, he might escape the same fate and his latter days will be even greater than the beginning (8:5-7). Ironically, Job receives twice the blessing as before once he seeks God's mercy *for his friends* (42:10, 12). This undermines the charge that Job and his children were punished for their sinfulness but also upholds Bildad's claim that if Job is pure and upright, God will restore his rightful dwelling place (8:6).

Eliphaz's outline of the righteous also fits Job's family restoration. He starts by describing the happy man who receives correction because God wounds but also heals (5:17-18). When he describes the righteous man's family, he claims that his descendants will be as numerous as grass, and he will die full of years (5:25-26). Job's story ends with him having ten children and twice the normal life span.[25] Not only does he have children and a long life, but he has enough wealth for both his daughters and sons to have inheritances, and he lives long enough to see four generations (42:13-17). Though Eliphaz was warning Job not to despise God's discipline, he was more accurate in the description of Job's future than he may have realized. Job would receive God's vindication and God would call him righteous.

The blessing in the epilogue appears to be the replacement of Job's children in the prologue. However, God's blessing was progeny and the continuation of his household rather than the children themselves. The friends frequently reference emptiness and a forgotten household as the curses of God. In each of the passages examined, the friends mention the entire household being destroyed, not just one generation or a specific child. The ANE literature also calls for the gods to make transgressors' households empty and forgotten and for the gods to bless the righteous with descendants in perpetuity.

Job's new children, then, are not replacements of the previous family but a return to fertility.[26] Even the animals in Job's care are twice as fertile as in the prologue, which coincides with Job's description of God's blessing, "his ox mates without fail, his cow calves and does not abort. They send forth their little ones like the flock, and their children skip about" (Job 21:10-11).

Hartley, *Book of Job*, 128.

25. Clines, *Job 38-42*, 1239; Alden, *Job*, 414; Hartley, *Book of Job*, 543; Habel, *Book of Job*, 585; Driver and Gray, *Critical and Exegetical Commentary on Job*, 376.

26. For discussions of the importance of fertility in the names of the daughters, see Wilcox, *Bitterness of Job*, 221-24.

Though Job questions the retribution principle, God repays Job with progeny and enough inheritance to provide all his children with property. God asserts his ability to act as he pleases in the divine speeches but still blesses Job with the greatest gift in the ANE: heirs and an enduring name.

Conclusion

The children of Job become a tool for the friends to apply the retribution principle. They discuss the divine destruction in Job 1 and explain how God is punishing Job through his household. Job's responses indicate that he sees their descriptions of God destroying the progeny of the wicked as attacks upon the tragedies within his own household. This theme shows that the deaths in chapter 1 are more than background narrative. His family does not just appear at the beginning and end of the story but features in the debates over divine interaction with the world. The friends tie the death of children to their father's sinfulness and so claim that Job's state is the result of divine justice and only an appeal to the divine can restore his household.

Much like the male-centric family death narratives of the ANE, Job appeals to God for the restoration of his family, and his friends recommend a divine appeal as well. Job is unique in the HB as the only male-centric family death narrative. However, this also creates a connection between the HB and ANE narratives. Job's divine appeal shows that appealing to men is not a HB phenomenon but a female protagonist response. Therefore, Job illustrates that in the experience of family death, the HB and ANE agree that men should appeal to the divine. However, the female-centric narratives of the HB demonstrate that women appeal to men when facing the same situation. The reason for the differing responses to the same crisis will be discussed in chapter 7.

CHAPTER 6

BARRENNESS NARRATIVES IN THE HB AND ANE

This chapter will treat the second group of texts, the barrenness narratives, with similar criteria to the family death narratives. The texts selected contain barrenness (entire household or an individual in the household), the character(s) or narrator attributing their situation to God, and the restoration of the family (whole or partial).[1] Like the family death narratives, each barrenness narrative must contain at least two of these criteria to be included.

The HB narratives that will be discussed are Sarah in Gen 18, Rebekah in Gen 25, Rachel in Gen 30, Manoah's wife in Judg 13, and Hannah in 1 Sam 1. In each of these texts, the wives are involved in the conversation with the divine, but the husbands are only occasionally involved. Even in the texts where husbands appeal to the divine, the wives also directly interact with God, unlike the family death narratives. Since only one ANE text fits the barrenness category criteria, it will be treated within this chapter alongside the HB texts. The ANE barrenness narrative discussed in this chapter is the Myth of Etana. Though the husband is more central in this narrative than in the HB narratives, Etana's wife interacts with the gods and receives a divine dream, unlike the women in the family death narratives.

The structure of analysis in this chapter is threefold: description of barrenness, interaction with the divine, and restoration. The first and last

---

1. Though outside the scope of this work, God appears to be directly involved in the lives of women servants who resolve the barrenness of their barren female masters (specifically Hagar, Bilhah, Zilpah). For a detailed study, also including Leah, see Starr-Morris, "Leah and Hagar," 384–401.

elements are quite similar to the family death narratives, but the second is different. Land inheritance is significant in the family death narratives because the ones who are supposed to maintain the ancestral land have died. Inheritance is also important in the barrenness narratives because the women desire to produce an heir, but ancestral land issues are less common in these narratives.[2] However, I have included the interaction with the divine in this chapter to show that women appeal to the divine in barrenness narratives, unlike the family death narratives. Therefore, the second element in this framework shows how women, and sometimes men, interact directly with the divine, rather than the women's concern for inheritance.

Sarah

The promise of Isaac takes place over several chapters in Genesis (15–21) with several other narratives spliced between.[3] Since the focus is upon Sarah's interaction with the divine, chapter 18 will be the primary text of this study. In this chapter, Yahweh meets with Sarah and Abraham by the oaks of Mamre. The nature of the three divine figures has been widely debated, especially in Christian circles. The traditional Christian interpretations are pre-incarnate Christ with two angels or an early type of the Trinity. For our purposes, their identification as divine figures is sufficient, because the focus is on how the human characters interact with the divine not the representation of the divine.[4] The text suggests that Abraham believes that three

---

2. Blessing claims, "The barren matriarch is barren through no fault of her own. The point of the barrenness is to show that the people of God are perpetuated by a sovereign act of God, in God's time. *The emphasis is on a fruitful future.*" Blessing, "Desolate Jerusalem and Barren Matriarch," 53, italics original.

3. Since Isaac's birth is announced multiple times within these chapters, the categorization of Gen 18:1–15 has been debated.

Some have called it an Annunciation Narrative. See Coats, *Genesis*, 137; Wenham, *Genesis 16–50*, 40; Irvine, "'Is Anything Too Hard for Yahweh?,'" 295–97; Rosenberg, "כעת חיה," 701–20; Fuchs, "Literary Characterization of Mothers," 117–36; Williams, "Beautiful and the Barren," 110.

Others have claimed it is a Fellowship Narrative since the birth was already announced in the previous chapter. See Ross, *Creation and Blessing*, 343; Sailhamer, "Genesis," 21–332. In my opinion, the narrative contains both elements.

Robert Neff categorizes 18:9–15 and 21:1 as a healing narrative. Neff, "Birth and Election of Isaac," 5–18.

4. For further discussion of the divine figures, see Grypeou and Spurling, "Abraham's Angels," 181–203; Bucur, "Early Christian Reception," 245–72; Benevich, "Maximus Confessor's Interpretation," 43–52. For a discussion of the reception history of Gen 18, see D'Alès, "Théophanie de Mambré," 150–60; Thunberg, "Early Christian Interpretation," 560–70; Stemberger, *Patriarchenbilder der Katakombe*, 21–33; Boulnois, "'Trois

men were at his tent[5] initially,[6] but the divine nature of these men quickly becomes apparent (vv. 2–3, 13–15). Some interpreters have even claimed that the angels visited to test Abraham's hospitality. In this view, they are revealed as divine and promised a son after he passes this test.[7] However,

---

Hommes et un Seigneur,'" 193–202; Bunge, *Rublev Trinity*; Louth, "Oak of Mamre, the Fathers," 90–100; Doerfler, "Entertaining the Trinity Unawares," 485–503; D'Costa, "Trinity and Other Religions," 5–31; Jericke, *Abraham in Mamre*, 159; Gnuse, "Divine Messengers in Genesis 18–19," 66–79; Filler, "Philo's Threefold Divine Vision," 93–113.

5. For the importance of the tent, as opposed to the trees, in this narrative see Ska, "Arbre et la Tente," 383–89.

6. Alston, "Genesis 18:1–11," 398; Collins, "Pleasure of Sarah," 22n32; Hamori, "When Gods Were Men," 83–94; Speiser, *Genesis*, 131; Greenstein, "God of Israel," 57; Sarna, *Genesis = בראשית*, 128; Hamilton, *Book of Genesis*, 8–11; de Regt, *Participants in Old Testament Texts*, 76–77; Kugel, *God of Old*, 10–12; Bolin, "Role of Exchange," 44–47; Cotter, *Genesis*, 117–19; Savran, *Encountering the Divine*, 47, 79; Wenham, *Genesis 16–50*, 45; Hamori, "Divine Embodiment in the Hebrew Bible," 161–83; Sommer, *Bodies of God*, 40; Gossai, *Power and Marginality*, 31; Smith, "Three Bodies of God," 471–88; Potter, *Angelology*, 31; Kugel, *Great Shift*, 5–7, 12.

However, Westermann claims, "There is no way in which one can consider the present event an appearance of God, though the majority of exegetes speak of it in this way." Westermann, *Genesis 12–36*, 275. Von Rad is more open than Westermann, but he says, "The interpretation given by the early church that the trinity of visitors is a reference to the Trinity has been universally abandoned by recent exegesis." Von Rad, *Genesis*, 204, 206.

Ahn Sang Keun and Pieter Venter "uphold the position of Abraham's immediate recognition of the divinity of his visitors. According to this view, the purpose of God's visit was to share covenantal fellowship with Abraham and his household. Receiving Isaac was the result of the Lord's covenantal faithfulness who keeps his promise, not the reward for Abraham's hospitality (Gn 17:17; 18:13, 15)." Keun and Venter, "Analytical Perspective on the Fellowship Narrative," 1. See also Ross, *Creation and Blessing*, 343–46; Sailhamer, "Genesis," 148; Stein, "Cognitive Factors as a Key," 545–89; Keil and Delitzsch, *Biblical Commentary on the Old Testament*, 1:228–32; Sailhamer, *Pentateuch as Narrative*, 161–65; Lyons, *Canon and Exegesis*, 159–61, 265.

7. For a discussion of Abraham's preparation of the calf for the simple meal that was promised (vv. 4–5, 7), see Abela, "Difficulties for Exegesis and Translation," 1–4. For the food offered in the meal in comparison with Aqhat, see Xella, "Épisode de Dnil et Kothar." For a discussion of angels eating and the non-kosher combination of meat and milk in early Jewish exegesis, see van der Horst, "Aan Abrahams dis," 207–14. For broader discussions of the hospitality shown by Abraham and Sarah, see Allard, "In the Shade of the Oaks of Mamre," 414–24; Arterbury, "Abraham's Hospitality," 359–76; Thunberg, "Early Christian Interpretation," 560–70; Cohen, "Abraham's Hospitality," 168–72; Bolin, "Role of Exchange," 37–56; Barnes, "Space of Meeting," 146–71; Monge, "Life Together," 101–10; Sánchez, "Church Is the House," 23–39; Schwartz, "God and the Stranger," 33–48. Irvine claims that the blessing of a son is a repayment of Abraham's hospitality. Irvine, "'Is Anything Too Hard for Yahweh?,'" 295–96. See also West et al., "From Homosexuality to Hospitality," 5–23; Espinosa Arce, "Hospitalidad en el Ciclo de Abraham," 731–40. Herzog reads Abraham's hospitality against the lack of hospitality in Sodom and analyzes the influence of violence at Sodom on Abraham's reception

the connection between Abraham's hospitality and the promise of an heir is unclear in the text.

Though Abraham initially greets the visitors, their initial question is, "Where is Sarah your wife?" (v. 9). The divine visitors then promise that they will return next year, and Sarah will have a son.[8] At this point, Sarah is listening but not interacting with the visitors. However, her internal dialogue, which is disbelief that she is able to bear children at her age, is noticed by the visitors, and they call to her directly.

The nature of her laughter at the promise of a son is somewhat unclear. Many have regarded it as her mocking or disbelief.[9] However, the New Testament authors regarded her as a model of faith.[10] In addition, some modern scholars have regarded it as excusable because she had not been told about the promises to Abraham.[11] In fact, Eitan Mayer claims that this is a moral failing on the part of Abraham:

> No wonder, then, that as we arrive at Genesis 18, Abraham, who is still hoping God will relent and accept Ishmael, continues to conceal the news from Sarah—for as long as she never hears of her intended majestic role, she will not be hurt. God's plan can still be changed. Knowing Abraham is desperate to keep His plan from Sarah, God plays on Abraham's "weakness"—his compassion, his hospitality, even for strangers—and angelically sneaks into Abraham's home and hearth to guarantee that Sarah now receives the news and end Abraham's campaign for Ishmael .... When He asks, "Why is Sarah laughing," He is rebuking Abraham, not Sarah: "Tell me, Abraham, why is your wife so

---

at Mamre. Herzog, "Lecture de l'hospitalité Biblique," 1–25. For the traditional position that the Lord's visit in human form was to test Abraham's hospitality, see Brueggemann, *Theology of the Old Testament*, 166; Calvin, *Genesis*, 468; Gunkel, *Genesis*, 193; Hamilton, *Book of Genesis*, 9; Hartley, *Genesis*, 177; Oden, *Ancient Christian Commentary on Scripture*, 2:62–64; Ross, *Creation and Blessing*, 338; Wenham, *Genesis 16–50*, 45.

8. For a discussion of the grammar of this phrase ("this time next year"), see Loretz, "K't Ḥyh—«wie Jetzt ums Jahr»," 75–78.

9. Brueggemann, *Genesis*, 158–59. See also Westermann, *Genesis 12–36*, 281; Shkop, "And Sarah Laughed . . .," 44–46; Clanton, *Daring, Disreputable, and Devout*, 55; Sternberg, *Poetics of Biblical Narrative*, 91; Rosenberg, *Ancestral Queerness*, 126–31, 135–37. Irvine claims it is disbelief because it aligns with the sons-in-law's disbelief of the Sodom narrative in Gen 19:14, using variations on the same root מצחק in 19:14 and צחק in 18:11–15. Irvine, "'Is Anything Too Hard for Yahweh?,'" 299. So also Levine, "Sarah/Sodom," 132.

10. The NT views Sarah as a model of faith (Rom 9:9; 1 Pet 3:6). See also Collins, "Pleasure of Sarah," 24–27; Briggs, "Sarah 1/Sarai," 152; Box, *Virgin Birth of Jesus*, 232–33; Origen, *Homilies on Genesis and Exodus*, §4.4.

11. Jeansonne, *Women of Genesis*, 22.

surprised at this news that she is gripped by disbelief? We all know: It is because you, hoping to see your plan realized, never reported My news!"[12]

Regardless of the disbelief or failures of Abraham or Sarah, the promise of a son is repeated directly to Sarah before the men rise to leave.[13] The fulfillment of this divine promise comes in Gen 21:1, where Yahweh notices Sarah as he had promised and causes her to conceive a son.

Description of Barrenness

Sarah's barrenness is a feature of much of the narrative of Abraham and Sarah. It is the reason why Sarah gave Hagar to Abraham and the cause of strife between Sarah and Hagar after Ishmael is born (Gen 15–17, 21).[14] As Tammi Schneider notes:

> Sarah's use of legal language may relate to legal precedents in the ancient Near East. According to the Code of Hammurabi: "If a man marries a *nadītu*, and she gives a slave woman to her husband, and she (the slave) then bears children, after which that slave woman aspires to equal status with her mistress—because she bore children, her mistress will not sell her; she shall place upon her the slave-hairlock, and she shall reckon her with the slave women."

Schneider notes that the HB does not give Sarah *nadītu* status, but this law code records a similar strife between a barren wife and fertile slave or secondary wife.[15]

Sarah's barrenness is not attributed to God, but it is God who brings fertility. The stated cause of Sarah's barrenness is old age (ninety years old in Gen 17:17), but the reason for her lack of children at a younger age is unknown, though it is clearly distressing and disruptive for the household.

Sarah's question in Gen 18:12 is, "After I have worn out, shall I have pleasure to myself and my lord who is old?" Many questions about the meaning of the word "pleasure" (עֶדְנָה) have been raised. Claassens, among

---

12. Mayer, "No News Is Bad News," 110–11.

13. Her reaction in fear has been seen as parallel to Lot's hiding in a cave in fear in Gen 19:30. See Levine, "Sarah/Sodom," 136.

14. For a discussion of the social implications of these disputes and Sarah's abusive actions, see Mbuwayesango, "Childlessness and Woman-to-Woman Relationships," 27–36.

15. Schneider, *Mothers of Promise*, 28.

others, claims that Sarah's laughter has sexual overtones and invites dialogue from God by breaking traditional interactions.[16] Others claim that the word refers to rainfall and thereby moisture and oil applied to the skin.[17] Still other scholars believe that it is a reference to the menstrual cycle.[18] Finally, some scholars argue that it refers to pregnancy or the pleasure of progeny.[19] Since this speech is responding to the promise of an heir, it is likely that Sarah is referring to conception or childbirth rather than simply age or sexual pleasure, though these might be secondary concerns in the conception of children.

Interaction with the Divine

Abraham is promised a son several times (Gen 15–17) but now Sarah is also promised a son. In Gen 18:9–15, Yahweh has a dialogue with Abraham and

16. Claassens, "Laughter and Tears," 300. Collins also argues that Sarah's laughter and her question whether she will have pleasure again (v. 12) has sexual connotations. Collins, "Pleasure of Sarah," 20–34. See also Westermann, *Genesis 12–36*, 281; Nowell, *Women in the Old Testament*, 9; Ben-Amos, "From Eden to Ednah," 58; Davidson, *Genesis 12–50*, 64; Bal, *Lethal Love*, 41; Alter, *Five Books of Moses*, 87; Letellier, *Day in Mamre, Night in Sodom*, 98; Mathews, *Genesis 11:27–50:26*, 218. Most lexicon and dictionary entries agree with a sexual interpretation of this term: "lust" (Koehler and Baumgartner, "עֶדְנָה," 793), "delight (sexual)" (Brown et al., "עֶדְנָה," 726), "(sexual) pleasure" (Clines, "עֶדְנָה," 284), "sexual desire" (Kedar-Kopfstein, "עֵדֶן 'eḏen," 10:486).

17. Greenfield, "Touch of Eden," 223. See Sarna, *Genesis = בראשית*, 130. Freshness of skin or oil applied to skin is a common interpretation in rabbinic sources. Neusner, *Babylonian Talmud*, 14:403, folio 87a (IV.16B); Hammer, *Sifre*, Piška 306 p. 304 (refreshing plants). Talmud Pesaḥim uses the term for skin rejuvenation with olive oil. Epstein, *Hebrew-English Edition of the Babylonian Talmud*, 5:43a. See also Tigay, "לא נס לחה 'He Had Not Become Wrinkled,'" 345–50; Cassuto, *Commentary on the Book of Genesis*, 107–8; Hess, "Eden," 28–33; Plaut, *Torah*, 124; Millard, "Etymology of Eden," 103–6; Rosenbaum and Silbermann, *Pentateuch with Targum Onkelos*, 1:72 (Rashi's comment on 18:12).

18. See Macintosh, "Third Root עדה in Biblical Hebrew," 454–73. Genesis Rabbah associates עדנה with adornment (עדי), the feminine cycle (Aramaic: עידן), and conception (Aramaic and Mishnaic Hebrew עדה). Neusner, *Genesis Rabbah*, 2:192, §48.17. Also, Chrysostom, *Homilies on Genesis 18–45*, homily 41; Stetkevych, "Sarah and the Hyena," 13–41. Targum Onqelos renders the term "youth," which Grossfeld understands as a respectful euphemism. Grossfeld, *Targum Onqelos to Genesis*, 76, 76n5.

19. Neusner, *Genesis Rabbah*, §48.17. Targum Neofiti renders it "pregnancies." McNamara, *Targum Neofiti 1*, 104. Targum Pseudo-Jonathan does as well and Michael Maher notes, "The Targums do not translate the biblical phrase 'shall I have pleasure?' literally. They felt that this phrase had sexual connotations and it was unworthy of Sarah." Maher, *Targum Pseudo-Jonathan*, 67, 67n20. See also Hartley, *Genesis*, 179. Andrew Davis claims the term is an echo of Gen 2–3 and the Noah narrative. Davis, "Eden Revisited," 611–31.

Sarah individually and repeats the promise to each of them. In addition, though Abraham greets the visitors, they specifically ask for Sarah (v. 9). In fact, some scholars hypothesize that the original text had God speaking to Sarah first, but later editors reversed the order.[20] Ahn Keun and Pieter Venter note, "They pay direct attention to Sarah for the first time in her life in this episode (Gn 18:9–15). In this unique way, the narrator tells his story in a dramatic fashion that highlights God's special relationship with his beloved covenant partners."[21] Axelrod even translates verse 10, "Then one of them said—formally to Abraham but loudly enough so that Sarah could hear, for it was really to Sarah that he was wanting to speak, the news he was carrying was not news for Abraham."[22] So, the divine figures are clearly focused upon Sarah rather than Abraham in this passage. As Brueggemann notes, "In v. 9, the strangers speak abruptly. They ask an unseemly question about Abraham's wife. And the question is more of a threat because they know too much, even her name. Abraham answers tersely to stop the embarrassing probe (v. 9). But the probe will not be stopped. It will continue with irresistible power and authority in v. 10."[23]

---

20. Zakovitch hypothesizes that the text originally had God speaking to Sarah first, but a later editor switched the order. Zakovitch, "Woman in Biblical Narrative," 14–32. See also Daniely, "'And Sarah Heard It in the Tent Door,'" 26–42; Neff, "Birth and Election of Isaac," 6–7.

21. Keun and Venter, "Analytical Perspective on the Fellowship Narrative," 2. See also Hamilton, *Book of Genesis*, 17; Ross, *Creation and Blessing*, 343; Sailhamer, "Genesis," 144.

22. Axelrod, "Abraham's Plea for Justice," 63. See also Bott, "Sarah as the 'Weaker Vessel,'" 257–58.

Westermann claims that the annunciation story focused on Sarah was once an independent narrative and the remnants of it can be found in verses 11–15. Westermann, *Genesis 12–36*, 275. Coats agrees with Westermann and claims this is part of the texts about divine annunciation healing a barren wife. Coats, *Genesis*, 138. See also Knight, "Apparitions and Appellations," 99.

23. Brueggemann, "'Impossibility' and Epistemology," 618. Likewise, Mayer claims, "Putting ourselves in Abraham's shoes, the strangers' initial question could seem both rude and jarring. Women in the ancient world probably did not socialize with strange men who came to the door; for strangers to boldly inquire after the woman of the house might well have been a violation of manners and modesty. But for these strangers to also somehow know the name of his wife must seem ominous to Abraham—these strangers are strange to him, but apparently he and Sarah are not unknown to them." Mayer, "No News Is Bad News," 107.

Interestingly, though the men ask about Sarah, she is still in the tent[24] not joining their conversation or meal.[25] In addition, the men do not directly address her until after the narrative records her laughing, so the messengers-Sarah dialogue is in some sense initiated by Sarah.[26] Also, the designation for the messenger changes immediately after Sarah's laughter.[27] Previously it was Adonai, but when responding to Sarah's laughter, it changes to Yahweh (18:12–13).[28]

The husband and wife have each have reported speech with the divine, but Abraham calls for the men to come to their tent[29] while the men address Sarah by name twice (vv. 9, 13).

---

24. For a discussion of being inside the tent as a feminine locale and at the tent opening or outside as a male locale in biblical narrative, see Seeman, "'Where Is Sarah Your Wife?,'" 107–8.

25. For the early church fathers and Martin Luther, the morality of Sarah was an important topic of discussion. Most believed that Sarah was the paragon of faith and displayed the correct form of hospitality and humility in her preparation of the meal and work within the tent. However, they are split on whether she showed appropriate faith in her laughter and denial to the divine messengers. Some considered it a flaw while others, like Martin Luther, claimed that it was understandable given her situation and God's graceful response (rather than a rebuke). Mattox, "Sancta Sara, Mater Ecclesiae," 295–320.

Contrary to these interpretations, Islamic authors resoundingly understand Sarah's reaction to the divine messengers as impious and unseemly. Mazuz, "Polemical Treatment of the Story," 252–62.

26. Claassens, "Laughter and Tears," 298.

27. The divine speech also changes Sarah's wording (Gen 18:13). The reason for this change has been debated. Some say it is changing to more polite language. Neusner, *Genesis Rabbah*, §48:18; Neusner, *Babylonian Talmud*, Mesi'a §87a (IV.16B); Neusner, *Babylonian Talmud*, Yebamot §65b. Rashi claims they are altered "for the sake of peace." Rosenbaum and Silbermann, *Pentateuch with Targum Onkelos*, 18:13. See also Alter, *Five Books of Moses*, 87; Cotter, *Genesis*, 118; von Rad, *Genesis*, 202; Wenham, *Genesis 16–50*, 49; Davidson, *Genesis 12–50*, 64–65.

Sternberg claims the differences between verses 12–13 reflect "two levels of awareness": narrator, Yahweh, and the reader are omniscient but Sarah's perspective is limited. Sternberg, *Poetics of Biblical Narrative*, 91.

28. Collins, "Pleasure of Sarah," 30. Though it should be noted that the first response question is directed to Abraham (vv. 13–14) and Sarah is only addressed after her denial (v. 15).

29. Brueggemann notes that Abraham has the initiative, and the visitors are passive in the first eight verses, but in verse 9, the narrative slows down and the visitors take control. Brueggemann, "'Impossibility' and Epistemology," 616–17.

Restoration

The fulfillment of the promise comes in Gen 21, though movement toward restoration happens in chapter 18. As Seeman notes:

> Thresholds (or "tent openings") are therefore a natural focal point for biblical narrative, because they represent a site for the mediation of blessing and barrenness. Abraham and Sarah's continuous movement toward openness and exteriority in the narrative of Isaac's conception signals the movement toward new fertility and the covenantal promise of progeny that they receive.[30]

The explicit announcement of conception in Gen 21 is centered on Yahweh's interaction with Sarah, just like the dialogue of Gen 18:1–15.[31] Yahweh took note of her and fulfilled his promise to her (v. 1). As Rosenberg claims, noting the prominence of Sarah, "'he did for [ל] her as he had promised.' The preposition ל that is translated here as 'for' can also easily take the meaning 'to': 'he did to her as he had promised.' Commentators ancient and modern have noted this unique component of Sarah's conception and used it to challenge Abraham's paternity."[32] Sarah also acknowledges God's hand in her conception in her reported speech that claims, "God has made laughter for me" (v. 6).[33] So, just as the Lord spoke directly to Sarah when he promised her a son, he also remembered her and his promise to her when he caused her to conceive.

Rebekah

Genesis 25:21–24 describes the birth of Jacob and Esau. There are clear parallels between Rebekah and Sarah in the text including Isaac bringing her into Sarah's tent (Gen 24:67).[34] Initially Isaac prays to Yahweh because Rebekah is barren. Interestingly, though, he prays to Yahweh "for his wife" (v. 21). Then the Lord answers and Rebekah conceives. However, the interactions with Yahweh continue. Rebekah's pregnancy is difficult, and she

---

30. Seeman, "'Where Is Sarah Your Wife?,'" 109.

31. Claassens, "Laughter and Tears," 301; Neff, "Birth and Election of Isaac," 15; Carden, "Endangered Ancestress Revisited," 7–11; Huizenga, *New Isaac*, 144–51; Rosenberg, *Ancestral Queerness*, 141–43.

32. Rosenberg, "כעת חיה," 714.

33. For a discussion of the theme of laughter in the birth and life of Isaac, see Paseggi, "He Who Laughs Last," 61–65; Zucker, "Isaac," 105–10.

34. See also Sarna, *Genesis* = בראשית, 170; Seeman, "'Where Is Sarah Your Wife?,'" 115; Neusner, *Genesis Rabbah*, §60.16.

asks the Lord about it. Most scholars interpret her inquiring of the Lord as being through some kind of divination, but the exact method is unclear.[35] Erin Fleming argues persuasively that the text indicates Rebekah performed the divination herself rather than through an intermediary.[36] I believe this interpretation is correct and will not assume or refer to an intermediary. However, the use of an intermediary does not lessen the force of my argument that it is Rebekah who is seeking out and communing with the divine not Isaac. Yahweh then responds to her in a reported speech that she has two nations in her womb and the older child will serve the younger (v. 23). As Lawrence Turner notes, "This oracle is important not only because divine utterances are rare in the Jacob narrative, but also because it fits the pattern of announcements of plot found at the beginning of the other major blocks in Genesis."[37]

Description of Barrenness

Rebekah's barrenness is mentioned only briefly. In fact, the passage begins with "Isaac prayed," and Rebekah's barrenness is the reason for his prayer (25:21). Yahweh is not credited with her barrenness, but Yahweh does answer the prayer and cause her to conceive. Also, the length of time that Rebekah was barren is unknown because the passage goes immediately from their marriage to her barrenness (vv. 20–21), but it can be deduced that she was barren for twenty years because Isaac married her when he was forty and he was sixty when she gave birth to the twins (Gen 25:20, 26).[38] However, Targum Pseudo-Jonathan claims that she was barren for twenty-two years (while strangely still claiming Isaac was forty at their marriage and sixty at the birth).[39] Whether twenty or twenty-two years, the barrenness appears to have been experienced for a long time.

---

35. Von Rad, *Genesis*, 260; Hartley, *Genesis*, 235–36; Coats, *Genesis*, 184; Fokkelman, *Narrative Art in Genesis*, 88n; Wagner, "דָּרַשׁ Dārash; מִדְרָשׁ Midhrāsh," 302; Westermann, *Genesis 12–36*, 413.

36. Fleming, "'She Went to Inquire of the Lord,'" 1–10; Hamilton, *Book of Genesis*, 177; Frymer-Kensky, *Reading the Women of the Bible*, 16.

37. Turner, "Disappointed Expectations," 55. See also Kellenberger, "Wie sind Geburtsorakel und Betrugs-Erzählung aufeinander bezogen?," 241–55.

38. Chung, "Jeremiah's Call and Jacob's Birth," 328.

39. For a discussion of this discrepancy, see Zhakevich, "Apparent Contradiction," 42–63.

Interaction with the Divine

Isaac prays for Rebekah's barrenness, but it is not in reported speech and the Lord's response is also in narrative rather than speech. However, immediately after the conception, Rebekah asks God the reason why the pregnancy is difficult in reported speech, and he responds to her in reported speech as well. Richard Clifford even claims, "Her question is genuine for it prompts her to seek an oracle of Yahweh. The oracular answer is probably given to her alone, for in Genesis 25:28 and throughout chapter 27 Isaac seems unaware of the boys' divinely determined destinies."[40] Many traditional Jewish authors also claimed she was the first woman that God spoke directly to (which assumes the three men speaking to Sarah were angels, not God).[41] So, in this narrative Isaac and Rebekah interact with the divine, but Isaac's prayer and response is only narrated while Rebekah's prayer and Yahweh's response is in reported speech.[42] As Mary Turner notes:

> Although the failure of the couple to bear offspring is usually the critical issue, here it is not. The long years of waiting for a child which receive much attention in the stories of Sarah and Abraham are dismissed in one short verse. Simply, Rebekah is barren and conceives. The critical issues of this story comes into play as Rebekah suffers through her pregnancy. The children struggle within her and, presumably on the basis of her discomfort, Rebekah "inquires (darash) of the Lord." This phrase is of great importance in the Old Testament. Only the great prophets

---

40. Clifford, "Genesis 25:19–34," 399. Reiss states, "Isaac prayed for her, and finally she did conceive. Was she aware of Isaac's intervention? She decided to seek an oracle about the difficulties of her pregnancy. Did she consult with Isaac about this? We are never told anything of communication or lack of communication between them." Reiss, "Archetypes in the Patriarchal Family," 14. See also Spero, "Jacob and Esau," 246; Snyman, "Readers' Disgust in the Case of Rebekah," 455–56.

Many commentators claim that Rebekah is the first person to seek God. Zornberg, *Murmuring Deep*; Tsymbalyuk and Melnik, "Rediscovering the Ancient Hermeneutic," 2.

For a discussion of the ambiguity of the final clause of the oracle, see Eichler, "Oracle of Rebekah," 584–93. For a discussion of emendations to resolve the (apparent) metric issue of the speech, see Kraft, "Note on the Oracle of Rebecca," 318–20.

41. Tsymbalyuk and Melnik, "Rediscovering the Ancient Hermeneutic," 2; Neusner, *Genesis Rabbah*, Parashah 57.2, Parashah 63.7; Friedman, *Commentary on the Torah*, 87.

42. Interestingly, in the retelling of this narrative in Jubilees Abraham tells Rebekah of God's choice, while in Josephus the prophecy is told to Isaac instead of Rebekah. Dunn, "Tertullian and Rebekah," 123–24; Josephus, *Jewish Antiquities*, 1.257–258; Jubilees 19:16–18.

like Moses and Elisha and the greatest kings of Israel inquire of the Lord.[43]

So, the barrenness is mentioned but Rebekah's inquiry is emphasized. The description of her inquiring of the Lord and the divine response places her in league with the most important characters of the HB.

Restoration

Yahweh causes Rebekah to conceive and explains how the difficult pregnancy is a double blessing of twins.[44] The brevity of this account does not allow for a detailed analysis of the themes, but the involvement of Rebekah in conversations with the divine is clear. Yahweh causes her to conceive and then responds directly to Rebekah to explain the fulfillment in more detail: not only does she conceive but she conceives twins and they will become nations (Gen 25:23). Naomi Steinberg describes this as the second "disequilibrium." First, Rebekah was barren, which jeopardized Isaac's lineage. Then she conceived twins, "but this seemingly harmonious situation raises a problem for the family. If a man has two sons—born moments apart by the same woman—how is he to decide which one will be the heir if custom decrees that a man's lineage may pass only through one offspring?" Both disharmonies are resolved (to a degree) by the divine. God causes her to conceive, and the divine oracle somewhat resolves the issue of priority for the two sons.[45]

Rachel

The series of births between Rachel, Leah, and their servants is complicated in Gen 30:1–24.[46] First, Rachel's barrenness appears to be connected to

---

43. Turner, "Rebekah," 44.

44. This divine reassurance has been compared with the prophetic call of Jeremiah (Jer 1:6). Chung, "Jeremiah's Call and Jacob's Birth," 329–30.

45. Steinberg, "Gender Roles in the Rebekah Cycle," 179.

46. Williams claims this is an example of the "agon (conflict) of the barren wife" type-scene. Williams, "Beautiful and the Barren," 109. For a discussion of the bicola about struggle in Gen 30:8, see Andersen, "Note on Genesis 30:8," 200; Krueger, "Vreugde en Verdriet in die Huis van Jakob," 935–57; Meurer, "Gebärwettstreit zwischen Lea und Rahel," 93–108.
Some have also connected the struggle between Rachel and Leah with the struggle between Jacob and Esau. Pardes, *Countertraditions in the Bible*, 63–67; Fokkelman, *Narrative Art in Genesis*, 131–35.

Jacob's preference for her (Gen 29:31). It is interesting that the initial description is the barrenness and fertility of the wives, not that Jacob has no children.[47] However, after Leah bore four children, Rachel confronts Jacob in a reported speech. She tells him to provide a child for her or she will die (Gen 30:1). However, Jacob gets angry with Rachel and asks, "Am I in the place of God who has withheld from you the fruit of the womb?" (30:2).[48] Rachel then provides her servant Bilhah, who has children in her stead,[49] but finally, after several more children from two servants and Leah, Rachel has her own son in Gen 30:22.[50] Here it states that God remembered her, listened to her, and opened her womb.[51] She then bore a son and named him Jacob. Karolina Olszewska notes Leah "is also the first woman who gives names to her children on the pages of the Holy Bible. In the first generation of patriarchs, Abraham names his sons (Gen 16:15; 21:3). In the second generation, Isaac and Rebecca do this together (Gen 25:25–26). In the third generation, names are given by both Leah and Rachel (Gen. 29:32–35;

---

47. Bailey, "Intimate Moments," 1. Leshem connects this preference for the barren wife with Manoah and Hannah in 1 Sam 1. Leshem, "Two Biblical Families," 1–15.

Karolina Olszewska notes, "In the biblical text, the name of Jacob is linked with the name of Rachel and the name of God with the name of Leah. Moreover, God does for Leah things he does not do for Rachel. Therefore, it can be said that the narrator here shows God and Leah as spouses in an intimate relationship. Leah is the one who has the privilege of being in the heart of God's care. It is God who initiates the change that takes place towards the 'hated-innocent.'" Olszewska, "Biblical Narrative About Leah," 351. See also Ross-Burstall, "Leah and Rachel," 166–67.

Hamilton also notes that Jacob is not mentioned at all in Leah's conception of children in Gen 29:31–35, which highlights the distance from her husband. Hamilton, *Book of Genesis*, 266.

48. For a discussion of this phrase in connection with the theological concept of God as the giver of life, see Rastoin, "Suis-je à la Place de Dieu, Moi?," 333–47.

49. Wilda Gafney terms these servants as "womb-slaves." Gafney, *Womanist Midrash*, 70–71. See also Jeffress, "Three's Company Too," 575–76.

50. Claassens notes how traumatic this narrative is as both wives are given to Jacob without their input, Leah fights for/laments her husband's affection, Rachel fights for/laments fertility, and two servants are given as surrogate mothers for the two primary wives without any voice of their own in the narrative. Claassens, "Reading Trauma Narratives," 22–23.

Sweeney claims that the children of Leah and the servants are marginalized tribes, but Rachel's children, Joseph and Benjamin, become the most important tribes in the divided monarchy period. His point is that this organization shows a northern/Ephraimite origin for the narrative. Sweeney, "Jacob Narratives," 246–47.

51. Seeman, "'Where Is Sarah Your Wife?,'" 116.

30:6.8. etc.)."⁵² Leah then thanks God for him and requests additional children (vv. 23–24).⁵³

Description of Barrenness

Though Rachel confronts Jacob about her lack of children, Jacob defers to God. He claims not only that God is the only one who can return her to fertility but also that God is the cause of her infertility (30:2). The reason why Rachel might be blaming Jacob could be situational since he was already able to have children with Leah. As Bailey speculates:

> When Rachel blames Jacob, she is simply indicating that she is unable to become pregnant because Jacob is either not sleeping with her or that he is unable to copulate with her when he does. In the face of Rachel's challenge, Jacob blames God. Elohim, he claims, not he, "has withheld from you the fruit of the womb" (Gen 30:2). Notice that Jacob says "from you" not "from us." There is no "us" in the Jacob and Rachel portion of the narrative. Jacob has four sons by Leah and producing children with Rachel does not appear to be a concern of his. The likely conclusion is that Jacob no longer loves Rachel having found her to be difficult to live with. The narrative, after all, opens with her quarreling with him.⁵⁴

Rachel does not respond to Jacob's assertion, but her statement "God has taken away my reproach" when she finally conceives a child indicates that she agrees with the divine origin of fertility and possibly also Jacob's claim of the divine origin of her barrenness (30:23).

In addition to the characters' claims, the narrator clearly attributes the barrenness to God. Genesis 29:31 states that God opened Leah's womb

---

52. Olszewska, "Biblical Narrative About Leah," 354.

53. Alter describes this as an annunciation type-scene: initial barrenness, divine intervention, and birth of a son. Alter, "How Convention Helps Us Read," 119.

54. Bailey, "Intimate Moments," 8. Bailey elsewhere speculates that the lack of children might be because Rachel was prepubescent when they were married since she was the younger daughter. See Bailey, "Baby Becky, Menarche and Prepubescent Marriage," 113–37.

Jonathan Crane explains, "Rachel's challenge infuriates Jacob, not least because he has indeed sired children through Leah: *he* is not infertile." Crane, "Who's Your Mama Now?," 95.

because she was unloved,[55] but Rachel was barren.[56] Then when Rachel finally has a child, the narrator claims that God remembered her and opened her womb (30:22). So, the barrenness is connected with Jacob's preferential treatment of Rachel but also directly attributed to God.

Interaction with the Divine

In the birth narratives of Gen 30, none of the characters directly engage with the divine. They are not recorded praying or having a divine encounter. However, when children are born, the mothers frequently have reported speeches attributing the births to God (29:32, 33, 35; 30:6, 18, 20, 23, 24).[57] The narrative is entirely focused upon the wives and Jacob is, at best, passive and, at worse, absent.[58]

In addition, in two birth announcements, the narrator attributes the conception to God (30:17, 22).[59] The locations of these announcements are significant. The first announcement is "God listened to Leah, and she conceived and bore Jacob a fifth son." This is the first child Leah conceived

---

55. Many understand שנואה literally. So, Leah is hated for some reason; perhaps she is hated for deceiving him on her wedding night as in the view of Nachmanides. See von Rad, *Genesis*, 294; Westermann, *Genesis 12–36*, 265–66.

However, the opinion that Leah was only less loved than Rachel seems more probable, since the expression is "and he loved Rachel more than Leah" (Gen 29:30). So, Jacob loved Rachel more than Leah but did not necessarily hate Leah in a despising or repulsive sense. Lea Jacobsen cites rabbinic authors in support of this view: "Radak on the verse under discussion: 'Jacob did not hate her. He actually loved her. But since he loved Rachel more than Leah, she was called "hated"—meaning that she was hated in comparison with Rachel.' Similarly, Shadal explained: '"Hated"—this is not to be understood literally, since before that it is stated that "he loved Rachel more than Leah," rather the word "hate" sometimes refers to a relatively lesser degree of love.' However, although Jacob did not truly hate Leah, her inferior standing in comparison with Rachel was sufficient reason for Reuben to interfere on the behalf of his mother." Jacobsen, "'And Reuben Went,'" 203n8. See also Luzzatto, *Commentary on the Pentateuch*, 120–21; Tigay, *Deuteronomy*, 2:534–35; Wenham, *Genesis 16–50*, 243.

56. Joel Wolowelsky summarizes, "In any event, we are told that God gave children to Leah because she was *senu'ah*, but 'Rachel remained barren.' No explanation is given for Rachel's infertility. Surely being the preferred wife is no reason to be inflicted with barrenness." Wolowelsky, "Rachel, a Mother of Israel," 11. It is noteworthy that Rachel's feelings about Jacob are unstated. See Gafney, *Womanist Midrash*, 61.

57. These phrases reflect the naming by Eve in Gen 4. Bailey, "Intimate Moments," 5.

58. Bailey, "Intimate Moments," 1–3.

59. Wenham notes these phrases as part of the structure of the narrative. Wenham, *Genesis 16–50*, 241.

after the narrator stated that she stopped bearing children (29:35).[60] The second time that the narrator attributes the conception to God is in Gen 30:22 where Rachel is remembered, listened to, and has her womb opened.[61] This is Rachel's first biological child, reversing the barrenness stated earlier (29:31).[62] Interestingly, the narrator does not simply say that God remembered the barren women, but specifically that God listened to them. These statements come after the women are declared to be barren but not when they bear other children. This likely indicates that each of them had appealed to the divine to reverse their barrenness.

Restoration

Initially, Rachel uses her own methods to gain fertility. However, she does not use Jacob to fulfill her desires, though she does ask him about it; she uses her servant Bilhah.[63] In fact, her reported speech with Jacob is less of a question than a demand for children. In this way, Rachel does not defer or attempt to coerce the favor of her husband or another man but uses her servant to enact her will.[64]

---

60. This birth also comes after an exchange of mandrakes, which not only purchased Leah's night with Jacob but are symbols of fertility and aphrodisiacs in the ANE. See Beuken, "'Please Give Me Some of Your Son's Love-Fruits,'" 220; Dresner, "Rachel and Leah," 154; Moss and Baden, *Reconceiving Infertility*, 24. Gafney describes the reference to mandrakes in the text as "love-fruit," which was thought to be "within bounds of legitimate health care." Gafney, *Womanist Midrash*, 58. Radak explains, "Reuben may have heard about the common belief that they [the mandrakes] help women to become pregnant, and since his mother had ceased giving birth he brought them to her." Kimchi, *Radak on Genesis*, comment on 30:14. See also von Rad, *Genesis*, 295; Westermann, *Genesis 12-36*, 475; Jacobsen, "'And Reuben Went,'" 205; Lavie, *Plants of the Bible*, 48; Amar, *Flora of the Bible*, 89-91; Olszewska, "Biblical Narrative About Leah," 353.

Wenham argues that the phrase shows "that though Rachel and Leah may think conception is aided by mandrakes, the text insists that children are God's gift." Wenham, *Genesis 16-50*, 247. See also Sarna, *Genesis = בראשית*, 209.

61. This phrase is not only significant for my argument that this is one of two places in this narrative where the narrator claims God listened to the woman and opened her womb. It was also very significant in the ancient world and was used frequently in fertility incantations. See Salzer, *Magie der Anspielung*, 33, 68; Naveh and Shaked, *Magic Spells and Formulae*, 189-209; Bhayro, "Aramaic Magic Bowl for Fertility," 106-11.

62. Mathews notes, "The important story line is the absence of children by Rachel, Jacob's beloved wife. By God's intervention, her tormented life will be graciously reversed (30:22)." Mathews, *Genesis 11:27-50:26*, 477.

63. Jacobs, *Gender, Power, and Persuasion*, 167; Claassens, "Reading Trauma Narratives," 21. For a discussion of the phrase "building of my house" through the servant by Sarah and Rachel, see Leder, "Who Builds the House of Israel?," 5-26.

64. Gruber, "Genesis 21.12," 174; Kramer, "Biblical Women That Come in Pairs,"

Once Bilhah has children, Rachel's responses and the names of the children no longer reference Jacob but God (Gen 30:6, 8). As Crane states, "Though earlier she was certain Jacob had something to do with her infertility, she now glosses over him altogether. His role is but a bit part. For one reason or another, God has rewarded her with offspring and in so doing she has achieved that elusive status of motherhood."[65] So, Jacob's role in Rachel's return to fertility, even in the surrogacy of Bilhah, is minimized.

However, even using her servant Bilhah to bear children in her name is not full restoration.[66] Once Rachel bears her own child, she claims that her reproach has been taken away, which indicates that she believed she had not fully obtained her goal of children even though Bilhah had provided two sons for her (30:23).[67] So, the full restoration of Rachel comes when God listens to her and opens her womb (30:22).[68]

222–23.

65. Crane, "Who's Your Mama Now?," 96.

66. Landau claims that Bilhah "giving birth on her knees" may have originally been a method of sympathetic magic to restore fertility to the barren woman but by the time of Gen 30, it has become a method of showing ownership over the child. Landau, "Giving Birth on Someone's Knees," 211–29. For a discussion of the phrase by Sarah, see Landau, "What Does I Will Be Built From/Through Her in Genesis 16:2 and 30:3 Mean?" 40–56. For the authority over or adoption of a servant's child, see Lee, "Two Translations of HSS V 67," 59–63; Dresner, "Rachel and Leah," 154; Speiser, *Genesis*, 230; Skinner, *Critical and Exegetical Commentary on Genesis*, 386–87; von Rad, *Genesis*, 294–95.

67. As Pardes claims, "The son she names is Bilhah's son. Her womb is still closed. This naming-speech is more the delusion of a desperate woman, trying to find comfort in the offspring of her maid." Pardes, *Countertraditions in the Bible*, 65. See also Moss and Baden, *Reconceiving Infertility*, 35, 39; Jacobsen, "'And Reuben Went,'" 208.

Crane explains, "What was her disgrace? Taking the names of her earlier sons into consideration, she apparently felt disgraced vis-à-vis her maternal status in contradistinction to her sister Leah, as well as to her handmaiden Bilhah and even to Zilpah. In Rachel's view, only biological motherhood could cut down and reap such disparate sites of her comparative disgrace." Crane, "Who's Your Mama Now?," 98.

Chaudhry, Muers, and Rashkover claim that the children are attempts for the women to increase their worth and fill an empty marriage or lack of connection with the covenant. Chaudhry et al., "Women Reading Texts on Marriage," 206–7.

68. Brueggemann, *Genesis*, 255. The phrase "he opened her womb" appears only twice in the Hebrew Bible, first with Yahweh as the subject and Leah being the one opened (Gen 29:31) and second, Elohim as the subject and Rachel being the one opened (Gen 30:22). See Bailey, "Intimate Moments," 6.

Manoah's Wife

In Judg 13, the birth narrative of Samson begins with a description of his father and mother. His mother is unnamed,[69] but she is described as barren and childless (13:2).[70] An angel of Yahweh visits her and tells her that she will have a son[71] and that he will take Nazirite vows and deliver Israel

---

69. The woman's namelessness is strange because she is clearly the primary protagonist in the birth narrative, and she is the only woman in the HB barrenness narratives that is unnamed. See Reinhartz, "Samson's Mother," 25–37; Johnson, "What Type of Son Is Samson?," 273; Mollo, "Did It Please God to Kill Them?," 91; Greenstein, "Riddle of Samson," 240; Crenshaw, "Samson Saga," 473; Soggin, *Judges*, 233; Exum, "Promise and Fulfillment," 45; Smith, "Failure of the Family in Judges," 426; Hartman, "Feminine Gender as a Literary Device," 163. Though she is nameless, she becomes important in later Jewish writings. See Zucker, "Romanticizing Samson's Mother," 1–19.

70. A connection between this narrative and the visitation to Abraham and Sarah in Gen 18 has been argued by scholars. Crenshaw, *Samson*, 161n9. One specific aspect noted by Brueggemann is the use of "impossible" in the name of the angel (Judg 13:18) and the response to Sarah of the Lord's ability to cause her to conceive (Gen 18:14). Brueggemann, "'Impossibility' and Epistemology," 620. See also Chisholm, "Role of Women," 42; Smit and Fowl, *Judges and Ruth*, 147.

A connection to the angelic visitation in the Gideon narrative in Judg 6 has also been argued to the point that some have claimed it was written by the same author. See Moore, *Critical and Exegetical Commentary on Judges*, 316; Boling, *Judges*, 219.

Williams claims this is part of the "promise to the barren wife" type-scene like Abraham and Sarah in Gen 18. Williams, "Beautiful and the Barren," 110. Benjamin Johnson also calls it a "son of a barren woman" type-scene. Johnson, "What Type of Son Is Samson?" See also Niditch, "Samson as Cultural Hero," 609–12; Ross, "Type-Casting the Samson Family," 237–52; Smith, "Failure of the Family in Judges," 425; Rzepka, "Nazireo dal Grembo Materno," 352.

For a discussion of the Greek Heracles narratives as a potential background for the Samson narrative and the dating implications of this, specifically Judg 13–16 as a late insertion, see Gnuse, "Samson and Heracles Revisited," 1–19.

71. The syntax in verse 5 could be understood as "you are pregnant," which leads to the possibility that she became pregnant by the messenger or at the messenger's announcement rather than by intercourse with Manoah. See Chisholm, "Identity Crisis," 148–50; Brettler, *Book of Judges*, 44–49; Reinhartz, "Why Ask My Name?," 98–101; Margalith, "More Samson Legends," 400–401; Guillaume, *Waiting for Josiah*, 166–67; Spronk, "Book of Judges as a Late Construct," 26; Reinhartz, "Samson's Mother," 166–68; Kozlovic, "Constructing the Motherliness of Manoah's Wife," 4–5; Zakovitch, "Strange Biography of Samson," 24–26.

This might be related to Manoah's jealousy and distrust as recurring themes in Josephus's retelling of the narrative. Josephus, *Jewish Antiquities*, 5.276–285. See also Butler, *Judges*, 325–26; Soggin, *Judges*, 231–32; Klein, *Triumph of Irony in Judges*, 111–14; Bal, *Death and Dissymmetry*, 266n9.

Some scholars agree with the translation "you are pregnant" but believe that she is pregnant by Manoah at the time the angel visits. Block, *Judges, Ruth*, 402; Boling, *Judges*, 220; Moore, *Critical and Exegetical Commentary on Judges*, 317; Butler, *Judges*, 311.

from the Philistines (vv. 3–5).[72] The woman then goes and tells her husband about the divine encounter and speech in another reported speech (vv. 6–7).[73] Manoah, the husband, immediately asks God to send the angel again to give more directions, but when the angel arrives, he again visits Manoah's wife alone and she has to bring her husband to him (vv. 8–14).[74]

After the angel reiterates the message to Manoah, he offers a sacrifice to Yahweh and the angel ascends in the flame.[75] At this point, the two fully realize they had an encounter with God and survived (vv. 22–23). The woman then gives birth to a son and names him Samson, and he grows up blessed by Yahweh (v. 24).

Description of Barrenness

The narrator and the angel claim that the woman was barren and had not borne children (Judg 13:2–3). However, neither of these descriptions attribute the barrenness to God or any other cause. The text also does not directly attribute her return to fertility to God.[76] The angel announces that

---

For a survey of these views see Crenshaw, *Samson*, 14–17; Brettler, *Book of Judges*, 40–58; Mobley, *Samson and the Liminal Hero*, 7–12.

72. Interestingly, the Septuagint uses the term "holy one" (ἅγιος) instead of "Nazirite." For a discussion of this lexical switch, see Chepey, "Samson the 'Holy One,'" 97–99.

73. The woman does not report the messenger's speech precisely and changes some of the details about Samson's Nazirite vows. The angel also omits some details in the speech to Manoah (vv. 13–14). See Davis, "Eden Revisited," 612; Alter, *Art of Biblical Narrative*, 127–28; Kim, *Structure of the Samson Cycle*, 190; Burney, *Book of Judges*, 347; Block, *Judges, Ruth*, 408; Exum, "Promise and Fulfillment," 52; Zakovitch, *Life of Samson (Judges 13–16)*, 39–42. The Numbers Rabbah claims, "She did not want to disclose her imperfection" (barrenness) to her husband. Slotki, *Midrash Rabbah*, §10.5. See also Mobley, *Empty Men*, 178–79; Reinhartz, "Samson's Mother," 31; Bal, *Death and Dissymmetry*, 75, 146.

Some scholars have wondered if the woman deceived her husband, specifically about Samson's military calling. See Gunn and Fewell, *Narrative in the Hebrew Bible*, 68; Savran, *Telling and Retelling*, 83–84.

James Wharton claims that this verse is a late addition, stating, "Looking back at 13:5, 7bb, we discover that adding these verses to the story complicates and confuses the narrative." Wharton, "Secret of Yahweh," 59.

74. John Roskoski claims that the inclusion of landmarks like the field where the angel visits the woman (Judg 13:9) and the rock where they sacrificed (v. 19) shows a familiarity with local Danite landmarks. Roskoski, "Recurring Theme of 'Beginning,'" 45.

75. For a discussion of the grammar of verses 20–21 and what caused Manoah to recognize that it was an angel, see Chisholm, "Note on Judges 13:20–21," 10–12.

76. Though the phrasing indicates that it is God who brings the blessing, or at least announces the blessing. See Boling, *Judges*, 219.

she will conceive a son but does not claim that God is providing her with the child nor does the narrator claim God gave her a son (vv. 3, 7, 24).[77] So, the lack of explicit attribution for the barrenness and fertility could imply that divine control was assumed by the author. In any event, the barrenness is not attributed to any negative actions on the part of Manoah or his wife.

Interaction with the Divine

The interaction with the divine is initiated by Yahweh not by the woman. The narrative does not indicate whether the woman sought help for her barrenness or simply accepted it.[78] However, though an appeal to the divine is not present, the centrality of the woman in the divine interaction is clear.[79] The angel appears to the woman first, and even when Manoah asks Yahweh to bring the angel back, the angel arrives when Manoah is away (Judg 13:3, 8–9). After Manoah arrives, the interaction with the angel centers upon the woman as the angel states that she must do everything that the angel previously commanded (vv. 13–14).[80]

---

77. Brueggemann does question whether the messenger announcing the birth is also the one causing the pregnancy. Brueggemann, "'Impossibility' and Epistemology," 620.

78. Kim, *Structure of the Samson Cycle*, 181; Chisholm, "Identity Crisis," 152n16; Moss and Baden, *Reconceiving Infertility*, 48; Jones, "Three Blind Vices?," 186n54; Ross, "Type-Casting the Samson Family," 240; Exum, "Promise and Fulfillment," 47–48; Crenshaw, *Samson*, 43; Amit, *Book of Judges*, 298; O'Connell, *Rhetoric of the Book of Judges*, 224; Johnson, "What Type of Son Is Samson?," 274; Smith, "Failure of the Family in Judges," 426; Smit and Fowl, *Judges and Ruth*, 148.

79. Soggin, *Judges*; Evans, "Invisibility of Women," 38–39; Exum, "Mother of Samson," 246; Exum and Yee, "Feminist Criticism," 78–79; Crenshaw, *Samson*, 70; Camp, *Wise, Strange, and Holy*, 111; Amit, "'Manoah Promptly Followed His Wife'"; Zakovitch, *Life of Samson (Judges 13–16)*, 23–24.

80. Boling, *Judges*; Pressler, *Joshua, Judges, and Ruth*, 214–15; Evans, *Judges and Ruth*, 149; Phillips, *Judges, Ruth*, 209; Lias, *Book of Judges*, 157; Cundall and Morris, *Judges and Ruth*, 158; Lewis, *Judges and Ruth*, 176; Gorospe and Ringma, *Judges*, 179; Burney, *Book of Judges*, 342–43; Bertheau, *Buch der Richter und Rut*; Stewart, *Book of Judges*; Walpole, *Handbook to Judges and Ruth*, 133; Frolov, *Judges*; Moore, *Critical and Exegetical Commentary on Judges*, 319–20.

However, it should be noted that all versions of the Septuagint have the verbs and pronouns in third person masculine, presumably referencing the infant, or possibly Manoah, rather than the woman. Soggin, *Judges*, 234; Bodine, *Greek Text of Judges*; Marcos, *Biblia Hebraica Quinta*, 90; Harlé, *Juges*, 200–201.

Meshel claims that the Hebrew verbs could be read as third feminine singular or second masculine singular creating an ambiguity as to whether the angel is commanding Manoah or his wife to follow his commands. Meshel, "Too Much in the Sun," 55–72.

The woman's understanding of the divine also appears to be clearer than Manoah as he fears they will be killed for seeing God, but she reminds him of their interaction with the divine (and the promises made) to reassure him that they will live (vv. 22-23).[81] So, though neither the man nor the woman appeals to the divine, the woman is more central in the interactions with the divine.

Restoration

The woman has a son just as the angel promised (Judg 13:24). However, the text does not claim that Yahweh caused her to conceive or provided her with the child. Instead, the child was born according to the promise of Yahweh rather than through an explicit act of God. As noted above, neither the barrenness nor the return to fertility is explicitly attributed to the divine so it is possible that the author assumed divine action, or even subtly hinted at it, without directly stating it.[82] Barry Webb notes, "The birth announced so simply here is in fact momentous, and what the whole chapter has been leading up to. It is much less dramatic than the messenger's fiery ascent in verse 20, but like it, it does not belong to the category of ordinary things . . . . The barren woman gives birth, as Yahweh's messenger said she would."[83] The HB and ANE background could show this assumption of divine control over fertility, but also the visitation and promise by the divine messenger is an indicator of God's involvement in her ability to conceive after being barren. As Chisholm notes, "The language used to describe the angel's visit plays off the idiomatic expression 'come to,' understood in a sexual sense, to emphasize that God is the one who enabled Samson's mother to conceive."[84]

---

81. Evans, "Invisibility of Women," 38; Moss and Baden, *Reconceiving Infertility*, 48; Jones, "Three Blind Vices?," 187; Kim, "More to the Eye," 3; Amit, "'Manoah Promptly Followed His Wife,'" 148-49; Reinhartz, "Samson's Mother," 32-33; Niditch, "Samson as Cultural Hero," 611; Reiss, "Samson," 136; Ross, "Type-Casting the Samson Family," 245.

82. Benjamin Crisp claims, "From the beginning of Samson's narrative, his judicial purpose could only be achieved through divine intervention. Even his birth required a divine messenger to a barren wife (Judg 13:2-7)." Crisp, "Samson's Blindness and Ethical Sight," 240.

83. Webb, *Book of Judges*, 358. See also Butler, *Judges*, 330.

84. Chisholm, "Identity Crisis," 150.

Hannah

The barrenness narrative in 1 Sam 1 shares many literary elements with the Manoah and his wife narrative in Judg 13[85] but also the competition aspect of the Leah and Rachel narrative in Gen 30.[86] Elkanah had two wives, Peninnah and Hannah. He loved Hannah but she was barren while Peninnah had multiple children.[87] Peninnah provoked Hannah because she was childless while Elkanah attempted to soothe her (1 Sam 1:6–8). So, after

---

85. Mollo, "Did It Please God to Kill Them?"; Gilmour, *Representing the Past*, 50; Johnson, "What Type of Son Is Samson?," 272; Ackerman, "Who Can Stand Before Yhwh?," 2.
Brian Peterson shows many parallels between God's choosing of David and Samson, through the angel's visit to his mother, but claims, "Of course the Judge/prophet Samuel had a similar beginning; however, Hannah dedicated him to the Lord, as opposed to the Lord calling him from birth." Peterson, "Samson," 38n73. Interestingly, Wénin connects this with Abraham's offering of his son Isaac in Gen 22. Wénin, "'Sacrifices' d'Abraham et d'Anne," 513–27.

86. Williams claims this is an example of the "agon (conflict) of the barren wife" type-scene along with the Leah and Rachel narrative. Williams, "Beautiful and the Barren," 109. See also Gaiser, "Sarah, Hagar, Abraham—Hannah, Peninnah, Elkanah"; Klein, "Hannah"; Leitch, "Redeeming Peninnah"; Leshem, "Two Biblical Families."
For the view that it is the birth of the hero or annunciation type-scene, see Brenner, "Female Social Behaviour," she also connects it with the conflict between wives narratives; Muñoz Iglesias, "Procedimiento Literario del Anuncio," 58; Tatko, "Vowing Mothers and Avowed Sons"; Cook, *Hannah's Desire, God's Design*, 10; You, "Historian's Heroines," 181; Willis, "Cultic Elements," 40; Roskoski, "Isaac and Samson."

87. Gilmour states, "Favouritism of the barren wife is another motif in birth narratives, for example, in the story of Rachel and Leah. Although Elkanah does not explicitly love Hannah more than Peninnah, it is implied through a series of suggestions." Gilmour, *Representing the Past*, 51.

the meal at the temple[88] of Yahweh,[89] Hannah prayed to God for a son in a reported speech (vv. 10–11).[90] The priest, Eli, saw her and believed that she was drunk, but when he learned that she was praying, he gave her a blessing that God would grant her request. When Elkanah and his family returned home, God remembered Hannah and she conceived and gave birth to a son, Samuel (vv. 19–20).

Description of Barrenness

The narrative states that "Yahweh closed her womb" (1 Sam 1:5-6). The characters in the narrative do not explicitly engage with the divine origin of Hannah's barrenness. However, both wives and Elkanah engage with the problem of Hannah's barrenness even to the point of calling it an affliction (v. 11). Peninnah's provocation of Hannah is said to be "because Yahweh

---

88. The use of the word "temple" (הֵיכַל) in verse 9 is confusing because the temple had not been built yet (cf. 2 Sam 7; 1 Kgs 6). Henry Smith claims, "The structure seems to have been a solid building, otherwise it could not be called *a temple*." Smith, *Critical and Exegetical Commentary on Samuel*, 9, italics original. See also Omanson and Ellington, *Handbook on the Books of Samuel*, 1:33. Bergen adds that this permanent structure had "a traditional tripartite Semitic temple design." To reconcile this with the lack of tent references in Josh 18, 19 and 2 Sam 7, he suggests, "Perhaps the earlier tabernacle set up at Shiloh in Joshua's day had been supplemented by a building during the days of the Judges; alternatively, a smaller ceremonial tent may have housed the ark within the holy of holies." Bergen, *1, 2 Samuel*, 68. See also Baldwin, *1 and 2 Samuel*, 65–68. Bill Arnold argues that it is a semipermanent porch with doors and doorposts at the entrance to the tabernacle. Arnold, *1 and 2 Samuel*, 55n6. See also Keil and Delitzsch, *Biblical Commentary on the Books of Samuel*, 23, 50–51.

David G. Firth claims that temple and palace imagery are being conflated here, as are the throne and the seat that Eli is sitting upon. Firth, *1 and 2 Samuel*, 56; Hutzli, "Coutumes et Lois Cultuelles," 110–11; Polzin, *Samuel and the Deuteronomist*, 2:23, 61, 64. Frank Spina claims it shows Eli is taking an illegitimate rulership position. Spina, "Eli's Seat," 67–75. For a discussion of the motif of doorways/doorposts, see Janzen, "'Samuel Opened the Doors,'" 89–96; Meredith, "Case of Open and Shut," 137–57.

89. For a discussion of the phrasing of "a double portion" for Hannah, sometimes identified as "single portion," "special portion," or even, according to Sipilä, "angry portion," see Aberbach, "מנה אחת אפים (1 Sam I 5)," 350–53; McCarter, *1 Samuel*, 60; Tsumura, *First Book of Samuel*, 113; Murphy, *1 Samuel*, 7; Omanson and Ellington, *Handbook on the Books of Samuel*, 27–28; Steinmann, *1 Samuel*, 45; Deist, "'APPAYIM (1 Sam. I 5) < *PYM?," 205–9; Sipilä, "On Portions, Nostrils, and Anger," 75–81; van Zyl, "Hannah's Share, Once More," 364–66; Werline, "Prayer, Politics, and Power," 9.

90. Stefanie Rembold notes that her petition takes place outside the sanctuary, by the doorpost, and claims, "Hannah's position outside of the sanctuary highlights her effort to maintain the boundaries and sanctity of the temple. By remaining outside while she prayed, Hannah kept her assumed pollution and yet positioned to gain purity in the process." Rembold, "Hannah in Stages and Places," 75.

had closed her womb," but it is unclear whether Peninnah knows that the barrenness is divine or simply that she is provoking Hannah because she is barren, and the narrator alone is acknowledging the divine origin (v. 6).[91] Hannah's call for Yahweh to remember her and see her affliction could indicate that she knows God is the origin of her barrenness, but she could also be referring to Peninnah's provocation as her affliction (v. 11). The challenge for the interpreter is that fertility solves both issues: Hannah's womb will no longer be closed and Peninnah will no longer be able to provoke her. Elkanah's response to the barrenness indicates his inability to bring fertility but does not address the divine origin (v. 8).[92] His response is that Hannah should not be upset that she has no children because he is better than ten sons.[93] So, the narrator states Yahweh closed Hannah's womb, and the responses by Hannah and Peninnah might indicate that they are aware of the divine origin, but this is unclear. Elkanah does not address the origin of Hannah's barrenness but seems to acknowledge his inability to provide children for her.[94]

Interaction with the Divine

God does not speak within the barrenness narrative of 1 Sam 1, but God does respond to Hannah within the narrative (v. 19). The interaction with the divine for Hannah's fertility only involves Hannah.[95] Though Elkanah

---

91. It is possible that part of the provocation is that Elkanah married Peninnah because of Hannah's sonlessness. For a discussion of this practice, see Abasili, "Hannah's Ordeal of Childlessness," 581–605; Bodner, *1 Samuel*, 72; Marsman, *Women in Ugarit and Israel*, 126; Klein, *1 Samuel*, 6; Cartledge, *1 and 2 Samuel*, 28; Tsumura, *First Book of Samuel*, 108; Ackroyd, *First Book of Samuel*, 19.

92. Brueggemann, "1 Samuel 1," 35.

93. Most commentators believe this shows Elkanah's ignorance or at least inability to sympathize with the seriousness of her situation. Evans, *1 and 2 Samuel*, 15; Amit, "'Am I Not More Devoted,'" 68–76; Mulzac, "Hannah," 212; Fewell and Gunn, *Gender, Power, and Promise*, 137.

His lack of sympathy may come from the fact that he already has several children and heirs through Peninnah. See Evans, *1 and 2 Samuel*, 15; Steinmann, *1 Samuel*, 53–54; Kim, "Story of Hannah," 3.

94. Hamilton notes that it is logical to consider childlessness as God's affliction if fertility is a divine blessing. Hamilton, "6829 עָקָר," 509.

95. Alter notes that "in this instance the standard biblical story beginning, *there was a man*, is in part a false lead because the real protagonist of the story is Elkanah's wife Hannah." Alter, *David Story*, 3. See also Johnson, "What Type of Son Is Samson?," 272; Ackerman, "Who Is Sacrificing at Shiloh?," 43; Meyers, "Hannah and Her Sacrifice," 101; Crawford, "Struggle for Female Authority," 20; Olyan, *Rites and Rank*, 115–17; De Andrado, "Hannah's Agency in Catalyzing Change," 271–89; Calabro, "Lord of Hosts,"

performs sacrifices and feasts at the house of Yahweh, the text does not record him praying for Hannah's barrenness.[96] The verbs describing her prayer[97] and vow are all feminine singular and, within her vow, she promises to give her son[98] to Yahweh in first person singular, which indicates that only Hannah is involved in the appeal to God (vv. 10–12).[99]

When Hannah leaves the meal to pray and weep,[100] Eli's response indicates that she is acting alone (vv. 12–14). The narrator states that she was

---

25; Chisholm, "Yahweh Versus the Canaanite Gods," 177; Meyers, "Ethnoarchaeological Analysis of Hannah's Sacrifice," 80; Meyers, "Hannah Narrative in Feminist Perspective," 117–26; Bronner, *Stories of Biblical Mothers*, 31.

For a discussion of ideological distinctions in Hannah's portrayal and centrality in the LXX, MT, and 4QSam versions of the narrative, see Parry, "Hannah in the Presence," 53–74; Trebolle, "Textual Criticism and the Composition History," 264–65; Walters, "Hannah and Anna," 385–412.

96. Berlin connects this with Elkanah's speech to Hannah about being worth more than ten sons: "I see him as an unusually sensitive husband. No other husband of a barren woman in the Bible reacts this way. On the other hand, Elkanah seems to have given up hope that Hannah will bear a child, or to not care (perhaps because he already had children); he does not entreat God on her behalf, as Isaac does in Gen 25:21." Berlin, "Hannah and Her Prayers," 228.

97. For a discussion of the variants between the MT, LXX, and later quotations of Hannah's prayer and response to Eli, see Friesen, "Getting Samuel Sober," 453–78; Friesen, "Translating Misfortune," 649–53.

98. Her request for a male child is consistent with the other barrenness and family death narratives as well as broader ANE culture. See Hertzberg, *I and II Samuel*, 25; Abasili, "Hannah's Ordeal of Childlessness," 595; Ademiluka, "Hannah's Prayer for a Male Child," 1–8; De-Whyte, *Wom(b)an*, 179; Payne, "1 and 2 Samuel," 296–333; Evans, *1 and 2 Samuel*, 16. Many translations also emphasize the male aspect of the request: NET (New English Translation) "a male child," NJB (New Jerusalem Bible) "a boy," NKJV "a male child," EIN (Einheitsübersetzung) "einen männlichen Nachkommen," LEE (Isaac Leeser Jewish Bible) "Man-child."
Contra Michael Carasik, who argues that the "phrase in 1 Sam 1:11 can be interpreted conclusively as Hannah's profound prayer to be blessed with a mortal offspring." Carasik, "Why Did Hannah Ask," 435. See also Paul, "Rejoinder Concerning 1 Samuel 1:11," 45.

99. Scholars note that she separates from the rest of the family to present herself to God. Tsumura, *First Book of Samuel*, 115; Martens, "7756 קוּם," 902; Abasili, "Hannah's Ordeal of Childlessness," 594; Brueggemann, *First and Second Samuel*, 13.

100. Ackermann claims that her actions of fasting, praying, and weeping are attempts at inducing a divine oracle. Ackerman, "Hannah's Tears," 24. See also Ackerman, "Ritual Undertones in Genesis 21:9–21?," 19–26. The name "Shiloh" might also indicate a place where divine oracles occur according to Nadav Na'aman. Na'aman, "Samuel's Birth Legend," 51–61. Silber, dubiously, claims, "Hanna, by praying silently in the presence of the High Priest instead of bringing a sacrifice, breaks with the temple's sacrificial tradition: she is, in a sense, rejecting the order which Eli's family has corrupted. Even when her husband, Elkana, brings sacrifices, Hanna refuses at first to eat; she will not participate in Shilo's established rituals." Silber, "Kingship, Samuel and the Story," 66.

silently moving her lips while Eli watched, so it was a personal prayer rather than public or family prayer. In addition, Eli's speech was only addressed to Hannah. The narrative states that he spoke "to her" (אֵלֶיהָ), and all the verbs in his initial speech are feminine singular (v. 14).[101] Eli's blessing is also addressed specifically to Hannah. This is shown by the second person feminine singular suffix on "your petition" (שֵׁלָתֵךְ) and the second person feminine singular verb "you asked" (שָׁאָלְתְּ) in Eli's blessing (v. 17).

Hannah is the only character appealing to God about her barrenness. This is confirmed through the description of Hannah's plea and vow.[102] It is also shown in Eli's questioning of Hannah's actions and his subsequent blessing of her request.

Restoration

After Elkanah and his family returned to their hometown, Ramah, the narrator states, "Elkanah knew Hannah, his wife, and Yahweh remembered her" (1 Sam 1:19). This is a direct response to the reported prayer by Hannah where she asked Yahweh to "remember me and not forget your maidservant" (v. 11). Hannah confirms this after she gives birth to Samuel because she claims, "because I have asked for him from Yahweh" (v. 20).[103] God never speaks to the characters in this narrative but is portrayed as the one who arranges events in the background.[104] So, the narrator claims that Yahweh fulfilled the request that Hannah made, and Hannah's speech also confirms that her son was given because she had asked God for him.[105]

Reed Carlson claims that Hannah falls into an ecstatic or trance-like experience at the altar and this is part of the reason why Eli believes she is intoxicated. Carlson, "Hannah at Pentecost," 245–58.

101. For discussions about Hannah's response describing herself as אִשָּׁה קְשַׁת־רוּחַ, see Ahlström, "1 Samuel 1,15," 254; Caquot and de Robert, *Livres de Samuel*, 33; Muraoka, "1 Sam 1,15 Again," 98–99.

102. Steinberg claims that Hannah's vow to give Samuel to the temple from infancy could be considered abandonment and child abuse. Steinberg, "1 Samuel 1, the United Nations Convention," 1–23.

103. Samuel was dedicated as a Nazirite by his mother even before his birth, though others have claimed the dedication was made official by Elkanah. See discussion of Hannah's ability to make a vow and the role of her husband in Backon, "Prooftext That Elkanah Rather Than Hannah Consecrated Samuel," 52–53; Smith, *Critical and Exegetical Commentary on Samuel*, 9; Fidler, "Wife's Vow," 374–88; Hyman, "Four Acts of Vowing," 231–38; Roi, "Conditional Vows," 3–24.

104. Moyo, "Karanga Perspective on Fertility," 82–83; Abasili, "Hannah's Ordeal of Childlessness," 591; Scharbert and Hentschel, *Rut, 1 Samuel*, 49.

105. Firth, *1 and 2 Samuel*, 58; Cartledge, "Hannah Asked, and God Heard," 143–44.

Myth of Etana

The Etana narrative has more mythic elements than the HB barrenness narratives, including trips to heaven and talking animals.[106] However, beyond these mythic elements, Etana still follows the pattern that humans appeal to the divine to overcome barrenness. In the story, Etana is a king who has great prospects for his rule except that he has no children.[107] The only solution to this problem is to get the birth plant from heaven and bring it to earth. This connection between human fertility and life and natural (plants and animals) fertility and life was shown in the Tale of Aqhat when he dies and suddenly there is a drought, as well as many other ANE texts.[108]

To obtain the fertility plant, Etana asks an eagle for help getting to heaven, but the eagle is in a pit because he betrayed his former friend, a serpent. Etana frees the eagle and, as a reward, he is taken on a trip to heaven. They make it to the realm of the gods but, unfortunately, the extant texts are badly damaged, so scholars have debated what takes place in heaven and their return trip to earth.[109] However, the Sumerian King List contains the name of Etana's son and heir, so they were apparently successful in the end, even though the restoration of his family in the extant Etana texts is debated.[110]

---

106. For a discussion about the authorship and date of the various versions of the narrative, see Lambert, "Ancestors, Authors, and Canonicity," 1–14.
Tradition attributed the authorship of the legend to a Sumerian demi-sage, Lu-Nanna. Dalley, *Myths from Mesopotamia*, 189.

107. I am not discussing the snake and eagle interactions earlier in the narrative as it is only loosely related to the second part of the narrative. For a discussion of the minimal connection between the two halves of the epic, see Kirk, *Myth*, 125; Verderame, *Letterature Dell'antica Mesopotamia*, 65; Kinnier Wilson, *Legend of Etana*; Haul, *Etana-Epos*, 249; Helle, "Two-Act Structure," 201–4.

108. Leick, *Sex and Eroticism*, 36.

109. Helle notes, "It is worth considering whether this parallel means that the two acts had similar outcomes as well. Does the eagle betray Etana as it had betrayed the snake? Or does the epic rather hinge on a contrast between its betrayal in the first act and its reformed loyalty in the second? Until the ending of the epic is recovered, there is no way to know for sure." Helle, "Two-Act Structure," 204. See also Horowitz, "Two Notes on Etana's Flight," 511–17; Dalley, *Myths from Mesopotamia*, 190–200.

110. Speiser, "Etana," 118n50; Glassner, *Mesopotamian Chronicles*, 120–21; Jacobsen, *Sumerian King List*; Winitzer, "Etana," 57–59.
Etana as a literary work operates according to different assumptions and conventions than the historiographic work of the Sumerian King List. So, Etana's son in the list does not necessarily force an ending on the narrative. In addition, the historicity of genealogies in the king list has been questioned by many. See Marchesi, "Sumerian King List," 231–48; Winitzer, "Etana in Eden," 456; Dick, "Royal Dynasticism as Divine Legitimization," 188.

Description of Barrenness

The beginning of the Etana narrative is a lengthy argument between the eagle and the snake. Etana's barrenness plea comes into the narrative after the snake has trapped the eagle in a pit. Etana begins by claiming he has offered daily sacrifices, and Shamash has accepted them, and now Shamash needs to remove his burden of barrenness and provide him an heir through the plant of birth (C-3:68–73).[111] Etana, then, claims that performing the proper cultic rites should provoke divine favor so that he can have a son. However, he does not directly blame Shamash for the barrenness, only for not acting to provide fertility.

However, Shamash speaks to the eagle immediately before Etana's entrance into the narrative. When the eagle calls to Shamash for help getting out of the snake's pit, Shamash responds, "Thou art evil and hast grieved me gravely! The detested of the gods (and) the forbidden thou didst eat. Though thou hast sworn, I will not come to thee! (But) lo, a man that I will send to thee, he will take thy hand!" (C-3:63–66). Shamash's immediate response to Etana's plea for an heir is that Etana needs to go to the pit to find the eagle (C-3:75–79). Within this narrative, it is likely that Shamash either caused Etana's barrenness or allowed it to continue in order to fulfill Shamash's promise to the eagle. So, barrenness is resolved by acquiring divine favor, but the gods also use Etana's barrenness as part of Shamash's plan for rescuing the eagle.

Interaction with the Divine

Etana's initial speech is a prayer to Shamash, and Shamash responds in a reported speech as well, introduced by "Shamash opened his mouth, saying to Etana" (C-3:75). Not only does Etana engage in a reported speech with Shamash, but he also speaks to the eagle, which is a mythical creature, though it is unclear what type of divinity or mythical being the eagle and snake are.[112] Beyond the speeches with mythical beings and Shamash, Etana goes to the realm of the gods. Once he rescues the eagle, the eagle takes him

---

111. His appointment as king was also provided by the gods at the beginning of the narrative. Haubold, "'Shepherds of the People,'" 253; Helle, "Two-Act Structure," 201. For a discussion of the grammatical difficulties in this section, see Lambert, "Line 10 of the Old Babylonian Etana Legend," 81–85; Sulyok, "Breach of Treaties," 34–35; Streck, "Notes on the Old Babylonian Epics," 484–85.

112. Though the eagle is described as an Anzû in II:72, see Noegel, "When Animals Speak," 111n11; Valk, "Eagle and the Snake," 889–900; Winitzer, "Etana in Eden," 453–54.

"to the heaven of An[u] . . . to the gate of Anu, Enlil, and Ea" (C-5:36–37).[113] Etana, then, appeals directly to the god Shamash and Shamash responds to him in reported speech. Etana follows Shamash's instructions to find the fertility plant and obtain an heir.[114]

James Kinnier Wilson suggested a new reading of the Old Version tablet 1 with new fragments that indicate Etana's wife (named either Sherbi'anni or Muanna) received a vision of the plant of birth.[115] Earlier translators did not include the vision by Etana's wife in the Standard Babylonian Version, but several subsequent scholars have accepted these texts belong to the Old Version.[116] Regardless of which version this reading belongs to, the involvement of the wife follows the biblical narratives. Though this is still male-centered—Etana is the one who interacts with the eagle and flies into the heavens—the wife has a divine interaction through the dream and her dream initiates the quest for fertility. So, Etana aligns with the other barrenness narratives because the barren wife has a divine interaction through the prophetic dream even though Etana is the one performing most of the actions.

Restoration

The ending of the narrative appears to show Etana's restoration, but the text is broken. As the text currently stands, the eagle takes Etana to the heavens and then returns him to the earth.[117] Presumably, this trip to the divine realm was the way for Etana to obtain the fertility plant[118] and for the eagle

---

113. Animals saving national heroes is a common theme in the ANE and ancient world more generally. George, "Gilgamesh and the Literary Traditions," 457.

114. Frauke Weiershäuser claims, "The subject of the Etana-tale is this quest of the male hero: his adventures, and his bravery. The sadness and concern of his wife who stays at home, unable to bear a son for her husband, her feelings and emotions, these are not the concern of this kind of Akkadian heroic literature." Weiershäuser, "Narrating About Men," 275.

115. Kinnier Wilson, *Studia Etanaica*, 16–17.

116. Kinnier Wilson, "Further Contributions to the Legend," 237–49; Konstantopoulos, "Women and the Interpretation of Dreams," 89–108; Winitzer, "Etana in Eden," 444; Dick, "Royal Dynasticism as Divine Legitimization," 187–88; Koubková, "Fortune and Misfortune," 373; Hallo, "Birth of Kings," 46; Novotny, *Standard Babylonian Etana Epic*, xi. However, Kinnier Wilson's edition from 1985 does not have the wife fragments. Kinnier Wilson, *Legend of Etana*, 33.

117. For the rhetorical value of counting the distance in this journey, see Freedman, "Counting Formulae in the Akkadian Epics," 70–71; Horowitz, "Two Notes on Etana's Flight," 511–17.

118. The purpose of the fertility plant has been debated. Many scholars believe that

to fulfill his promise to Etana that he would provide offspring for him.[119] Most scholars believe that the text would resolve with Etana succeeding and receiving an heir if it was complete.[120] So, the restoration comes by following Shamash's instructions and receiving a blessing, or plant, that only the gods possess.[121]

Conclusion

The HB barrenness narratives discussed in this chapter are Sarah in Gen 18, Rebekah in Gen 25, Rachel in Gen 30, Manoah's wife in Judg 13, and Hannah in 1 Sam 1. The ANE barrenness narrative is the Myth of Etana. Though the husband is more central in Etana than the HB narratives, shared themes can be ascertained. First, the women interact with the divine. Even in Etana, his wife has a prophetic dream and spurs him to interact with the divine beings. Second, the solution to the barrenness crisis comes through divine action in each narrative rather than human or social action. Finally, in comparison to the family death narratives, barrenness narratives overwhelmingly focus upon the plight of the women experiencing the crisis and their initiatives, apart from male influence, to overcome it.

---

the plant is for conception. See Stol, *Birth in Babylonia and the Bible*, 55–56. However, other scholars claim that it is for delivery rather than fertility, and Wilson claims this based upon the fragments about the pregnancy that he believes should be included within the narrative. See Kinnier Wilson, *Studia Etanaica*, 46; Bottéro, "Antiquités Assyro-Babyloniennes," 117. This detail appears more significant than it is for my argument. Regardless of the biological function of the plant, the goal is to provide an heir for a childless Etana. Therefore, it is a barrenness narrative whether the plant aides in birth or in conception.

119. Sasson claims that the journey to heaven and back is indicative of "a favored theme, the immortality of the human species (but not of individuals)." Sasson, "Comparative Observations," 229.

120. Speiser, "Etana," 118n50; Sulyok, "Breach of Treaties," 35; Kinnier Wilson, *Legend of Etana*, 13; Stol, *Birth in Babylonia and the Bible*, 55. But some are uncertain. See Haul, *Etana-Epos*, 32; Henkelman, "Birth of Gilgameš," 841, 841n78; Foster, *Before the Muses*, 438; Foster, *From Distant Days*, 103; Koubková, "Fortune and Misfortune," 377.

121. Kinnier Wilson has argued that two Sultantepe fragments (346 and 351) are part of the Etana narrative, and, in his reconstruction, they detail the pregnancy and Etana's attempts to ward off demons. Kinnier Wilson, *Studia Etanaica*, 43–46. Dick agrees with this suggestion. Dick, "Royal Dynasticism as Divine Legitimization," 188.

CHAPTER 7

COMPARISON OF THE PORTRAYAL OF PROGENY IN BARRENNESS AND FAMILY DEATH NARRATIVES

IN THIS CHAPTER, I will begin with a summary and comparison of the barrenness and family death narratives. I will then discuss cultural views and, particularly, laws for marriage and overcoming childlessness in the HB and ANE. These laws and practices will be used to understand the different literary conventions in the categories of family death and barrenness narratives. I will then conclude with a discussion about the validity of separating the narratives into these categories.

Alhena Gadotti notes that in Old Babylonian Sumerian literature, "the portrayal of women in Sumerian literature had everything to do with real women."[1] In fact, in a later article, Gadotti claims that "the divine feminine replicates on a divine level the biological, social and cultural roles women had in 'real life.'"[2] The intention of this chapter is more modest. I am not intending to argue that all or even most women are having divine visions or that men are conversing with the gods. The goal is to show that cultural norms are reflected within the roles of these idealized and mythological characters. The responses of the men and women in the narratives reflect the social and religious roles of men and women within families. So, the characterization of these individuals is based upon the expected roles of people within society.

1. Gadotti, "Portraits of the Feminine," 195.
2. Gadotti, "Feminine in Myths and Epic," 28.

Barrenness and Family Death

		Type of Narrative	
		Barrenness	Family Death
Primary Character/ Protagonist	Female	Sarah, Rebekah, Rachel, Manoah's wife, Hannah	Lot's daughters, Tamar, Zelophehad's daughters, Ruth
	Male	Etana	Job, *Kirta*, *Aqhat*, *Babylonian Theodicy*

Table 1. Barrenness and Family Death

The family death narratives are Ruth, Job, Lot's daughters, Judah and Tamar, and Zelophehad's daughters in the HB and the Kirta Epic, the Story of Aqhat, and the Babylonian Theodicy in the ANE. The barrenness narratives are Sarah, Rebekah, Rachel, Manoah's wife, and Hannah in the HB and the Myth of Etana in the ANE. A challenge for identifying themes that categorize these texts is that the HB narratives are centered on women, except Job, and the ANE narratives are centered on men.

However, these different gender focuses still show a basic pattern. The women in the family death narratives, Ruth, Lot's daughters, Tamar, and Zelophehad's daughters, appeal to men. They also lack dialogue with the divine. On the other hand, the family death narratives that center upon men, Job, Kirta, Aqhat, and the Babylonian Theodicy, appeal to the divine and the men interact with the divine in reported speech, except in the Babylonian Theodicy.

In the barrenness narratives, however, every central character appeals to the divine. The women of the HB barrenness narratives not only appeal to God but have reported speeches with the divine. The male protagonist of Etana engages mythical beings and travels to heaven to find a cure for barrenness. Even more intriguing, his wife recounts her prophetic dream to initiate the sequence of divine encounters.

The HB and ANE texts emphasize dialogue over narration to show the importance of the character and their relationship to the subject. Robert Alter notes "the highly subsidiary role of narration in comparison to direct speech by the characters."[3] This emphasis on reported speech has been used

---

3. Alter, *Art of Biblical Narrative*, 81. Jerome Walsh claims, "Biblical narrative is often little more than extensive dialogue connected by a minimum of narrative transitions." Walsh, *Old Testament Narrative*, 56. Robert Kawashima affirms, "Hence, as has already been demonstrated by others, dialogue becomes a medium for the Bible's cunning and subtle characterizations." Kawashima, *Biblical Narrative and the Death*, 75–76.

in this analysis to demonstrate which characters are central to the narrative and identify their primary concerns and desired solutions. As noted, the men in the family death narratives have reported speech with the divine. In addition, the women in the barrenness narratives have reported speech appealing to the divine, including Etana's wife whose recounting of the prophetic dream is in reported speech.

Splitting the ANE and HB texts, both barrenness and family death ANE texts are all male-centered and all appeal to the divine. However, the HB texts are almost all female-centered narratives. The women of the barrenness narratives interact with the divine as does the man, Job, in the family death narrative. However, the women of the family death narratives do not appeal to the divine. This shows a peculiar feature of women's actions in family death narratives as opposed to barrenness narratives: women appeal to men in family death crises but to God in barrenness situations.

Marriage and Barrenness

The responses of the women in the family death and barrenness narratives illuminate the differences in the cultural understanding of these events. The social aspects of marriage and barrenness are important for understanding why the family death narratives resolve differently from barrenness narratives. As Robert Alter claims, "A literary convention may in some instances reflect certain social or cultural realities but is bound to offer a highly mediated, stylized image of such realities: in the literary convention, culture has been transformed into text."[4] In this section, I will discuss marriage customs and the description of female barrenness in the HB and ANE. The emphasis will be upon contracts and law codes in the HB and ANE to show the cultural understanding of these crises.

Marriage

HB

As the head of the household or, to use the more biblical term, "the father's house," the family ties revolve around the father and husband.[5] J. Andrew Dearman argues, "The Hebrew term closest to 'family' is *bêt'āb*, literally

---

4. Alter, "How Convention Helps Us Read," 119.
5. For the archaeological evidence of this household organization, see Stager, "Archaeology of the Family," 17–23; King and Stager, *Life in Biblical Israel*, 36–40. A more social study is presented in Clifton, *Family and Identity*, 13–40.

rendered as 'father's house,' reflecting a male-headed, multigenerational household as the basic kinship unit in ancient Israel. A household was shaped by endogamous marriage rites, patrilineal succession, and inheritance customs that privileged the eldest son."[6] As Daniel Block summarizes:

> Biblical genealogies trace descent through the male line; a married couple resided within the household of the groom; in references to a man and his wife or a man and his children, the man is generally named first (Gen 7:7); children were born to the father (Gen 21:1–7); fathers negotiated family disputes (Gen 13:1–13; 31:1–55); God generally addressed the heads of the household; when families worshiped, the head of the household took the initiative; and when men died without descendants their "name" died.[7]

The centrality of the father impacts not only the functioning of the household but also the practice of marriage. As noted by Block, the married couple resided within the groom's house. Even more significant than joining the patriarch's household, parents arranged the marriages for their children.[8] Most often the father arranged the marriages, though mothers are involved in their sons' marriages in several cases (cf. Gen 21:21; 27:46; Judg 14). The arrangement of the marriages did not just unite the couple but united households and clans.[9]

---

6. Dearman, "Family in the Old Testament," 117. See also LaCocque, *Feminine Unconventional*, 7; Ackerman, "Women's Rites of Passage," 21; Mathias, *Paternity, Progeny, and Perpetuation*, 164–89.

7. Block, "Marriage and Family," 42. See also Faust and Bunimovitz, "House and the World," 148.

8. Block, "Marriage and Family," 56; Borowski, *Daily Life in Biblical Times*, 82. Raphael Patai claims, "Since the wife of a son became incorporated into his father's family, the choice of a wife was, under usual circumstances, made, not by the son, but by the father or one of his trusted representatives." Patai, *Sex and Family*, 49. See also Shafer-Elliott, "All in the Family," 39; Stone, "Marriage and Sexual Relations," 173–88.

9. Block, "Marriage and Family," 56. See also the laws on people groups that Israelites could not marry (Exod 34:10–17; Deut 7:1–5; Josh 23:12; Ezra 9:2); also, the punishment meted out to the tribe of Benjamin and the (recommended!) kidnapping of women that reversed the marriage ban (Judg 21). Guenther, "Typology of Israelite Marriage," 387–407; Lehmann, "Reconstructing the Social Landscape," 141–93; Donaldson, "Kinship Theory in the Patriarchal Narratives," 77–87; Prewitt, "Kinship Structures and the Genesis Genealogies," 87–98; Oden, "Jacob as Father, Husband," 189–205; Fox, *Marriage and Kinship*, 208.

However, the purpose of marriage could also be based upon an in-group, endogamy, or a desired genealogical lineage. See Steinberg, *Kinship and Marriage in Genesis*, 8–11; Steinberg, "Alliance or Descent?," 45–55.

This arrangement by parents and move to the husband's household leads Fewell and Gunn to claim, "Daughters are 'given' (though in actuality 'sold') to other families. They invest in other fathers' families as the wives of other sons. Because a daughter will eventually be lost to the family anyway, the lack of daughters is never viewed with the same disappointment as the lack of sons. Understood this way, daughters-in-law assume an interesting priority over actual daughters."[10] Though the priority of daughters-in-law over daughters is debatable, the priority of sons is clear. In addition, the use of children to build the house of the groom's father is an important aspect of marriage arrangements in the HB. Consideration of ancestry and potential heirs is part of the legal decision by Moses concerning families with daughters and no sons (Num 36), and building the house of the husband's family, rather than wife's, is evident in the blessing of Ruth's marriage (Ruth 4:11–12).[11]

Borowski goes so far as to claim that the exchanging of gifts by the families of the married couple makes the marriage "a business transaction." He considers the requirement of a letter for divorce as another piece of evidence for this business relationship between the families.[12] Though considering the marriage a business transaction might be overstated, the involvement of the father's households in giving gifts and bringing together the couple, rather than just the vows or desires of the couple, shows the importance of the parents in the marriage arrangement.[13] Several scholars claim that women are the sexual property of men and so daughters are the sexual creation of their father acquired as sexual property by their

---

10. Fewell and Gunn, *Gender, Power, and Promise*, 71. Kimberly Russaw argues, "In the world of the text, the daughter's social status (or class) is dictated by her gender and her father's power and prestige (wealth) in the community." Russaw, *Daughters in the Hebrew Bible*, 37.

11. For a comparison between the blessing for Ruth's marriage and the blessing for Kirta's marriage, which both include building a house and references to ancestors, see Parker, "Marriage Blessing in Israelite and Ugaritic Literature," 23–30.

12. Borowski, *Daily Life in Biblical Times*, 82. For similar arguments for a primarily economic basis of marriage and divorce, see Epstein, *Jewish Marriage Contract*, 53; Jackson, "'Institutions' of Marriage and Divorce," 221–51.

T. M. Lemos questions, "What is also clear is that in Exodus 22 and Deuteronomy 22, the giving of the *mōhar* is one of the main rituals that actualizes marriage. Whether it is *the* ritual that actualizes marriage is yet another of the uncertainties presented by these passages." Lemos, *Marriage Gifts and Social Change*, 40, italics original.

13. Gruber claims, "As minors, Israelite women were married off without informed consent, and they remained under the legal authority of their husbands." Gruber, "Women in the Ancient Levant," 143. See also Blenkinsopp, "Household in Ancient Israel," 170; Emmerson, "Women in Ancient Israel," 384.

husband.[14] The degree to which women, specifically wives, were property[15] is beyond my argument. The necessary observation is that women did not arrange their own marriages, and, most often, it was the fathers that made the arrangement for their children. In addition, when mothers are involved in the matching of the couple, it is the mother of the son and not the mother of the daughter in the HB examples. So, fathers, as head of the household, negotiate a marriage for their son or daughter and, occasionally, a mother will participate in the negotiation of a marriage for her son.

ANE

Most ANE societies were also organized around the father's household, though in the absence or death of the father, the eldest son could fulfill the head of the household role.[16] Within this system, "the father or the eldest brother negotiated the arrangement of marriage with the bride's parents or 'guardians.'"[17] This arrangement of the marriage by the father and the daughter moving from her paternal household to the household of her husband upon marriage is found in Mesopotamian texts as well as Ugaritic texts.[18] Occasionally, it appears that a man could negotiate the marriage on his own if his father died or he was an adult, head of household.[19] Just like the HB marriages, the goal was to develop social ties and economic connections between the families.[20] As Karen Rhea Nemet-Nejat states, "The

14. Rashkow, "Daughters and Fathers in Genesis," 254; Feinstein, *Sexual Pollution in the Hebrew Bible*, 159; Laffey, *Wives, Harlots and Concubines*, 158–60.

15. See further Lemos, "Were Israelite Women Chattel?," 227–42; Lemos, *Violence and Personhood*; Jacobs, "'Disposable Wife' as Property," 337–56.

16. Matthews, "Marriage and Family," 1–2; van der Toorn, *Family Religion in Babylonia*, 21; Gelb, "Household and Family," 1–97; Nemet-Nejat, *Daily Life in Ancient Mesopotamia*, 127.

17. Matthews, "Marriage and Family," 7. See also Greengus, "Old Babylonian Marriage Ceremonies," 59; Justel, "Women, Gender and Law," 79.

18. Yon, "Women's Daily Lives," 454; McGeough, "'Will Womankind Now Be Hunting?,'" 477–78, 481–82. For a discussion of this in Hittite sources, see Bryce, "Role and Status of Women," 310–11.

19. Matthews, "Marriage and Family," 7.
In special cases like women who were priestesses or women who had no male guardian, they occasionally appear to negotiate their own marriage or the marriage of other women in the household. However, it should be noted these are not found in law codes but in contracts and are quite rare. See examples from Lagash, Ur, and Emar in Justel, "Women, Gender and Law," 79–80.

20. Lemos explains that "it was typical for the groom to bring bridewealth to his father-in-law, but that this fact alone was not enough to constitute marriage; instead it effected the intermediary state of betrothal or inchoate marriage . . . the status of

bride married into her husband's family; she did not marry an individual."[21] Unlike the descriptions in the HB, social class and economic standing are important parts of the negotiation, which highlights the business contract aspect of the marital arrangements.[22] The HB restricts marriages for Levites and priests but, other than that, the social class of marriage partners is not explicitly mentioned. This does not mean social class or economic standing was not part of the selection but simply that it is not the focus of the text.

The standard process of marriage negotiation in the ANE typically begins with the family of the groom making a request to the bride's father for consent to marriage. In the laws of Eshnunna, the requirement of the consent of the parents is stated explicitly:

> If a man takes a(nother) man's daughter without asking the permission of her father and her mother and concludes no *formal marriage contract* with her father and her mother, even though she may live in his house for a year, she is not a housewife. *On the other hand*, if he concludes a formal contract with her father and her mother and cohabits with her, she is a housewife.[23]

So, without a contract with the parents of the wife, the marriage was not considered legitimate. Therefore, the individuals involved in marriage contracts in the ANE are quite similar to those in the HB.[24] The head of

---

inchoate marriage was one in which, vis-à-vis the bride's parents, the groom had the right to perform the action(s) necessary to effect actual marriage." Lemos, *Marriage Gifts and Social Change*, 142. Giving gifts between the families was also common as was legislation for the division of property and wealth on death or dissolution of the marriage (137–52).

21. Nemet-Nejat, "Women in Ancient Mesopotamia," 88.

22. For discussion of social class and marriage in the ANE, see Matthews, "Marriage and Family," 7; Westbrook, *Old Babylonian Marriage Law*, 66; Bryce, "Role and Status of Women," 310–11.

Old Babylonian *seriktum* and Egyptian Demotic deeds for daughters have similar regulations for dowries and other wealth transmission with the daughter's inheritance share going to her children after her death. See Porten, *Archives from Elephantine*, 229n85; Driver and Miles, *Babylonian Laws*, 1:272, 336. A similar clause, *benin dikhrin*, can be found in Dead Sea papyri and the Mishnah (e.g., P. Mur. 21:12–14, P. Mur. 116:4–7, P. Mur. 115:12–14, P. Yad 10:12–13, P. XHev/Se 2:11–13; Ketubot 4:10). This focus upon transmission of property and wealth is also found in the neo-Babylonian period. Roth, *Babylonian Marriage Agreements*, 24–28. See also Jackson, "'Institutions' of Marriage and Divorce," 244.

23. Goetze, "Laws of Eshnunna," 162, §27–28; Yaron, *Laws of Eshnunna*, 32–33; Greengus, "Old Babylonian Marriage Ceremonies," 62.

24. It should be noted that texts at Ugarit record women initiating divorce and owning property separate from their husbands, which are not allowed in the HB. However, this does not indicate that they were able to initiate or ratify a marriage contract. See

household, which is typically the father, negotiates the contract, though the mother can also be involved in the process. In any case, it seems that the wife, or wife-to-be, does not select the husband or negotiate the marriage contract.

Barrenness

HB

Pnina Galpaz-Feller claims, "Biblical writings show how important it was for every married couple to have children. It may even be said that the purpose of the marriage was to produce offspring. Prior to her marriage, a bride often received her family's blessing that she produce many offspring (Genesis 24:60)."[25]

Within the HB, women are the ones described as barren.[26] Male fertility was obviously part of the conception process, but a lack of children was typically attributed to the woman's infertility.[27] As Alice Yafeh-Deigh claims, "Women are valued mostly as those who carry the biological burden of procreation; having children is a social duty and obligation, not a choice."[28] Fertility as the duty of women is shown by the cultural practices and the women's response in the HB.

First, barrenness lowered the social standing of the woman just as children raised their standing.[29] Juliana Claassens claims that barrenness is "a great threat to her status in a society that places great value on women's

---

McGeough, "'Will Womankind Now Be Hunting?,'" 482, 485; Vita, "Society of Ugarit," 478–79; Wilson, *Women of Canaan*, 54–59, 90.

25. Galpaz-Feller, "Pregnancy and Birth," 42. See also Sakenfeld, *Just Wives?*, 11–15.

26. Yafeh-Deigh, "Children, Motherhood, and the Social Death," 611; Patai, *Sex and Family*, 74–75.

27. Koepf Taylor notes that men's infertility is never clearly mentioned in the HB, though advanced age in the case of Abraham and the Shunammite woman's husband might hint at this. Koepf Taylor, *Give Me Children*, 38.

28. Yafeh-Deigh, "Children, Motherhood, and the Social Death," 611.

Tikva Frymer-Kensky claims, "Women are portrayed as more loyal to their husbands than to their birth-families, desirous of having children and concerned with their well-being, and eager for the welfare and peace of Israel. These goals were not uniquely 'female.' On the contrary, Israel actively promoted the nuclear family, and was determinedly pronatalistic." Frymer-Kensky, "Ideology of Gender," 186. It is true that concern for children occurs throughout the HB but the burden of producing children, and perhaps blame for a lack of children, often fell upon women rather than men.

29. Koepf Taylor notes that the birth of sons is important throughout the HB but the birth of daughters is absent or barely mentioned. So, having children is valued, but having sons is even more valuable. Koepf Taylor, *Give Me Children*, 37.

ability to bear children."[30] Kristine Garroway goes further, claiming, "Barrenness was an undesirable state, akin to having a disability or a curse."[31] This drop in status or view of the barren woman as accursed shows that procreation was, primarily, the woman's responsibility.[32] Cheryl Exum goes even further, claiming, "Genesis portrays the matriarchs' lives as revolving around their sons, for it was through bearing children that women achieved status and gained some security for themselves in the patriarchal society of ancient Israel."[33] The men with barren wives did not necessarily suffer socially because of the barrenness, though their household was endangered by the lack of heirs.[34]

Second, when barrenness is experienced, husbands often took second wives, or their wife offered a servant as a surrogate.[35] This method

---

30. Claassens, "Just Emotions," 2. See also Emmerson, "Women in Ancient Israel," 684; Fewell and Gunn, *Gender, Power, and Promise*, 45, 68–70. For a discussion of bearing children as empowering women in the Sarah-Hagar narratives and the Rachel and Leah narrative, see Jacobs, *Gender, Power, and Persuasion*, 129–55, 157–75.

31. Garroway, *Growing Up in Ancient Israel*, 28.

32. The importance of childbearing is shown in the life expectancy differences between men and women in Iron Age Israel. Complications from pregnancy caused a ten-year difference in average lifespan, forty years for men and thirty years for women, as calculated from skeletons in archaeological digs. See Nakhai, "World of Possibilities," 377; Nakhai, "Female Infanticide in Iron II," 258; Kloner and Davis, "Burial Cave," 110.

Carol Meyers claims that this short life expectancy for women implies that "it would have been a demographic impossibility for most men to have had multiple spouses." Meyers, *Rediscovering Eve*, 109.

33. Exum, *Fragmented Women*, 104. See also Bird, "Images of Women," 51–55, 61–71.

34. Van der Toorn claims, "In prayers for women, childlessness and infertility are frequently mentioned as a source of anxiety and sorrow. To men, however, such flaws were not nearly such a threat as to women; a man was theoretically free to take a second wife, younger and hopefully more productive." Van der Toorn, "Torn Between Vice and Virtue," 2.

35. This section is focused upon non-royal marriages and second marriages in the instance of barrenness. Royals in the HB, especially David and Solomon, took many wives to secure political alliances and display wealth. However, this chapter is not concerned about political marriages. For information on royal wives and queen mothers, see Nakhai, "World of Possibilities," 374–80; Gruber, "Women in the Ancient Levant," 138–42.

The patriarchs likely represent elites rather than the average household size. However, the narratives portray a more intimate family dynamic than a royal harem. Therefore, they are used as background for Israelite practice even as they are acknowledged as being larger and wealthier households than the average Israelite. See Meyers, *Rediscovering Eve*, 109–10; Zorn, "Estimating the Population Size," 33; Stager, "Archaeology of the Family," 18. Blenkinsopp claims, "The ancestors of Israel whose life-stories are related in Genesis 12–50 were wealthy as well as pious and god-fearing, and therefore hardly typical of the average anonymous Israelite family. Though these stories are paradigmatic

of overcoming barrenness is shown in Sarah giving Abraham her servant Hagar (Gen 16), Rachel giving Bilhah to Jacob and Leah giving him Zilpah (Gen 30), and, potentially, Elkanah's fertile (second?) wife Peninnah in contrast to his (first?) barren wife Hannah (1 Sam 1).[36] This surrogacy practice indicates that barrenness was considered the affliction of women rather than men.[37] Surrogacy was not codified into law in the HB, but the narratives show that the practice was known.[38] Also, the practice recorded in the HB, just like in the rest of the ANE, was for a surrogate wife rather than husband.[39] In fact, the word for barren (עקר) is almost exclusively applied to women (except Deut 7:14 where it is men and women).[40]

The use of surrogates or second wives for the return to fertility and the potential rise in social status for childbearing women in the HB indicates that the problem of barrenness was more severe for women. In addition, the use of surrogates shows that they did not view men as the source of barrenness nor were men able to physically solve the problem for the women.

---

rather than strictly historical, their descriptions of household management and the pattern of relationships within households are not implausible." Blenkinsopp, "Household in Ancient Israel," 172. See also Meyers, "Women's Daily Life," 492–93.

36. Yafeh-Deigh, "Children, Motherhood, and the Social Death," 614. It should also be noted that strife between these wives is a common theme and usually related to barrenness/fertility and the husband's affection. See Trible, *Texts of Terror*, 12.

Co-wives and polygynous relationships are different. The strife between co-wives is between women of equal(ish) status whereas a wife to a concubine, servant, or secondary wife are women of different statuses within the family. See Patai, *Family, Love and the Bible*, 37–38.

37. Meyers notes that the patriarchs are depicted as elites, just like the later royals of Judah and Israel, so having multiple wives might stem from their status and not be reflective of the average Israelite's household dynamic. As Meyers claims, "Virtually no ordinary Israelite in the Hebrew Bible seems to have had more than one wife except Elhanan, whose two wives are necessary for the literary dynamic of the narrative (1 Sam 1). Also, one wife (Hannah) is barren; given the critical importance of offspring for a household's livelihood and continuity, having and infertile wife was likely grounds for even a peasant man to take a second one." Meyers, *Rediscovering Eve*, 109.

38. Yafeh-Deigh, "Children, Motherhood, and the Social Death," 615. For the social settings that may have led to polygynous practices in the HB see Leeb, "Polygyny," 50–65; Steinberg, "Kinship and Gender," 46–56.

39. The term for this type of marriage is polycoity as the second wife is a lower status than the primary wife. Polygyny is also found in the HB (e.g., Rachel and Leah, the wives of Lamech, Adah and Zillah), but this is typically not marrying a second wife because the first wife is barren, though barrenness or the husband's affection often causes strife between the wives. See discussion in Steinberg, *Kinship and Marriage in Genesis*, 15–17.

40. In some barrenness narratives, the phrase "without children" is used rather than "barren," but this phrase also overwhelmingly refers to women (cf. 1 Sam 1). Klein, "עקר," 483; White, "Deconstructing Barrenness," 42; Kramer, "Barrenness," 23.

Instead, they could solve the issue socially, but it was through a surrogate for the barren woman, not a surrogate for the man.

ANE

Just like the HB, many ANE texts place barrenness upon women rather than men.[41] As Tikva Frymer-Kensky claims:

> Women who did not give birth were considered "barren" and unfortunate, and a woman who did not want to have children was somehow unnatural, unwomanly, devoid of the "maternal instinct." Society had a vested interest in women's wombs and sought to guard them by excluding women from occupations that might endanger the reproductive powers.[42]

One of the primary ways that this is demonstrated is through the use of a surrogate or second wife.[43] Unlike the HB, ANE law codes contain regulations for obtaining a second wife when the first wife is barren.[44] In addition, Nuzi adoption tablets provide restrictions for husbands marrying second wives. For example, "If Gilimninu bears children, Shennima shall not take another wife. But if Gilimninu fails to bear children, Gilimninu shall get for Shennima a woman from the Lullu country (a slave girl) as a concubine. In that case, Gilimninu herself shall have authority over the offspring."[45]

---

41. Erectile dysfunction was an identified problem in the Middle Babylonian period. However, the magical and medicinal cures appear to target the inability to have intercourse rather than an inability to impregnate. That is, the dysfunction does not appear to be male sterility but a lack of arousal. Budin, "Sexuality," 4. See the Hittite, Ugaritic, and Middle Kingdom Egypt practices for this in Budin, "Fertility and Gender," 32, 42–43. Also, there are inferences about male impotence and fertility in the myths about deities. Budin, "Phallic Fertility in the Ancient Near East," 25–38; Stol, "Birth," 4:3–4; Stol, *Women in the Ancient Near East*, 148–51.

42. Frymer-Kensky, *Motherprayer*, xvi. See also Beckman, "Birth and Motherhood," 320.

43. Nemet-Nejat, "Women in Ancient Mesopotamia," 88. See the discussion of Nuzi contracts in Walton, *Ancient Israelite Literature*, 54–55.
Adelina Albà notes that "there were two ways to do this. First, they might adopt, or second the husband might beget a son with a secondary wife or a slave; the child of this union would, for legal purposes, be the child of the married couple." Albà, "Women in the Hebrew Bible," 359.

44. For example, the Hammurapi code has the barren wife obtaining a second wife for the husband, but if he divorces the barren wife, he has to return the dowry. Davies, *Codes of Hammurabi and Moses*, law 138, p. 65.

45. Speiser, *Genesis*, 120. See also Yafeh-Deigh, "Children, Motherhood, and the Social Death," 615; Meek, "Mesopotamian Legal Documents," 220.

Therefore, the second wife is not for additional children but to overcome the barrenness of the first wife. Even more importantly, the children of the second wife are considered as heirs for the first wife.[46]

Another aspect of the second wife laws is status. Bearing children restricts the ability of the husband to take a second wife.[47] Beyond this, if the first wife has children, according to the Nuzi texts, she can recoup her dowry if the husband marries a second wife: "If Kelim-ninu bears (children) and Shennima takes another wife, she may take her dowry and leave."[48] Likewise, the Laws of Eshnunna state, "If a man divorces his wife after having made her bear children and takes [ano]ther wife, he shall be driven from his house and from whatever he owns and may go after him who will accept him."[49] Also, Lipit-Ishtar indicates the importance of children, as even non-wives receive financial support if they bear children and their children can even become heirs: "If a man's wife has not borne him children (but) a harlot (from) the public square has borne him children, he shall provide grain, oil, and clothing for that harlot; the children which the harlot has borne him shall be his heirs, and as long as his wife lives the harlot shall not live in the house with his wife."[50]

These laws and legal contracts show that barrenness changed the status of women.[51] In fact, some law codes explicitly state that the second wife must not be considered equal to the first wife, even after the second wife has borne children.[52] This explicit maintenance of status within the household is necessary because the social status of the barren wife is compromised.[53]

46. Steinberg explains, "The term polycoity refers to a marriage pattern in which a man takes an additional wife, beyond his primary wife, who is of lower social status than the primary wife." Steinberg, "Zilpah." See also Yafeh-Deigh, "Children, Motherhood, and the Social Death," 614.
Polycoity is also found in Mesopotamian texts. See Van Seters, "Problem of Childlessness," 401–8.
Glassner argues that the line between prostitution and polygyny is not as clear in Mesopotamian literature as many have tried to assert. Glassner, "Polygynie ou Prostitution," 151–64.

47. Nemet-Nejat, "Women in Ancient Mesopotamia," 91.

48. Meek, "Mesopotamian Legal Documents," 220.

49. Goetze, "Laws of Eshnunna," line 59, p. 163.

50. Kramer, "Lipit-Ishtar Lawcode," line 27, p. 160.

51. Some texts indicate that marriages were only divinely blessed once they produced children. Imparati, "Private Life Among the Hittites," 575; Marsman, *Women in Ugarit and Israel*, 47–48; van der Toorn, *From Her Cradle to Her Grave*, 70–73; Willis, "Barren, Barrenness," 400–401.

52. See specifically the Code of Hammurapi line 146. Meek, "Code of Hammurabi," 172.

53. In the ANE, a marriage was not secure until the couple had children, which

Barrenness is attributed to women and overcome through surrogacy and adoption of other children by the barren wife.

Divine and Human Responses: Barrenness and Family Death

With the background of marriage and barrenness, the responses of women in the family death and barrenness narratives can be set within their cultural background. In this section, I will analyze the narratival themes through the law codes that were examined in the previous section. My argument is that the two narrative categories demonstrate that men control marriage, but God controls the womb.[54] Barrenness primarily affects women, and men are unable to physically reverse it (though they can compensate socially through additional wives). However, family death affects all people and can only be overcome through the creation of a new family. Therefore, when the family dies, women must appeal to the arranger of marriages, men, whereas when they are unable to produce children, they appeal to the opener of wombs, God.

Barrenness

The barrenness narratives are primarily female centered. Even the ANE text, Etana, has Etana's wife receiving a prophetic dream to begin the search for the fertility plant. These narratives have women appealing to the divine in every instance.[55] Etana's wife speaks to Etana but does not appeal to him directly. She asks him to appeal to the divine and presents the plan for resolving the issue from her vision.

This appeal to the divine by women shows that barrenness is seen primarily as a problem for women and outside the control of men.[56] As Jacob responded to Rachel when asked for sons, "Am I in the place of God, who

---

places the barren wife in a precarious situation. Delaney, "Seeds of Honor," 35–48; Esler, *Sex, Wives, and Warriors*, 60–61; Fontaine, "Sage in Family and Tribe," 160–61.

54. Knibb, "Life and Death," 395–415.

55. Dietmar Neufeld claims that Sarai and Hannah experience trance states or altered consciousness to improve their damaged social status of barrenness in polygamous marriages. Neufeld, "Barrenness," 128–41.

56. Baab, "Barrenness," 359. Yafeh-Deigh claims, "The stigmatization of infertility is primarily due to prenatal social norms but can function as a moral judgment against an infertile woman." Yafeh-Deigh, "Children, Motherhood, and the Social Death," 613n17. See also Baden, "Be Fruitful and Multiply," 4–8; Baden, "Nature of Barrenness," 20.

has held back from you the fruit of the womb?" (Gen 30:2). As the practice of second wives and surrogate heirs shows, the women of the barrenness narratives benefited the most from having their own biological children. It would secure their status as the senior or sole wife and provide them with a higher level of status as they fulfilled the expected role as mother. It also, according to the ANE laws, allowed the women a certain level of security as the husbands could not immediately divorce them or keep their dowry and marry another once they had children.

The background of second wives and the adoption of their children also shows men's inability to bring fertility. As noted earlier in the barrenness narratives chapter, the women interact with the divine rather than with their husbands. This divine appeal follows from the laws about adoption and marrying additional wives. The men can return fertility to the household, but this does not reverse the issue for the women. They still suffer the shame of not bearing children, and adoption, though allowing them to obtain heirs, is not the same as bearing children.

Hannah claimed her affliction of childlessness even though Elkanah's household was not childless (1 Sam 1). Likewise, Rachel was jealous of her sister because she was bearing children to Jacob (Gen 30:1). Sarah feared Hagar's son receiving part of the inheritance after she gave birth, even though Sarah was the one who suggested Abraham have a child with Hagar as a way to provide an heir for her (Gen 16:2; 21:10).

Though the Hammurapi law code claims that the second wife should not be equal with the first wife, the Lipit-Ishtar laws require a man to provide food for a prostitute that bears his child, and those children become heirs if his wife does not have children. This relationship in the Lipit-Ishtar laws puts the first wife in a precarious position. However, the husband does not have the same level of suffering. When he marries another wife or concubine, he obtains heirs and an enduring household.

The struggle of the barren wives is shown through the law codes and the barrenness narratives. The husbands are relatively unaffected and therefore have secondary roles (except Etana). As Frauke Weiershäuser notes about Etana's wife, "The king's longing for a son is understandable, but one suspects that his wife felt equal pressure to become the mother of a boy."[57] The women appeal to the divine because the husbands cannot physically return their fertility. Even more troubling for the wives, the men's solution for barrenness would be to marry additional wives, which restores fertility to the household but jeopardizes the barren wives' status.

---

57. Weiershäuser, "Narrating About Men," 274.

Family Death

The family death narratives split between female oriented and male oriented narratives. This split indicates the more universal concern of household destruction. Barrenness affects women but death affects all. In addition, men are able to overcome household barrenness through additional wives, but they cannot raise the dead. Therefore, the men must appeal to God to restore their fortunes.

The method for restoration in the male-centered narratives, though, leads to the reason for the women's appeals. Job, Kirta, and Aqhat restore their households by obtaining new wives and heirs. As noted in the marriage practices above, parents typically arranged marriages, but men could arrange their own marriages as well. The challenge for the women is that they cannot arrange their own marriages. The women appeal to men in order to restore the family unit. They do not appeal directly to the divine because, to use De-Whyte's terminology, the barrenness is not physical but social.[58] The women appeal to the arrangers of marriages, men, rather than the opener of wombs, God.[59]

Family death is a social concern that affects all members of the household. Restoration is brought through the social customs of the day. When a household dies, a new household must be created. This comes through marriage and children. Men arrange marriages for themselves and their children. Patriarchs were also the ones "officially adopting a baby into the household when it was born."[60] In this way, they can resolve the family death crisis for themselves unless no suitable options exist for recreating the family (cf. widespread death in Job and the Babylonian Theodicy and the search

---

58. Specifically, Tamar, Ruth, and Naomi. De-Whyte, *Wom(b)an*, 242–52.

59. The lack of divine appeal in the restoration of the family can be shown through an example from Ruth. As Jack Sasson explains, "Of the twenty-four references to a divine figure, only two could be considered as contributing to the development of the tale. These two instances, it is interesting to note, occur at the tale's extremities: The first occurs in 1:6, in which God's grace to the Bethlehemites sets Naomi (and the story) in motion; the second is recorded in 4:13, in which Ruth's pregnancy is permitted by God." Ruth and Naomi appeal to and are answered primarily by men. Sasson, *Ruth*, 221.

Hubbard concurs: "Thus, at first glance, the women's praise seems simply to reinforce the point that Yahweh had provided the newborn. In my view, however, it offers a terse theological commentary on the book's entire prior chain of events. Granted, Yahweh's help enabled Ruth to conceive. But there would be no birth at all without human actions—sexual consummation by the newlyweds (4:13), Boaz's day in court (4:1–12), the meetings of Ruth and Boaz (chaps. 2 and 3), and her migration to Judah (chap. 1). In short, the book implies that divine guidance lay behind everything, even the actions of human characters." Hubbard, "Goʾel in Ancient Israel," 18.

60. Shafer-Elliott, "All in the Family," 38.

for a wife and heir in Kirta and Aqhat).⁶¹ If a woman is left without a father, or brother or other male family member, to offer a dowry and match her with a new husband, then she must appeal to a social leader or head of household to remedy the situation.⁶²

Women's Relation to the Divine

Scholars have argued about women's roles in temple rituals and cultic observance, especially in the HB, which appears to have an entirely male-dominated cult.⁶³ The rest of the ANE appears less gender restricted, though the

---

61. Note that Obed is the redeemer/restorer of Naomi, and Ruth, whereas God is the restorer of Job in the family death narratives. Mangrum notes, "The macro-narrative featuring the *return* and *restoration* of Naomi function as a kind of death and resurrection. She has now returned from the bitter land of the dead to a life of fullness, this restoration becomes evident in the fact that the women of Bethlehem in the concluding section say *to Naomi*, 'May he also be to you a *restorer of life* and a sustainer of your old age' (4:27). Obed's designation as 'restorer' comes from the popular verb of the first chapter, *šub* ('return'). This is the last and fifteenth use of the word in the book. In this instance of the term, Obed is stylized as the 'fullness' that brings Naomi from death to life by being the 'wealth' of Ruth offered to her mother-in-law; as a matter of fact, the connotation of a resurrection of life in some cases accompanies the action of the verb *šub* (c.f. 2 Sam 12:23; 1 Kgs 13:6)." Mangrum, "Bringing 'Fullness' to Naomi," 76, italics original.

Jacobson makes the comparison: "When Ruth returns home and reports what has transpired in the field, Naomi exclaims in response, 'Blessed be he by the LORD, whose kindness has not forsaken the living or the dead! . . . The man is a relative of ours, one of our nearest kin' (2:20). The word here translated 'nearest kin' is the Hebrew word *goʾel*. It can also be translated 'redeemer,' as in Job 19:25, 'I know that my Redeemer lives.' The role of the nearest kin is to redeem the family. In the final two chapters of Ruth, the word occurs as a verb (*gʾl* is the root) or a noun (*goʾel*) twenty-one times." Jacobson, "Redefining Family in Ruth," 8.

Angel concurs: "This story is parallel to Job: Like Job, Naomi first complained about her God-given lot (1:20–21), but was restored to happiness by the end of the narrative. From this point of view, the deaths and suffering at the outset of Ruth are theologically significant, but the reader is not told how. Unlike Job, however, where God's direct involvement is discussed in the beginning and end of the book, in Ruth it is not. Additionally, the human characters in Ruth played an active role in changing their fate, whereas Job did not. It is unclear whether Ruth was intended to parallel Job, or whether the two books were meant to be contrasted, with the characters in Ruth held more responsible for their original suffering, and given more credit for their eventual happiness." Angel, "Midrashic View of Ruth," 92–93, 97–98.

62. McKeown, *Ruth*, 126. See also McKeown's discussion of God's hiddenness in Ruth as opposed to Job as shown in her complaint to townspeople versus his complaint to God (110–11).

63. Peritz, "Woman in the Ancient Hebrew Cult," 111–48; Otwell, *And Sarah Laughed*, 152–78; Vos, *Woman in Old Testament Worship*; Beer, *Soziale und Religiöse*

precise roles that women could fulfill in each local context are not always clear. As Marten Stol summarizes:

> We know much about the particular responsibilities the "religious women" held because they occupied important positions and their activities are well documented. They were highly placed women whom we reverently call priestesses since they played a role in the cult worship. In the Old Babylonian period there were other women whom we call nuns. They had religious tasks, such as praying and perhaps making offerings for the dead, and often lived in special building complexes. Because we call them nuns, the place where they lived as a group we naturally call a convent. They had no (biological) children.[64]

In the barrenness narratives, though, almost all of the women appealing to God are involved in private prayer rather than cultic worship in a sacred location. Sarah, Rebekah, Rachel, Manoah's wife, and even Etana's wife have encounters with the divine in their homes. The divine figure(s) come to Sarah, Manoah's wife, and Etana's wife seemingly unprovoked while Rebekah and Rachel pray to God privately and receive a response. None of these women are recorded as being in official sacred spaces, though Manoah builds an altar *after* the divine encounter, nor engaging with cultic personnel.

The exception to this is Hannah. However, her pilgrimage to the temple is initiated by her husband as part of an annual event, not as part of the process for relieving her barrenness. The narrator records that Elkanah goes up to the temple annually and his wives come with him (1 Sam 1:3), and his response to Hannah's distress, "Am I not better to you than ten sons?" (v. 8), shows his lack of concern for her plight. So, the trip to the temple is not for Hannah's barrenness but an annual observance for the family.

In addition, Hannah's prayer appears to be outside of the normal practice in the temple. First, she leaves the dinner alone to pray (1 Sam 1:9). Second, her prayer is observed by the high priest, who is confused to the point of thinking she is intoxicated in the temple (which apparently was more expected than a woman praying alone?). So, though Hannah is within the sacred precinct and among the priests, she is acting outside of the common cultic practice.

Stellung der Frau; Nakhai, "Women in Israelite Religion," 1–11; Ackerman, "Women in Ancient Israel"; Winter, *Frau und Göttin*; Meyers, "From Household to House of Yahweh," 277–303.

64. Stol, *Women in the Ancient Near East*, 555; Crawford, "Exploration of the World," 22–23; Collins, "Women in Hittite Ritual," 246–71; Roth, "Women and Law," 144–74.

These observations fit within recent HB and archaeological studies. For example, Beth Alpert Nakhai claims, "Extensive archaeological evidence has clarified what the Bible only hints at, by means of condemnation (e.g., 2 Kgs 17:9-11), that religion was practiced not only in state-sponsored sanctuaries, but also in community and domestic settings, and at burial sites."[65] Meyers argues that "women's religious culture would have empowered them as major religious actors in their households. Indeed, in their access to the supernatural in the religious culture of the households, women may have experienced power that countered other, male-specific, cultural forms."[66] The women in the barrenness narratives are not primarily involved in official cultic practices but appear to converse with the deity in domestic settings.[67]

Conversely, the men appealing to the divine go to cultic locations. Both Kirta and Aqhat begin with sacrifices in the temple. Aqhat offers sacrifices six days in a row to receive a divine vision while Kirta is commanded by El to perform sacrifices in the shrine before besieging the town of Udum. Job begins consecrating and offering sacrifices for his children (Job 1:4-5) and ends with God commanding the friends to ask Job to make sacrifices and pray for them (Job 42:8). In the Babylonian Theodicy, part of the sufferer's complaint is that he has followed the cultic rites, made the appropriate sacrifices, and prayed the required prayers but has not been given success and divine favor (stanzas VII and XIII).[68] Though the success of cultic practices and sacrifices varies between the texts, the expectation that the men perform cultic rites is found in each text.

This does not indicate that women were uninvolved in cultic practice, but their involvement in formal cultic activities in the barrenness and family death texts is limited. This is a recurring theme in biblical texts, as Marc Zvi

65. Nakhai, "Women in Israelite Religion," 6. Bird claims that women initially had central roles in the Israelite cult but over time, as the religious community became specialized and hierarchical, women were pushed out of official cultic roles. Bird, "Place of Women" (1999), 3–20

66. Meyers, "From Household to House of Yahweh," 301.

67. Albertz and Schmitt, "Personal Names and Family Religion," 273–74; Bird, "Place of Women" (1987), 408–10; Ackerman, "At Home with the Goddess," 461–65; Meyers, *Households and Holiness*, 13–17; van der Toorn, *From Her Cradle to Her Grave*, 92.

68. Though not every text indicates the location of the sacrifice, this is usually understood as part of a formal worship setting or at least formal enough to have a large altar and sacred space surrounding it. For example, Albertz claims, "Although women would likely have played prominent roles in the domestic cult, blood sacrifices would only have been offered at local or regional sanctuaries under male control and authority." Albertz and Schmitt, "Introduction," 6. See also Gerstenberger, *Theologien im Alten Testament*, 39.

Brettler explains, "analogies suggest the possible existence of a whole type of specifically female prayer or ritual, which the Bible, due to its nature and ideology, would not reflect."[69] So, their formal or informal roles in religious practice are rarely represented in the biblical texts. This is not true of ANE texts, though the textual sources are not as codified and redacted as the HB. For example, the majority of the surviving prophetic oracles from Ninevah are from female prophets and the known Assyrian prophets in general are predominantly women.[70] In another example, from Early Dynastic II to the end of the Neo-Sumerian period, women of different social status are often named as important actors within cultic rituals.[71] The sources and focus of the ANE texts versus the HB likely account for some of the divergence in women's religious representation (i.e., ritual texts or individual prophetic oracles versus a compiled and edited text).

However, this lack of involvement in official cult practices in the HB is complicated by the fact that the women have a relationship with the divine. Though none of them appear to be acting within the official cultic sphere, they all receive divine communication.[72] It is also challenging because women appear to have cultic roles in the priesthood and as prophets in many other parts of the ANE. Perhaps Etana's wife was involved in an incubation ritual that is not recorded in the text (or is in one of the lacunas). It could also be that rituals and prayers for barrenness took place within a domestic setting or less formal cultic location.[73] It seems likely that women

---

69. Brettler, "Women and Psalms," 56. Meyers also suggests that women had much more pronounced social and religious roles than the HB indicates and the male-dominated worldview developed in later (Iron Age II) Israelite society. Meyers, "Procreation, Production, and Protection," 489–514. See also Meyers, "In the Household and Beyond," 20; Bird, "Women in the Ancient Mediterranean World," 44. For iconography that hints at a more feminine influenced cultic establishment in Israel than the biblical text indicates, see Schroer, "Gender und Ikonographie," 107–24.

Fontaine notes that history in the ANE is handed down by the "winners," that is, elite males. Fontaine, "Heifer from Thy Stable" (1999), 159.

70. Nissinen, *Prophets and Prophecy*, 99–100; Nemet-Nejat, "Women in Neo-Assyrian Inscriptions," 240–45.

71. Asher-Greve, "'Golden Age' of Women?," 57–58. See also Hittite religious practices that seem to have equality in terms of male and female cultic roles. Collins, "Women in Hittite Religion," 329–42. See also the discussion of Hittite priests and priestesses in local cultic activities in Cammarosano, *Hittite Local Cults*, 155–58; Meyers, "Roots of Restriction," 93–94.

72. As Schneider identifies with biblical women, "the [d]eity plays an active role in helping the matriarchs become mothers of those who inherit the promise." Schneider, *Mothers of Promise*, 218.

73. Women have roles within the family/domestic religion but, as van der Toorn notes, "When addressing a woman, the Babylonians would speak either of 'the god of your father' or 'the god of your husband.' Women worship the god of the man under

would take a central role in overcoming barrenness that is afflicting their own bodies and, with the other indications that women were active in domestic worship practices, performing their fertility rituals within the home or other less formal cultic locations is reasonable.[74]

Regardless of what roles women were allowed to fulfill in the official cultic sphere, they clearly had a relationship with the divine. The authors did not place them within cultic locations nor with the performance of sacrifices, but they also did not deny them the ability to communicate with the divine. Most married women likely performed religious rituals within the household and for success during conception and childbirth.[75] These practices overlap with the domestic setting and female protagonists of the barrenness narratives. In the barrenness narratives, then, the women have private divine encounters while in the family death narratives, the men appeal to the gods with sacrifices and rituals, usually at sacred locations.

Conclusion

Rather than simply narrative tropes, the family death and barrenness narrative categories reflect idealized responses to crises. The reactions, specifically by the women, demonstrate the cultural background of the narratives. Finding a new husband or sexual partner can restore a family after the

---

whose authority they fall; his god is by definition their god as well. As long as they are unmarried, their devotion is to the god of their father; in wedlock, they worship the god of their husband." Van der Toorn, "Family Religion," 29.

74. Meyers defines Israelite religion as "an umbrella term for the religions of various groups with different albeit overlapping beliefs, activities, [and] liturgies." She continues that "rituals surrounding pregnancy, labor, and birth, along with those securing fertility before pregnancy and those dealing with post-partum lactation, infant care, and circumcision . . . constitutes the religious culture of women more than men." Meyers, "From Household to House of Yahweh," 281, 283. Also, Dever, *Did God Have a Wife?*, 241; Zevit, *Religions of Ancient Israel*, 175–76; Albertz and Schmitt, "Introduction," 10; van der Toorn, *From Her Cradle to Her Grave*; Stol, *Women in the Ancient Near East*, 627–39.

75. For cultic roles in conception and childbirth, see Bachvarova, "Hurro-Hittite Stories," 272–306; Olyan, "Family Religion in Israel," 123n14. Albertz argues, "Rituals took place in connection with the distress of infertility, pregnancy, and birth; here the mother of the house stood at the center of the domestic cult." Albertz, "Family Religion in Ancient Israel," 98.

For women's religious roles within the household, see Michel, "Akkadian Texts," 205–12. For their roles in contributing to household shrines and worship practice in ancient Israel, see Ackerman, "Household Religion, Family Religion," 138–40, 148–49. Referring to the Aqhat narrative, Lewis claims, "one of the story's central tenets: the importance of the religion that took place within the home." Lewis, "Family, Household, and Local Religion," 71.

children have died, but that type of social response does not relieve the issue of barrenness. Since barrenness was commonly assumed to be a struggle for women in the ancient world, the dominance of women appealing to God in the barrenness narratives is expected. They are responding according to the understanding that men cannot restore fertility, except through the use of additional wives or adoption, and so those suffering must appeal to the divine. Therefore, this narrative categorization reflects common ancient views of fertility, death, and methods for finding restoration.

APPENDIX

FOUR NEAR MISSES
THE SHUNAMMITE WOMAN, THE TALE OF APPU, THE OLD MAN AND THE YOUNG GIRL, AND THE DOOMED PRINCE

IN SELECTING TEXTS, FOUR narratives must be addressed that are often categorized under the heading of "barrenness": the Hurrian-Hittite Tale of Appu, the biblical Shunammite woman, the Tale of the Egyptian Doomed Prince, and the Old Man and the Young Girl. However, these lack narrative elements that would lead to this classification. In this appendix, I will show that the story of the Shunammite woman is not focused upon overcoming barrenness but, rather, showing the power of Elisha. The Tale of Appu and the Old Man and the Young Girl also fall outside of the barrenness narratives because it appears that impotence or sexual inexperience by the male character, Appu or the old man, is the focus of the narrative rather than infertility. Finally, the Doomed Prince is focused upon the actions of the prince, and the description of his birth does not clearly indicate that barrenness preceded it.

The Shunammite Woman

In 2 Kgs 4:8–17, an unnamed woman invites Elisha to stay at her house when he is passing through because he is "a holy man of God" (v. 9). In return for the hospitality, Elisha asks, through Gehazi, what he can offer the woman.¹ She refuses his initial offer to speak to senior military officials on her behalf,² but Elisha's servant Gehazi suggests that she might desire a son because she and her husband have no sons and are old (vv. 14–16). Elisha tells the woman that she will have a son, and she (miraculously?) conceives and gives birth to one.³ However, immediately after this birth narrative, the son dies, and Elisha is summoned. Elisha prays and performs a ritual, and the boy comes back to life (vv. 18–37).⁴ Within this narrative, the Shunammite woman, her husband, and her son remain unnamed, and they are only mentioned once outside of this short pericope (2 Kgs 8:1–6; the woman sojourns in Philistia during a famine at the recommendation of Elisha and Gehazi).

The story of the Shunammite woman is often classified in the barrenness type-scene, especially by those calling it the "annunciation type-scene."⁵ In fact, Alter claims that this is the narrative that explains all the later variations of the annunciation trope.⁶ However, this has considerable variance with the annunciation model that Alter proposes and especially with the barrenness category that I have described.⁷ However, Alter claims "the annunciation type-scene begins with the plight of barrenness of the future mother of the hero."⁸ So, with Alter's three elements, initial barrenness,

1. For the contrast between the woman's gift with no expectation for receiving something in return and Elisha's expectation of exchange, see Plate and Rodríguez Mangual, "Gift That Stops Giving," 119–23; Fewell, "Gift," 113–14.

2. Burke Long notes that Elisha speaks to the woman through Gehazi in this narrative, but she consistently speaks directly to Elisha. Long, "Framing Repetitions in Biblical Historiography," 390–91. See the discussion of the conversation and the difficulty of the woman coming to Elisha twice in Slager, "Where Is the Wealthy Lady," 198–201; Park, *2 Kings*, 45–49; Yannai, "Elisha and the Shunammite," 123–35.

3. Gershon Hepner claims that Elisha commits adultery with the woman, which makes him worse than Abimelech with Sarah and further confirms the parallel of the child's death and resurrection with the sacrificing of Isaac, but this seems to go far beyond the text. Hepner, "Three's a Crowd in Shunem," 387–400. See also the parentage question in Graybill, "Elisha's Body and the Queer Touch," 36.

4. For recent discussions of the ritual see Riemersma, "Hoe een Jong Mens Weer tot Leven Komt," 21–34; Rebiger, "Magic Touch," 104–21; Graybill, "Elisha's Body and the Queer Touch," 32–40; Pietsch, "Prophet als Magier," 343–80; Richelle, "D'une Formule d'incantation Ougaritique," 241–59; Spoelstra, "Queens, Widows, and Mesdames," 181–82; Hobbs, *2 Kings*, 52; Nelson, *First and Second Kings*, 174.

5. Alter, "How Convention Helps Us Read," 126; Ackerman, *Warrior, Dancer, Seductress, Queen*, 185; Williams, "Beautiful and the Barren," 110; Shields, "Subverting a Man of God," 59–69.

6. Alter, "How Convention Helps Us Read," 126.

7. For a critique of this view from a "birth of a hero" viewpoint, see Johnson, "What Type of Son Is Samson?," 270n7.

8. Alter, "How Convention Helps Us Read," 119.

divine promise, and birth of a son, this text misses the significant/heroic child and the initial barrenness.[9] The boy is not named in the story and does not appear to do anything noteworthy for his nation, city, or family (besides being resurrected by Elisha). In addition, the Shunammite woman is never said to be barren;[10] she is only described as "a great woman" (2 Kgs 4:8).[11]

The lack of barrenness terminology leads to additional issues for the barrenness type-scene as I have defined it. First, the woman is without a son (בן v. 14) not without children entirely (cf. 1 Sam 1:2, 5).[12] So, it is possible that the couple were not childless but missing a son and heir.[13]

Second, the woman does not appeal to God or to Elisha to change her situation.[14] The desire for a son is presumed by Gehazi but not requested by the woman or her husband (2 Kgs 4:14). In addition, her claim to Elisha when her son dies is, "Did I ask for a son?" (v. 28). As Plate and Rodríguez Mangual interpret it, "She protests the second offer as well, 'No, my lord, O man of God; do not lie to your maidservant.' . . . She immediately says 'No' to the prophet, and later on in 2 Kgs 4:28 the great woman reiterates that she did not ask for a son. One wonders how many times a woman should have to say 'No' before readers start to hear her?"[15] Mary Shields notes, "The particular construction used here—*lō* occurring twice, followed first by an address to someone else, and second by a verb—occurs only two other times

---

9. Plate and Rodríguez Mangual also note that, unlike the other annunciation type-scenes, "a man of God is visiting and announces the woman's future birth, but he has not come specifically for that reason." Plate and Rodríguez Mangual, "Gift That Stops Giving," 125.

10. Parker, *Valuable and Vulnerable*, 150.

11. Becking, "'Touch for Health,'" 34–35; Rice, "Great Woman of Ancient Israel," 70–71; Jobling, "Bettered Woman," 179.

Contra Josef Tropper who claims גדולה means "old woman." Tropper, "Elischa und die 'grosse' Frau aus Schunem," 71–80.

12. Wray Beal, *1 and 2 Kings*, 322; Winslow, *1 and 2 Kings*, 176.

Plate and Rodríguez Mangual are close when they claim, "The Shunammite is unable to bear children, but unlike all the other annunciations, the 2 Kings text does not explicitly say that she is barren, only that she has no children and her husband is old." The text is even further from the annunciation type-scene because it does not claim that she has no children. Plate and Rodríguez Mangual, "Gift That Stops Giving," 125.

13. Contra the claim that they were childless by House, *1, 2 Kings*, 211; Konkel, *1 and 2 Kings*, 414; Olley, *Message of Kings*, 230.

14. Hens-Piazza, *1–2 Kings*, 251–52; Park, *2 Kings*, 49–50; Parker, "You Are a Bible Child," 65.

15. Plate and Rodríguez Mangual, "Gift That Stops Giving," 126. See also, Becking, "'Touch for Health,'" 35–36; van Dijk-Hemmes, "Great Woman of Shunem," 223; Camp, "1 and 2 Kings," 107.

in the OT, both of which are rape contexts."[16] Therefore, the woman does not appeal to overturn the barrenness or lack of sons. She may have desired a son (or children), but she does not voice this within the narrative and in fact protests receiving the child several times.

Finally, the narrative is focused upon Elisha, not the woman or the child. Though Manoah's wife remains unnamed, she receives most of the prophecies from the angel and her speeches drive the interpretation of events in the narrative. In addition, the children in the narratives are all named, and the naming is typically significant in the birth narrative.[17] In 2 Kgs 4:17, the birth is narrated but neither the mother nor son receives a name.[18] In addition, the narrative does not record any speeches by the husband or wife at the birth of the child that provide any indication that the child was longed for or is significant within the text. It appears that the birth of the child and the resurrection of the child are meant to highlight the supernatural power of Elisha rather than the significance of the family or son.[19]

---

16. Shields, "Subverting a Man of God," 62. See also Davison, *More than a Womb*, 15; Heller, *Characters of Elijah and Elisha*, 142.

17. Dean Erickson states, "The birth and growth of the son are relegated to scenery as the narrative speeds to the son's sudden death. An unnamed servant is sent by the unnamed father to carry the boy to his mother. It is striking in this quickly developing crisis that the servant and husband are unnamed while Gehazi will be titled servant and named, as at the beginning of the story (v. 11), when the scene again shifts to Elisha in verse 25." Erickson, "Gospel According to Gehazi," 284.

18. Plate and Rodríguez Mangual, "Gift That Stops Giving," 125.

19. Fricke, *Zweite Buch von den Königen*, 54–61; Hentschel, *2 Könige*, 20; Würthwein, *Bücher der Könige*, 2:294; Nelson, *First and Second Kings*, 170–76; Long, "Shunammite Woman," 12–25; Hobbs, *2 Kings*, 41–54; Montgomery, *Critical and Exegetical Commentary on Kings*, 366–69; Farrar, *Second Book of Kings*, 40–49; Brodie, "Luke 7:36–50 as an Internalization," 457–85.

Yairah Amit states, "Let me start by advancing the thesis that one of the aims of the story of the Shunammite, as it stands—if not its main aim—was to show the prophet being tested, to subject him to criticism, even to cut him down to size and show him to be a mere instrument of God." Amit, "Prophet Tested," 281. See also Riemersma, "Elisa en de verborgen God"; Simon, *Reading Prophetic Narratives*, 227–62; Roncace, "Elisha and the Woman of Shunem," 109–27; Hobbs, "Man, Woman, and Hospitality," 91–100.

Contra the interpretation that the purpose of the narrative is to present the Shunammite woman as a typological representation of King David. Jero, "Mother-Child Narratives and the Kingdom of God," 164–65.

The Tale of Appu

The Tale of Appu, also called Appu and His Two Sons,[20] describes a rich Hittite man named Appu living in Sudul.[21] He has wealth and property but does not have any children.[22] The text portrays him as an outsider among the other wealthy families[23] and indicates a level of sexual ignorance by noting that he goes to bed fully clothed (§5 (1 i 22–26)). His wife asks if he has found success, presumably sexual performance,[24] but when she asks him, he tells her that she is an ignorant woman and leaves.[25] Appu makes a sacrifice

---

20. The ANE or Indo-European background of the text has been debated. Beckman thinks they are highly Mesopotamian/ANE influenced, but with lots of native diversity. Beckman, "Birth and Motherhood Among the Hittites," 320–21. Similarly, Haas, *Hethitische Literatur*, 193.

Frederico Giusfredi and Valerio Pisaniello claim, "Despite some parallels with the songs of the Kumarbi cycle, there is no compelling evidence to assign the Tale of Appu and his sons (CTH 360) to the Hurrian cultural milieu. It is preserved in 12 manuscripts in Hittite that date to the Empire period, although linguistic data show that the composition is older." Giusfredi and Pisaniello, "Hurrians and Hurrian in Hittite Anatolia," 269. Similarly, Siegelová, *Appu-Märchen Und Ḫedammu-Mythus*, 33–34.

Itamar Singer claims the text has nothing compelling for Mesopotamian origin. Singer, "Some Thoughts on Translated and Original Hittite Literature," 125.

Hans G. Güterbock appears to have changed his mind about the Hurrian origins of the narrative: "I included both the Appu story and the tale of the Cow among Hittite texts of Hurrian origin, and both Friedrich and Hoffner followed me in this. But Siegelová showed that there is no evidence for Hurrian origin in these two tales, and the repertory of preserved Hurrian mythological fragments published by M. Salvini does not include a Hurrian text on Appu or the Cow story." Güterbock, "Hurro-Hittite Hymn to Ishtar," 155.

Matteo Vigo claims the story is one of several written by Hittite scribes with Hurrian influence and "at least the so-called *Tale of Appu* presents some features of the 14th century BC." Vigo, "Sources for the Study," 330n7.

21. For a discussion of the introductory line about the justice of the gods, see Hoffner, "Theodicy in Hittite Texts," 96–97; Curtis, "Structure of Hospitality Type-Scenes," 29–30; De Vries, "Style of Hittite Epic," 37–38; Hoffner, "Hittite Mythological Texts," 139–40.

22. This has been compared to the biblical Job. Grottanelli, "Observations sur l'histoire d'Appou," 49–57; Beckman, "Proverbs and Proverbial Allusions in Hittite," 26.

23. Beckman, "Birth and Motherhood Among the Hittites," 320; Beckman, *Hittite Birth Rituals*, 2–3.

24. Hoffner, *Hittite Myths*, 83. Vigo even translates this "never had intercourse before." Vigo, "Sources for the Study," 331. Birgit Christiansen translates this as "'touch her (from) below' (*katta ep-*)." Christiansen, "Love and Affection in Hittite Texts," 729. Jaan Puhvel translates this "never did you perform; what about now?" Puhvel, "Genus and Sexus in Hittite," 549. Similarly, Peled, "Contempt and Related Emotions," 602.

25. Beckman, "Hittite and Hurrian Epic," 259; Beckman, "Old Woman," 48–57.

to the Sun God[26] who tells him to get drunk and sleep with his wife[27] and he will bear a son. At this point the text breaks off, but it resumes again with his wife giving birth to two sons in quick succession, named Wrong and Right.[28] The narrative continues with the sons arguing before the gods about land and property divisions, but the resolution of the trial before the gods is missing.[29]

This text has been described as an infertility or barrenness narrative.[30] However, the lack of children is not ascribed to the woman. In fact, Appu does not appear to be suffering from impotence either.[31] The description of his lack of success by his wife might imply that he is unable to consummate their marriage because of a physical issue,[32] but his actions and the resolution hint at inexperience rather than physical impotence. As Ioannis M. Konstantakos says, "Apparently, the two of them do not even know how to go about the task, given that they lie on their bed fully dressed."[33] Additionally, Birgit Christiansen claims, "Unlike the biblical Abraham or

26. This is one of the few times in Hittite literature where the Sun God is explicitly said to take a human form to interact with a human outside of a temple. See Hundley, "God Collectors," 176–200. The Sun God is unnamed here and in many other Hittite texts. See Bryce, *Life and Society in the Hittite World*, 141.

27. For a discussion of Hittite use of alcohol in festivals and to perform actions that are otherwise difficult, including in the Appu story, see Francia, "Plant-Based Potions," 142–43.

28. Though these names describe the later actions of the sons, the name Wrong might be a critique of the use of drunkenness to conceive the son. See Hoffner, "Birth and Name-Giving," 202. For a further discussion of the naming in the text, see Haas, *Geschichte der Hethitischen Religion*, 307–09; Hutter, "Personennamen der Hethitischen Großreichszeit als Quellen Religiöser Verhältnisse," 506–07.

29. For a discussion of the ending, see Walcot, "Hesiod and the Didactic Literature," 34–35; De Vries, "Style of Hittite Epic," 41.

30. Marsman, *Women in Ugarit and Israel*, 192–93; Moss and Baden, *Reconceiving Infertility*, 36–37; Beckman, *Hittite Birth Rituals*, 2–3; Collins, *Hittites and Their World*, 148–49; Beckman, "Hittite Literature," 235; Puhvel, "Genus and Sexus in Hittite," 549; Imparati, *Studi Sulla Società*, 610.

Singer even suggests that Appu (or Abu) is a hypocoristic form resembling the West Semitic name Abra(ha)m. Singer, "Hittites and the Bible Revisited," 753. Similar suggestion in Singer, "Some Thoughts on Translated and Original Hittite Literature," 125.

31. Stol claims that infertility was ascribed to the woman, but in the Appu narrative, the wife blames him for not "tak[ing] me correctly," which indicates some kind of dysfunction or lack of skill in the act of consummation. Stol, "Embryology in Babylonia," 150.

32. Vigo, "Sources for the Study," 331.

33. Konstantakos, "Maiden Who Knew Nothing," 450.

Contra Bert de Vries, "Appu's going to bed with his shoes on, joined by his wife fully dressed may be a symbolic act to enhance conception. Appu has to cleanse himself after a ritually impure act." De Vries, "Style of Hittite Epic," 197n150.

Isaac, Appu's childlessness is not explained by his wife's infertility. Rather, Appu has no child because he does not have sexual intercourse with his wife. Apparently for the amusement of the audience, this circumstance is illustrated by the depiction of Appu going to sleep with his boots on."[34] So, Appu, apparently oblivious to how to procreate, goes to bed dressed and his wife joins him, also fully clothed. The Sun God does not prescribe a ritual or medicine to overcome impotence but alcohol. This would not cure physical impotence, but overcome inhibitions, which are implied by Appu going to bed fully clothed. Therefore, this narrative is not physical barrenness but a coming-of-age narrative about a wealthy, but sexually inexperienced, man who overcomes his inhibitions through divine instruction and alcohol to receive children and heirs.

The Old Man and the Young Girl

The story of the Old Man and the Young Girl comes from the Old Babylonian period but is found in several texts from Nippur with a couple versions possibly from other locations, though their origin is unknown.[35] The narrative begins with an old man proposing marriage to a young girl. She hesitates and asks her friend for advice, who cautions against the marriage, but eventually she accepts the proposal. The man lost his virility, which was what the friend had noted, and even after marrying the young girl, he could not regain it.[36] Since the girl already married the old man, she appealed to the king to resolve the impotency problem.[37] The king consulted a court woman about the problem, but her response is damaged in the text. The king then asks the old man why he is unable to consummate the marriage and have children, and the old man laments his lost youth. The king then allows the young girl to sleep with her slave. However, she interprets this decree to mean that promiscuous behavior generally is approved, which

---

34. Christiansen, "Love and Affection in Hittite Texts," 729. See also Leick, "Appu," 11.

35. For a discussion of the dating and the arrangement of the tablets, see Alster, *Studies in Sumerian Proverbs*, 90–97. See also the versions of the text and discussion in Matuszak, "Complete Reconstruction, New Edition," 184–87.

36. In other texts young women revitalize old men. The young girl, then, might have assumed that he would regain his virility through marrying her. See Crenshaw, *Old Testament Wisdom*, 265–66; Harris, *Gender and Aging in Mesopotamia*, 55; Curchin, "Old Age in Sumer," 63.

37. For the king's role in mediation, see Lipiński, "King's Arbitration," 137–42.

angers the king. The narrative ends with the king punishing the girl and running her out of the house.[38]

Though infertility in old age is an aspect of some of the barrenness narratives (e.g., Sarah in Gen 18), the issue does not appear to be infertility but impotence from old age. The friend asks about felling poplar trees (a common phallic symbol), and the narrative then describes that after the marriage, the old man is unable "to open her beloved womb" (lines 9–13).[39] The discussion with the king also describes the old man's inability to consummate the marriage, despite the fertility of the young girl ("fine is my vegetable bed but he has not luck there," lines 16–17, 22–23), and the old man's description of his incontinence[40] ("My urine, which used to pierce a solid wall—now it trickles uncontrollably," line 37).[41]

Therefore, much like Appu, the old man is suffering from an inability to complete his sexual obligation rather than infertility.[42] The descriptions of the situation by the young girl and the response of the old man indicate that the problem is an inability to consummate the marriage (which the slave would be able to perform) rather than lacking children after fulfilling the sexual expectations. This, then, is not a barrenness narrative but a narrative about male impotence and the mismatching of a young (fertile) girl and an old (impotent) man.

---

38. This summary follows the translation in Matuszak, "Complete Reconstruction, New Edition," 201–02.
Previous translations of the text have a wise woman or nun joining the couple together and places some of the complaints of impotence in the mouth of the old man rather than the young girl. Matuszak added new tablets to the extant versions of the narrative and arranged them in an order that, I think, makes the plot development more logical. However, regardless of the version used, the discussions of impotence and age-related sexual dysfunction are prominent. For earlier versions, see Alster, *Studies in Sumerian Proverbs*, 90–97; Alster, *Wisdom of Ancient Sumer*, 384–90; Alster, *Sumerian Proverbs in the Schøyen Collection*, 96–122.

39. See commentary on these lines in Matuszak, "Complete Reconstruction, New Edition," 204.

40. The old man also references his inability to support a child and slave girl, which some have speculated to be a wife and concubine that he can no longer sexually satisfy. See Harris, *Gender and Aging in Mesopotamia*, 56; Crenshaw, "Youth and Old Age in Qoheleth," 3; Curchin, "Old Age in Sumer," 62.

41. Matuszak, "Complete Reconstruction, New Edition," 201-2.

42. This focus on impotency has even drawn comparisons to David and Abishag in 1 Kings. Alster, *Studies in Sumerian Proverbs*, 94; Alster, *Wisdom of Ancient Sumer*, 385; Meek, "Abishag Episode," 1–14; Schreiner, "'But He Could Not Warm Himself,'" 121–30.

The Tale of the Doomed Prince

A New Kingdom Egyptian papyrus, P. Harris 500, contains the narrative of a prince who must overcome his fate of an early death.[43] The narrative begins with a king who has no son. He prays to the gods and they declared that he should have a son. So, he sleeps with his wife and she has a son. This son, however, was fated to die by a dog, a snake, or a crocodile by the Hathor goddesses.[44] The remainder of the narrative describes the prince outwitting the dog and snake, but the final outcome of his battle with the crocodile is missing in the text.

This text focuses on the actions of the prince, but several scholars have found the motif of childlessness in it and compared it to the narratives of Kirta, Aqhat, and Abraham.[45] However, the birth of the prince is narrated in only a couple lines.[46] As Martin Pehal notes:

---

43. Wente, "Tale of the Doomed Prince," 75. For the claim that the narrative dates to the late Dynasty 18, see Helck, "Erzählung vom Verwunschenen Prinzen," 218–25; Frandsen, "Aspects of Kingship in Ancient Egypt," 53; Spalinger, "Transformations in Egyptian Folktales," 138. Camilla Di Biase-Dyson claims, "The only preserved manuscript of the story follows The Taking of Joppa on the verso of Papyrus Harris 500, which dates to the earlier part of the reign of Ramesses II." Di Biase-Dyson, *Foreigners and Egyptians*, 121. See also Loprieno, "Travel and Fiction in Egyptian Literature," 43. Georg Möller dates the papyrus to the nineteenth century. Möller, *Hieratische Lesestücke Für Den Akademischen Gebrauch*, 2:21. Maspero claims it comes from the end or middle of twentieth dynasty "at the very earliest" because of the writing style. Maspero, *Popular Stories of Ancient Egypt*, 154.

44. These are specific animals sent to destroy him and have supernatural powers like speech. Eyre, "Fate, Crocodiles and the Judgement," 105.

45. McAfee claims, "The motif of childlessness is widespread in folklore. Dorothy Irvin, applying Stith Thompson's classificatory scheme to the mythology of the ancient Near East, has identified several texts in which childlessness forms a part of the 'Traditional Birth Episode.' In addition to the texts being examined in this thesis, Irvin includes the Akkadian myth of Etana, the Hittite myth of Appu, and the Egyptian tale of The Doomed Prince. Irvin's work is useful in providing a literary context for my examination of the problem of childlessness in the epics of Dan'el, Kirta, and Abraham, all part of what I understand to have emerged from a single cultural continuum, namely, Late Bronze Age Canaanite culture." McAfee, "Patriarch's Longed-for Son," 15–16. This has also been interpreted as two separate connections: children coming from royal households and the parents being sterile. See Hubai, "Einer Literarische Quelle der Ägyptischen Religionsphilosophie?," 297; Di Biase-Dyson, *Foreigners and Egyptians*, 128.

46. For a discussion of the plot and devices used to move it forward and focus upon the prince's actions as an adult, see Lazaridis, "Physical Characterization in Ancient Egyptian," 126. Spalinger does not even include the birth narrative in the components of the narrative but instead begins with hiding the child. Spalinger, "Transformations in Egyptian Folktales," 150.

> The Egyptian brevity is understandable as the motif of the childless pharaoh is virtually non-existent in ancient Egyptian literature and probably did not represent a motif worth developing for the Egyptian reader/listener. Even the mention of the Hathors—having been adapted to the Egyptian taste—follows the birth of the hero as opposed to the Ugaritic story where the Katharat arrive before the conception itself. The "foreign" and "exotic" setting of the story plot was therefore clearly indicated already at the beginning but was limited to the bare minimum and altered where possible.[47]

More importantly, the text does not say that the couple is childless but only that the king lacks a son. The possibility of the king having daughters is left open.[48] In addition, there is a lacuna immediately before the appeal to the gods so that the text reads, "to whom no son had been born [. . .] requested a son for himself."[49] The missing text could indicate a length of time that the couple was childless or infertile. However, it could also be a simple introductory formula, like "but when His Majesty requested."[50]

A more basic interpretation of this story is that it acknowledges the gods are in control of fertility. As noted in the previous chapter, the gods enable childbirth for all couples, not just barren or infertile ones. Alys Cox argues when discussing the narrative of the Doomed Prince, "the type of power given to the gods can be determined by characters' reactions to their presence. Moreover, the relationship between humanity, the deities and divine power can illustrate how aspects of Egyptian theology were believed to function in actuality."[51] So, the king's appeal to the gods and their granting of his request are ways that the myth makes explicit what was understood to take place in the divine realm every time a family conceived a child. The text does not indicate that barrenness or any other special circumstance brought this appeal. Asking, or hoping, the gods to grant a child would be the standard procedure for having children since the gods are ultimately in control of fertility and conception.

47. Pehal, "Ancient Egyptian Mythological Narratives," v.
48. Di Biase-Dyson, *Foreigners and Egyptians*, 128n49.
49. Lichtheim, "Doomed Prince," 535; Wente, "Tale of the Doomed Prince," 76.
50. So translated by Wente, "Tale of the Doomed Prince," 76.
51. Cox, "Gods, Knowledge and Power," 28.

BIBLIOGRAPHY

Aaron, David H. "The Ruse of Zelophehad's Daughters." *HUCA* 80 (2009) 1–38.

Abasili, Alexander I. "Genesis 38: The Search for Progeny and Heir." *SJOT* 25.2 (2011) 276–88.

———. "Hannah's Ordeal of Childlessness: Interpreting 1 Samuel 1 Through the Prism of a Childless African Woman in a Polygynous Family." *OTE (New Series)* 28.3 (2015) 581–605.

Abela, Anthony. "Difficulties for Exegesis and Translation: The Inversion in Genesis 18.7a." *BT* 60.1 (2009) 1–4.

Aberbach, David. "מנה אחת אפים" (1 Sam I 5): A New Interpretation." *VT* 24.3 (1974) 350–53.

Ackerman, James S. "Who Can Stand Before Yhwh, This Holy God? A Reading of 1 Samuel 1–15." *Prooftexts* 11.1 (1991) 1–24.

Ackerman, Susan. "At Home with the Goddess." In *Symbiosis, Symbolism, and the Power of the Past: Canaan, Ancient Israel, and Their Neighbors from the Bronze Age Through Roman Palaestina*, edited by William G. Dever and Seymour Gitin, 455–68. Winona Lake, IN: Eisenbrauns, 2003.

———. "The Deception of Isaac, Jacob's Dream at Bethel, and Incubation on an Animal Skin." In *Priesthood and Cult in Ancient Israel*, edited by Gary A. Anderson and Saul M. Olyan, 92–120. JSOT Supplement Series 125. Sheffield: JSOT, 1991.

———. "Hannah's Tears." In *Celebrate Her for the Fruit of Her Hands: Essays in Honor of Carol L. Meyers*, edited by Susan Ackerman et al., 13–26. Winona Lake, IN: Eisenbrauns, 2014.

———. "Household Religion, Family Religion, and Women's Religion in Ancient Israel." In *Household and Family Religion in Antiquity*, edited by John Bodel and Saul M. Olyan, 127–58. The Ancient World: Comparative Histories. Malden, MA: Blackwell, 2008.

———. "Ritual Undertones in Genesis 21:9–21?" *JHS* 19 (2019) 19–26.

———. *Warrior, Dancer, Seductress, Queen: Women in Judges and Biblical Israel*. Anchor Bible Reference Library. New York: Doubleday, 1998.

———. "Who Is Sacrificing at Shiloh? The Priesthood of Ancient Israel's Regional Sanctuaries." In *Levites and Priests in Biblical History and Tradition*, edited by Mark A. Leuchter and Jeremy M. Hutton, 25–43. Ancient Israel and Its Literature 9. Atlanta: SBL, 2011.

———. "Women in Ancient Israel and the Hebrew Bible (or Women in Ancient Israel and the Old Testament)." In *Oxford Research Encyclopedia of Religion*. Oxford: Oxford University Press, 2016. https://doi.org/10.1093/acrefore/9780199340378.013.45.

———. "Women's Rites of Passage in Ancient Israel: Three Case Studies (Birth, Coming of Age, and Death)." In *Family and Household Religion: Toward a Synthesis of Old Testament Studies, Archaeology, Epigraphy, and Cultural Studies*, edited by Rainer Albertz et al., 1–32. Winona Lake, IN: Eisenbrauns, 2014.

Ackroyd, Peter R. *The First Book of Samuel*. Cambridge Bible Commentary. New York: Cambridge University Press, 1971.

Adelman, Rachel E. *The Female Ruse: Women's Deception and Divine Sanction in the Hebrew Bible*. Hebrew Bible Monographs 74. Sheffield: Sheffield Phoenix, 2015.

———. "Seduction and Recognition in the Story of Judah and Tamar and the Book of Ruth." *Nashim: A Journal of Jewish Women's Studies and Gender Issues* 23 (2012) 87–109.

Ademiluka, Solomon O. "Hannah's Prayer for a Male Child: Interpreting 1 Samuel 1:11 in the Nigerian Context." *IDS* 55.1 (2021) 1–8.

Ahiamadu, Amadi. "A Functional Equivalence Translation of the Zelophehad Narrative in Num 27:1–11." *Scriptura* 93 (2006) 293–304.

Ahlström, Gösta W. "1 Samuel 1, 15." *Biblica* 60.2 (1979) 254.

Aistleitner, Joseph. *Die Mythologischen Und Kultischen Texte Aus Ras Schamra*. Bibliotheca Orientalis Hungarica 8. Budapest: Akadémiai Kiadó, 1959.

Aitken, Kenneth T. *The Aqhat Narrative: A Study in the Narrative Structure and Composition of an Ugaritic Tale*. Journal of Semitic Studies Monograph 13. Manchester: University of Manchester, 1990.

———. "Structure and Theme in the Aqhat Narrative." PhD diss., University of Edinburgh, 1978.

Albà, Adelina Millet. "Women in the Hebrew Bible: Real or Literary Characters? The Case of Some Matriarchs in Genesis." In *Gender and Methodology in the Ancient Near East: Approaches from Assyriology and Beyond*, edited by Stephanie Lynn Budin et al., 357–67. Barcino Monographica Orientalia 10. Barcelona: Universitat de Barcelona Edicions, 2019.

Albertson, R. G. "Job and Ancient Near Eastern Wisdom Literature." In *Scripture in Context II: More Essays on the Comparative Method*, edited by William W. Hallo et al., 210–30. Winona Lake, IN: Eisenbrauns, 1983.

Albertz, Rainer. "Family Religion in Ancient Israel and Its Surroundings." In *Household and Family Religion in Antiquity*, edited by John Bodel and Saul M. Olyan, 89–112. The Ancient World: Comparative Histories. Malden, MA: Blackwell, 2008.

Albertz, Rainer, and Rüdiger Schmitt. "Introduction." In *Family and Household Religion in Ancient Israel and the Levant*, 1–20. Winona Lake, IN: Eisenbrauns, 2012.

———. "Personal Names and Family Religion." In *Family and Household Religion in Ancient Israel and the Levant*, 245–386. Winona Lake, IN: Eisenbrauns, 2012.

Alden, Robert L. *Job*. New American Commentary 11. Nashville: Broadman & Holman, 1993.

Allard, Silas Webster. "In the Shade of the Oaks of Mamre: Hospitality as a Framework for Political Engagement Between Christians and Muslims." *Political Theology* 13.4 (2012) 414–24.

Alster, Bendt. *Studies in Sumerian Proverbs*. Mesopotamia 3. Copenhagen: Akademisk Forlag, 1975.

———. *Sumerian Proverbs in the Schøyen Collection.* Cornell University Studies in Assyriology and Sumerology/Manuscripts in the Schøyen Collection: Cuneiform Texts 2. Bethesda, MD: CDL, 2007.

———. *Wisdom of Ancient Sumer.* Bethesda, MD: CDL, 2005.

Alston, Wallace M. "Genesis 18:1–11." *Interpretation* 42.4 (1988) 397–402.

Alter, Robert. *The Art of Biblical Narrative.* Rev. ed. New York: Basic, 2011.

———. *The David Story: A Translation with Commentary of 1 and 2 Samuel.* New York: Norton, 1999.

———. *The Five Books of Moses: A Translation with Commentary.* New York: Norton, 2004.

———. "How Convention Helps Us Read: The Case of the Bible's Annunciation Type-Scene." *Prooftexts* 3.2 (1983) 115–30.

———. "Sodom as Nexus: The Web of Design in Biblical Narrative." In *The Book and the Text: The Bible and Literary Theory,* edited by Regina M. Schwartz, 146–60. Oxford: Blackwell, 1990.

———. *Strong as Death Is Love: The Song of Songs, Ruth, Esther, Jonah, and Daniel: A Translation with Commentary.* New York: Norton, 2015.

Amar, Zohar. *Flora of the Bible: A New Investigation Aimed at Identifying All of the Plants of the Bible in Light of Sources and Scientific Research.* Jerusalem: Rubin Mass, 2012.

Amit, Yairah. "'Am I Not More Devoted to You Than Ten Sons?' (1 Samuel 1:8): Male and Female Interpretations." In *A Feminist Companion to Samuel and Kings,* edited by Athalya Brenner, 68–76. The Feminist Companion to the Bible 5. Sheffield: Sheffield Academic, 1994.

———. *The Book of Judges: The Art of Editing.* Biblical Interpretation Series 38. Leiden: Brill, 1999.

———. "'Manoah Promptly Followed His Wife' (Judges 13:11): On the Place of the Woman in Birth Narratives." In *A Feminist Companion to Judges,* edited by Athalya Brenner, 146–56. A Feminist Companion to the Bible 4. Sheffield: Sheffield Academic, 1993.

———. "Progression as a Rhetorical Device in Biblical Literature." *JSOT* 28.1 (2003) 3–32.

———. "A Prophet Tested: Elisha, the Great Woman of Shunem, and the Story's Double Message." *BibInt* 11.3/4 (2003) 279–94.

Andersen, Francis I. *Job: An Introduction and Commentary.* Tyndale Old Testament Commentaries 14. Downers Grove, IL: IVP Academic, 2015.

———. "Note on Genesis 30:8." *JBL* 88.2 (1969) 200.

Andrew, M. E. "Moving from Death to Life: Verbs of Motion in the Story of Judah and Tamar in Gen 38." *ZAW* 105.2 (1993) 262–69.

Angel, Hayyim. "A Midrashic View of Ruth Amidst a Sea of Ambiguity." *Jewish Bible Quarterly* 33.2 (2005) 91–99.

Arbeitman, Yoël L. "Tamar's Name or Is It? (Gen 38)." *ZAW* 112.3 (2000) 341–55.

Arnold, Bill T. *1 and 2 Samuel: The NIV Application Commentary from Biblical Text to Contemporary Life.* NIV Application Commentary. Grand Rapids, MI: Zondervan, 2003.

———. *Genesis.* New Cambridge Bible Commentary. Cambridge: Cambridge University Press, 2009.

Arterbury, Andrew E. "Abraham's Hospitality Among Jewish and Early Christian Writers: A Tradition History of Gen 18:1–16 and Its Relevance for the Study of the New Testament." *Perspectives in Religious Studies* 30.3 (2003) 359–76.

Aschkenasy, Nehama. "The Book of Ruth as Comedy: Classical and Modern Perspectives." In *Scrolls of Love: Ruth and the Song of Songs*, edited by Peter S. Hawkins and Lesleigh Cushing Stahlberg, 31–45. New York: Fordham University Press, 2006.

———. "Language as Female Empowerment in Ruth." In *Reading Ruth: Contemporary Women Reclaim a Sacred Story*, edited by Judith A. Kates and Gail Twersky Reimer, 111–24. New York: Ballantine, 1994.

Asher-Greve, Julia M. "'Golden Age' of Women? Status of Gender in Third Millennium Sumerian and Akkadian Art." In *Images and Gender: Contributions to the Hermeneutics of Reading Ancient Art*, edited by Silvia Schroer, 41–81. Orbis Biblicus et Orientalis 220. Göttingen: Vandenhoeck & Ruprecht, 2006.

Ashley, Elana. "The 'Epic of AQHT' and the 'RPUM Texts': A Critical Interpretation (Parts One and Two)." PhD diss., New York University, 1977.

Ashmon, Scott A. *Birth Annunciations in the Hebrew Bible and Ancient Near East: A Literary Analysis of the Forms and Functions of the Heavenly Foretelling of the Destiny of a Special Child*. Lewiston, NY: Edwin Mellen, 2012.

Avishur, Yitzhak. "The 'Duties of the Son' in the 'Story of Aqhat' and Ezekiel's Prophecy on Idolatry (Ch. 8)." *Ugarit-Forschungen* 17 (1986) 49–60.

Axelrod, C. D. "Abraham's Plea for Justice: A Commentary on Genesis Chapter 18." *Journal of Biblical Theology* 4.1 (2021) 61–78.

Baab, O. J. "Barrenness." In *The Interpreter's Dictionary of the Bible: An Illustrated Encyclopedia*, edited by George Arthur Buttrick, 1:358–59. Nashville: Abingdon, 1962.

Bachvarova, Mary. "Hurro-Hittite Stories and Hittite Pregnancy and Birth Rituals." In *Women in the Ancient Near East: A Sourcebook*, edited by Mark W. Chavalas, 272–306. Routledge Sourcebooks for the Ancient World. New York: Routledge, 2014.

Backon, Joshua. "Prooftext That Elkanah Rather Than Hannah Consecrated Samuel as a Nazirite." *Jewish Bible Quarterly* 42.1 (2014) 52–53.

Baden, Joel S. "Be Fruitful and Multiply: The Dangers of Divine Blessing." *Communitas: Journal of Education Beyond the Walls* 14 (2018) 4–8.

———. "The Nature of Barrenness in the Hebrew Bible." In *Disability Studies and Biblical Literature*, edited by Candida R. Moss and Jeremy Schipper, 13–28. New York: Palgrave Macmillan, 2011.

Bailey, Randall C. "Why Do Readers Believe Lot? Genesis 19 Reconsidered." *OTE* 23.3 (2010) 519–48.

Bailey, Wilma Ann. "Baby Becky, Menarche and Prepubescent Marriage in Ancient Israel." *The Journal of the Interdenominational Theological Center* 37.1–2 (2011) 113–37.

———. "Intimate Moments: A Study of Genesis 29:31–30:21." *Proceedings—Eastern Great Lakes and Midwest Biblical Societies* 29 (2009) 1–14.

Bal, Mieke. *Death and Dissymmetry: The Politics of Coherence in the Book of Judges*. Chicago Studies in the History of Judaism. Chicago: University of Chicago Press, 1988.

———. *Lethal Love: Feminist Literary Readings of Biblical Love Stories*. Indiana Studies in Biblical Literature. Bloomington: Indiana University Press, 1987.

Baldwin, Joyce G. *1 and 2 Samuel: An Introduction and Commentary.* Tyndale Old Testament Commentaries 8. Downers Grove, IL: InterVarsity, 1988.

Balentine, Samuel E. *Job.* Smyth and Helwys Bible Commentary 15. Macon, GA: Smyth & Helwys, 2006.

Barnes, Michael. "The Space of Meeting: Learning to Be Host and Guest." *Communio Viatorum* 58.2 (2016) 146–71.

Barré, Michael L. "'Fear of God' and the World View of Wisdom." *Biblical Theology Bulletin* 11.2 (1981) 41–43.

Barrett, Judy. "Ruth vs Job." *JudyBarrettBlog* (blog), Aug. 17, 2017. https://judybarrettblog.com/2017/08/17/ruth-vs-job/.

Barton, George A. "Danel, a Pre-Israelite Hero of Galilee." *JBL* 60.3 (1941) 213–25.

Bauckham, Richard. "The Book of Ruth and the Possibility of a Feminist Canonical Hermeneutic." *BibInt* 5.1 (1997) 29–45.

Baylis, Charles P. "Naomi in the Book of Ruth in Light of the Mosaic Covenant." *Bibliotheca Sacra* 161.644 (2004) 413–31.

Bazaq, Amnon. "עולם חסד בנה' - בין מגילת רות לספר איוב' ['A World of Kindness Will Be Built'—Between the Scroll of Ruth and the Book of Job]." *Megadim* 18 (1993) 169–75.

Beattie, D. R. G. "Book of Ruth as Evidence for Israelite Legal Practice." *VT* 24.3 (1974) 251–67.

———. "Kethibh and Qere in Ruth 4:5." *VT* 21.4 (1971) 490–94.

Beaulieu, Paul-Alain. "The Social and Intellectual Setting of Babylonian Wisdom Literature." In *Wisdom Literature in Mesopotamia and Israel*, edited by Richard J. Clifford, 3–19. Symposium Series (Society of Biblical Literature) 36. Atlanta: SBL, 2007.

Bechmann, Ulrike. "Prophetische Frauen Am Zweiten Tempel?: Ein Vorschlag, Die Töchter Zelofhads (Num 27) Als Kultprophetinnen Zu Verstehen." *Biblische Notizen* 119/120 (2003) 52–62.

Becking, Bob. "'Touch for Health...': Magic in II Reg 4,31–37 with a Remark on the History of Yahwism." *ZAW* 108.1 (1996) 34–54.

Beckman, Gary. "Birth and Motherhood Among the Hittites." In *Women in Antiquity: Real Women Across the Ancient World*, edited by Stephanie Lynn Budin and Jean MacIntosh Turfa, 319–28. New York: Routledge, 2016.

———. "Hittite and Hurrian Epic." In *A Companion to Ancient Epic*, edited by John Miles Foley, 255–63. Blackwell Companions to the Ancient World. Malden, MA: Blackwell, 2005.

———. *Hittite Birth Rituals.* 2nd ed. Studien zu den Boğazköy-Texten 29. Wiesbaden: Otto Harrassowitz, 1983.

———. "Hittite Literature." In *From an Antique Land: An Introduction to Ancient Near Eastern Literature*, edited by Carl S. Ehrlich, 215–54. Lanham, MD: Rowman & Littlefield, 2009.

———. "The Old Woman: Female Wisdom as a Resource and a Threat in Hittite Anatolia." In *Audias Fabulas Veteres: Anatolian Studies in Honor of Jana Součková-Siegelová*, edited by Šárka Velhartická, 48–57. Culture and History of the Ancient Near East 79. Leiden: Brill, 2016.

———. "Proverbs and Proverbial Allusions in Hittite." *Journal of Near Eastern Studies* 45.1 (1986) 19–30.

Beer, Georg. *Die Soziale und Religiöse Stellung der Frau im Israelitischen Altertum*. Tübingen: Mohr Siebeck, 1919.

Belnap, Daniel. *Fillets of Fatling and Goblets of Gold: The Use of Meal Events in the Ritual Imagery in the Ugaritic Mythological and Epic Texts*. Gorgias Ugaritic Studies 4. Piscataway, NJ: Gorgias, 2008.

Ben-Amos, Dan. "From Eden to Ednah: Lilith in the Garden." *BAR* 42.3 (2016) 54–58.

Ben-Barak, Zafrira. *Inheritance by Daughters in Israel and the Ancient Near East: A Social, Legal and Ideological Revolution*. Jaffa, Israel: Archaeological Center Publications, 2006.

Bendor, Shunya. *The Social Structure of Ancient Israel: The Institution of the Family (Beit 'ab) from the Settlement to the End of the Monarchy*. Jerusalem Biblical Studies 7. Jerusalem: Simor, 1996.

Benevich, Grigory. "Maximus Confessor's Interpretation of Abraham's Hospitality in Genesis 18 and the Preceding Orthodox Tradition." *Scrinium* 13 (2017) 43–52.

Bergen, Robert D. *1, 2 Samuel*. New American Commentary 7. Nashville: Broadman & Holman, 1996.

Berger, Yitzhak. "Ruth and Inner-Biblical Allusion: The Case of 1 Samuel 25." *JBL* 128.2 (2009) 253–72.

Berlejung, Angelika. "Sin and Punishment: The Ethics of Divine Justice and Retribution in Ancient Near Eastern and Old Testament Texts." *Interpretation* 69.3 (2015) 272–87.

Berlin, Adele. "Hannah and Her Prayers." *Scriptura* 87 (2004) 227–32.

———. *Poetics and Interpretation of Biblical Narrative*. Bible and Literature Series 9. Sheffield: Almond, 1983.

Berman, Samuel A., trans. *Midrash Tanhuma-Yelammedenu*. Hoboken, NJ: KTAV, 1996.

Bernstein, Moshe J. "Two Multivalent Readings in the Ruth Narrative." *JSOT* 50 (1991) 15–26.

Berquist, Jon L. "Role Dedifferentiation in the Book of Ruth." *JSOT* 18.57 (1993) 23–37.

Bertheau, Ernst. *Das Buch Der Richter Und Rut*. Kutzgefasstes Exegetisches Handbuch Zum Alten Testament. Leipzig: Weidmann, 1845.

Bertman, Stephen. "Symmetrical Design in the Book of Ruth." *JBL* 84.2 (1965) 165–68.

Beuken, Willem A. M. "'Please Give Me Some of Your Son's Love-Fruits' (Gen 30:14): Apportioning or Sharing God's Election?" *Louvain Studies* 23.3 (1998) 203–20.

Bhayro, Siam. "An Aramaic Magic Bowl for Fertility and Success in Childbirth: Lisboa, Musen Da Farmacia (Lisbon, Pharmacy Museum), Inv. No. 10895." *Aramaic Studies* 15.1 (2017) 106–11.

Bird, Phyllis. "The Harlot as Heroine: Narrative Art and Social Presupposition in Three Old Testament Texts." Edited by Miri Amihai et al. *Semeia* 46 Narrative Research on the Hebrew Bible (1989) 119–39.

———. "The Harlot as Heroine: Narrative Art and Social Presupposition in Three Old Testament Texts." In *Women in the Hebrew Bible: A Reader*, edited by Alice Bach, 99–118. New York: Routledge, 1999.

———. "Images of Women in the Old Testament." In *Religion and Sexism: Images of Woman in the Jewish and Christian Traditions*, edited by Rosemary Radford Ruether, 41–88. New York: Simon and Schuster, 1974.

———. "The Place of Women in the Israelite Cultus." In *Ancient Israelite Religion: Essays in Honor of Frank Moore Cross*, edited by Patrick D. Miller et al., 397–419. Philadelphia: Fortress, 1987.

———. "The Place of Women in the Israelite Cultus." In *Community, Identity, and Ideology: Social Science Approaches to the Hebrew Bible*, edited by Charles E. Carter and Carol L. Meyers, 515–36. Winona Lake, IN: Eisenbrauns, 1996.

———. "The Place of Women in the Israelite Cultus." In *Women in the Hebrew Bible: A Reader*, edited by Alice Bach, 3–20. New York: Routledge, 1999.

———. "Women in the Ancient Mediterranean World: Ancient Israel." *Biblical Research* 39 (1994) 31–45.

Black, James. "Ruth in the Dark: Folktale, Law and Creative Ambiguity in the Old Testament." *Literature and Theology* 5.1 (1991) 20–36.

Trible, Joseph. "The Household in Ancient Israel and Early Judaism." In *The Blackwell Companion to the Hebrew Bible*, edited by Leo G. Perdue, 169–85. Blackwell Companions to Religion. Malden, MA: Blackwell, 2005.

Blessing, Kamila. "Desolate Jerusalem and Barren Matriarch: Two Distinct Figures in the Pseudepigrapha." *Journal for the Study of the Pseudepigrapha* 18 (1998) 47–69.

Block, Daniel I. *Judges, Ruth*. New American Commentary 6. Nashville: Broadman & Holman, 1999.

———. "Marriage and Family in Ancient Israel." In *Marriage and Family in the Biblical World*, edited by Ken M. Campbell, 33–102. Downers Grove, IL: InterVarsity, 2003.

———. *Ruth: A Discourse Analysis of the Hebrew Bible*. Zondervan Exegetical Commentary on the Old Testament 8. Grand Rapids, MI: Zondervan, 2015.

Bodine, Walter Ray. *The Greek Text of Judges: Recensional Developments*. Harvard Semitic Monographs 23. Chico, CA: Scholars Press, 1980.

Bodner, Keith. *1 Samuel: A Narrative Commentary*. Hebrew Bible Monographs 19. Sheffield: Sheffield Phoenix, 2008.

Bolin, Thomas M. "The Role of Exchange in Ancient Mediterranean Religion and Its Implications for Reading Genesis 18–19." *JSOT* 29.1 (2004) 37–56.

Boling, Robert G. *Judges*. Anchor Bible 6A. Garden City, NY: Doubleday, 1975.

Borowski, Oded. *Daily Life in Biblical Times*. Archaeology and Biblical Studies 5. Atlanta: SBL, 2003.

Bott, Nicholas T. "Sarah as the 'Weaker Vessel': Genesis 18 and 20 in 1 Peter's Instructions to Husbands in 1 Pet 3:7." *Trinity Journal* 36.2 (2015) 243–59.

Bottéro, Jean. "Antiquités Assyro-Babyloniennes." In *Annuaire de l'école Pratique des Hautes Études. 4e Section, Sciences Historiques et Philologique*, 87–129. Paris: École pratique des hautes études, 1971.

Boulnois, Marie-Odile. "'Trois Hommes et un Seigneur': Lectures Trinitaires de la Théophanie de Mambré dans l'exégèse et l'iconographie." In *Studia Patristica Vol. XXXIX: Papers Presented at the Fourteenth International Conference on Patristic Studies Held in Oxford 2003*, edited by F. Young et al., 193–202. Leuven: Peeters, 2006.

Bovell, Carlos. "Symmetry, Ruth and Canon." *JSOT* 28.2 (2003) 175–91.

Box, George Herbert. *The Virgin Birth of Jesus: A Critical Examination of the Gospel-Narratives of the Nativity, and Other New Testament and Early Christian Evidence, and the Alleged Influence of Heathen Ideas*. Reprint. Whitefish, MT: Kessinger, 2009.

Braber, Marieke den, and Jan-Wim Wesselius. "The Unity of Joshua 1–8, Its Relation to the Story of King Keret, and the Literary Background to the Exodus and Conquest Stories." *SJOT* 22.2 (2008) 253–74.

Branch, Robin Gallaher. "Handling a Crisis via a Combination of Human Initiative and Godly Direction: Insights from the Book of Ruth." *IDS* 46.2 (2012) 1–11.

Braulik, Georg. "The Book of Ruth as Intra-Biblical Critique on the Deuteronomic Law." *Acta Theologica* 19.1 (1999) 1–20.

———. "Das Deuteronomium und die Bücher Ijob, Sprichwörter, Rut: Zur Frage Früher Kanonizität des Deuteronomiums." In *Die Tora Als Kanon für Juden und Christen*, edited by Erich Zenger, 61–138. Herders Biblische Studien 10. New York: Herder, 1996.

Brenner, Athalya, ed. "Female Social Behaviour: Two Descriptive Patterns Within the 'Birth of the Hero' Paradigm." *VT* 36.3 (1986) 257–73.

———. *A Feminist Companion to Ruth*. Feminist Companion to the Bible 3. Sheffield: Sheffield Academic, 1993.

———. *The Israelite Woman: Social Role and Literary Type in Biblical Narrative*. 2nd ed. London: Bloomsbury, 2015.

———. "Naomi and Ruth." *VT* 33.4 (1983) 385–97.

———. "Naomi and Ruth." In *A Feminist Companion to Ruth*, edited by Athalya Brenner, 70–84. Feminist Companion to the Bible 3. Sheffield: Sheffield Academic, 1993.

———. "Naomi and Ruth: Further Reflections." In *A Feminist Companion to Ruth*, edited by Athalya Brenner, 140–44. Feminist Companion to the Bible 3. Sheffield: Sheffield Academic, 1993.

———, ed. *Ruth and Esther: A Feminist Companion to the Bible*. Feminist Companion to the Bible 2nd Series 3. Sheffield: Sheffield Academic, 1999.

———. "Ruth as a Foreign Worker and the Politics of Exogamy." In *Ruth and Esther: A Feminist Companion to the Bible*, edited by Athalya Brenner, 158–62. Feminist Companion to the Bible 2nd Series 3. Sheffield: Sheffield Academic, 1999.

Brettler, Marc Zvi. *The Book of Judges*. Old Testament Readings. New York: Routledge, 2002.

———. "Women and Psalms: Toward an Understanding of the Role of Women's Prayer in the Israelite Cult." In *Gender and Law in the Hebrew Bible and the Ancient Near East*, edited by Victor H. Matthews et al., 25–56. JSOT Supplement Series 262. Sheffield: Sheffield Academic, 1998.

Bricker, Daniel P. "Innocent Suffering in Mesopotamia." *Tyndale Bulletin* 51.2 (2000) 193–214.

Briggs, Sheila. "Sarah 1/Sarai." In *Women in Scripture: A Dictionary of Named and Unnamed Women in the Hebrew Bible, the Apocryphal/Deuterocanonical Books, and the New Testament*, edited by Carol Meyers et al., 150–52. Boston: Houghton Mifflin, 2000.

Brison, Ora. "Aggressive Goddesses, Abusive Men: Gender Role Change in Near Eastern Mythology." *Studi Micenei Ed Egeo-Anatolici* 49 (2007) 67–74.

Brodie, Thomas L. "Luke 7:36–50 as an Internalization of 2 Kings 4:1–37: A Study in Luke's Use of Rhetorical Imitation." *Biblica* 64.4 (1983) 457–85.

Bronner, Leila Leah. *Stories of Biblical Mothers: Maternal Power in the Hebrew Bible*. New York: University Press of America, 2004.

———. "A Thematic Approach to Ruth in Rabbinic Literature." In *A Feminist Companion to Ruth*, edited by Athalya Brenner, 146–69. Feminist Companion to the Bible 3. Sheffield: Sheffield Academic, 1993.
Brown, Francis, et al. "בַּת." In BDB 123.
———. "עֶדְנָה." In BDB 726.
Bruckner, James K. *Implied Law in the Abraham Narrative: A Literary and Theological Analysis*. JSOT Supplement Series 335. London: Sheffield Academic, 2001.
Brueggemann, Walter. "1 Samuel 1: A Sense of a Beginning." *ZAW* 102.1 (1990) 33–48.
———. *First and Second Samuel*. Interpretation: A Bible Commentary for Teaching and Preaching. Louisville, KY: John Knox, 1990.
———. *Genesis*. Interpretation: A Bible Commentary for Teaching and Preaching. Atlanta: John Knox, 1982.
———. "'Impossibility' and Epistemology in the Faith Tradition of Abraham and Sarah (Gen 18:1–15)." *ZAW* 94.4 (1982) 615–34.
———. *Theology of the Old Testament: Testimony, Dispute, Advocacy*. Minneapolis: Fortress, 1997.
Bryce, Trevor. *Life and Society in the Hittite World*. Reprint. Oxford: Oxford University Press, 2012.
———. "The Role and Status of Women in Hittite Society." In *Women in Antiquity: Real Women Across the Ancient World*, edited by Stephanie Lynn Budin and Jean MacIntosh Turfa, 303–18. New York: Routledge, 2016.
Bucur, Bogdan G. "The Early Christian Reception of Genesis 18: From Theophany to Trinitarian Symbolism." *Journal of Early Christian Studies* 23.2 (2015) 245–72.
Budin, Stephanie Lynn. "Fertility and Gender in the Ancient Near East." In *Sex in Antiquity: Exploring Gender and Sexuality in the Ancient World*, edited by Mark Masterson et al., 30–49. New York: Routledge, 2015.
———. "Gender in the Tale of Aqhat." In *Studying Gender in the Ancient Near East*, edited by Saana Svärd and Agnès Garcia-Ventura, 51–72. University Park, PA: Eisenbrauns, 2018.
———. "Phallic Fertility in the Ancient Near East and Egypt." In *Reproduction: Antiquity to the Present Day*, edited by Nick Hopwood et al., 25–38. Cambridge: Cambridge University Press, 2018.
———. "Sexuality: Ancient Near East (Except Egypt)." In *The International Encyclopedia of Human Sexuality*, edited by Patricia Whelehan and Anne Bolin, 1–5. Malden, MA: John Wiley & Sons, 2015. https://doi.org/10.1002/9781118896877.wbiehs477.
Bunge, Gabriel. *The Rublev Trinity: The Icon of the Trinity by the Monk-Painter Andrei Rublev*. Crestwood, NY: St. Vladimir's Seminary Press, 2007.
Burney, Charles F. *The Book of Judges: With Introduction and Notes, And Notes on the Hebrew Text of the Books of Kings: With an Introduction and Appendix*. New York: KTAV, 1970.
Bush, Frederic W. "Ruth 4:17: A Semantic Wordplay." In *'Go to the Land I Will Show You': Studies in Honor of Dwight W. Young*, edited by Joseph E. Coleson and Victor H. Matthews, 3–14. Winona Lake, IN: Eisenbrauns, 1996.
———. *Ruth–Esther*. Word Biblical Commentary 9. Waco, TX: Word, 1996.
Butler, Trent. *Judges*. Word Biblical Commentary 8. Nashville: Thomas Nelson, 2009.

Calabro, David. "The Lord of Hosts and His Guests: Hospitality on Sacred Space in Exodus 29 and 1 Samuel 1." *Proceedings—Eastern Great Lakes and Midwest Biblical Societies* 27 (2007) 19–29.

Calvin, John. *Genesis*. Translated by John King. Geneva Series Commentary. Carlisle, PA: Banner of Truth Trust, 1992.

Cammarosano, Michele. *Hittite Local Cults*. Writings from the Ancient World 40. Atlanta: SBL, 2018.

Camp, Claudia V. "1 and 2 Kings." In *The Women's Bible Commentary*, edited by Carol A. Newsom and Sharon H. Ringe, exp. ed., 102–16. Louisville, KY: Westminster John Knox, 1998.

———. "Daughters, Priests, and Patrilineage: A Feminist and Gender-Critical Interpretation of the End of the Book of Numbers." In *Feminist Frameworks and the Bible: Power, Ambiguity, and Intersectionality*, edited by L. Juliana Claassens and Carolyn J. Sharp, 177–94. Library of Hebrew Bible/Old Testament Studies 630. New York: Bloomsbury T&T Clark, 2017.

———. *Wise, Strange, and Holy: The Strange Woman and the Making of the Bible*. JSOT Supplement Series 320. Sheffield: Sheffield Academic, 2000.

Campbell, Edward F., Jr. *Ruth: A New Translation with Introduction, Notes, and Commentary*. Anchor Bible 7. Garden City, NY: Doubleday, 1975.

Campbell, Nicholas J. "God and Heirs: The Theme of Progeny in Job." *SJOT* 36.1 (2022) 150–62.

Caquot, André. "Traits Royaux dans le Personnage de Job." In *Maqqél Shâqédh, La Branche d'amandier: Hommage à Wilhelm Vischer*, 32–45. Montpellier: Causse, Graille, Castelnau, 1960.

Caquot, André, and Philippe de Robert. *Les Livres de Samuel*. Commentaire de l'Ancien Testament 6. Genève: Labor et Fides, 1994.

Caquot, André, et al. *Textes Ougaritiques*. Vol. 1: *Mythes et Legendes: Introduction, Traduction, Commentaire*. Littératures Anciennes Du Proche-Orient 7. Paris: Cerf, 1974.

Carasik, Michael. "Why Did Hannah Ask for the 'Seed of Men'?" *JBL* 129.3 (2010) 433–36.

Carden, Michael. "Endangered Ancestress Revisited: Sarah's Miraculous Motherhood and the Restoration of Eden." *The Bible and Critical Theory* 1.3 (2005) 1–14.

———. "Genesis." In *The Queer Bible Commentary*, edited by Mona West and Robert E. Shore-Goss, 2nd ed., 21–60. London: SCM, 2022.

Carlson, Reed. "Hannah at Pentecost: On Recognizing Spirit Phenomena in Early Jewish Literature." *Journal of Pentecostal Theology* 27.2 (2018) 245–58.

Carmichael, Calum. "Inheritance in Biblical Sources." *Law and Literature* 20.2 (2008) 229–42.

Carroll, Nora. "Tragedy and Theodicy: The Role of the Sufferer from Job to Ahab." MA thesis, The City University of New York, 2018.

Cartledge, Tony W. *1 and 2 Samuel*. Smyth and Helwys Bible Commentary. Macon, GA: Smyth & Helwys, 2001.

———. "Hannah Asked, and God Heard." *Review and Expositor* 99.2 (2002) 143–44.

Case, M. L. "The Inheritance Injunction of Numbers 36: Zelophehad's Daughters and the Intersection of Ancestral Land and Sex Regulation." In *Sexuality and Law in the Torah*, edited by Hilary Lipka and Bruce Wells, 194–216. New York: T&T Clark, 2020.

Caspi, Mishael Maswari, and Rachel S. Havrelock. *Women on the Biblical Road: Ruth, Naomi, and the Female Journey*. Lanham, MD: University Press of America, 1996.

Cassuto, Umberto. *A Commentary on the Book of Genesis*. Translated by Israel Abrahams. 2 vols. Jerusalem: The Perry Foundation for Biblical Research, 1961.

———. "The Seven Wives of King Keret." *Bulletin of the American Schools of Oriental Research* 119 (1950) 18–20.

Cazelles, H. "Book Review: Canaanite Myths and Legends by G. R. Driver." *VT* 7.4 (1957) 420–30.

Chan, Chi Wai. "The Ultimate Trickster in the Story of Tamar from a Feminist Perspective." *Feminist Theology* 24.1 (2015) 93–101.

Chaudhry, Ayesha Siddiqua, et al. "Women Reading Texts on Marriage." *Feminist Theology* 17.2 (2009) 191–209.

Chepey, Stuart D. "Samson the 'Holy One': A Suggestion Regarding the Reviser's Use of Ἅγιος in Judg 13,7; 16,17 LXX Vaticanus." *Biblica* 83.1 (2002) 97–99.

Childs, Brevard S. *Introduction to the Old Testament as Scripture*. Philadelphia: Fortress, 1979.

Chisholm, Robert B., Jr. "Identity Crisis: Assessing Samson's Birth and Career." *Bibliotheca Sacra* 166.662 (2009) 147–62.

———. "A Note on Judges 13:20–21: Sorting Out the Syntax." *Jewish Bible Quarterly* 38.1 (2010) 10–12.

———. "The Role of Women in the Rhetorical Strategy of the Book of Judges." In *Integrity of Heart, Skillfulness of Hands: Biblical and Leadership Studies in Honor of Donald K. Campbell*, edited by Charles H. Dyer and Roy B. Zuck, 34–49. Grand Rapids, MI: Baker, 1994.

———. "Yahweh Versus the Canaanite Gods: Polemic in Judges and 1 Samuel 1–7." *Bibliotheca Sacra* 164.654 (2007) 165–80.

Cho, Paul Kang-Kul. "The Integrity of Job 1 and 42:11–17." *The Catholic Biblical Quarterly* 76.2 (2014) 230–51.

Christiansen, Birgit. "Love and Affection in Hittite Texts." In *The Routledge Handbook of Emotions in the Ancient Near East*, edited by Karen Sonik and Ulrike Steinert, 725–38. London: Routledge, 2023.

Chrysostom, John. *Homilies on Genesis 18–45*. Translated by Robert C. Hill. Reprint. Fathers of the Church 82. Washington, DC: Catholic University of America, 2001.

Chung, Il Seung. "Jeremiah's Call and Jacob's Birth: A Test Case for Investigating Prophetic Influence on the Book of Genesis." *The Expository Times* 128.7 (2017) 325–33.

Churnai, Varunaj. "Beyond Justice: Death and the Retribution Principle in the Book of Job." PhD diss., Concordia Seminary, 2010.

Claassens, L. Juliana. "'Give Us a Portion Among Our Father's Brothers': The Daughters of Zelophehad, Land, and the Quest for Human Dignity." *JSOT* 37.3 (2013) 319–37.

———. "Just Emotions: Reading the Sarah and Hagar Narrative (Genesis 16, 21) Through the Lens of Human Dignity." *Verbum et Ecclesia* 34.2 (2013) 1–6.

———. "Laughter and Tears: Carnivalistic Overtones in the Stories of Sarah and Hagar." *Perspectives in Religious Studies* 32.3 (2005) 295–308.

———. "Reading Trauma Narratives: Insidious Trauma in the Story of Rachel, Leah, Bilhah and Zilpah (Genesis 29–30) and Margaret Atwood's The Handmaid's Tale." *OTE (New Series)* 33.1 (2020) 10–31.

———. "Resisting Dehumanization: Ruth, Tamar, and the Quest for Human Dignity." *Catholic Biblical Quarterly* 74.4 (2012) 659–74.

———. *Writing and Reading to Survive: Biblical and Contemporary Trauma Narratives in Conversation*. Bible in the Modern World 74. Sheffield: Sheffield Phoenix, 2020.

Clanton, Dan W., Jr. *Daring, Disreputable, and Devout: Interpreting the Bible's Women in the Arts and Music*. New York: T&T Clark, 2009.

Clarke, Benjamin. "Misery Loves Company: A Comparative Analysis of Theodicy Literature in Ancient Mesopotamia and Israel." *Intermountain West Journal of Religious Studies* 2.1 (2010) 78–92.

Clifford, Richard J. "Genesis 25:19–34." *Interpretation* 45.4 (1991) 397–401.

Clifton, Bruno J. *Family and Identity in the Book of Judges*. Studies in Cultural Contexts of the Bible 7. Paderborn, Germany: Brill Schöningh, 2022.

Clines, David J. A., ed. *Job 1–20*. Word Biblical Commentary 17. Nashville: Thomas Nelson, 2011.

———. *Job 21–37*. Word Biblical Commentary 18A. Nashville: Thomas Nelson, 2006.

———. *Job 38–42*. Word Biblical Commentary 18B. Nashville: Thomas Nelson, 2011.

———, ed. "עֶדְנָה." In *The Dictionary of Classical Hebrew*, 6:284. Sheffield: Sheffield Phoenix, 2007.

Coats, George W. *Genesis: With an Introduction to Narrative Literature*. The Forms of the Old Testament Literature 1. Grand Rapids, MI: Eerdmans, 1983.

———. "Lot: A Foil in the Abraham Saga." In *Understanding the Word: Essays in Honor of Bernhard W. Anderson*, edited by James T. Butler et al., 113–32. JSOT Supplement Series 37. Sheffield: JSOT, 1985.

———. "Widow's Rights: A Crux in the Structure of Genesis 38." *Catholic Biblical Quarterly* 34.4 (1972) 461–66.

Cobb, Kirsi. "'Look at What They've Turned Us Into': Reading the Story of Lot's Daughters with Trauma Theory and the Handmaid's Tale." *Open Theology* 7.1 (2021) 208–23.

Cohen, Jeffrey M. "Abraham's Hospitality." *Jewish Bible Quarterly* 34.3 (2006) 168–72.

Cohen, Yoram, and Nathan Wasserman. "Mesopotamian Wisdom Literature." In *The Oxford Handbook of Wisdom and the Bible*, edited by Will Kynes, 121–40. Oxford: Oxford University Press, 2021.

Coleson, Joseph E. "The Peasant Woman and the Fugitive Prophet: A Study in Biblical Narrative Settings." In *'Go to the Land I Will Show You': Studies in Honor of Dwight W. Young*, edited by Joseph E. Coleson and Victor H. Matthews, 27–44. Winona Lake, IN: Eisenbrauns, 1996.

Collins, Billie Jean. *The Hittites and Their World*. Archaeology and Biblical Studies 7. Atlanta: SBL, 2007.

———. "Women in Hittite Religion." In *Women in Antiquity: Real Women Across the Ancient World*, edited by Stephanie Lynn Budin and Jean MacIntosh Turfa, 329–42. New York: Routledge, 2016.

———. "Women in Hittite Ritual." In *Women in the Ancient Near East: A Sourcebook*, edited by Mark W. Chavalas, 246–71. Routledge Sourcebooks for the Ancient World. New York: Routledge, 2014.

Collins, Sandra Ladick. "The Pleasure of Sarah: Recovering Eden Again." *Conversations with the Biblical World* 38 (2018) 20–34.

———. *Weapons upon Her Body: The Female Heroic in the Hebrew Bible*. Newcastle upon Tyne, UK: Cambridge Scholars, 2012.

Coogan, Michael David, ed. *Stories from Ancient Canaan*. Philadelphia: Westminster, 1978.
Cook, Joan E. "Four Marginalized Foils—Tamar, Judah, Joseph and Potiphar's Wife: A Literary Study of Genesis 38-39." *Proceedings—Eastern Great Lakes and Midwest Biblical Societies* 21 (2001) 115-28.
———. *Hannah's Desire, God's Design: Early Interpretations of the Story of Hannah*. JSOT Supplement Series 282. Sheffield: Sheffield Academic, 1999.
———. "Hannah's Initiative, God's Fulfillment." *Proceedings—Eastern Great Lakes and Midwest Biblical Societies* 18 (1998) 11-21.
Cook, Stephen L. "Death, Kinship, and Community: Afterlife and the Ideal חסד in Israel." In *The Family in Life and in Death: The Family in Ancient Israel: Sociological and Archaeological Perspectives*, edited by Patricia Dutcher-Walls, 106-21. Library of Hebrew Bible/Old Testament Studies 504. New York: T&T Clark International, 2009.
Cotter, David W. *Genesis*. Berit Olam. Collegeville, MN: Liturgical, 2003.
Cox, Alys. "Gods, Knowledge and Power in Ancient Egyptian Tales: Narratology and the Story of The Doomed Prince." In *Cult and Belief in Ancient Egypt: Proceedings of the Fourth International Congress for Young Egyptologists 25-27 September 2012, Sofia*, edited by Teodor Lekov and Emil Buzov, 25-29. Sofia, Bulgaria: East West, 2014.
Crane, Jonathan K. "Who's Your Mama Now? Rachel, Leah, and Rabbinic Views on Their Procreative Possibilities." *Journal of Jewish Ethics* 3.1 (2017) 92-117.
Crawford, Cory D. "The Struggle for Female Authority in Biblical and Mormon Theology." *Dialogue* 48.2 (2015) 1-66.
Crawford, Harriet. "An Exploration of the World of Women in Third-Millennium Mesopotamia." In *Women in the Ancient Near East: A Sourcebook*, edited by Mark W. Chavalas, 10-27. Routledge Sourcebooks for the Ancient World. New York: Routledge, 2014.
Crenshaw, James L. *Old Testament Wisdom: An Introduction*. 3rd ed. Louisville, KY: Westminster John Knox, 2010.
———. *Samson: A Secret Betrayed, a Vow Ignored*. Atlanta: John Knox, 1978.
———. "The Samson Saga: Filial Devotion or Erotic Attachment." *ZAW* 86.4 (1974) 470-504.
———. "Youth and Old Age in Qoheleth." *Hebrew Annual Review* 10 (1986) 1-13.
Crisp, Benjamin. "Samson's Blindness and Ethical Sight." *Journal of Biblical Perspectives in Leadership* 9.1 (2019) 233-45.
Cross, Frank Moore. *Canaanite Myth and Hebrew Epic: Essays in the History of the Religion of Israel*. Cambridge, MA: Harvard University Press, 1973.
Cundall, Arthur E., and Leon Morris. *Judges and Ruth: An Introduction and Commentary*. Tyndale Old Testament Commentaries 7. Downers Grove, IL: InterVarsity, 2008.
Curchin, Leonard. "Old Age in Sumer: Life Expectancy and Social Status of the Elderly." *Florilegium* 2.1 (1980) 61-70.
Curtis, Silvio. "The Structure of Hospitality Type-Scenes in Homer and Hittite Mythology: Evidence for an Eastern Mediterranean Tradition." MA thesis, University of Georgia, 2015.
D'Alès, Adhémar. "La Théophanie de Mambré Devant la Tradition des Pères." *Recherches de Science Religieuse* 20 (1930) 150-60.

Dalley, Stephanie. *Myths from Mesopotamia: Creation, the Flood, Gilgamesh, and Others.* Rev. ed. Oxford World's Classics. Oxford: Oxford University Press, 2000.

Daniely, Dvora Lederman. "'And Sarah Heard It in the Tent Door' (Genesis 18, 10): Uncovering Sarah's Covenant." *Feminist Theology* 27.1 (2018) 26–42.

Davidson, Robert. *Genesis 12–50.* Cambridge Bible Commentary. Cambridge: Cambridge University Press, 1979.

Davies, Eryl W. "Inheritance Rights and the Hebrew Levirate Marriage (Part 1)." *VT* 31.2 (1981) 138–44.

———. "Judah, Tamar, and the Law of Levirate Marriage." In *Sexuality and Law in the Torah*, edited by Hilary Lipka and Bruce Wells, 111–22. Library of Hebrew Bible/Old Testament Studies 675. London: Bloomsbury, 2020.

Davies, W. W. *The Codes of Hammurabi and Moses: With Copious Comments, Index, and Bible References.* Cincinnati: Jennings and Graham, 1905.

Davis, Andrew R. "Eden Revisited: A Literary and Theological Reading of Genesis 18:12–13." *Catholic Biblical Quarterly* 78.4 (2016) 611–31.

———. "The Literary Effect of Gender Discord in the Book of Ruth." *JBL* 132.3 (2013) 495–513.

Davis, Ellen F. *Who Are You, My Daughter? Reading Ruth Through Image and Text.* Louisville, KY: Westminster John Knox, 2003.

Davison, Lisa Wilson. *More Than a Womb: Childfree Women in the Hebrew Bible as Agents of the Holy.* Eugene, OR: Cascade, 2021.

Day, John. "The Daniel of Ugarit and Ezekiel and the Hero of the Book of Daniel." *VT* 30.2 (1980) 174–84.

D'Costa, Gavin. "The Trinity and Other Religions: Genesis 18, Judaism and Hinduism in Two Works of Art." *Gregorianum* 80.1 (1999) 5–31.

De Andrado, Paba Nidhani. "Hannah's Agency in Catalyzing Change in an Exclusive Hierarchy." *JBL* 140.2 (2021) 271–89.

Dearman, J. Andrew. "The Family in the Old Testament." *Interpretation* 52.2 (1998) 117–29.

Decker, Timothy L. "Contrastive Characterization in Ruth 1:6–22: Three Ways to Return from Exile." *OTE (New Series)* 32.3 (2019) 908–35.

Deist, Ferdinand. "'APPAYIM (1 Sam. I 5) < *PYM?" *VT* 27.2 (1977) 205–9.

Delaney, Carol. "Seeds of Honor, Fields of Shame." In *Honor and Shame and the Unity of the Mediterranean*, edited by David D. Gilmore, 35–48. A Special Publication of the American Anthropological Association 22. Washington, DC: American Anthropological Association, 1987.

Delitzsch, Franz. *A New Commentary on Genesis.* Translated by Sophia Taylor. Vol. 2. Edinburgh: T&T Clark, 1889.

del Olmo Lete, Gregorio. *Mitos y Leyendas de Canaan: Según la Tradición de Ugarit.* Fuentes de la Ciencia Bíblica 1. Madrid: Ediciones Cristianidad Institución San Jerónimo, 1981.

del Olmo Lete, Gregorio, and Joaquín Sanmartín. *A Dictionary of the Ugaritic Language in the Alphabetic Tradition.* Edited by Wilfred G. E. Watson. 3rd ed. Handbook of Oriental Studies 112. Boston: Brill, 2015.

de Moor, Johannes C., ed. *An Anthology of Religious Texts from Ugarit.* Nisaba 16. Leiden: Brill, 1987.

———. "Contributions to the Ugaritic Lexicon." *Ugarit-Forschungen* 11 (1979) 639–53.

———. "Ugarit and the Origin of Job." In *Ugarit and the Bible: Proceedings of the International Symposium on Ugarit and the Bible, Manchester, September 1992*, edited by George J. Brooke, 225–57. Ugaritisch-Biblische Literatur 11. Münster: Ugarit-Verlag, 1994.

de Moor, Johannes C., and Klaas Spronk. "Problematical Passages in the Legend of Kirtu (I)." *Ugarit-Forschungen* 14 (1982) 153–71.

Denning-Bolle, Sara J. *Wisdom in Akkadian Literature: Expression, Instruction, Dialogue*. Mededelingen en Verhandelingen van Het Vooraziatish-Egyptisch Genootschap "Ex Oriente Lux" 28. Leiden: Ex Oriente Lux, 1992.

de Regt, L. J. *Participants in Old Testament Texts and the Translator: Reference Devices and Their Rhetorical Impact*. Studia Semitica Neerlandica 39. Assen, Netherlands: Van Gorcum, 1999.

de Vaal-Stanton, Milda. "The Meaning and Implications of Ruth 4:5: A Grammatical, Socio-Cultural and Juridical Investigation." *OTE (New Series)* 28.3 (2015) 674–93.

Dever, William G. *Did God Have a Wife? Archaeology and Folk Religion in Ancient Israel*. Grand Rapids, MI: Eerdmans, 2005.

de Villiers, Gerda. "Ecodomy: Taking Risks and Overstepping Boundaries in the Book of Ruth." *Verbum et Ecclesia* 38.3 (2017) 35–50.

De Vries, Bert. "The Style of Hittite Epic and Mythology." PhD diss., Brandeis University, 1967.

De-Whyte, Janice P. *Wom(b)an: A Cultural-Narrative Reading of the Hebrew Bible Barrenness Narratives*. Leiden: Brill, 2018.

Di Biase-Dyson, Camilla. *Foreigners and Egyptians in the Late Egyptian Stories: Linguistic, Literary and Historical Perspectives*. Probleme der Ägyptologie 32. Leiden: Brill, 2013.

Dick, Michael B. "Royal Dynasticism as Divine Legitimization." In *Enigmas and Images: Studies in Honor of Tryggve N. D. Mettinger*, edited by Göran Eidevall and Blaženka Scheuer, 163–202. Coniectanea Biblica Old Testament Series 58. Winona Lake, IN: Eisenbrauns, 2011.

Dickman, Nathan Eric, and Joy Spann. "Dialogue or Narrative? Exploring Tensions Between Interpretations of Genesis 38." *Religions* 12.11 (2021) 1–13.

Dietrich, Manfried, and Oswald Loretz. "Das Aqhat-Epos." In *Mythen Und Epen IV*, edited by Otto Kaiser, 3:1254–305. Texte aus der Umwelt des Alten Testaments 6. Gütersloh: Gütersloher Verlagshaus, 1997.

———. "Das Keret-Epos." In *Mythen Und Epen IV*, edited by Otto Kaiser, 3:1213–53. Texte Aus der Umwelt des Alten Testaments 6. Gütersloh: Gütersloher Verlagshaus, 1997.

———. "Der Prolog des KRT-Epos (CTA 14 I 1–35)." In *Wort und Geschichte: Festschrift für Karl Elliger zum 70sten Geburtstag*, edited by Hartmut Gese and Hans Peter Rüger, 31–36. Alter Orient und Altes Testament 18. Kevelaer: Butzon and Bercker, 1973.

Doane, Sébastien. "An Ass in a Lion's Skin: The Subversion of Judah's Hegemonic Masculinity in Genesis 38." *Postscripts* 11.2 (2020) 237–55.

Doerfler, Marie E. "Entertaining the Trinity Unawares: Genesis XVIII in Western Christian Interpretation." *Journal of Ecclesiastical History* 65.3 (2014) 485–503.

Donaldson, Laura E. "The Sign of Orpah: Reading Ruth Through Native Eyes." In *Ruth and Esther: A Feminist Companion to the Bible*, edited by Athalya Brenner, 130–

44. Feminist Companion to the Bible 2nd Series 3. Sheffield: Sheffield Academic, 1999.

Donaldson, Mara E. "Kinship Theory in the Patriarchal Narratives: The Case of the Barren Wife." *Journal of the American Academy of Religion* 49.1 (1981) 77–87.

Doniger, Wendy. *The Bedtrick: Tales of Sex and Masquerade*. Chicago: University of Chicago Press, 2000.

———. *The Implied Spider: Politics and Theology in Myth*. Columbia Classics in Religion. New York: Columbia University Press, 2011.

Dresner, Samuel H. "Rachel and Leah." *Judaism* 38.2 (1989) 151–59.

Dressler, Harold H. P. "The Evidence of the Ugaritic Tablet CTA 19 (KTU 1.19): A Reconsideration of the Kinnereth Hypothesis." *VT* 34.2 (1984) 216–21.

———. "The Identification of the Ugaritic Dnil with the Daniel of Ezekiel." *VT* 29.2 (1979) 152–61.

———. "Is the Bow of Aqhat a Symbol of Virility?" *Ugarit-Forschungen* 7 (1975) 217–25.

———. "Problems in the Collation of the Aqht-Text, Column One." *Ugarit-Forschungen* 15 (1983) 43–46.

Driver, G. R. *Canaanite Myths and Legends*. Vol. 3. Old Testament Studies. Edinburgh: T&T Clark International, 1956.

Driver, G. R., and John C. Miles. *The Babylonian Laws*. Vol. 1: *Legal Commentary*. Oxford: Clarendon, 1952.

Driver, Samuel R., and George Buchanan Gray. *A Critical and Exegetical Commentary on the Book of Job Together with a New Translation*. Reprint. International Critical Commentary 14. Edinburgh: T&T Clark, 1986.

Dube, Musa W. "The Unpublished Letters of Orpah to Ruth." In *Ruth and Esther: A Feminist Companion to the Bible*, edited by Athalya Brenner, 145–50. Feminist Companion to the Bible 2nd Series 3. Sheffield: Sheffield Academic, 1999.

Dunn, Geoffrey D. "Tertullian and Rebekah: A Re-Reading of an 'Anti-Jewish' Argument in Early Christian Literature." *Vigiliae Christianae* 52.2 (1998) 119–45.

Ehrlich, Ernst Ludwig. *Der Traum im Alten Testament*. Beiheft zur ZAW 73. Berlin: Töpelmann, 1953.

Eichler, Raanan. "The Oracle of Rebekah: An Ambiguous Etiology." *Biblica* 100.4 (2019) 584–93.

Eissfeldt, Otto. "Sohnespflichten im Alten Orient." *Syria* 43.1 (1966) 39–47.

Ellerby, Petra. "May the Grass Grow Long: Hierarchy and Destruction in Ancient Mesopotamian Lamentation." *Aisthesis: The Interdisciplinary Honors Journal* 12.1 (2021) 1–14.

Embry, Brad. "Legalities in the Book of Ruth: A Renewed Look." *JSOT* 41.1 (2016) 31–44.

———. "'Redemption-Acquisition': The Marriage of Ruth as a Theological Commentary on Yahweh and Yahweh's People." *Journal of Theological Interpretation* 7.2 (2013) 257–73.

Emmerson, Grace I. "Women in Ancient Israel." In *The World of Ancient Israel: Sociological, Anthropological and Political Perspectives: Essays by Members of the Society for Old Testament Study*, edited by R. E. Clements, 371–94. Cambridge: Cambridge University Press, 1989.

Engnell, Ivan. *Studies in Divine Kingship in the Ancient Near East*. 2nd ed. Oxford: Blackwell, 1967.

Epstein, I., ed. *Hebrew-English Edition of the Babylonian Talmud*. Translated by H. Freedman. Vol. 5: *Pesaḥim*. New ed. London: Soncino, 1983.

Epstein, Louis M. *The Jewish Marriage Contract: A Study in the Status of the Woman in Jewish Law*. New York: Jewish Theological Seminary of America, 1927.

Erickson, Dean M. "The Gospel According to Gehazi." *Word and World* 40.3 (2020) 281–89.

Eskenazi, Tamara Cohn, and Tikva Frymer-Kensky. *Ruth = רות: The Traditional Hebrew Text with the New JPS Translation*. JPS Torah Commentary. Philadelphia: Jewish Publication Society, 2011.

Esler, Philip F. "'All That You Have Done . . . Has Been Fully Told to Me': The Power of Gossip and the Story of Ruth." *JBL* 137.3 (2018) 645–66.

———. *Sex, Wives, and Warriors: Reading Old Testament Narrative with Its Ancient Audience*. Cambridge: James Clarke, 2012.

Espinosa Arce, Juan Pablo. "La Hospitalidad en el Ciclo de Abraham: Una Propuesta de Lectura desde el Análisis Narrativo." *Cauriensia* 11 (2016) 731–40.

Evans, Mary J. *1 and 2 Samuel*. New International Biblical Commentary Old Testament 6. Peabody, MA: Hendrickson, 2000.

———. "The Invisibility of Women: An Investigation of a Possible Blind Spot for Biblical Commentators." *The Journal of the Christian Brethren Research Fellowship* 122 (1990) 37–40.

———. *Judges and Ruth: An Introduction and Commentary*. Tyndale Old Testament Commentaries 7. Downers Grove, IL: InterVarsity, 2017.

Exum, J. Cheryl. "Desire Distorted and Exhibited: Lot and His Daughters in Psychoanalysis, Painting, and Film." In *"A Wise and Discerning Mind": Essays in Honor of Burke O. Long*, edited by Saul M. Olyan and Robert C. Culley, 83–108. Brown Judaic Studies 325. Providence, RI: Brown Judaic Studies, 2000.

———. *Fragmented Women: Feminist (Sub)Versions of Biblical Narratives*. 2nd ed. Cornerstones. New York: Bloomsbury T&T Clark, 2016.

———. "Mother of Samson." In *Women in Scripture: A Dictionary of Named and Unnamed Women in the Hebrew Bible, the Apocryphal/Deuterocanonical Books, and the New Testament*, edited by Carol Meyers et al., 245–46. Boston: Houghton Mifflin, 2000.

———. "The Mothers of Israel: The Patriarchal Narratives from a Feminist Perspective." *Bible Review* 2.1 (1986) 60–67.

———. *Plotted, Shot, and Painted: Cultural Representations of Biblical Women*. JSOT Supplement Series 215. Sheffield: Sheffield Academic, 1996.

———. "Promise and Fulfillment: Narrative Art in Judges 13." *JBL* 99.1 (1980) 43–59.

Exum, J. Cheryl, and Johanna W. H. Van Wijk-Bos, eds. "Reasoning with the Foxes: Female Wit in a World of Male Power." *Semeia* 42 (1988).

Exum, J. Cheryl, and Gale A. Yee. "Feminist Criticism: Whose Interests Are Being Served?" In *Judges and Method: New Approaches in Biblical Studies*, 65–90. Minneapolis: Fortress, 1995.

Eyre, Chris. "Fate, Crocodiles and the Judgement of the Dead: Some Mythological Allusions in Egyptian Literature." *Studien zur Altägyptischen Kultur* 4 (1976) 103–14.

Farrar, F. W. *The Second Book of Kings*. London: Hodder and Stoughton, 1894.

Faust, Avraham, and Shlomo Bunimovitz. "The House and the World: The Israelite House as a Microcosm." In *Family and Household Religion: Toward a Synthesis* of *Old Testament Studies, Archaeology, Epigraphy, and Cultural Studies*, edited by Rainer Albertz et al., 143–64. Winona Lake, IN: Eisenbrauns, 2014.

Feder, Yitzhaq. "Morality Without Gods? Retribution and the Foundations of the Moral Order in the Ancient Near East." In *Teaching Morality in Antiquity Wisdom: Texts, Oral Traditions, and Images*, edited by T. M. Oshima, 253–64. Orientalische Religionen in der Antike 29. Tübingen: Mohr Siebeck, 2018.

Feinstein, Eve Levavi. *Sexual Pollution in the Hebrew Bible*. New York: Oxford University Press, 2014.

Fensham, F. Charles. "The Obliteration of the Family as Motif in the Near Eastern Literature." *Annali Istituto Orientale Di Napoli (Nueva Serie)* 29 (1969) 191–99.

———. "Remarks on Certain Difficult Passages in Keret." *Journal of Northwest Semitic Languages* 1 (1971) 11–22.

Fewell, Danna Nolan. "The Gift: World Alteration and Obligation in 2 Kings 4:8–37." In *"A Wise and Discerning Mind": Essays in Honor of Burke O. Long*, edited by Saul M. Olyan and Robert C. Culley, 109–24. Brown Judaic Studies 325. Providence, RI: Brown Judaic Studies, 2000.

Fewell, Danna Nolan, and David M. Gunn. "Boaz, Pillar of Society: Measures of Worth in the Book of Ruth." *JSOT* 14.45 (1989) 45–59.

———. *Compromising Redemption: Relating Characters in the Book of Ruth*. Louisville, KY: Westminster John Knox, 1990.

———. *Gender, Power, and Promise: The Subject of the Bible's First Story*. Nashville: Abingdon, 1993.

———. "'A Son Is Born to Naomi!' Literary Allusions and Interpretation in the Book of Ruth." *JSOT* 13.40 (1988) 99–108.

———. "'A Son Is Born to Naomi!' Literary Allusions and Interpretation in the Book of Ruth." In *Women in the Hebrew Bible: A Reader*, edited by Alice Bach, 233–40. New York: Routledge, 1999.

Fidler, Ruth. "A Wife's Vow—The Husband's Woe? The Case of Hannah and Elkanah (1 Samuel 1,21.23)." *ZAW* 118.3 (2006) 374–88.

Fields, Weston W. *Sodom and Gomorrah: History and Motif in Biblical Narrative*. JSOT Supplement Series 231. Sheffield: Sheffield Academic, 1997.

Filler, Elad. "Philo's Threefold Divine Vision and the Christian Trinity." Translated by Michael Carasik. *HUCA* 87 (2016) 93–113.

Finkel, Irving L. "The Dream of Kurigalzu and the Tablet of Sins." *Anatolian Studies* 33 (1983) 75–80.

Finkel, Joshua. "A Mathematical Conundrum in the Ugaritic Keret Poem." *HUCA* 26 (1955) 109–49.

Finlay, Timothy D. *The Birth Report Genre in the Hebrew Bible*. Forschungen zum Alten Testament 12. Tübingen: Mohr Siebeck, 2005.

Firth, David G. *1 and 2 Samuel*. Apollos Old Testament Commentary 8. Downers Grove, IL: InterVarsity, 2009.

Fisch, Harold. "Ruth and the Structure of Covenant History." *VT* 32.4 (1982) 425–37.

Fischer, Irmtraud. "The Book of Ruth: A 'Feminist' Commentary to the Torah?" In *Ruth and Esther: A Feminist Companion to the Bible*, edited by Athalya Brenner, 24–49. Feminist Companion to the Bible 2nd Series 3. Sheffield: Sheffield Academic, 1999.

———. "The Book of Ruth as Exegetical Literature." *European Judaism* 40.2 (2007) 140–49.

———. "On the Significance of the 'Women Texts' in the Ancestral Narratives." In *Torah*, edited by Irmtraud Fischer et al., 251–94. Bible and Women 1. Atlanta: SBL, 2011.

———. *Rut*. Herders Theologischer Kommentar zum Alten Testament. Freiburg im Breisgau: Herder, 2001.

Fleming, Daniel E. "Job: The Tale of Patient Faith and the Book of God's Dilemma." *VT* 44.4 (1994) 468–82.

Fleming, Erin E. "'She Went to Inquire of the Lord': Independent Divination in Genesis 25:22." *Union Seminary Quarterly Review* 60.3–4 (2007) 1–10.

Floyd, Michael H. "Welcome Back, Daughter of Zion!" *Catholic Biblical Quarterly* 70.3 (2008) 484–504.

Fokkelman, J. P. *Narrative Art in Genesis: Specimens of Stylistic and Structural Analysis*. 2nd ed. Studia Semitica Neerlandica 17. Sheffield: JSOT, 1991.

Fontaine, Carole R. "A Heifer from Thy Stable: On Goddesses and the Status of Women in the Ancient Near East." In *The Pleasure of Her Text: Feminist Readings of Biblical and Historical Texts*, edited by Alice Bach, 69–95. Philadelphia: Trinity, 1990.

———. "A Heifer from Thy Stable: On Goddesses and the Status of Women in the Ancient Near East." In *Women in the Hebrew Bible: A Reader*, edited by Alice Bach, 159–78. New York: Routledge, 1999.

———. "The Sage in Family and Tribe." In *The Sage in Israel and the Ancient Near East*, edited by John G. Gammie and Leo G. Perdue, 155–64. Winona Lake, IN: Eisenbrauns, 1990.

Foster, Benjamin R. *Akkadian Literature of the Late Period*. Guides to the Mesopotamian Textual Record 2. Münster: Ugarit-Verlag, 2007.

———. *Before the Muses: An Anthology of Akkadian Literature: Archaic, Classical, Mature*. Vol. 1. Bethesda, MD: CDL, 1993.

———. *From Distant Days: Myths, Tales, and Poetry of Ancient Mesopotamia*. Bethesda, MD: CDL, 1995.

Fox, Robin. *Marriage and Kinship: An Anthropological Perspective*. Cambridge Studies in Social Anthropology 50. Cambridge: Cambridge University Press, 1967.

Francia, Rita. "Plant-Based Potions and Ecstatic States in Hittite Rituals." In *The Routledge Companion to Ecstatic Experience in the Ancient World*, edited by Diana Stein et al., 138–52. London: Routledge, 2022.

Frandsen, Paul John. "Aspects of Kingship in Ancient Egypt." In *Religion and Power: Divine Kingship in the Ancient World and Beyond*, edited by Nicole Brisch, 2nd ed., 47–73. Oriental Institute Seminars 4. Chicago: Oriental Institute of the University of Chicago, 2012.

Freedman, R. David. "Counting Formulae in the Akkadian Epics." *Journal of the Ancient Near Eastern Society* 3.2 (1970) 65–81.

Frevel, Christian. *Das Buch Rut*. Neuer Stuttgarter Kommentar: Altes Testament 6. Stuttgart: Verlag Katholisches Bibelwerk, 1992.

Fricke, Klaus Dietrich. *Das Zweite Buch von den Königen*. Die Botschaft des Alten Testaments 12/11. Stuttgart: Calwer, 1972.

Friedman, Richard Elliott. *Commentary on the Torah: With a New English Translation*. San Francisco: HarperSanFrancisco, 2001.

Friesen, Courtney J. P. "Getting Samuel Sober: The 'Plus' of LXX 1 Samuel 1:11 and Its Religious Afterlife in Philo and the Gospel of Luke." *Journal of Theological Studies* 67.2 (2016) 453–78.

———. "Translating Misfortune: The Textual Problem of 1 Samuel 1:15 in the MT and the LXX." *VT* 65.4 (2015) 649–53.

Frolov, Serge. *Judges*. Forms of the Old Testament Literature 6B. Grand Rapids, MI: Eerdmans, 2013.

Frymer-Kensky, Tikva. "The Ideology of Gender in the Bible and the Ancient Near East." In *DUMU-E2-DUB-BA-A: Studies in Honor of Åke W. Sjöberg*, edited by Hermann Behrens et al., 185–91. Occasional Publications of the Samuel Noah Kramer Fund 11. Philadelphia: University of Pennsylvania Press, 1989.

———. *Motherprayer: The Pregnant Woman's Spiritual Companion*. New York: Riverhead, 1995.

———. *Reading the Women of the Bible: A New Interpretation of Their Stories*. New York: Schocken, 2002.

Fuchs, Esther. "The Literary Characterization of Mothers and Sexual Politics in the Hebrew Bible." In *Women in the Hebrew Bible: A Reader*, edited by Alice Bach, 127–40. New York: Routledge, 1999.

———. *Sexual Politics in the Biblical Narrative: Reading the Hebrew Bible as a Woman*. JSOT Supplement Series 310. Sheffield: Sheffield Academic, 2000.

———. "Status and Role of Female Heroines in the Biblical Narrative." In *Women in the Hebrew Bible: A Reader*, edited by Alice Bach, 77–84. New York: Routledge, 1999.

Gadotti, Alhena. "The Feminine in Myths and Epic." In *Women in the Ancient Near East: A Sourcebook*, edited by Mark W. Chavalas, 28–58. Routledge Sourcebooks for the Ancient World. New York: Routledge, 2014.

———. "Portraits of the Feminine in Sumerian Literature." *Journal of the American Oriental Society* 131.2 (2011) 195–206.

Gafney, Wilda. *Womanist Midrash: A Reintroduction to the Women of the Torah and the Throne*. Louisville, KY: Westminster John Knox, 2017.

Gaiser, Frederick J. "Sarah, Hagar, Abraham—Hannah, Peninnah, Elkanah: Case Studies in Conflict." *Word and World* 34.3 (2014) 273–84.

Galpaz-Feller, Pnina. "Pregnancy and Birth in the Bible and Ancient Egypt (Comparative Study)." *Biblische Notizen* 102 (2000) 42–53.

Garroway, Kristine Henriksen. *Growing Up in Ancient Israel: Children in Material Culture and Biblical Texts*. Archaeology and Biblical Studies 23. Atlanta: SBL, 2018.

Gaster, Theodor H. *Thespis: Ritual, Myth, and Drama in the Ancient Near East*. 2nd ed. New York: Anchor, 1961.

Gelb, I. J. "Household and Family in Early Mesopotamia." In *State and Temple Economy in the Ancient Near East: Proceedings of the International Conference Organized by the Katholieke Universiteit Leuven from the 10th to the 14th of April 1978*, edited by Edward Lipiński, 1:1–97. Orientalia Lovaniensia Analecta 5. Leuven: Departement Oriëntalistiek, 1979.

George, A. R. "Gilgamesh and the Literary Traditions of Ancient Mesopotamia." In *The Babylonian World*, edited by Gwendolyn Leick, 447–59. The Routledge Worlds. New York: Routledge, 2008.

Gerstenberger, Erhard S. *Theologien im Alten Testament: Pluralität und Synkretismus Alttestamentlichen Gottesglaubens*. Stuttgart: W. Kohlhammer, 2001.

Gevaryahu, Gilad J. "The Root G-R-A in the Bible: The Case of the Daughters of Zelophehad and Beyond." *Jewish Bible Quarterly* 41.2 (2013) 107–12.

Gibson, J. C. L. *Canaanite Myths and Legends*. 2nd ed. New York: T&T Clark International, 1978.

———. "Myth, Legend and Folk-Lore in the Ugaritic Keret and Aqhat Texts." In *Congress Volume: Edinburgh, 1974*, 60–68. Supplements to VT 28. Leiden: Brill, 1975.

Gilmour, Rachelle. *Representing the Past: A Literary Analysis of Narrative Historiography in the Book of Samuel*. Supplements to VT 143. Leiden: Brill, 2011.

Ginsberg, Harold L. "The Legend of King Keret." In *ANET* 142–48.

———. *The Legend of King Keret: A Canaanite Epic of the Bronze Age*. Bulletin of the American Schools of Oriental Research Supplemental Studies 2–3. New Haven, CT: American Schools of Oriental Research, 1946.

———. "The North-Canaanite Myth of Anath and Aqhat." *Bulletin of the American Schools of Oriental Research* 97 (1945) 3–10.

———. "The Tale of Aqhat." In *ANET* 149–55.

Giusfredi, Frederico, and Valerio Pisaniello. "Hurrians and Hurrian in Hittite Anatolia." In *Contacts of Languages and Peoples in the Hittite and Post-Hittite World*, 1. The Bronze Age and Hatti:259–83. Ancient Languages and Civilizations 4. Leiden: Brill, 2023.

Gladson, Jerry A. *A Critical and Exegetical Commentary on the Book of Ruth*. Lewiston, NY: Edwin Mellen, 2012.

Glanzman, George S. "The Origin and Date of the Book of Ruth." *Catholic Biblical Quarterly* 21.2 (1959) 201–7.

Glassner, Jean-Jacques. *Mesopotamian Chronicles*. Writings from the Ancient World 19. Atlanta: SBL, 2004.

———. "Polygynie ou Prostitution: Une Approche Comparative de la Sexualité Masculine." In *Sex and Gender in the Ancient Near East: Proceedings of the 47th Rencontre Assyriologique Internationale, Helsinki, July 2–6, 2001*, edited by S. Parpola and R. M. Whiting, 1:151–64. Helsinki: Neo-Assyrian Text Corpus Project, 2002.

Glover, Neil. "Your People, My People: An Exploration of Ethnicity in Ruth." *JSOT* 33.3 (2009) 293–313.

Gnuse, Robert Karl. "Divine Messengers in Genesis 18–19 and Ovid." *SJOT* 31.1 (2017) 66–79.

———. *Dreams and Dream Reports in the Writings of Josephus: A Traditio-Historical Analysis*. Arbeiten zur Geschichte des Antiken Judentums und des Urchristentums 36. New York: Brill, 1996.

———. "Samson and Heracles Revisited." *SJOT* 32.1 (2018) 1–19.

Goetze, Albrecht. "The Laws of Eshnunna." In *ANET* 161–63.

Gordon, Cyrus H. "Notes on the Legend of Keret." *Journal of Near Eastern Studies* 11.3 (1952) 212–13.

———. *Ugarit and Minoan Crete: The Bearing of Their Texts on the Origins of Western Culture*. New York: Norton, 1966.

———. *Ugaritic Literature: A Comprehensive Translation of the Poetic and Prose Texts*. Scripta Pontificii Instituti Biblici 98. Rome: Pontificium Institutum Biblicum, 1949.

Gorospe, Athena E., and Charles R. Ringma. *Judges: A Pastoral and Contextual Commentary*. Asia Bible Commentary Series. Manila: Langham, 2016.

Gossai, Hemchand. *Power and Marginality in the Abraham Narrative*. Lanham, MD: University Press of America, 1995.

Goswell, Gregory R. "The Book of Ruth and the House of David." *Evangelical Quarterly* 86.2 (2014) 116–29.

Gray, John. "The Book of Job in the Context of Near Eastern Literature." *ZAW* 82.2 (1970) 251–69.

———. "Canaanite Kingship in Theory and Practice." *VT* 2.3 (1952) 193–220.

———. *The Krt Text in the Literature of Ras Shamra: A Social Myth of Ancient Canaan.* 2nd ed. Documenta et Monumenta Orientis Antiqui 5. Leiden: Brill, 1964.

———. *The Legacy of Canaan: The Ras Shamra Texts and Their Relevance to the Old Testament.* 2nd ed. Supplements to VT 5. Leiden: Brill, 1965.

Graybill, Rhiannon. "Elisha's Body and the Queer Touch of Prophecy." *Biblical Theology Bulletin* 49.1 (2019) 32–40.

Graybill, Rhiannon, and Peter J. Sabo. "Caves of the Hebrew Bible: A Speleology." *BibInt* 26.1 (2018) 1–22.

Green, Barbara. "The Plot of the Biblical Story of Ruth." *JSOT* 7.23 (1982) 55–68.

———. "A Study of Field and Seed Symbolism in the Biblical Story of Ruth." PhD diss., Graduate Theological Union, 1980.

Greenberger, Chaya. "Judah and Tamar: Self-Esteem Lost and (Partially) Redeemed." *Jewish Bible Quarterly* 48.1 (2020) 23–32.

Greenfield, Jonas C. "Aspects of Aramean Religion." In *Ancient Israelite Religion: Essays in Honor of Frank Moore Cross*, edited by Patrick D. Miller et al., 67–78. Philadelphia: Fortress, 1987.

———. "Keret's Dream: 'ḎHRT' and 'HDRT.'" *Bulletin of the School of Oriental and African Studies* 57.1 (1994) 87–92.

———. "Some Glosses on the Keret Epic." *Eretz-Israel: Archaeological, Historical and Geographical Studies* 9 (1969) 60–65.

———. "Studies in Aramaic Lexicography I." *Journal of the American Oriental Society* 82.3 (1962) 290–99.

———. "A Touch of Eden." In *Orientalia J. Duchesne-Guillemin Emerito Oblata*, 219–24. Acta Iranica 23. Leiden: Brill, 1984.

Greengus, Samuel. "Old Babylonian Marriage Ceremonies and Rites." *Journal of Cuneiform Studies* 20.2 (1966) 55–72.

Greenstein, Edward L. "The God of Israel and the Gods of Canaan: How Different Were They?" In *Proceedings of the Twelfth World Congress of Jewish Studies, Jerusalem, July 29–August 5, 1997*, edited by Ron Margolin, 1:47–58. Jerusalem: World Union of Jewish Studies, 1999.

———. "Kirta." In *Ugaritic Narrative Poetry*, edited by Simon B. Parker, 9–48. Writings from the Ancient World / Society of Biblical Literature 9. Atlanta: Scholars Press, 1997.

———. "Reading Strategies and the Story of Ruth." In *Women in the Hebrew Bible: A Reader*, edited by Alice Bach, 211–32. New York: Routledge, 1999.

———. "The Riddle of Samson." *Prooftexts* 1.3 (1981) 237–60.

———. "The Role of the Reader in Ugaritic Narrative." In *"A Wise and Discerning Mind": Essays in Honor of Burke O. Long*, edited by Saul M. Olyan and Robert C. Culley, 139–51. Brown Judaic Studies 325. Providence, RI: Brown Judaic Studies, 2000.

———. "Wisdom in Ugaritic." In *Language and Nature: Papers Presented to John Huehnergard on the Occasion of His 60th Birthday*, edited by Rebecca Hasselbach-

Andee and Na'ama Pat-El, 69–90. Studies in Ancient Oriental Civilization 67. Chicago: Oriental Institute of the University of Chicago, 2012.

Gregory, Mark Wesson. "Narrative Time in the Keret Epic and the Succession Narrative." PhD diss., The Southern Baptist Theological Seminary, 1988.

Grohmann, Marianne. "Barrenness: Ancient Near East and Biblical Texts." In *Encyclopedia of the Bible and Its Reception*, edited by Hans-Josef Klauck et al., 4:546–48. Boston: De Gruyter, 2011.

Grossfeld, Bernard. *The Targum Onqelos to Genesis*. The Aramaic Bible 6. Wilmington, DE: Michael Glazier, 1988.

Grossman, Jonathan. "'Associative Meanings' in the Character Evaluation of Lot's Daughters." *Catholic Biblical Quarterly* 76.1 (2014) 40–57.

———. "Divine Command and Human Initiative: A Literary View on Numbers 25–31." *BibInt* 15.1 (2007) 54–79.

———. "'Gleaning Among the Ears'—'Gathering Among the Sheaves': Characterizing the Image of the Supervising Boy (Ruth 2)." *JBL* 126.4 (2007) 703–16.

———. *Ruth: Bridges and Boundaries*. Alte Testament im Dialog 9. Bern: Peter Lang, 2015.

Grottanelli, Cristiano. "Observations sur l'histoire d'Appou." *Revue Hittite et Asianique* 36 (1978) 49–57.

Gruber, Mayer I. "Akkadian *labān appi* in the Light of Art and Literature." *Journal of the Ancient Near Eastern Society* 7.1 (1975) 73–83.

———. "Genesis 21.12: A New Reading of an Ambiguous Text." In *Genesis*, edited by Athalya Brenner, 172–79. Feminist Companion to the Bible 2nd Series 1. Sheffield: Sheffield Academic, 1998.

———. "Women in the Ancient Levant." In *Women's Roles in Ancient Civilizations: A Reference Guide*, edited by Bella Vivante, 115–54. Westport, CT: Greenwood, 1999.

Grypeou, Emmanouela, and Helen Spurling. "Abraham's Angels: Jewish and Christian Exegesis of Genesis 18–19." In *The Exegetical Encounter Between Jews and Christians in Late Antiquity*, edited by Emmanouela Grypeou and Helen Spurling, 181–203. Jewish and Christian Perspectives Series 18. Leiden: Brill, 2009.

Guenther, Allen. "A Typology of Israelite Marriage: Kinship, Socio-Economic, and Religious Factors." *JSOT* 29.4 (2005) 387–407.

Guillaume, Philippe. *Waiting for Josiah: The Judges*. JSOT Supplement Series 385. New York: T&T Clark, 2004.

Gunkel, Hermann. *Genesis*. Translated by Mark E. Biddle. Macon, GA: Mercer University Press, 1997.

———. "Rut." In *Die Religion in Geschichte und Gegenwart: Handwörterbuch für Theologie und Religionswissenschaft*, edited by Hans D. Betz et al., 4:2180–82. Tübingen: Mohr Siebeck, 2007.

Gunn, David M., and Danna Nolan Fewell. *Narrative in the Hebrew Bible*. Oxford Bible. Oxford: Oxford University Press, 1993.

Güterbock, Hans G. "A Hurro-Hittite Hymn to Ishtar." *Journal of the American Oriental Society* 103.1 (1983) 155–64.

Haas, Volkert. *Geschichte der Hethitischen Religion*. Handbuch der Orientalistik. Erste Abteilung, Nahe und der Mittlere Osten 15. Leiden: Brill, 1994.

———. *Die Hethitische Literatur: Texte, Stilistik, Motive*. Berlin: De Gruyter, 2006.

Habel, Norman C. *The Book of Job: A Commentary*. Old Testament Library. Philadelphia: Westminster, 1985.
Hallo, William W. "The Birth of Kings." In *Love and Death in the Ancient Near East: Essays in Honor of Marvin H. Pope*, edited by John H. Marks and Robert M. Good, 45–52. Guilford, CT: Four Quarters, 1987.
Halton, Charles. "An Indecent Proposal: The Theological Core of the Book of Ruth." *SJOT* 26.1 (2012) 30–43.
Hamilton, Victor P. "6829 עָקַר." In *New International Dictionary of Old Testament Theology and Exegesis*, edited by Willem A. VanGemeren, 3:509–10. Grand Rapids, MI: Zondervan, 1997.
———. *The Book of Genesis: Chapters 18–50*. New International Commentary on the Old Testament. Grand Rapids, MI: Eerdmans, 1995.
Hamlin, E. John. *Surely There Is a Future: A Commentary on the Book of Ruth*. International Theological Commentary. Grand Rapids, MI: Eerdmans, 1996.
Hammer, Reuven, trans. *Sifre: A Tannaitic Commentary on the Book of Deuteronomy*. Yale Judaica Series 24. New Haven, CT: Yale University Press, 1986.
Hamori, Esther J. "Divine Embodiment in the Hebrew Bible and Some Implications for Jewish and Christian Incarnational Theologies." In *Bodies, Embodiment, and Theology of the Hebrew Bible*, edited by S. Tamar Kamionkowski and Wonil Kim, 161–83. Library of Hebrew Bible/Old Testament Studies 465. New York: T&T Clark, 2010.
———. *"When Gods Were Men": The Embodied God in Biblical and Near Eastern Literature*. Beihefte zur ZAW 384. Berlin: De Gruyter, 2008.
Harlé, Paul. *Les Juges*. La Bible d'Alexandrie 7. Paris: Cerf, 1999.
Harris, Rivkah. *Gender and Aging in Mesopotamia: The Gilgamesh Epic and Other Ancient Literature*. Red River Books. Norman, OK: University of Oklahoma Press, 2003.
Hartley, John E. *The Book of Job*. New International Commentary on the Old Testament. Grand Rapids, MI: Eerdmans, 1988.
———. *Genesis*. New International Biblical Commentary 1. Peabody, MA: Hendrickson, 2000.
———. "Job 2: Ancient Near Eastern Background." In *Dictionary of the Old Testament: Wisdom, Poetry and Writings: A Compendium of Contemporary Biblical Scholarship*, edited by Tremper Longman III and Peter Enns, 871–906. IVP Bible Dictionary Series 3. Downers Grove, IL: IVP Academic, 2008.
Hartman, Harvey D. "The Feminine Gender as a Literary Device in the Narrative of Judges." ThD diss., Grace Theological Seminary, 1992.
Haubold, Johannes. "'Shepherds of the People': Greek and Mesopotamian Perspectives." In *Mesopotamia in the Ancient World: Impact, Continuities, Parallels. Proceedings of the Seventh Symposium of the Melammu Project Held in Obergurgl, Austria, November 4–8, 2013*, edited by Robert Rollinger and Erik van Dongen, 245–54. Melammu Symposia 7. Münster: Ugarit-Verlag, 2015.
Haul, Michael. *Das Etana-Epos: Ein Mythos von der Himmelfahrt des Königs von Kiš*. Göttinger Arbeitshefte zur Altorientalischen Literatur 1. Göttingen: Seminar für Keilschriftforschung, 2000.
Havrelock, Rachel. "The Myth of Birthing the Hero: Heroic Barrenness in the Hebrew Bible." *BibInt* 16.2 (2008) 154–78.

Hawk, L. Daniel. *Ruth*. Apollos Old Testament Commentary 7B. Downers Grove, IL: InterVarsity, 2015.
Hayes, C. E. "The Midrashic Career of the Confession of Judah (Genesis Xxxviii 26): Part I The Extra-Canonical Texts, Targums and Other Versions." *VT* 45.1 (1995) 62–81.
Healey, John F. "The Pietas of an Ideal Son in Ugarit." *Ugarit-Forschungen* 11 (1979) 353–56.
Helck, Wolfgang. "Die Erzählung vom Verwunschenen Prinzen." In *Form und Maß: Beiträge zur Literatur, Sprache und Kunst des Alten Ägypten: Festschrift für Gerhard Fecht zum 65. Geburtstag Am 6. Februar 1987*, edited by Jürgen Osing and Günter Dreyer, 218–25. Ägypten und Altes Testament 12. Weisbaden: Otto Harrassowitz, 1987.
Helle, Sophus. "The Two-Act Structure: A Narrative Device in Akkadian Epics." *Journal of Ancient Near Eastern Religions* 20.2 (2020) 190–224.
Heller, Roy L. *The Characters of Elijah and Elisha and the Deuteronomic Evaluation of Prophecy: Miracles and Manipulation*. Library of Hebrew Bible/Old Testament Studies 671. New York: Bloomsbury T&T Clark, 2018.
Hendel, Ronald S. *The Epic of the Patriarch: The Jacob Cycle and the Narrative Traditions of Canaan and Israel*. Harvard Semitic Monographs 42. Atlanta: Scholars Press, 1987.
———. *Remembering Abraham: Culture, Memory, and History in the Hebrew Bible*. New York: Oxford University Press, 2005.
Henkelman, Wouter F. M. "The Birth of Gilgameš (Ael. NA XII.21): A Case-Study in Literary Receptivity." In *Altertum und Mittelmeerraum: Die Antike Welt Diesseits und Jenseits der Levante: Festschrift für Peter W. Haider zum 60. Geburtstag*, edited by Robert Rollinger and Brigitte Truschnegg, 807–56. Oriens et Occidens 12. Stuttgart: F. Steiner, 2006.
Hens-Piazza, Gina. *1–2 Kings*. Abingdon Old Testament Commentaries. Nashville: Abingdon, 2006.
Hentschel, Georg. *2 Könige*. Die Neue Echter Bibel: Kommentar zum Alten Testament mit der Einheitsübersetzung 11. Würzburg: Echter Verlag, 1985.
Hepner, Gershon. "Three's a Crowd in Shunem: Elisha's Misconduct with the Shunamite Reflects a Polemic Against Prophetism." *ZAW* 122.3 (2010) 387–400.
Herman, Judith Lewis. *Father-Daughter Incest*. 2nd ed. Cambridge, MA: Harvard University Press, 2000.
Hertzberg, Hans Wilhelm. *I and II Samuel*. Translated by J. S. Bowden. Old Testament Library. Philadelphia: Westminster, 1964.
Herzog, Annabel. "Lecture de l'hospitalité Biblique." *Revue des Études Juives* 171.1-2 (2012) 1–25.
Hess, Richard S. "Eden—A Well Watered Place." *Bible Review* 7.6 (1991) 28–33.
Hillers, Delbert R. "The Bow of Aqhat: The Meaning of a Mythological Theme." In *Poets Before Homer: Collected Essays on Ancient Literature*, edited by F. W. Dobbs-Allsopp, 207–21. Winona Lake, IN: Eisenbrauns, 2015.
———. "A Proposal for a Difficult Line in Keret Lm Ank Ksp." In *Poets Before Homer: Collected Essays on Ancient Literature*, edited by F. W. Dobbs-Allsopp, 222–24. Winona Lake, IN: Eisenbrauns, 2015.
Hobbs, T. R. *2 Kings*. Word Biblical Commentary 13. Waco, TX: Word, 1985.

———. "Man, Woman, and Hospitality—2 Kings 4:8–36." *Biblical Theology Bulletin* 23.3 (1993) 91–100.

Hoffman, Yair. "Ancient Near Eastern Literary Conventions and the Restoration of the Book of Job." *ZAW* 103.3 (1991) 399–411.

Hoffner, Harry A., Jr. "Birth and Name-Giving in Hittite Texts." *Journal of Near Eastern Studies* 27.3 (1968) 198–203.

———. "Hittite Mythological Texts: A Survey." In *Unity and Diversity: Essays in the History, Literature, and Religion of the Ancient Near East*, edited by Hans Goedicke and J. J. M. Roberts, 136–45. Johns Hopkins Near Eastern Studies. Baltimore, MD: Johns Hopkins University, 1975.

———. *Hittite Myths*. 2nd ed. Writings from the Ancient World 2. Atlanta: Scholars Press, 1998.

———. "Symbols for Masculinity and Femininity: Their Use in Ancient Near Eastern Sympathetic Magic Rituals." *JBL* 85.3 (1966) 326–34.

———. "Theodicy in Hittite Texts." In *Theodicy in the World of the Bible: The Goodness of God and the Problem of Evil*, edited by Antti Laato and Johannes C. de Moor, 90–107. Leiden: Brill, 2003.

Holbert, J. C. "'The Skies Will Uncover His Iniquity': Satire in the Second Speech of Zophar (Job XX)." *VT* 31.2 (1981) 171–79.

Holm, Tawny L. "Ancient Near Eastern Literature: Genres and Forms." In *A Companion to the Ancient Near East*, edited by Daniel C. Snell, 2nd ed., 269–88. Blackwell Companions to the Ancient World. Malden, MA: Blackwell, 2007.

Honig, Bonnie. "Ruth, the Model Emigrée: Mourning and the Symbolic Politics of Immigration." In *Ruth and Esther: A Feminist Companion to the Bible*, edited by Athalya Brenner, 50–74. Feminist Companion to the Bible 2nd Series 3. Sheffield: Sheffield Academic, 1999.

Horowitz, Wayne. "Two Notes on Etana's Flight to Heaven." *Orientalia* 59.4 (1990) 511–17.

House, Paul R. *1, 2 Kings: An Exegetical and Theological Exposition of Holy Scripture*. New American Commentary 8. Nashville: Broadman & Holman, 1995.

Hubai, Péter. "Einer Literarische Quelle der Ägyptischen Religionsphilosophie? Das Märchen vom Prinzen, der Drei Gefahren zu Überstehen Hatte." In *The Intellectual Heritage of Egypt: Studies Presented to László Kákosy by Friends and Colleagues on the Occasion of His 60th Birthday*, edited by Ulrich Luft, 277–300. Studia Aegyptiaca 14. Budapest: Chaire d'Égyptologie de l'Université Eötvös Loránd de Budapest, 1992.

Hubbard, Robert L., Jr. *The Book of Ruth*. New International Commentary on the Old Testament. Grand Rapids, MI: Eerdmans, 1988.

———. "The Go'el in Ancient Israel: Theological Reflections on an Israelite Institution." *Bulletin for Biblical Research* 1 (1991) 3–19.

Huizenga, Leroy A. *The New Isaac: Tradition and Intertextuality in the Gospel of Matthew*. Supplements to Novum Testamentum 131. Leiden: Brill, 2009.

Hundley, Michael B. "The God Collectors: Hittite Conceptions of the Divine." *AoF* 41.2 (2015) 176–200.

Hunt, Joel H. "Book Review: Babylonian Poems of Righteous Sufferers: Ludlul Bēl Nēmeqi and the Babylonian Theodicy." *Journal of the American Oriental Society* 137.2 (2017) 418–20.

Hurowitz, Victor Avigdor. "*ᵈNarru* and *ᵈZulumaar* in the Babylonian Theodicy." *Journal of the American Oriental Society* 124.4 (2004) 777–78.
Husser, Jean-Marie. "The Birth of a Hero: Form and Meaning of KTU 1.17 i–Ii." In *Ugarit, Religion and Culture: Proceedings of the International Colloquium on Ugarit, Religion and Culture, Edinburgh, July 1994: Essays Presented in Honour of Professor John C. L. Gibson*, edited by N. Wyatt et al., 85–98. Ugaritisch-Biblische Literatur 12. Münster: Ugarit-Verlag, 1996.

———. *Dreams and Dream Narratives in the Biblical World*. Biblical Seminar 63. Sheffield: Sheffield Academic, 1999.

———. "La Mort d'Aqhat: Chasse et Rites de Passage à Ugarit." *Revue de l'histoire des Religions* 3 (2008) 323–45.

———. *Le Songe et la Parole: Etude Sur le Rêve et Sa Fonction dans l'ancien Israël*. Beiheft zur ZAW 210. Berlin: De Gruyter, 1994.

Hutter, Manfred. "Personennamen der Hethitischen Großreichszeit als Quellen Religiöser Verhältnisse." In *Hrozný and Hittite: The First Hundred Years. Proceedings of the International Conference Held at Charles University, Prague, 11–14 November 2015*, edited by Ronald I. Kim et al., 506–17. Culture and History of the Ancient Near East 107. Leiden: Brill, 2020.

Hutzli, Jürg. "Coutumes et Lois Cultuelles dans les Livres de Samuel." *Judaïsme Ancien* 4 (2016) 105–22.

Hyman, Ronald T. "Four Acts of Vowing in the Bible." *Jewish Bible Quarterly* 37.4 (2009) 231–38.

Imparati, Fiorella. "Private Life Among the Hittites." In *Civilizations of the Ancient Near East*, edited by Jack M. Sasson, 1:572–80. New York: Charles Scribner's Sons, 1995.

———. *Studi Sulla Società e Sulla Religione Degli Ittiti*. Eothen 12. Bivigliano, Italy: LoGisma, 2004.

Irvine, Stuart A. "'Is Anything Too Hard for Yahweh?' Fulfillment of Promise and Threat in Genesis 18–19." *JSOT* 42.3 (2018) 285–302.

Irwin, Brian P. "Removing Ruth: Tiqqune Sopherim in Ruth 3.3–4?" *JSOT* 32.3 (2008) 331–38.

Jackson, Bernard S. "The 'Institutions' of Marriage and Divorce in the Hebrew Bible." *Journal of Semitic Studies* 56.2 (2011) 221–51.

Jackson, Melissa A. *Comedy and Feminist Interpretation of the Hebrew Bible: A Subversive Collaboration*. Oxford: Oxford University Press, 2012.

———. "Lot's Daughters and Tamar as Tricksters and the Patriarchal Narratives as Feminist Theology." *JSOT* 26.4 (2002) 29–46.

Jacobs, Mignon R. *Gender, Power, and Persuasion: The Genesis Narratives and Contemporary Portraits*. Grand Rapids, MI: Baker Academic, 2007.

Jacobs, Sandra. "'The Disposable Wife' as Property in the Hebrew Bible." In *Gender and Methodology in the Ancient Near East: Approaches from Assyriology and Beyond*, edited by Stephanie Lynn Budin et al., 337–56. Barcino Monographica Orientalia 10. Barcelona: Universitat de Barcelona Edicions, 2019.

Jacobsen, Lea. "'And Reuben Went' (Gen 30,14–18; 35,22a): For His Mother's Sake or for His Own?" *SJOT* 34.2 (2020) 201–20.

Jacobsen, Thorkild. *The Sumerian King List*. Assyriological Studies 11. Chicago: University of Chicago, 1939.

Jacobson, Diane. "Redefining Family in the Book of Ruth." *Word and World* 33.1 (2013) 5–11.

James, Elaine T. "Land and Community in the Book of Ruth." In *Rooted and Grounded: Essays on Land and Christian Discipleship*, edited by Ryan Dallas Harker and Janeen Bertsche Johnson, 29–39. Studies in Peace and Scripture: Institute of Mennonite Studies. Eugene, OR: Pickwick, 2016.

Janzen, J. Gerald. "'Samuel Opened the Doors of the House of Yahweh' (1 Samuel 3:15)." *JSOT* 8.26 (1983) 89–96.

Jeansonne, Sharon Pace. *The Women of Genesis: From Sarah to Potiphar's Wife*. Minneapolis: Fortress, 1990.

Jeffers, Ann. *Magic and Divination in Ancient Palestine and Syria*. Studies in the History and Culture of the Ancient Near East 8. New York: Brill, 1996.

Jeffress, Jean. "Three's Company Too: A Midrash on Everyday Misogyny, Leah, Rachel, Jacob, and the Comedy of Errors of This Hebrew Bible Dysfunctional Family." *Review and Expositor* 115.4 (2018) 572–76.

Jeremiah, Anderson. "Reclaiming 'Her' Right: Rereading the Story of Tamar (Genesis 38:1–27) from Dalit Women Perspective." *Bangalore Theological Forum* 38.1 (2006) 145–56.

Jericke, Detlef. *Abraham in Mamre: Historische und Exegetische Studien zur Region von Hebron und zu Genesis 11,27–19,38*. Culture and History of the Ancient Near East 17. Leiden: Brill, 2003.

Jero, Christopher. "Mother-Child Narratives and the Kingdom of God: Authorial Use of Typology as an Interpretive Device in Samuel-Kings." *Bulletin for Biblical Research* 25.2 (2015) 155–69.

Jirku, Anton. *Kanaanäische Mythen und Epen aus Ras Schamra-Ugarit*. Gütersloh: Gütersloher Verlagshaus, 1962.

Jobling, David. "A Bettered Woman: Elisha and the Shunammite in the Deuteronomic Work." In *The Labour of Reading: Desire, Alienation, and Biblical Interpretation*, edited by Fiona C. Black et al., 177–92. Semeia Studies 36. Atlanta: SBL, 1999.

Johnson, Benjamin J. M. "What Type of Son Is Samson? Reading Judges 13 as a Biblical Type-Scene." *Journal of the Evangelical Theological Society* 53.2 (2010) 269–86.

Johnson, Elisabeth Ann. "Barrenness, Birth, and Biblical Allusions in Luke 1–2." PhD diss., Princeton Theological Seminary, 2000.

Jones, K. L. "Three Blind Vices? Vision and Blindness in the Samson Cycle (Judges 13–16)." *BibInt* 28.2 (2020) 175–201.

Joo, Heun-Kyu. "The Literary Inner Logic of Genesis 38 by Means of Sexual Incontinence and Deception Motifs." *Canon and Culture* 12.2 (2018) 105–30.

Josephus, Flavius. *Jewish Antiquities*. Translated by H. St. J. Thackeray. Vol. 1, *Books 1–3*. Loeb Classical Library 242. Cambridge, MA: Harvard University Press, 1998.

———. *Jewish Antiquities*. Translated by H. St. J. Thackeray. Vol. 2, *Books 4–6*. Loeb Classical Library 490. Cambridge, MA: Harvard University Press, 1998.

Justel, Josué J. "Women, Gender and Law at the Dawn of History: The Evidence of the Cuneiform Sources." In *Women in Antiquity: Real Women Across the Ancient World*, edited by Stephanie Lynn Budin and Jean MacIntosh Turfa, 77–100. New York: Routledge, 2016.

Kalmanofsky, Amy. *Dangerous Sisters of the Hebrew Bible*. Minneapolis: Fortress, 2014.

Kawashima, Robert S. *Biblical Narrative and the Death of the Rhapsode*. Indiana Studies in Biblical Literature. Bloomington: Indiana University Press, 2004.

Kedar-Kopfstein, B. "עֵדֶן 'eḏen." In *Theological Dictionary of the Old Testament*, edited by G. Johannes Botterweck et al., translated by Douglas W. Stott, 10:481–90. Grand Rapids, MI: Eerdmans, 1999.
Keefer, Arthur. "The Meaning of Life in Ecclesiastes: Coherence, Purpose, and Significance from a Psychological Perspective." *Harvard Theological Review* 112.4 (2019) 447–66.
Keil, C. F., and F. Delitzsch. *Biblical Commentary on the Books of Samuel*. Translated by James Martin. Clark's Foreign Theological Library 9. Edinburgh: T&T Clark, 1866.
———. *Biblical Commentary on the Old Testament*. Translated by James Martin. Vol. 1: *The Pentateuch*. Edinburgh: T&T Clark, 1885.
Keita, Schadrac, and Janet W. Dyk. "The Scene at the Threshing Floor: Suggestive Readings and Intercultural Considerations on Ruth 3." *BT* 57.1 (2006) 17–32.
Kellenberger, Edgar. "Wie sind Geburtsorakel und Betrugs-Erzählung Aufeinander Bezogen? Auslegungsgeschichtliche und Narratologische Überlegungen zu Gen 25,23 und 27,1ff." *Communio Viatorum* 58.3 (2016) 241–55.
Keun, Ahn Sang, and Pieter M. Venter. "An Analytical Perspective on the Fellowship Narrative of Genesis 18:1–15." *HTS Teologiese Studies/Theological Studies* 66.1 (2010) 1–8.
Kim, Dohyung. "From Lot's Daughters to Bathsheba: Thematic Commonalities of Tamar and Other Specific Women in the Primary Narrative (Genesis–2 Kings)." *Korean Journal of Christian Studies* 97 (2015) 47–68.
———. "The Structure of Genesis 38: A Thematic Reading." *VT* 62.4 (2012) 550–60.
Kim, Jichan. *The Structure of the Samson Cycle*. Kampen, Netherlands: Kok Pharos, 1993.
Kim, Koowon. *Incubation as a Type-Scene in the Aqhatu, Kirta, and Hannah Stories: A Form-Critical and Narratological Study of KTU 1.14 I–1.15 III, 1.17 I–II, and 1 Samuel 1:1–2:11*. Supplements to VT 145. Leiden: Brill, 2011.
Kim, Uriah Y. "More to the Eye Than Meets the Eye: A Protest Against Empire in Samson's Death?" *BibInt* 22.1 (2014) 1–19.
Kim, Yung Suk. "The Story of Hannah (1 Sam 1:1–2:11) from a Perspective of Han: The Three-Phase Transformative Process." *The Bible and Critical Theory* 4.2 (2008) 1–9.
Kimchi, David. *Radak on Genesis*. Safaria, 2009. https://www.sefaria.org/Radak_on_Genesis?tab=contents.
King, Greg A. "Ruth 2:1–13." *Interpretation* 52.2 (1998) 182–84.
King, Philip J., and Lawrence E. Stager. *Life in Biblical Israel*. Library of Ancient Israel. Louisville, KY: Westminster John Knox, 2001.
Kinnier Wilson, James V. "Further Contributions to the Legend of Etana." *Journal of Near Eastern Studies* 33.2 (1974) 237–49.
———. *The Legend of Etana: A New Edition*. Warminster, England: Aris & Phillips, 1985.
———. *Studia Etanaica: New Texts and Discussions*. Alter Orient und Altes Testament 338. Münster: Ugarit-Verlag, 2007.
Kirk, G. S. *Myth: Its Meaning and Functions in Ancient and Other Cultures*. Sather Classical Lectures 40. Cambridge: Cambridge University Press, 1970.
Kislev, Itamar. "Numbers 36,1–12: Innovation and Interpretation." *ZAW* 122.2 (2010) 249–59.

———. "What Happened to the Sons of Korah? The Ongoing Debate Regarding the Status of the Korahites." *JBL* 138.3 (2019) 497–511.

Kitchen, K. A., and Paul Lawrence. *Treaty, Law and Covenant in the Ancient Near East*. Vol. 1. 3 vols. Wiesbaden: Harrassowitz Verlag, 2012.

Klein, Ernest. "עקר." In *A Comprehensive Etymological Dictionary of the Hebrew Language for Readers of English*. New York: Macmillan, 1987.

Klein, Lillian R. "Hannah: Marginalized Victim and Social Redeemer." In *A Feminist Companion to Samuel and Kings*, edited by Athalya Brenner, 77–92. The Feminist Companion to the Bible 5. Sheffield: Sheffield Academic, 1994.

———. *The Triumph of Irony in the Book of Judges*. JSOT Supplement Series 68. Sheffield: Almond, 1988.

Klein, Ralph W. *1 Samuel*. 2nd ed. Word Biblical Commentary 10. Nashville: Thomas Nelson, 2008.

Kloner, Amos, and David Davis. "A Burial Cave of the Late First Temple Period on the Slope of Mount Zion." In *Ancient Jerusalem Revealed*, edited by Hillel Geva, reprint and exp. ed., 107–10. Jerusalem: Israel Exploration Society, 2000.

Kluger, Yehezkel. *A Psychological Interpretation of Ruth: In the Light of Mythology, Legend and Kabbalah*. Einsiedeln, Switzerland: Daimon, 1999.

Knibb, Michael A. "Life and Death in the Old Testament." In *The World of Ancient Israel: Sociological, Anthropological and Political Perspectives: Essays by Members of the Society for Old Testament Study*, edited by R. E. Clements, 395–415. Cambridge: Cambridge University Press, 1989.

Knight, Stacy A. "Apparitions and Appellations: Questions Regarding the Identity of the Visitors in Gen. 18:1–15." *Proceedings—Eastern Great Lakes and Midwest Biblical Societies* 16 (1996) 95–105.

Knoppers, Gary N. "Dissonance and Disaster in the Legend of Kirta." *Journal of the American Oriental Society* 114.4 (1994) 572–82.

Koch, Klaus. "Die Sohnesverheißung an den Ugaritischen Daniel." *Zeitschrift für Assyriologie und Vorderasiatische Archäologie* 58 (1967) 211–21.

Koehler, Ludwig, and Walter Baumgartner. "בַּת." In *HALOT* 1:165–66.

———. "עֶדְנָה." In *HALOT* 2:793.

Koepf Taylor, Laurel W. *Give Me Children or I Shall Die: Children and Communal Survival in Biblical Literature*. Emerging Scholars. Minneapolis: Fortress, 2013.

Köhler, Ludwig. "Die Adoptionsform von Rt 4." *ZAW* 29.4 (1909) 312–14.

Köhlmoos, Melanie. *Ruth*. Das Alte Testament Deutsch 9/3. Göttingen: Vandenhoeck & Ruprecht, 2010.

Konkel, August H. *1 and 2 Kings: From Biblical Text—To Contemporary Life*. NIV Application Commentary. Grand Rapids, MI: Zondervan, 2006.

———. *Job*. Cornerstone Biblical Commentary 6. Carol Stream, IL: Tyndale House, 2006.

Konstantakos, Ioannis M. "The Maiden Who Knew Nothing About Sex: A Scabrous Theme in Novella and Comedy." In *Sex and the Ancient City: Sex and Sexual Practices in Greco-Roman Antiquity*, edited by Andreas Serafim et al., 445–70. Trends in Classics—Supplementary Volumes 126. Berlin: De Gruyter, 2022.

Konstantopoulos, Gina. "Women and the Interpretation of Dreams in Sumerian and Akkadian Literature." *Journal of Cuneiform Studies* 74.1 (2022) 89–108.

Koosed, Jennifer L. *Gleaning Ruth: A Biblical Heroine and Her Afterlives*. Columbia: University of South Carolina Press, 2011.

Korpel, Marjo. *The Structure of the Book of Ruth*. Pericope 2. Assen, Netherlands: Van Gorcum, 2001.

Korpman, Matthew J. "Can Anything Good Come from Sodom? A Feminist and Narrative Critique of Lot's Daughters in Gen. 19.30-38." *JSOT* 43.3 (2019) 334-42.

Koubková, Evelyne. "Fortune and Misfortune of the Eagle in the Myth of Etana." In *Fortune and Misfortune in the Ancient Near East: Proceedings of the 60th Rencontre Assyriologique Internationale at Warsaw 21-25 July 2014*, edited by Olga Drewnowska and Małgorzata Sandowicz, 371-82. Winona Lake, IN: Eisenbrauns, 2017.

Kozlovic, Anton Karl. "Constructing the Motherliness of Manoah's Wife in Cecil B. DeMille's Samson and Delilah (1949)." *Women in Judaism* 4.1 (2006) 1-20.

Kraft, Robert A. "Note on the Oracle of Rebecca (Gen 25:23)." *The Journal of Theological Studies* 13.2 (1962) 318-20.

Kramer, Dale E. "Barrenness: A Consideration of YHWH's Modus Operandi Within Cultic Covenantal Renewal for the Establishment, Sustainability, and Fulfillment of Divine Purpose." MA thesis, Regent University, 2018.

Kramer, Phyllis Silverman. "Biblical Women That Come in Pairs: The Use of Female Pairs as a Literary Device in the Hebrew Bible." In *Genesis*, edited by Athalya Brenner, 217-31. Feminist Companion to the Bible 2nd Series 1. Sheffield: Sheffield Academic, 1998.

Kramer, S. N. "Lipit-Ishtar Lawcode." In *ANET* 159-61.

Krueger, Paul. "Vreugde en Verdriet in die Huis van Jakob." *HTS Theological Studies* 64.2 (2008) 935-57.

Krüger, Thomas. "Morality and Religion in Three Babylonian Poems of Pious Sufferers." In *Teaching Morality in Antiquity: Wisdom Texts, Oral Traditions, and Images*, edited by T. M. Oshima, 182-88. Orientalische Religionen in der Antike 29. Tübingen: Mohr Siebeck, 2018.

Kruschwitz, Jonathan. "Tamar Among the Matriarchs: Godless and Perhaps Closer to God." *Review and Expositor* 115.4 (2018) 542-55.

Kugel, James L. *The God of Old: Inside the Lost World of the Bible*. New York: Free Press, 2003.

———. *The Great Shift: Encountering God in Biblical Times*. Boston: Mariner, 2018.

LaCocque, André. "Date et Milieu du Livre de Ruth." *Revue d'histoire et de Philosophie Religieuses* 59.3-4 (1979) 583-93.

———. *The Feminine Unconventional: Four Subversive Figures in Israel's Tradition*. Overtures to Biblical Theology. Minneapolis: Fortress, 1990.

———. *Ruth: A Continental Commentary*. Translated by K. C. Hanson. Continental Commentaries. Minneapolis: Fortress, 2004.

———. "Subverting the Biblical World: Sociology and Politics in the Book of Ruth." In *Scrolls of Love: Ruth and the Song of Songs*, edited by Peter S. Hawkins and Lesleigh Cushing Stahlberg, 20-30. New York: Fordham University Press, 2006.

Laffey, Alice L. *Wives, Harlots and Concubines: The Old Testament in Feminist Perspective*. London: SPCK, 1990.

Lambert, W. G. "Ancestors, Authors, and Canonicity." *Journal of Cuneiform Studies* 11.1 (1957) 1-14.

———. *Babylonian Wisdom Literature*. Winona Lake, IN: Eisenbrauns, 1996.

———. "Line 10 of the Old Babylonian Etana Legend." *Journal of Cuneiform Studies* 32.2 (1980) 81-85.

Landau, Ephraim. "Giving Birth on Someone's Knees: The Meaning of Genesis 30:3." *Jewish Bible Quarterly* 48.4 (2020) 211–29.

———. "What Does I Will Be Built From/Through Her in Genesis 16:2 and 30:3 Mean?" *Jewish Bible Quarterly* 48.1 (2020) 40–56.

Lau, Peter H. W. *Identity and Ethics in the Book of Ruth: A Social Identity Approach*. Beihefte zur ZAW 416. New York: De Gruyter, 2011.

Lau, Peter H. W., and Gregory Goswell. *Unceasing Kindness: A Biblical Theology of Ruth*. New Studies in Biblical Theology 41. Downers Grove, IL: InterVarsity, 2016.

Lavie, David. *Plants of the Bible in Their Natural Surroundings*. Haifa: Dept. of Education and Culture, Municipality of Haifa, 1969.

Lazaridis, Nikolaos. "Physical Characterization in Ancient Egyptian Narrative Literature." *ENiM* 6 (2013) 123–37.

Leder, Arie C. "Who Builds the House of Israel? The Verb Bnh in Genesis 2:22; 16:2; 30:3." *Revue Biblique* 128.1 (2021) 5–26.

Lee, Kerry. "Two Translations of HSS V 67 and Their Significance for Genesis 16,21, and 30." *JBL* 134.1 (2015) 59–63.

Lee, Young Gil. "From Fertility to Manipulation: Female Characterizations and the Birth Narratives in the Hebrew Bible." PhD diss., University of Sheffield, 2021.

Leeb, Carolyn S. "Polygyny: Insights from Rural Haiti." In *Ancient Israel: The Old Testament in Its Social Context*, edited by Philip F. Esler, 50–65. Minneapolis: Fortress, 2006.

Leggett, Donald A. *The Levirate and Goel Institutions in the Old Testament: With Special Attention to the Book of Ruth*. Cherry Hill, NJ: Mack, 1974.

Lehmann, Gunnar. "Reconstructing the Social Landscape of Early Israel: Rural Marriage Alliances in the Central Hill Country." *Tel Aviv* 31.2 (2004) 141–93.

Leick, Gwendolyn. "Appu." In *A Dictionary of Ancient Near Eastern Mythology*, 11. New York: Taylor & Francis, 2003.

———. *Sex and Eroticism in Mesopotamian Literature*. New York: Routledge, 1994.

Leitch, Dane. "Redeeming Peninnah: A Freeing Translation of צרתה in 1 Samuel 1.6." *BT* 65.3 (2014) 280–91.

Lemos, T. M. *Marriage Gifts and Social Change in Ancient Palestine: 1200 BCE to 200 CE*. Cambridge: Cambridge University Press, 2010.

———. *Violence and Personhood in Ancient Israel and Comparative Contexts*. Oxford: Oxford University Press, 2017.

———. "Were Israelite Women Chattel? Shedding New Light on an Old Question." In *Worship, Women, and War: Essays in Honor of Susan Niditch*, edited by John J. Collins et al., 227–42. Brown Judaic Studies 357. Providence, RI: Brown University, 2015.

Leshem, Yossi. "Two Biblical Families and Their Differences." *HUCA* 81 (2010) 1–15.

Letellier, Robert Ignatius. *Day in Mamre, Night in Sodom: Abraham and Lot in Genesis 18 and 19*. Biblical Interpretation Series 10. Leiden: Brill, 1995.

Leuchter, Mark. "Genesis 38 in Social and Historical Perspective." *JBL* 132.2 (2013) 209–27.

Levine, Baruch A. *Numbers 21–36: A New Translation with Introduction and Commentary*. Anchor Bible 4A. New York: Doubleday, 2000.

Levine, Nachman. "Sarah/Sodom: Birth, Destruction, and Synchronic Transaction." *JSOT* 31.2 (2006) 131–46.

Levinson, Bernard M. *Legal Revision and Religious Renewal in Ancient Israel.* Cambridge: Cambridge University Press, 2008.
Lewis, Arthur H. *Judges and Ruth.* Everyman's Bible Commentary. Chicago: Moody Press, 1979.
Lewis, Theodore J. "Family, Household, and Local Religion at Late Bronze Age Ugarit." In *Household and Family Religion in Antiquity*, edited by John Bodel and Saul M. Olyan, 60-88. The Ancient World: Comparative Histories. Malden, MA: Blackwell, 2008.
———. "The Identity and Function of Ugaritic Sha'tiqatu: A Divinely Made Apotropaic Figure." *Journal of Ancient Near Eastern Religions* 14.1 (2014) 1-28.
———. "The Sha'tiqatu Narrative from the Ugaritic Story About the Healing of King Kirta." *Journal of Ancient Near Eastern Religions* 13.2 (2013) 188-211.
Lias, J. J. *The Book of Judges: With Map, Notes and Introduction.* Reprint. Cambridge: Cambridge University Press, 1906.
Lichtheim, Miriam, ed. "The Doomed Prince." In *Ancient Egyptian Literature*, 2:534-38. Oakland: University of California Press, 2019.
Lim, Timothy H. "How Good Was Ruth's Hebrew? Ethnic and Linguistic Otherness in the Book of Ruth." In *The "Other" in Second Temple Judaism: Essays in Honor of John J. Collins*, edited by Daniel C. Harlow et al., 101-15. Grand Rapids, MI: Eerdmans, 2011.
Linafelt, Tod. "Narrative and Poetic Art in the Book of Ruth." *Interpretation* 64.2 (2010) 118-29.
Linafelt, Tod, and Timothy K. Beal. *Ruth and Esther.* Berit Olam. Collegeville, MN: Liturgical, 1999.
Lipiński, Edward. "The King's Arbitration in Ancient Near Eastern Folk-Tale." In *Keilschriftliche Literaturen: Ausgewählte Vorträge der XXXII. Rencontre Assyriologique Internationale Münster, 8.-12.7.1985*, edited by Karl Hecker and Walter Sommerfeld, 137-42. Berliner Beiträge zum Vorderen Orient 6. Berlin: Reimer, 1986.
Litke, John D. "The Daughters of Zelophehad." *Currents in Theology and Mission* 29.3 (2002) 207-18.
Loader, J. A. "David and the Matriarch in the Book of Ruth." *IDS* 28.1 (1994) 25-35.
Long, Burke O. "Framing Repetitions in Biblical Historiography." *JBL* 106.3 (1987) 385-99.
———. "The Shunammite Woman: In the Shadow of the Prophet?" *Bible Review* 7.1 (1991) 12-25.
Longman, Tremper, III. *Job.* Baker Commentary on the Old Testament Wisdom and Psalms. Grand Rapids, MI: Baker Academic, 2012.
Loprieno, Antonio. "Travel and Fiction in Egyptian Literature." In *Mysterious Lands*, edited by David O'Connor and Stephen Quirke, 31-52. Encounters with Ancient Egypt. New York: Routledge, 2016.
Loretz, Oswald. "K't ⬚yh—«wie Jetzt ums Jahr» Gen 18,10." *Biblica* 43.1 (1962) 75-78.
Louth, Andrew. "The Oak of Mamre, the Fathers and St. Andrei Rublev: Patristic Interpretation of the Hospitality of Abraham and Rublev's Icon of the Trinity." In *The Trinity-Sergius Lavra in Russian History and Culture*, edited by Vladimir Tsurikov, 90-100. Readings in Russian Religious Culture 3. Jordanville, NY: Holy Trinity Seminary Press, 2005.

Low, Katherine B. "The Sexual Abuse of Lot's Daughters: Reconceptualizing Kinship for the Sake of Our Daughters." *Journal of Feminist Studies in Religion* 26.2 (2010) 37–54.

Luzzatto, S. D. *Commentary on the Pentateuch*. Tel Aviv: Dvir, 1965.

Lyons, William John. *Canon and Exegesis: Canonical Praxis and the Sodom Narrative*. JSOT Supplement Series 352. New York: Sheffield Academic, 2002.

Macintosh, A. A. "Third Root עדה in Biblical Hebrew." *VT* 24.4 (1974) 454–73.

Maher, Michael. *Targum Pseudo-Jonathan: Genesis*. The Aramaic Bible 1B. Collegeville, MN: Liturgical, 1992.

Mangrum, Benjamin. "Bringing 'Fullness' to Naomi: Centripetal Nationalism in The Book of Ruth." *Horizons in Biblical Theology* 33.1 (2011) 62–81.

Marchesi, Gianni. "The Sumerian King List and the Early History of Mesopotamia." In *Ana Turri Gimilli: Studi Dedicati al Padre Werner R. Mayer, S.J., Da Amici e Allievi*, edited by M. G. Biga and M. Liverani, 231–48. Vicino Oriente Quaderno 5. Rome: Universita degli Studi di Roma La Sapienza, 2010.

Marcos, Natalio Fernández. *Biblia Hebraica Quinta: Judges*. Gesamtwerk zur Fortsetzung 7. Stuttgart: Deutsche Bibelgesellschaft, 2011.

Margalit, Baruch. "John Day and the 'Kinnereth Hypothesis.'" *VT* 31.3 (1981) 373–75.

———. "Studia Ugaritica II: Studies in Krt and Aqht." *Ugarit-Forschungen* 8 (1976) 137–92.

———. *The Ugaritic Poem of AQHT: Text, Translation, Commentary*. Beiheft zur ZAW 182. New York: De Gruyter, 1989.

Margalith, Othniel. "More Samson Legends." *VT* 36.4 (1986) 397–405.

Marsman, Hennie J. *Women in Ugarit and Israel: Their Social and Religious Position in the Context of the Ancient Near East*. Oudtestamentische Studiën 49. Leiden: Brill, 2003.

Martens, Elmer A. "7756 קום." In *New International Dictionary of Old Testament Theology and Exegesis*, edited by Willem A. VanGemeren, 3:902–5. Grand Rapids, MI: Zondervan, 1997.

Masenya, Madipoane J. "Kgarebe (Virgin) and Carnal Knowledge: Reading Genesis 19:30–38 from the Margins." *HTS Theological Studies* 77.3 (2021) 1–7.

———. "Stuck Between the Waiting Room and the Reconfigured Levirate Entity? Reading Ruth in Marriage-Obsessed African Christian Contexts." In *Feminist Frameworks and the Bible: Power, Ambiguity, and Intersectionality*, edited by L. Juliana Claassens and Carolyn J. Sharp, 163–76. Library of Hebrew Bible/Old Testament Studies 630. New York: Bloomsbury T&T Clark, 2017.

———. "Who Calls the Shots in Naomi's Life? Reading the Naomi-Ruth Story Within the African Religio-Cultural Context." *Acta Theologica* 24 (2016) 84–96.

Maspero, Gaston. *Popular Stories of Ancient Egypt*. Edited by Hasan El-Shamy. Santa Barbara, CA: ABC-CLIO, 2002.

Mathews, Kenneth A. *Genesis 11:27–50:26*. New American Commentary 1B. Nashville: Broadman & Holman, 2005.

Mathewson, Dan. *Death and Survival in the Book of Job: Desymbolization and Traumatic Experience*. Library of Hebrew Bible/Old Testament Studies 450. New York: T&T Clark, 2006.

Mathewson, Steven D. "An Exegetical Study of Genesis 38." *Bibliotheca Sacra* 146 (1989) 373–92.

Mathias, Steffan. *Paternity, Progeny, and Perpetuation: Creating Lives After Death in the Hebrew Bible*. Library of Hebrew Bible/Old Testament Studies 696. London: Bloomsbury T&T Clark, 2020.

Matskevich, Karalina. *Construction of Gender and Identity in Genesis: The Subject and the Other*. Library of Hebrew Bible/Old Testament Studies 647. New York: T&T Clark, 2019.

Matthews, Victor H. "The Determination of Social Identity in the Story of Ruth." *Biblical Theology Bulletin* 36.2 (2006) 49–54.

———. *Judges and Ruth*. New Cambridge Bible Commentary. New York: Cambridge University Press, 2004.

———. "Marriage and Family in the Ancient Near East." In *Marriage and Family in the Biblical World*, edited by Ken M. Campbell, 1–32. Downers Grove, IL: InterVarsity, 2003.

Mattingly, Gerald L. "The Pious Sufferer: Mesopotamia's Traditional Theodicy and Job's Counselors." In *The Bible in the Light of Cuneiform Literature*, edited by William W. Hallo et al., 305–48. Scripture in Context 3. Lewiston, NY: Edwin Mellen, 1990.

Mattox, Mickey L. "Sancta Sara, Mater Ecclesiae: Martin Luther's Catholic Exegesis of Genesis 18:11–15." *Pro Ecclesia* 10.3 (2001) 295–320.

Matuszak, Jana. "A Complete Reconstruction, New Edition and Interpretation of the Sumerian Morality Tale 'The Old Man and the Young Girl.'" *Zeitschrift für Assyriologie und Vorderasiatische Archäologie* 112.2 (2022) 184–218.

Mayer, Eitan. "No News Is Bad News: Beneath the Surface of Genesis 18." *Tradition* 53.4 (2021) 106–13.

Mazuz, Haggai. "Polemical Treatment of the Story of the Annunciation of Isaac's Birth in Islamic Sources." *The Review of Rabbinic Judaism* 17.2 (2014) 252–62.

Mbuwayesango, Dora R. "Childlessness and Woman-to-Woman Relationships in Genesis and in African Patriarc[h]al Society: Sarah and Hagar from a Zimbabwean Woman's Perspective (Gen 16:1–16; 21:8–21)." *Semeia* 78 (1997) 27–36.

McAfee, Eugene C. "The Patriarch's Longed-for Son: Biological and Social Reproduction in Ugaritic and Hebrew Epic." ThD diss., Harvard Divinity School, 1996.

McCarter, P. Kyle., Jr. *1 Samuel: A New Translation, Notes and Commentary*. Anchor Bible 8. Garden City, NY: Doubleday, 1980.

McDonnell, Eric D., Jr. "Will Womankind Now Go Hunting? Constructions of Gender in the Aqhat Epic." *Antiguo Oriente* 19 (2021) 41–64.

McGeough, Kevin M. "'Will Womankind Now Be Hunting?' The Work and Economic Lives of Women at Late Bronze Age Ugarit." In *Women in Antiquity: Real Women Across the Ancient World*, edited by Stephanie Lynn Budin and Jean MacIntosh Turfa, 476–87. New York: Routledge, 2016.

McKeown, James. *Ruth*. Two Horizons Old Testament Commentary. Grand Rapids, MI: Eerdmans, 2015.

McKinlay, Judith E. "A Son Is Born to Naomi: A Harvest for Israel." In *Ruth and Esther: A Feminist Companion to the Bible*, edited by Athalya Brenner, 151–57. Feminist Companion to the Bible 2nd Series 3. Sheffield: Sheffield Academic, 1999.

———. "Who's/Whose Sarah? Journeying with Sarah in a Chorus of Voices." In *Redirected Travel: Alternative Journeys and Places in Biblical Studies*, edited by Roland Boer and Edgar W. Conrad, 131–43. JSOT Supplement Series 382. New York: T&T Clark, 2003.

McNamara, Martin. *Targum Neofiti 1: Genesis*. The Aramaic Bible 1A. Collegeville, MN: Liturgical, 1992.

Meek, Russell L. "The Abishag Episode: Reexamining the Role of Virility in 1 Kings 1:1–4 in Light of the Kirta Epic and the Sumerian Tale 'The Old Man and the Young Woman.'" *Bulletin for Biblical Research* 24.1 (2014) 1–14.

Meek, Theophile J. "The Code of Hammurabi." In *ANET* 163–80.

———. "Mesopotamian Legal Documents." In *ANET* 217–22.

Melcher, Sarah J. "A Tale of Two Eunuchs: Isaiah 56:1–8 and Acts 8:26–40." In *Disability Studies and Biblical Literature*, edited by Candida R. Moss and Jeremy Schipper, 117–29. New York: Palgrave Macmillan, 2011.

Mendelsohn, Isaac. "Dream." In *The Interpreter's Dictionary of the Bible: An Illustrated Encyclopedia*, edited by George Arthur Buttrick, 1:868–69. Nashville: Abingdon, 1962.

Menn, Esther Marie. *Judah and Tamar (Genesis 38) in Ancient Jewish Exegesis: Studies in Literary Form and Hermeneutics*. Supplements to the Journal for the Study of Judaism 51. Leiden: Brill, 1997.

Meredith, Christopher. "A Case of Open and Shut: The Five Thresholds in 1 Samuel 1:1–7:2." *BibInt* 18.2 (2010) 137–57.

Meshel, Naphtali S. "Too Much in the Sun: Intentional Ambiguity in the Samson Narrative." *Hebrew Studies* 62 (2021) 55–72.

Meurer, Thomas. "Der Gebärwettstreit Zwischen Lea und Rahel: Der Erzählaufbau von Gen 29,31–30,24 als Testfall der Erzählerischen Geschlossenheit einer Zusammenhanglos Wirkenden Einheit." *Biblische Notizen* 107/108 (2001) 93–108.

Meyers, Carol L. "An Ethnoarchaeological Analysis of Hannah's Sacrifice." In *Pomegranates and Golden Bells: Studies in Biblical, Jewish, and Near Eastern Ritual, Law, and Literature in Honor of Jacob Milgrom*, edited by David P. Wright et al., 77–92. Winona Lake, IN: Eisenbrauns, 1995.

———. "From Household to House of Yahweh: Women's Religious Culture in Ancient Israel." In *Congress Volume Basel 2001*, edited by A. Lemaire, 277–303. Supplements to VT 92. Brill, 2002.

———. "Hannah and Her Sacrifice: Reclaiming Female Agency." In *A Feminist Companion to Samuel and Kings*, edited by Athalya Brenner, 93–104. The Feminist Companion to the Bible 5. Sheffield: Sheffield Academic, 1994.

———. "The Hannah Narrative in Feminist Perspective." In *"Go to the Land I Will Show You": Studies in Honor of Dwight W. Young*, edited by Joseph E. Coleson and Victor H. Matthews, 117–26. Winona Lake, IN: Eisenbrauns, 1996.

———. *Households and Holiness: The Religious Culture of Israelite Women*. Minneapolis: Fortress, 2023.

———. "In the Household and Beyond: The Social World of Israelite Women." *Studia Theologica* 63.1 (2009) 19–41.

———. "Procreation, Production, and Protection: Male-Female Balance in Early Israel." In *Community, Identity, and Ideology: Social Science Approaches to the Hebrew Bible*, edited by Charles E. Carter and Carol L. Meyers, 489–514. Winona Lake, IN: Eisenbrauns, 1996.

———. *Rediscovering Eve: Ancient Israelite Women in Context*. Oxford: Oxford University Press, 2013.

———. "Returning Home: Ruth 1.8 and the Gendering of the Book of Ruth." In *A Feminist Companion to Ruth*, edited by Athalya Brenner, 85–114. Feminist Companion to the Bible 3. Sheffield: Sheffield Academic, 1993.

———. "The Roots of Restriction: Women in Early Israel." *The Biblical Archaeologist* 41.3 (1978) 91–103.

———. "'Women of the Neighborhood' (Ruth 4.17): Informal Female Networks in Ancient Israel." In *Ruth and Esther: A Feminist Companion to the Bible*, edited by Athalya Brenner, 110–27. Feminist Companion to the Bible 2nd Series 3. Sheffield: Sheffield Academic, 1999.

———. "Women's Daily Life (Iron Age Israel)." In *Women in Antiquity: Real Women Across the Ancient World*, edited by Stephanie Lynn Budin and Jean MacIntosh Turfa, 488–500. New York: Routledge, 2016.

Michael, Matthew. "The Art of Persuasion and the Book of Ruth: Literary Devices in the Persuasive Speeches of Ruth 1: 6–18." *Hebrew Studies* 56 (2015) 145–62.

———. "Orpah and Her Interpreters: Evaluating the Justifications for the Traditional-Stereotyped Readings." *OTE (New Series)* 24.2 (2011) 390–413.

Michel, Cécile. "Akkadian Texts: Women in Letters, Old Assyrian Kaniš." In *Women in the Ancient Near East: A Sourcebook*, edited by Mark W. Chavalas, 205–12. Routledge Sourcebooks for the Ancient World. New York: Routledge, 2014.

Milgrom, Jacob. *Numbers = במדבר: The Traditional Hebrew Text with the New JPS Translation*. The JPS Torah Commentary. Philadelphia: Jewish Publication Society, 1990.

Millard, Alan R. "The Etymology of Eden." *VT* 34.1 (1984) 103–6.

Miller, James E. "Sexual Offences in Genesis." *JSOT* 25.90 (2000) 41–53.

Mobley, Gregory. *The Empty Men: The Heroic Tradition of Ancient Israel*. Anchor Bible Reference Library. New York: Doubleday, 2005.

———. *Samson and the Liminal Hero in the Ancient Near East*. Library of Hebrew Bible/Old Testament Studies 453. New York: T&T Clark, 2006.

Möller, Georg. *Hieratische Lesestücke für den Akademischen Gebrauch*. Vol. 2. Literarische Texte des Neuen Reiches. Berlin: Akademie-Verlag, 1961.

Mollo, Paolo. "Did It Please God to Kill Them? Literary Comparison Between the Birth Accounts of Samson and Samuel." *Henoch* 36.1 (2014) 86–105.

Monge, Claudio. "Life Together: Lessons in Hospitality from Mamre." *Toronto Journal of Theology* 29.1 (2013) 101–10.

Montgomery, James A. *A Critical and Exegetical Commentary on the Books of Kings*. International Critical Commentary. Edinburgh: T&T Clark, 1951.

Moore, E. "Ruth 2: Ancient Near Eastern Background." In *Dictionary of the Old Testament: Wisdom, Poetry and Writings: A Compendium of Contemporary Biblical Scholarship*, edited by Tremper Longman III and Peter Enns, 1685–99. IVP Bible Dictionary Series 3. Downers Grove, IL: IVP Academic, 2008.

Moore, George Foot. *A Critical and Exegetical Commentary on Judges*. International Critical Commentary 7. Edinburgh: T&T Clark, 1895.

Moore, Michael S. "Ruth the Moabite and the Blessing of Foreigners." *Catholic Biblical Quarterly* 60.2 (1998) 203–17.

———. "Two Textual Anomalies in Ruth." *Catholic Biblical Quarterly* 59.2 (1997) 234–43.

Moseley, James Allen. *Understanding the Books of Ruth and Job: Kindness, Morality, Suffering and Justice*. Independently published, 2020.

Moss, Candida R., and Joel S. Baden. *Reconceiving Infertility: Biblical Perspectives on Procreation and Childlessness*. Princeton, NJ: Princeton University Press, 2015.

Moyo, Chiropafadzo. "A Karanga Perspective on Fertility and Barrenness as Blessing and Curse in 1 Samuel 1:1–2:10." ThD diss., University of Stellenbosch, 2006.

Moyo, Fulata Lusungu. "'Traffic Violations': Hospitality, Foreignness, and Exploitation: A Contextual Biblical Study of Ruth." *Journal of Feminist Studies in Religion* 32.2 (2016) 83–94.

Mrozek, Andrzej. "Ugarycka Idea Boskiego Gniewu." *Verbum Vitae* 33 (2018) 129–52.

Mullen, E. Theodore, Jr. *The Divine Council in Canaanite and Early Hebrew Literature*. Harvard Semitic Monographs 24. Chico, CA: Scholars Press, 1980.

Müller, Hans-Peter. "Keilschriftliche Parallelen zum Biblischen Hiobbuch Möglichkeit und Grenze des Vergleichs." *Orientalia* 47.3 (1978) 360–75.

Mulzac, Ken. "Hannah: The Receiver and Giver of a Great Gift." *Andrews University Seminary Studies* 40.2 (2002) 207–17.

Muñoz Iglesias, Salvador. "El Procedimiento Literario del Anuncio Previo en la Biblia." *Estudios Bíblicos* 42.1–2 (1984) 21–70.

Muraoka, T. "1 Sam 1,15 Again." *Biblica* 77.1 (1996) 98–99.

Murphy, Francesca Aran. *1 Samuel*. Brazos Theological Commentary on the Bible. Grand Rapids, MI: Brazos, 2010.

Mwandayi, Canisius, and Sophia Chirongoma. "'Suspected Killer': Tamar's Plight (Gn 38) as a Lens for Illuminating Women's Vulnerability in the Legal Codes of Shona and Israelite Societies." *HTS Theological Studies* 76.3 (2020) 1–10.

Myers, Jacob M. *The Linguistic and Literary Form of the Book of Ruth*. Leiden: Brill, 1955.

Naicker, Linda. "Food, Sex and Text: Exploring Survival Sex in the Context of Food Insecurity Through Communal Readings of the Book of Ruth." PhD diss., University of the Western Cape, 2021.

Nakhai, Beth Alpert. "Female Infanticide in Iron II Israel and Judah." In *Sacred History, Sacred Literature: Essays on Ancient Israel, the Bible, and Religion in Honor of R. E. Friedman on His Sixtieth Birthday*, edited by Shawna Dolansky, 257–72. Winona Lake, IN: Eisenbrauns, 2008.

———. "Women in Israelite Religion: The State of Research Is All New Research." *Religions* 10.2 (2019) 1–11.

———. "A World of Possibilities: Jerusalem's Women in the Iron Age (1000–586 BCE)." In *Gender and Methodology in the Ancient Near East: Approaches from Assyriology and Beyond*, edited by Stephanie Lynn Budin et al., 369–89. Barcino Monographica Orientalia 10. Barcelona: Universitat de Barcelona Edicions, 2019.

Natan-Yulzary, Shirly. "Contrast and Meaning in the ⌈Aqhat Story." *VT* 62.3 (2012) 433–49.

———. "The Use of Resumptive Repetition for the Construction of Time and Space in the Ugaritic Epic of Aqhat." *Ugarit-Forschungen* 48 (2017) 373–90.

Naveh, Joseph, and Shaul Shaked. *Magic Spells and Formulae: Aramaic Incantations of Late Antiquity*. Jerusalem: Magnes, 1993.

Nazarov, Konstantin. "Focalization in the Old Testament Narratives with Specific Examples from the Book of Ruth." PhD diss., University of Chester, 2018.

Na'aman, Nadav. "Samuel's Birth Legend and the Sanctuary of Shiloh." *Journal of Northwest Semitic Languages* 43.1 (2017) 51–61.

Neff, Robert Wilbur. "Birth and Election of Isaac in the Priestly Tradition." *Biblical Research* 15 (1970) 5–18.
Nelson, Richard D. *First and Second Kings*. Interpretation: A Bible Commentary for Teaching and Preaching. Louisville, KY: John Knox, 1987.
Nemet-Nejat, Karen Rhea. *Daily Life in Ancient Mesopotamia*. Westport, CT: Greenwood, 1998.
———. "Women in Ancient Mesopotamia." In *Women's Roles in Ancient Civilizations: A Reference Guide*, edited by Bella Vivante, 85–114. Westport, CT: Greenwood, 1999.
———. "Women in Neo-Assyrian Inscriptions: Neo-Assyrian Oracles." In *Women in the Ancient Near East: A Sourcebook*, edited by Mark W. Chavalas, 240–45. Routledge Sourcebooks for the Ancient World. New York: Routledge, 2014.
Neufeld, Dietmar. "Barrenness: Trance as a Protest Strategy." In *Ancient Israel: The Old Testament in Its Social Context*, edited by Philip F. Esler, 128–41. Minneapolis: Fortress, 2006.
Neusner, Jacob. *The Babylonian Talmud: A Translation and Commentary*. Vol. 14: *Tractate Baba Mesi'a*. Peabody, MA: Hendrickson, 2005.
———. *The Babylonian Talmud: A Translation and Commentary*. Vol. 8: *Tractate Yebamot*. Peabody, MA: Hendrickson, 2005.
———. *Genesis Rabbah: The Judaic Commentary to the Book of Genesis: A New American Translation*. Vol. 2. Brown Judaic Studies 105. Atlanta: Scholars Press, 1985.
Newsom, Carol A. *The Book of Job: A Contest of Moral Imaginations*. Oxford: Oxford University Press, 2003.
Niditch, Susan. "Samson as Cultural Hero, Trickster, and Bandit: The Empowerment of the Weak." *Catholic Biblical Quarterly* 52.4 (1990) 608–24.
———. "The Wronged Woman Righted: An Analysis of Genesis 38." *Harvard Theological Review* 72 (1979) 143–49.
Nielsen, Kirsten. *Ruth: A Commentary*. Old Testament Library. Louisville, KY: Westminster John Knox, 1997.
Nissinen, Martti. *Prophets and Prophecy in the Ancient Near East*. 2nd ed. Writings from the Ancient World 41. Atlanta: SBL, 2019.
Noble, Paul R. "Esau, Tamar, and Joseph: Criteria for Identifying Inner-Biblical Allusions." *VT* 52.2 (2002) 219–52.
Noegel, Scott. "When Animals Speak." *Journal of the Ancient Near Eastern Society* 34.1 (2020) 107–35.
Nohrnberg, James. "The Keeping of Nahor: The Etiology of Biblical Election." In *The Book and the Text: The Bible and Literary Theory*, edited by Regina M. Schwartz, 161–88. Oxford: Blackwell, 1990.
Noth, Martin. *Numbers: A Commentary*. 2nd ed. Old Testament Library. London: SCM, 1980.
Novotny, Jamie R. *The Standard Babylonian Etana Epic: Cuneiform Text, Transliteration, Score, Glossary, Indices and Sign List*. State Archives of Assyria Cuneiform Texts 2. Helsinki: Neo-Assyrian Text Corpus Project, 2001.
Nowell, Irene. *Women in the Old Testament*. Collegeville, MN: Liturgical, 1997.
Nurullin, Rim, et al. "The Most Ancient Verse in the World (Sumerian, Akkadian, Hittite) Quantitative Analysis." In *Quantitative Approaches to Versification*, edited

by Petr Plecháč et al., 173–82. Institute of Czech Literature of the Czech Academy of Sciences, 2019.

Nwaoru, Emmanuel O. "The Case of the Daughters of Zelophehad (Num 27:1–11) and African Inheritance Rights." *Asia Journal of Theology* 16.1 (2002) 49–65.

Obermann, Daniel. *How Daniel Was Blessed with a Son: An Incubation Scene at Ugarit*. Supplement to the Journal of the American Oriental Society 6. Baltimore, MD: American Oriental Society, 1946.

O'Callaghan, Martin. "The Structure and Meaning of Gen 38—Judah and Tamar." *Proceedings of the Irish Biblical Association* 5 (1981) 72–97.

O'Connell, Robert H. *The Rhetoric of the Book of Judges*. Supplements to VT 63. Leiden: Brill, 1996.

O'Connor, Daniel J. "The Keret Legend and the Prologue-Epilogue of Job." *Irish Theological Quarterly* 55.1 (1989) 1–6.

———. "The Keret Legend and the Prologue-Epilogue of Job: A Postscript." *Irish Theological Quarterly* 55.3 (1989) 240–42.

O'Connor, Kathleen M. *Genesis 1–25A*. Smyth and Helwys Bible Commentary 1. Macon, GA: Smyth & Helwys, 2018.

Oden, Robert A., Jr. "Jacob as Father, Husband, and Nephew: Kinship Studies and the Patriarchal Narratives." *JBL* 102.2 (1983) 189–205.

Oden, Thomas C., ed. *Ancient Christian Commentary on Scripture: Old Testament*. Vol. 2: *Genesis 12–50*. Downers Grove, IL: InterVarsity, 2002.

Olley, John W. *The Message of Kings: God Is Present*. Bible Speaks Today. Downers Grove, IL: InterVarsity, 2011.

Olojede, Funlola. "Numbered with the Transgressors: The Story of the Daughters of Zelophehad as Retold by Noah." In *Transgression and Transformation: Feminist, Postcolonial and Queer Biblical Interpretation as Creative Interventions*, edited by L. Juliana Claassens et al., 11–19. Library of Hebrew Bible/Old Testament Studies 707. New York: Bloomsbury T&T Clark, 2021.

Olszewska, Karolina. "The Biblical Narrative About Leah, Jacob's Wife (Genesis 29:16–30:21; 31:4–16; 33:1–3)." *Biblica et Patristica Thoruniensia* 11.3 (2018) 347–58.

Olyan, Saul M. "Family Religion in Israel and the Wider Levant of the First Millennium BCE." In *Household and Family Religion in Antiquity*, edited by John Bodel and Saul M. Olyan, 113–26. The Ancient World: Comparative Histories. Malden, MA: Blackwell, 2008.

———. *Rites and Rank: Hierarchy in Biblical Representations of Cult*. Princeton, NJ: Princeton University Press, 2000.

Omanson, Roger L., and John E. Ellington. *A Handbook on the First and Second Books of Samuel*. Vol. 1. UBS Handbook Series. New York: United Bible Societies, 2001.

Origen. *Homilies on Genesis and Exodus*. Translated by Ronald E. Heine. Fathers of the Church 71. Washington, DC: Catholic University of America, 1982.

Osgood, S. Joy. "Women and the Inheritance of Land in Early Israel." In *Women in the Biblical Tradition*, 29–52. Studies in Women and Religion 31. Lewiston, NY: Edwin Mellen, 1992.

Oshima, Takayoshi. *Babylonian Poems of Pious Sufferers: Ludlul Bēl Nēmeqi and the Babylonian Theodicy*. Orientalische Religionen in der Antike 14. Tübingen: Mohr Siebeck, 2014.

———. "The Babylonian Theodicy: An Ancient Babylonian Discourse on Human Piety and Divine Justice." *Religion Compass* 9.12 (2015) 483–92.

———. *The Babylonian Theodicy: Introduction, Cuneiform Text and Transliteration with a Translation, Glossary and Commentary*. Publications of the Foundation for Finnish Assyriological Research 9. Helsinki: The Neo-Assyrian Text Corpus Project, 2013.

Ostriker, Alicia. "The Book of Ruth and the Love of the Land." *BibInt* 10.4 (2002) 343–58.

Ottosson, Magnus. "אָכַל 'ākhal." In *Theological Dictionary of the Old Testament*, edited by G. Johannes Botterweck and Helmer Ringgren, translated by John T. Willis, 1:236–41. Grand Rapids, MI: Eerdmans, 1974.

Otwell, John H. *And Sarah Laughed: The Status of Woman in the Old Testament*. Philadelphia: Westminster, 1977.

Pardee, Dennis. "The 'Aqhatu Legend (1.103)." In *The Context of Scripture: Canonical Compositions from the Biblical World*, edited by William W. Hallo, 1:343–56. Leiden: Brill, 1997.

———. "An Emendation in the Ugaritic Aqht Text." *Journal of Near Eastern Studies* 36.1 (1977) 53–56.

———. "Kirta Epic." In *Context of Scripture: Canonical Compositions from the Biblical World*, edited by William W. Hallo, 1:333–56. Leiden: Brill, 2003.

Pardes, Ilana. *Countertraditions in the Bible: A Feminist Approach*. Cambridge, MA: Harvard University Press, 1992.

Park, Grace J. "The Rhetorical Question in Ruth 1:17b." *Journal of Northwest Semitic Languages* 43.1 (2017) 87–103.

Park, Song-Mi Suzie. *2 Kings*. Wisdom Commentary. Collegeville, MN: Liturgical, 2019.

Parker, Julie Faith. *Valuable and Vulnerable: Children in the Hebrew Bible, Especially the Elisha Cycle*. Brown Judaic Studies 355. Providence, RI: Brown Judaic Studies, 2013.

———. "Women Warriors and Devoted Daughters: The Powerful Young Women in Ugaritic Narrative Poetry." *Ugarit-Forschungen* 38 (2006) 557–75.

———. "You Are a Bible Child: Exploring the Lives of Children and Mothers Through the Elisha Cycle." In *Women in the Biblical World: A Survey of Old and New Testament Perspectives*, edited by Elizabeth A. McCabe, 1:59–70. New York: University Press of America, 2009.

Parker, Simon B., ed. "Aqhat." In *Ugaritic Narrative Poetry*, 49–80. Writings from the Ancient World / Society of Biblical Literature 9. Atlanta: Scholars Press, 1997.

———. "Death and Devotion: The Composition and Theme of Aqht." In *Love and Death in the Ancient Near East: Essays in Honor of Marvin H. Pope*, edited by John H. Marks and Robert M. Good, 71–83. Guilford, CT: Four Quarters, 1987.

———. "The Historical Composition of KRT and the Cult of EL." *ZAW* 89.2 (1977) 161–75.

———. "Marriage Blessing in Israelite and Ugaritic Literature." *JBL* 95.1 (1976) 23–30.

———. *The Pre-Biblical Narrative Tradition: Essays on the Ugaritic Poems Keret and Aqhat*. Resources for Biblical Study 24. Atlanta: Scholars Press, 1989.

———. "Ugaritic Literature and the Bible." *Near Eastern Archaeology* 63.4 (2000) 228–31.

Parry, Donald W. "Hannah in the Presence of the Lord." In *Archaeology of the Books of Samuel: The Entangling of the Textual and Literary History*, edited by Philippe Hugo and Adrian Schenker, 53–74. Leiden: Brill, 2010.

Paseggi, Marcos. "He Who Laughs Last: Some Notes on Laughter in Isaac's Birth Story." *DavarLogos* 5.1 (2006) 61–65.

Patai, Raphael. *Family, Love and the Bible*. London: MacGibbon & Kee, 1960.

———. *Sex and Family in the Bible and the Middle East*. Garden City, NY: Doubleday, 1959.

Paul, Shalom M. "Psalm Xxvii 10 and the Babylonian Theodicy." *VT* 32.4 (1982) 489–92.

———. "A Rejoinder Concerning 1 Samuel 1:11." *JBL* 130.1 (2011) 45.

Payne, David F. "1 and 2 Samuel." In *New Bible Commentary: 21st Century Edition*, edited by G. J. Wenham et al., 296–333. Downers Grove, IL: InterVarsity, 1994.

Pehal, Martin. "Ancient Egyptian Mythological Narratives: Structural Interpretation of the Tale of Two Brothers, Tale of the Doomed Prince, the Astarte Papyrus, the Osirian Cycle, and the Anat Myth." PhD diss., Charles University in Prague, 2015.

Peled, Ilan. "Contempt and Related Emotions in Hittite and Akkadian Literary Texts." In *The Routledge Handbook of Emotions in the Ancient Near East*, edited by Karen Sonik and Ulrike Steinert, 597–613. London: Routledge, 2023.

Peleg, Yitzhak. "Why Didn't Ruth the Moabitess Raise Her Child? 'A Son Is Born to Naomi' (Ruth 4:17)." In *In the Arms of Biblical Women*, edited by John T. Greene and Mishael M. Caspi, 281–300. Biblical Intersections 13. Piscataway, NJ: Gorgias, 2013.

Perdue, Leo G. "The Household, Old Testament Theology, and Contemporary Hermeneutics." In *Families in Ancient Israel*, edited by Leo G. Perdue et al., 223–58. Louisville, KY: Westminster John Knox, 1997.

Peritz, Ismar J. "Woman in the Ancient Hebrew Cult." *JBL* 17.2 (1898) 111–48.

Petersen, John. *Reading Women's Stories: Female Characters in the Hebrew Bible*. Minneapolis: Fortress, 2004.

Peterson, Brian Neil. "Samson: Hero or Villain? The Samson Narrative in Light of David and Saul." *Bibliotheca Sacra* 174.693 (2017) 22–44.

———. "The Sin of Sodom Revisited: Reading Genesis 19 in Light of Torah." *Journal of the Evangelical Theological Society* 59.1 (2016) 17–31.

Phanon, Panthakan. "Double Ḥesed of God in Naomi's Life (Ruth 1:19–22)." *Asian Journal of Pentecostal Studies* 13.1 (2010) 20–39.

Phillips, W. Gary. *Judges, Ruth*. Holman Old Testament Commentary 5. Nashville: Broadman & Holman, 2004.

Pietersen, Leonore, and Willem Fourie. "The Bible, Culture and Ethics: Trickery in the Narrative of Judah and Tamar." *HTS Teologiese Studies/Theological Studies* 71.3 (2015) 1–8.

Pietsch, Michael. "Der Prophet als Magier: Magie und Ritual in den Elischaerzählungen." In *Zauber und Magie im Antiken Palästina und in Seiner Umwelt: Kolloquium des Deutschen Vereins zur Erforschung Palästinas vom 14. Bis 16. November 2014 in Mainz*, edited by Jens Kamlah et al., 343–80. Abhandlungen des Deutschen Palästina-Vereins 46. Wiesbaden: Harrassowitz, 2017.

Pitard, Wayne T. "The Reading of KTU 1.19:III:41: The Burial of Aqhat." *Bulletin of the American Schools of Oriental Research* 293 (1994) 31–38.

Plate, S. Brent, and Edna M. Rodríguez Mangual. "The Gift That Stops Giving: Hélène Cixous's 'Gift' and the Shunammite Woman." *BibInt* 7.2 (1999) 113–32.

Plaut, W. Gunther. *The Torah: A Modern Commentary*. Rev. ed. New York: Union for Reform Judaism, 2005.

Polhemus, Robert M. *Lot's Daughters: Sex, Redemption, and Women's Quest for Authority.* Stanford, CA: Stanford University Press, 2005.

Polzin, Robert. *Samuel and the Deuteronomist: A Literary Study of the Deuteronomic History.* Vol. 2: *1 Samuel.* Indiana Studies in Biblical Literature. Bloomington: Indiana University Press, 1993.

Pope, Marvin H. "The Cult of the Dead at Ugarit." In *Ugarit in Retrospect: Fifty Years of Ugarit and Ugaritic,* edited by Gordon D. Young, 159–79. Winona Lake, IN: Eisenbrauns, 1981.

———. *Job.* Anchor Bible 15. Garden City, NY: Doubleday, 1973.

Porten, Bezalel. *Archives from Elephantine: The Life of an Ancient Jewish Military Colony.* Berkeley: University of California Press, 1968.

Porter, J. R. "The Daughters of Lot." *Folklore* 89.2 (1978) 127–41.

Potter, Dylan David. *Angelology: Recovering Higher-Order Beings as Emblems of Transcendence, Immanence, and Imagination.* Cambridge: James Clarke, 2017.

Pressler, Carolyn. *Joshua, Judges, and Ruth.* Westminster Bible Companion. Louisville, KY: Westminster John Knox, 2002.

Preuss, H. D. "נוּחַ; מְנוּחָה." In *Theological Dictionary of the Old Testament,* edited by G. Johannes Botterweck et al., translated by David E. Green, 9:277–86. Grand Rapids, MI: Eerdmans, 1998.

Prewitt, Terry J. "Kinship Structures and the Genesis Genealogies." *Journal of Near Eastern Studies* 40.2 (1981) 87–98.

Prinsloo, W. S. "The Theology of the Book of Ruth." *VT* 30.3 (1980) 330–41.

Puhvel, Jaan. "Genus and Sexus in Hittite." In *Sex and Gender in the Ancient Near East: Proceedings of the 47th Rencontre Assyriologique Internationale, Helsinki, July 2–6, 2001,* edited by S. Parpola and R. M. Whiting, 2:547–50. Helsinki: Neo-Assyrian Text Corpus Project, 2002.

Pyeon, Yohan. *You Have Not Spoken What Is Right About Me: Intertextuality and the Book of Job.* Studies in Biblical Literature 45. New York: Peter Lang, 2003.

Rashkow, Ilona N. "Daddy-Dearest and the 'Invisible Spirit of Wine.'" In *Genesis: The Feminist Companion to the Bible,* edited by Athalya Brenner, 82–107. Second Series 1. Sheffield: Sheffield Academic, 1998.

———. "Daughters and Fathers in Genesis . . . Or, What Is Wrong with This Picture?" In *The New Literary Criticism and the Hebrew Bible,* edited by J. Cheryl Exum and David J. A. Clines, 250–65. JSOT Supplement Series 143. Sheffield: Sheffield Academic, 1993.

———. *The Phallacy of Genesis: A Feminist-Psychoanalytic Approach.* Literary Currents in Biblical Interpretation. Louisville: Westminster John Knox, 1993.

———. *Taboo or Not Taboo: Sexuality and Family in the Hebrew Bible.* Minneapolis: Fortress, 2000.

Rastoin, Marc. "Suis-Je à la Place de Dieu, Moi? Note sur Gn 30,2 et 50,19 et l'intention Théologique de la Genèse." *Revue Biblique* 114.3 (2007) 333–47.

Rauber, D. F. "The Book of Ruth." In *Literary Interpretations of Biblical Narratives,* edited by Kenneth R. R. Gros Louis et al., 163–76. Bible in Literature Courses. Nashville: Abingdon, 1974.

———. "Literary Values in the Bible: The Book of Ruth." *JBL* 89.1 (1970) 27–37.

Rebiger, Bill. "A Magic Touch: Performative Haptic Acts in Biblical and Medieval Jewish Magic." In *A Touch of Doubt: On Haptic Scepticism,* edited by Rachel Aumiller, 104–21. Studies and Texts in Scepticism 9. Berlin: De Gruyter, 2021.

Reinhartz, Adele. "Samson's Mother: An Unnamed Protagonist." *JSOT* 17.55 (1992) 25–37.

———. "Samson's Mother: An Unnamed Protagonist." In *A Feminist Companion to Judges*, edited by Athalya Brenner, 157–70. Feminist Companion to the Bible 4. Sheffield: JSOT, 1993.

———. *"Why Ask My Name?" Anonymity and Identity in Biblical Narrative*. New York: Oxford University Press, 1998.

Reiss, Moshe. "Archetypes in the Patriarchal Family." *Jewish Bible Quarterly* 28.1 (2000) 12–19.

———. "Samson: The Only Nazarite in the Hebrew Bible and His Women!" *SJOT* 28.1 (2014) 133–46.

Reiss, Moshe, and David J. Zucker. "Co-Opting the Secondary Matriarchs: Bilhah, Zilpah, Tamar, and Aseneth." *BibInt* 22.3 (2014) 307–24.

Rembold, Stefanie. "Hannah in Stages and Places: An Exploration of Narrative Space in 1 Samuel 1." *OTE (New Series)* 35.1 (2022) 68–83.

Resane, Kelebogile T. "Daughters of Zelophehad: Quest for Gender Justice in Land Acquisition and Ownership." *HTS Theological Studies* 77.2 (2021) 1–8.

Reuter, E. "שִׁפְחָה Šipḥâ." In *Theological Dictionary of the Old Testament*, edited by G. Johannes Botterweck et al., translated by David E. Green, 15:405–10. Grand Rapids, MI: Eerdmans, 2006.

Reyburn, William David. *A Handbook on the Book of Job*. New York: United Bible Societies, 1992.

Rice, Gene. "A Great Woman of Ancient Israel (2 Kings 4:8–37; 8:1–6)." *Journal of Religious Thought* 60.2 (2008) 69–85.

Richelle, Matthieu. "D'une Formule d'incantation Ougaritique à un Mystérieux Geste Prophétique Israélite." *Semitica* 59 (2017) 241–59.

Riemersma, Nico. "Elisa en de Verborgen God: 2 Koningen 4,8–37—Afbakening, Opbouw en Karakterisering." *Nico Riemersma: Kerkelijk Theoloog in Den Haag* (blog), Mar. 9, 2022. https://www.nicoriemersma.nl/blog/id/300/.

———. "Hoe Een Jong Mens Weer Tot Leven Komt: Een Close Reading van 2 Koningen 4:32–35." In *Elia and Elisa*, edited by Marieke den Braber and Willem van Wieringen, 21–34. Amsterdamse Cahiers Voor Exegese van de Bijbel en Zijn Traities 35. Amsterdam: Societas Hebraica Amstelodamensis, 2022.

Roberts, J. J. M. "Job and the Israelite Religious Tradition." *ZAW* 89.1 (1977) 107–14.

Robertson, Edward. "The Plot of the Book of Ruth." *Bulletin of the John Rylands Library* 32.2 (1950) 207–28.

Robinson, Margaret G. "Dreams in the Old Testament." PhD diss., Manchester University, 1987.

Roi, Micha. "Conditional Vows—Where They Are Made and Paid." *Biblische Notizen* 167 (2015) 3–24.

Ron, Zvi. "The Genealogical List in the Book of Ruth: A Symbolic Approach." *Jewish Bible Quarterly* 38.2 (2010) 85–92.

Roncace, Mark. "Elisha and the Woman of Shunem: 2 Kings 4.8–37 and 8.1–6 Read in Conjunction." *JSOT* 91 (2000) 109–27.

Roop, Eugene F. *Ruth, Jonah, Esther*. Believers Church Bible Commentary. Scottdale, PA: Herald, 2002.

Rooy, Herrie F. van. "Fertility as Blessing and Infertility as Curse in the Ancient Near East and the Old Testament." In *Archaeology and Fertility Cult in the*

Ancient Mediterranean: Papers Presented at the First International Conference on Archaeology of the Ancient Mediterranean, the University of Malta, 2–5 September 1985, edited by Anthony Bonanno, 225–36. Amsterdam: B. R. Grüner, 1986.

Rosenbaum, M., and A. M. Silbermann. *Pentateuch with Targum Onkelos, Haphtaroth and Rashi's Commentary*. Vol. 1: *Genesis*. London: Shapiro Vallentine, 1945.

Rosenberg, Gil. *Ancestral Queerness: The Normal and the Deviant in the Abraham and Sarah Narratives*. Hebrew Bible Monographs 80. Sheffield: Sheffield Phoenix, 2019.

———. "כעת חיה: An Allusion Connecting Genesis 18:10, 14 and 2 Kings 4:16–17." *JBL* 139.4 (2020) 701–20.

Rosenblatt, Naomi H., and Joshua Horwitz. *Wrestling with Angels: What Genesis Teaches Us About Our Spiritual Identity, Sexuality, and Personal Relations*. New York: Dell, 1996.

Roskoski, John. "Isaac and Samson: Sons of the Promises." *Journal of Biblical Theology* 2.4 (2019) 198–215.

———. "The Recurring Theme of 'Beginning' in the Samson Narratives." *Journal of Biblical Theology* 5.3 (2022) 38–54.

Ross, Allen P. *Creation and Blessing: A Guide to the Study and Exposition of the Book of Genesis*. Grand Rapids, MI: Baker, 1988.

Ross, Jillian L. "Type-Casting the Samson Family: Genesis Parodies in Judges 13–14." *Journal of the Evangelical Theological Society* 64.2 (2021) 237–52.

Ross-Burstall, Joan. "Leah and Rachel: A Tale of Two Sisters." *Word and World* 14.2 (1994) 162–70.

Roth, Martha Tobi. *Babylonian Marriage Agreements: 7th–3rd Centuries BC*. Alter Orient und Altes Testament 222. Kevelaer, Germany: Butzon & Bercker, 1989.

———. "Women and Law." In *Women in the Ancient Near East: A Sourcebook*, edited by Mark W. Chavalas, 144–74. Routledge Sourcebooks for the Ancient World. New York: Routledge, 2014.

Rowe, Ignacio Márquez. "The King's Men in Ugarit and Society in Late Bronze Age Syria." *Journal of the Economic and Social History of the Orient* 45.1 (2002) 1–19.

———. *The Royal Deeds of Ugarit: A Study of Ancient Near Eastern Diplomatics*. Alter Orient und Altes Testament 335. Münster: Ugarit-Verlag, 2006.

Rozmarin, Miri. "Staying Alive: Matricide and the Ethical-Political Aspect of Mother-Daughter Relations." *Studies in Gender and Sexuality* 17.4 (2016) 242–53.

Rummel, Stan. "Narrative Structures in the Ugaritic Texts." In *Ras Shamra Parallels: The Texts from Ugarit and the Hebrew Bible*, edited by Stan Rummel, 3:221–332. Rome: Pontificium Institutum Biblicum, 1981.

Russaw, Kimberly D. *Daughters in the Hebrew Bible*. Lanham, MD: Lexington, 2018.

Rzepka, Barbara. "Nazireo Dal Grembo Materno: La Finalità e i Tratti Particolari Del Racconto in Gdc 13 Alla Luce Dell'analisi Narrativa." *Biblical Annals* 5.2 (2015) 351–74.

Sabo, Peter J. "Blurred Boundaries in the Lot Story." In *History, Memory, Hebrew Scriptures: A Festschrift for Ehud Ben Zvi*, edited by Ian Douglas Wilson and Diana Edelman, 433–44. Winona Lake, IN: Eisenbrauns, 2015.

———. "Moabite Women, Transjordanian Women, and Incest and Exogamy: The Gendered Dimensions of Boundaries in the Hebrew Bible." *JSOT* 45.1 (2020) 93–110.

Sailhamer, John H. "Genesis." In *Genesis–Leviticus*, 21–332. The Expositor's Bible Commentary 1. Grand Rapids, MI: Zondervan, 2008.

———. *The Pentateuch as Narrative: A Biblical-Theological Commentary*. Grand Rapids, MI: Zondervan, 1992.

Sakenfeld, Katharine Doob. "At the Threshing Floor: Sex, Reader Response, and a Hermeneutic of Survival." *OTE (New Series)* 15.1 (2002) 164–78.

———. "Feminist Biblical Interpretation." *Theology Today* 46.2 (1989) 154–68.

———. *Just Wives? Stories of Power and Survival in the Old Testament and Today*. Louisville, KY: Westminster John Knox, 2003.

———. *Ruth*. Interpretation: A Bible Commentary for Teaching and Preaching. Louisville, KY: John Knox, 1999.

———. "Zelophehad's Daughters." *Perspectives in Religious Studies* 15.4 (1988) 37–47.

Saliba, George A. "A Cure for King Keret (IIK, Col. vi, 1–13)." *Journal of the American Oriental Society* 92.1 (1972) 107–10.

Salzer, Dorothea M. *Die Magie der Anspielung: Form und Funktion der Biblischen Anspielungen in den Magischen Texten der Kairoer Geniza*. Texte und Studien zum Antiken Judentum 134. Tübingen: Mohr Siebeck, 2010.

Sánchez, Leopoldo A. "The Church Is the House of Abraham: Reflections on Martin Luther's Teaching on Hospitality Toward Exiles." *Concordia Journal* 44.1 (2018) 23–39.

Sarna, Nahum M. *Genesis* = בראשית: *The Traditional Hebrew Text with New JPS Translation*. JPS Torah Commentary. Philadelphia: Jewish Publication Society, 1989.

Sasson, Jack M. "Comparative Observations on the Near Eastern Epic Traditions." In *A Companion to Ancient Epic*, edited by John Miles Foley, 215–32. Blackwell Companions to the Ancient World. Malden, MA: Blackwell, 2005.

———. "Genealogical 'Convention' in Biblical Chronography." *ZAW* 90.2 (1978) 171–85.

———. "Generation, Seventh." In *Interpreter's Dictionary of the Bible*, edited by Keith Crim, Supplementary:354–56. Nashville: Abingdon, 1976.

———. "The Issue of Ge'ullah in Ruth." *JSOT* 3.5 (1978) 52–64.

———. "Literary Criticism, Folklore Scholarship, and Ugaritic Literature." In *Ugarit in Retrospect: Fifty Years of Ugarit and Ugaritic*, edited by Gordon D. Young, 81–98. Winona Lake, IN: Eisenbrauns, 1981.

———. "The Numeric Progression in Keret I: 15–20. Yet Another Suggestion." *Studi Epigrafici e Linguistici Sul Vicino Oriente Antico* 5 (1988) 181–88.

———. *Ruth: A New Translation with a Philological Commentary and a Formalist-Folklorist Interpretation*. Johns Hopkins Near Eastern Studies. Baltimore, MD: Johns Hopkins University, 1979.

Savran, George W. *Encountering the Divine: Theophany in Biblical Narrative*. JSOT Supplement Series 420. New York: T&T Clark, 2005.

———. *Telling and Retelling: Quotation in Biblical Narrative*. Indiana Studies in Biblical Literature. Bloomington: Indiana University Press, 1988.

———. "The Time of Her Life: Ruth and Naomi." *Nashim* 30 (2016) 7–23.

Saxegaard, Kristin Moen. *Character Complexity in the Book of Ruth*. Forschungen zum Alten Testament 47. Tübingen: Mohr Siebeck, 2010.

———. "'More Than Seven Sons': Ruth as Example of the Good Son." *SJOT* 15.2 (2001) 257–75.

Scharbert, Josef, and Georg Hentschel. *Rut, 1 Samuel*. Neue Echter Bibel Altes Testament. Würzburg: Echter Verlag, 1994.

Schipper, Jeremy. "Healing and Silence in the Epilogue of Job." *Word and World* 30.1 (2010) 16–22.

———. *Ruth: A New Translation with Introduction and Commentary*. Anchor Bible 7D. New Haven, CT: Yale University Press, 2016.

———. "Translating the Preposition 'm in the Book of Ruth." *VT* 63.4 (2013) 663–69.

Schloen, J. David. *The House of the Father as Fact and Symbol: Patrimonialism in Ugarit and the Ancient Near East*. Studies in the Archaeology and History of the Levant 2. Winona Lake, IN: Eisenbrauns, 2001.

Schneider, Tammi J. *Mothers of Promise: Women in the Book of Genesis*. Grand Rapids, MI: Baker Academic, 2008.

Scholz, Susanne. *Sacred Witness: Rape in the Hebrew Bible*. Minneapolis: Fortress, 2010.

Schreiner, David B. "'But He Could Not Warm Himself': Sexual Innuendo and the Place of 1 Kgs 1,1–4." *SJOT* 32.1 (2018) 121–30.

Schroer, Silvia. "Gender und Ikonographie: Aus der Sicht Einer Feministischen Bibelwissenschaftlerin." In *Images and Gender: Contributions to the Hermeneutics of Reading Ancient Art*, edited by Silvia Schroer, 107–24. Orbis Biblicus et Orientalis 220. Göttingen: Vandenhoeck & Ruprecht, 2006.

Schwartz, G. David. "God and the Stranger." *Horizons in Biblical Theology* 20.1 (1998) 33–48.

Seeman, Don. "'Where Is Sarah Your Wife?' Cultural Poetics of Gender and Nationhood in the Hebrew Bible." *Harvard Theological Review* 91.2 (1998) 103–25.

Seifert, Elke. *Tochter und Vater im Alten Testament: Eine Ideologiekritische Untersuchung zur Verfügungsgewalt von Vätern über Ihre Töchter*. Neukirchener Theologische Dissertationen und Habilitationen 9. Neukirchen-Vluyn: Neukirchener, 1997.

Selms, A. van. *Marriage and Family Life in Ugaritic Literature*. Pretoria Oriental Series 1. London: Suzac and Company, 1954.

Seow, C. L. *Job 1–21: Interpretation and Commentary*. Illuminations. Grand Rapids, MI: Eerdmans, 2013.

Shafer-Elliott, Cynthia. "All in the Family: Ancient Israelite and Judahite Families in Context." In *Mishpachah: The Jewish Family in Tradition and in Transition*, edited by Leonard J. Greenspoon, 33–43. Studies in Jewish Civilization 27. West Lafayette, IN: Purdue University Press, 2016.

Sharon, Diane M. "Some Results of a Structural Semiotic Analysis of the Story of Judah and Tamar." *JSOT* 29.3 (2005) 289–318.

Sharp, Carolyn J. "Is This Naomi? A Feminist Reading of the Ambiguity of Naomi in the Book of Ruth." In *Feminist Frameworks and the Bible: Power, Ambiguity, and Intersectionality*, edited by L. Juliana Claassens and Carolyn J. Sharp, 149–62. Library of Hebrew Bible/Old Testament Studies 630. New York: Bloomsbury T&T Clark, 2017.

Shemesh, Yael. "A Gender Perspective on the Daughters of Zelophehad: Bible, Talmudic Midrash, and Modern Feminist Midrash." *BibInt* 15.1 (2007) 80–109.

Shields, Mary E. "'More Righteous Than I': The Comeuppance of the Trickster in Genesis 38." In *Are We Amused? Humour About Women in the Biblical Worlds*, edited by Athalya Brenner, 31–51. JSOT Supplement Series 383. New York: T&T Clark, 2003.

———. "Subverting a Man of God, Elevating a Woman: Role and Power Reversals in 2 Kings 4." *JSOT* 18.58 (1993) 59–69.
Shkop, Esther M. "And Sarah Laughed . . ." *Tradition* 31.3 (1997) 42–51.
Siegelová, Jana. *Appu-Märchen Und Ḫedammu-Mythus*. Studien zu den Boğazköy-Texten 14. Wiesbaden: Otto Harrassowitz, 1971.
Silber, David. "Kingship, Samuel and the Story of Hanna." *Tradition* 23.2 (1988) 64–75.
Simon, Uriel. *Reading Prophetic Narratives*. Translated by Lenn J. Schramm. Indiana Studies in Biblical Literature. Bloomington: Indiana University Press, 1997.
Singer, Itamar. "The Hittites and the Bible Revisited." In *"I Will Speak the Riddles of Ancient Times": Archaeological and Historical Studies in Honor of Amihai Mazar on the Occasion of His Sixtieth Birthday*, edited by Aren M. Maeir and Pierre de Miroschedji, 2:723–56. Winona Lake, IN: Eisenbrauns, 2006.
———. "Some Thoughts on Translated and Original Hittite Literature." In *Language and Culture in the Near East*, edited by Shlomo Izre'el and Rina Drory, 123–28. Israel Oriental Studies 15. Leiden: Brill, 1995.
Sipilä, Seppo. "On Portions, Nostrils, and Anger—A Crux Interpretum in 1 Samuel 1.5." *BT* 64.1 (2013) 75–81.
Siquans, Agnethe. "Foreignness and Poverty in the Book of Ruth: A Legal Way for a Poor Foreign Woman to Be Integrated into Israel." *JBL* 128.3 (2009) 443–52.
Ska, Jean Louis. "L'arbre et la Tente: La Fonction du Décor en Gn 18,1–15." *Biblica* 68 (1987) 383–89.
———. "L'Ironie de Tamar (Gen 38)." *ZAW* 100.2 (1988) 261–63.
Skinner, John. *A Critical and Exegetical Commentary on Genesis*. 2nd ed. International Critical Commentary 1. Edinburgh: T&T Clark, 1994.
Slager, Donald. "Where Is the Wealthy Lady of Shunem in 2 Kings 4.11–17?" *BT* 59.4 (2008) 198–201.
Slotki, Judah J., trans. *Midrash Rabbah: Numbers*. Midrash Rabbah 5. New York: Soncino, 1983.
Smit, Laura A., and Stephen E. Fowl. *Judges and Ruth*. Brazos Theological Commentary on the Bible. Grand Rapids, MI: Brazos, 2018.
Smith, Carol. "Challenged by the Text: Interpreting Two Stories of Incest in the Hebrew Bible." In *A Feminist Companion to Reading the Bible: Approaches, Methods and Strategies*, edited by Athalya Brenner and Carole Fontaine, 114–35. Sheffield: Sheffield Academic, 1997.
Smith, Henry Preserved. *A Critical and Exegetical Commentary on the Books of Samuel*. Reprint. International Critical Commentary 9. Edinburgh: T&T Clark, 1977.
Smith, Mark S. "The Three Bodies of God in the Hebrew Bible." *JBL* 134.3 (2015) 471–88.
———. "'Your People Shall Be My People': Family and Covenant in Ruth 1:16–17." *Catholic Biblical Quarterly* 69.2 (2007) 242–58.
Smith, Michael J. "The Failure of the Family in Judges, Part 2: Samson." *Bibliotheca Sacra* 162.648 (2005) 424–36.
Snaith, N. H. "Daughters of Zelophehad." *VT* 16.1 (1966) 124–27.
Snyman, Gerrie F. "Readers' Disgust in the Case of Rebekah, Jacob, Isaac, and Esau: Perverters of Justice." *OTE* 33.3 (2020) 445–72.
Soggin, J. Alberto. *Judges: A Commentary*. Old Testament Library. Philadelphia: Westminster, 1981.

Sommer, Benjamin D. *The Bodies of God and the World of Ancient Israel*. Cambridge: Cambridge University Press, 2009.

Southwood, Katherine E. "Will Naomi's Nation Be Ruth's Nation? Ethnic Translation as a Metaphor for Ruth's Assimilation Within Judah." *Humanities* 3.2 (2014) 102–31.

Spalinger, Anthony. "Transformations in Egyptian Folktales: The Royal Influence." *Revue d'Égyptologie* 58 (2007) 137–56.

Speiser, E. A. "Etana." In *ANET* 114–18.

———. *Genesis*. 3rd ed. Anchor Bible 1. Garden City, NY: Doubleday, 1983.

Spero, Shubert. "Jacob and Esau: The Relationship Reconsidered." *Jewish Bible Quarterly* 32.4 (2004) 245–50.

Spiegel, Shalom. "Noah, Danel, and Job: Touching on Canaanite Relics in the Legends of the Jews." In *Louis Ginzberg: Jubilee Volume on the Occasion of His Seventieth Birthday*, 305–56. New York: The American Academy for Jewish Research, 1945.

Spina, Frank Anthony. "Eli's Seat: The Transition from Priest to Prophet in 1 Samuel 1–4." *JSOT* 19.62 (1994) 67–75.

Spoelstra, Joshua Joel. "Queens, Widows, and Mesdames: The Role of Women in the Elijah-Elisha Narrative." *Journal for the Evangelical Study of the Old Testament* 3.2 (2014) 171–84.

Spronk, Klaas. "The Book of Judges as a Late Construct." In *Historiography and Identity (Re)Formulation in Second Temple Historiographical Literature*, edited by Louis Jonker, 15–28. Library of Hebrew Bible/Old Testament Studies 534. New York: T&T Clark, 2010.

Stager, Lawrence E. "The Archaeology of the Family in Ancient Israel." *Bulletin of the American Schools of Oriental Research* 260 (1985) 1–35.

Stahlberg, Lesleigh Cushing. "Sex and the Singular Girl: Dinah, Tamar, and the Corrective Art of Biblical Narrative." *Biblical Theology Bulletin* 47.4 (2017) 195–204.

Stanislav, Segert. "Vorarbeiten zur Hebräischen Metrik, III: Zum Problem der Metrischen Elemente im Buche Ruth." *Archiv Orientální* 25 (1957) 190–200.

Staples, W. E. "The Book of Ruth." *The American Journal of Semitic Languages and Literatures* 53.3 (1937) 145–57.

Starr-Morris, Ashley. "Leah and Hagar: An Intergenerational Conversation of Belonging." *Cross Currents* 69.4 (2019) 384–401.

Stein, David E. S. "Cognitive Factors as a Key to Plain-Sense Biblical Interpretation: Resolving Cruxes in Gen 18:1–15 and 32:23–33." *Open Theology* 4 (2018) 545–89.

Steinberg, Naomi A. "1 Samuel 1, the United Nations Convention on the Rights of Children, and 'The Best Interests of the Child.'" *Journal of Childhood and Religion* 1.3 (2010) 1–23.

———. "Alliance or Descent? The Function of Marriage in Genesis." *JSOT* 16.51 (1991) 45–55.

———. "Gender Roles in the Rebekah Cycle." *Union Seminary Quarterly Review* 39.3 (1984) 175–88.

———. "Kinship and Gender in Genesis." *Biblical Research* 39 (1994) 46–56.

———. *Kinship and Marriage in Genesis: A Household Economics Perspective*. Minneapolis: Fortress, 1993.

———. "Zilpah: Bible." In *The Shalvi/Hyman Encyclopedia of Jewish Women*. Jewish Women's Archive, Dec. 13, 1999. https://jwa.org/encyclopedia/article/zilpah-bible.

Steinmann, Andrew. *1 Samuel*. Concordia Commentary. St. Louis, MO: Concordia, 2016.
Stemberger, Günter. *Die Patriarchenbilder der Katakombe in der Via Latina im Lichte der Jüdischen Tradition*. Kairos 16. Freilassing: Otto Müller, 1974.
Sternberg, Meir. *The Poetics of Biblical Narrative: Ideological Literature and the Drama of Reading*. Indiana Literary Biblical Series. Bloomington: Indiana University Press, 1985.
Stetkevych, Suzanne Pinckney. "Sarah and the Hyena: Laughter, Menstruation, and the Genesis of a Double Entendre." *History of Religions* 36.1 (1996) 13–41.
Stewart, H. F. *Book of Judges*. 2nd ed. London: Rivingtons, 1913.
Stiebert, Johanna. *Fathers and Daughters in the Hebrew Bible*. Oxford: Oxford University Press, 2013.
Stinespring, W. F. "No Daughter of Zion: A Study of the Appositional Genitive in Hebrew Grammar." *Encounter* 26.2 (1965) 133–41.
Stol, Marten. "Birth: Ancient Near East and Hebrew Bible/Old Testament." In *Encyclopedia of the Bible and Its Reception*, edited by Hans-Josef Klauck et al., 4:1–6. Boston: De Gruyter, 2011.
———. *Birth in Babylonia and the Bible: Its Mediterranean Setting*. Cuneiform Monographs 14. Groningen: Styx, 2000.
———. "Embryology in Babylonia and the Bible." In *Imagining the Fetus: The Unborn in Myth, Religion, and Culture*, edited by Vanessa R. Sasson and Jane Marie Law, 137–55. American Academy of Religion Cultural Criticism Series. New York: Oxford University Press, 2009.
———. *Women in the Ancient Near East*. Translated by Helen Richardson and Mervyn Richardson. Berlin: De Gruyter, 2016.
Stone, Alison. "Stealing Lot's Wife and Daughters from the Bible: A Response to Rozmarin's 'Staying Alive.'" *Studies in Gender and Sexuality* 17.4 (2016) 254–61.
Stone, Ken. "Marriage and Sexual Relations in the World of the Hebrew Bible." In *The Oxford Handbook of Theology, Sexuality, and Gender*, edited by Adrian Thatcher, 173–88. Oxford: Oxford University Press, 2014.
Stone, Timothy J. "Six Measures of Barley: Seed Symbolism in Ruth." *JSOT* 38.2 (2013) 189–99.
Streck, Michael P. "Notes on the Old Babylonian Epics of Anzu and Etana." *Journal of the American Oriental Society* 129.3 (2009) 477–86.
Sulyok, Gábor. "Breach of Treaties in the Ancient Near East." *Journal of the History of International Law* 20.1 (2018) 31–56.
Sun, Chloe. *The Ethics of Violence in the Story of Aqhat*. Gorgias Ugaritic Studies. Piscataway, NJ: Gorgias, 2008.
Sutskover, Talia. "Lot and His Daughters (Gen 19:30–38): Further Literary and Stylistic Examinations." *JHS* 11 (2011) 2–11.
———. "The Themes of Land and Fertility in the Book of Ruth." *JSOT* 34.3 (2010) 283–94.
Sweeney, Marvin A. "The Jacob Narratives: An Ephraimitic Text?" *Catholic Biblical Quarterly* 78.2 (2016) 236–55.
Tatko, Victoria. "Vowing Mothers and Avowed Sons: Hannah's Annunciation Type-Scene (1 Sam. 1–2:10) As Interpretive Lens for Proverbs 31:1–9." *Presbyterion* 48.1 (2022) 132–50.

Thomas, Christine Neal. "Reconceiving the House of the Father: Royal Women at Ugarit." PhD diss., Harvard University, 2014.
Thompson, Thomas, and Dorothy Thompson. "Some Legal Problems in the Book of Ruth." *VT* 18.1 (1968) 79–99.
Thunberg, Lars. "Early Christian Interpretation of the Three Angels in Gen 18." In *Studia Patristica Vol. VII: Papers Presented to the Fourth International Conference on Patristic Studies Held at Christ Church Oxford, 1963*, edited by F. L. Cross, 560–70. Texte und Untersuchungen zur Geschichte der Altchristlichen Literatur 91. Berlin: Akademie-Verlag, 1966.
Tigay, Jeffrey H. *Deuteronomy*. Vol. 2. Mikra le-Yisraʼel. Jerusalem: Magnes, 2016.
———. "לא נם לחה 'He Had Not Become Wrinkled' (Deuteronomy 34:7)." In *Solving Riddles and Untying Knots: Biblical, Epigraphic, and Semitic Studies in Honor of Jonas C. Greenfield*, edited by Ziony Zevit et al., 345–50. Winona Lake, IN: Eisenbrauns, 1995.
Tonson, Paul. "Mercy Without Covenant: A Literary Analysis of Genesis 19." *JSOT* 26.1 (2001) 95–116.
Trebolle, Julio. "Textual Criticism and the Composition History of Samuel: Connections Between Pericopes in 1 Samuel 1–4." In *Archaeology of the Books of Samuel: The Entangling of the Textual and Literary History*, edited by Philippe Hugo and Adrian Schenker, 261–86. Leiden: Brill, 2010.
Trible, Phyllis. *God and the Rhetoric of Sexuality*. Overtures to Biblical Theology 2. Philadelphia: Fortress, 1978.
———. *Texts of Terror: Literary-Feminist Readings of Biblical Narratives*. Overtures to Biblical Theology 13. Philadelphia: Fortress, 1984.
———. "Two Women in a Man's World: A Reading of the Book of Ruth." *Soundings: An Interdisciplinary Journal* 59.3 (1976) 251–79.
Tropper, Josef. "Elischa und die 'Grosse' Frau aus Schunem (2 Kön 4,8–37)." In *Kleine Untersuchungen zur Sprache des Alten Testaments und Seiner Umwelt*, edited by Reinhard G. Lehmann, 3:71–80. Kamen, Germany: Harmut Spenner, 2002.
———. "Die Sieben Frauen des Königs Keret." *Ugarit-Forschungen* 27 (1995) 529–32.
Tsevat, Matitiahu. "The Canaanite God Šälaḥ." *VT* 4.1 (1954) 41–49.
Tsoffar, Ruth. "The Trauma of Otherness and Hunger: Ruth and Lot's Daughters." *Women in Judaism* 5.1 (2007) 1–13.
Tsumura, David Toshio. *The First Book of Samuel*. New International Commentary on the Old Testament. Grand Rapids, MI: Eerdmans, 2007.
Tsumura, David Toshio, and Prince Takahito Mikasa. "The Problem of Childlessness in the Royal Epic of Ugarit." In *Monarchies and Socio-Religious Traditions in the Ancient Near East: Papers Read at the 31st International Congress of Human Sciences in Asia and North Africa*, 11–20. Bulletin of the Middle Eastern Culture Center in Japan 1. Wiesbaden: Harrassowitz, 1984.
Tsymbalyuk, Oleg M., and Valery V. Melnik. "Rediscovering the Ancient Hermeneutic of Rebekah's Character." *HTS Theological Studies* 76.1 (2020) 1–8.
Turner, Laurence A. "Disappointed Expectations: A Narrative-Critical Reading of the Jacob Story." *Scripture Bulletin* 36.2 (2006) 54–63.
———. "Lot as Jekyll and Hyde: A Reading of Genesis 18–19." In *The Bible in Three Dimensions: Essays in Celebration of Forty Years of Biblical Studies in the University of Sheffield*, edited by David J. A. Clines et al., 85–101. JSOT Supplement Series 87. Sheffield: JSOT, 1990.

Turner, Mary Donovan. "Rebekah: Ancestor of Faith." *Lexington Theological Quarterly* 20.2 (1985) 42–50.

Uehlinger, Christoph. "Das Hiob-Buch im Kontext der Altorientalischen Literatur- Und Religionsgeschichte." In *Das Buch Hiob und seine Interpretationen: Beiträge zum Hiob-Symposium auf dem Monte Verità vom 14.–19. August 2005*, edited by Thomas Krüger et al., 97–163. ATANT 88. Zürich: Theologischer Verlag Zürich, 2007.

Ulrich, Dean R. "The Framing Function of the Narratives About Zelophehad's Daughters." *Journal of the Evangelical Theological Society* 41.4 (1998) 529–38.

Valk, Jonathan. "The Eagle and the Snake, or Anzû and Bašmu? Another Mythological Dimension in the Epic of Etana." *Journal of the American Oriental Society* 140.4 (2020) 889–900.

van Aarde, Tim. "The Semantic Relationship Between יְרֻשָּׁה and נַחֲלָה in Jeremiah 32 and Ruth 4." *Journal for Semitics* 24.2 (2015) 613–37.

van der Horst, Pieter W. "Aan Abrahams Dis: Joodse Interpretaties van Genesis 18:8." *Nederlands Theologisch Tijdschrift* 59.3 (2005) 207–14.

van der Toorn, Karel. *Family Religion in Babylonia, Syria, and Israel: Continuity and Change in the Forms of Religious Life*. Studies in the History and Culture of the Ancient Near East 7. Leiden: Brill, 1996.

———. "Family Religion in Second Millennium West Asia (Mesopotamia, Emar, Nuzi)." In *Household and Family Religion in Antiquity*, edited by John Bodel and Saul M. Olyan, 20–36. The Ancient World: Comparative Histories. Malden, MA: Blackwell, 2008.

———. *From Her Cradle to Her Grave: The Role of Religion in the Life of the Israelite and the Babylonian Woman*. Translated by Sara J. Denning-Bolle. Sheffield: JSOT, 1994.

———. "Torn Between Vice and Virtue: Stereotypes of the Widow in Israel and Mesopotamia." In *Female Stereotypes in Religious Traditions*, edited by Ria Kloppenborg and Wouter J. Hanegraaff, 1–13. Studies in the History of Religions 66. Leiden: Brill, 1995.

van Dijk-Hemmes, Fokkelien. "The Great Woman of Shunem and the Man of God: A Dual Interpretation of 2 Kings 4.8–37." In *A Feminist Companion to Samuel and Kings*, edited by Athalya Brenner, 218–30. Feminist Companion to the Bible 5. Sheffield: Sheffield Academic, 1994.

———. "Ruth: A Product of Women's Culture?" In *A Feminist Companion to Ruth*, edited by Athalya Brenner, 134–39. Feminist Companion to the Bible 3. Sheffield: Sheffield Academic, 1993.

Vandop, Steve. "Job, Naomi and Ruth." *Working Through the Word* (blog), Nov. 25, 2015. https://steveworkingthroughtheword.com/2015/11/25/job-naomi-and-ruth/.

Van Seters, John. "Problem of Childlessness in Near Eastern Law and the Patriarchs of Israel." *JBL* 87.4 (1968) 401–8.

Van Wijk-Bos, Johanna W. H. "Out of the Shadows: Genesis 38; Judges 4:17–22; Ruth 3." *Semeia* 42: "Reasoning with the Foxes: Female Wit in a World of Male Power" (1988) 37–67.

van Wolde, Ellen. *Aan de Hand van Ruth*. Kamen: Kok, 1993.

———. "Intertextuality: Ruth in Dialogue with Tamar." In *A Feminist Companion to Reading the Bible: Approaches, Methods and Strategies*, edited by Athalya Brenner and Carole Fontaine, 426–51. Sheffield: Sheffield Academic, 1997.

———. *Ruth and Naomi*. Macon, GA: Smyth & Helwys, 1997.
———. "Texts in Dialogue with Texts: Intertextuality in the Ruth and Tamar Narratives." *BibInt* 5 (1997) 1–28.
van Zyl, Danie C. "Hannah's Share, Once More 1 Samuel 1:5." *OTE (New Series)* 6.3 (1993) 364–66.
Vayntrub, Jacqueline. "Transmission and Mortal Anxiety in the Tale of Aqhat." In *Like ' Ilu Are You Wise: Studies in Northwest Semitic Languages and Literatures in Honor of Dennis G. Pardee*, edited by H. H. Hardy II et al., 73–90. Studies in Ancient Oriental Civilization 73. Chicago: Oriental Institute of the University of Chicago, 2017.
Verburg, Jelle. "Women's Property Rights in Egypt and the Law of Levirate Marriage in the LXX." *ZAW* 131.4 (2019) 592–606.
Verderame, Lorenzo. *Letterature Dell'antica Mesopotamia*. Milan: Mondadori, 2016.
Verreet, Eddy. "Der Keret-Prolog." *Ugarit-Forschungen* 19 (1987) 317–35.
Vigo, Matteo. "Sources for the Study of the Role of Women in the Hittite Administration." In *The Role of Women in Work and Society in the Ancient Near East*, edited by Brigitte Lion and Cécile Michel, 328–53. Studies in Ancient Near Eastern Records 13. Berlin: De Gruyter, 2016.
Virolleaud, Charles. *La Légende Phénicienne de Danel; Texte Cunéiforme Alphabétique avec Transcription et Commentaire, Précédé d'une Introduction à l'étude de la Civilisation d'Ugarit*. Bibliothèque Archéologique et Historique 21. Paris: Geuthner, 1936.
———. "Le Mariage du Roi Kéret (III K). Poème de Ras-Shamra." *Syria* 23.3/4 (43 1942) 137–72.
———. "Le Roi Kêret et Son Fils (II K). Poème de Ras Shamra." *Syria* 22.2 (1941) 105–36.
Vita, Juan-Pablo. "The Society of Ugarit." In *Handbook of Ugaritic Studies*, edited by Wilfred G. E. Watson and Nicolas Wyatt, 455–98. Handbuch der Orientalistik. Erste Abteilung, Nahe und der Mittlere Osten 39. Leiden: Brill, 1999.
Volgger, David. "Tamar, Rut und Dtn 25,5–10: Drei Biblische Wendepunkte." *Antonianum* 84.2 (2009) 235–50.
von Rad, Gerhard. *Genesis: A Commentary*. Philadelphia: Westminster, 1972.
Vos, Clarence J. *Woman in Old Testament Worship*. Delft, Netherlands: Judels & Brinkman, 1968.
Wagner, S. "דָּרַשׁ Dārash; מִדְרָשׁ Midhrāsh." In *Theological Dictionary of the Old Testament*, edited by G. Johannes Botterweck and Helmer Ringgren, translated by John T. Willis and Geoffrey W. Bromiley, 3:293–307. Grand Rapids, MI: Eerdmans, 1978.
Walcot, Peter. "Hesiod and the Didactic Literature of the Near East." *Revue des Études Grecques* 75.354/355 (1962) 13–36.
Walls, Neal H. *The Goddess Anat in Ugaritic Myth*. Dissertation Series (Society of Biblical Literature) 135. Atlanta: Scholars Press, 1992.
Walpole, G. H. S. *Handbook to Judges and Ruth: For the Use of Teachers and Students*. London: Rivingtons, 1901.
Walsh, Jerome T. *Old Testament Narrative: A Guide to Interpretation*. Louisville, KY: Westminster John Knox, 2009.
Walters, Stanley D. "Hannah and Anna: The Greek and Hebrew Texts of 1 Samuel 1." *JBL* 107.3 (1988) 385–412.

Walton, John H. *Ancient Israelite Literature in Its Cultural Context: A Survey of Parallels Between Biblical and Ancient Near Eastern Texts*. 2nd ed. Library of Biblical Interpretation. Grand Rapids, MI: Zondervan, 1990.

Warner, Megan. "Finding Lot's Daughters." *JHS* 19 (2019) 49–58.

Wassén, Cecilia. "The Story of Judah and Tamar in the Eyes of the Earliest Interpreters." *Literature and Theology* 8.4 (1994) 354–66.

Waters, Sonia E. "Reading Sodom Through Sexual Violence Against Women." *Interpretation* 71.3 (2017) 274–83.

Watson, Wilfred G. E. "Puzzling Passages in the Tale of Aqhat." *Ugarit-Forschungen* 8 (1976) 371–78.

Webb, Barry G. *The Book of Judges*. New International Commentary on the Old Testament. Grand Rapids, MI: Eerdmans, 2012.

Weiershäuser, Frauke. "Narrating About Men, Narrating About Women in Akkadian Literature." In *Gender and Methodology in the Ancient Near East: Approaches from Assyriology and Beyond*, edited by Stephanie Lynn Budin et al., 273–86. Barcino Monographica Orientalia 10. Barcelona: Universitat de Barcelona Edicions, 2019.

Weimar, Peter. "'Und Er Nannte Seinen Namen Perez' (Gen 38,29:) Erwägungen zu Komposition und Literarischer Gestalt von Gen 38 Teil 1." *Biblische Zeitschrift* 51.2 (2007) 193–215.

Weinfeld, Moshe. "Job and Its Mesopotamian Parallels: A Typological Analysis." In *Text and Context: Old Testament and Semitic Studies for F. C. Fensham*, edited by W. Claassen, 217–26. JSOT Supplement Series 48. Sheffield: JSOT, 1988.

Weingreen, Jacob. "Case of the Daughters of Zelophehad." *VT* 16.4 (1966) 518–22.

Weisberg, Dvora E. "The Widow of Our Discontent: Levirate Marriage in the Bible and Ancient Israel." *JSOT* 28.4 (2004) 403–29.

Wenham, Gordon J. *Genesis 16–50*. Word Biblical Commentary 2. Grand Rapids, MI: Zondervan, 2015.

Wénin, André. "La Ruse de Tamar (Gn 38): Une Approche Narrative." *Science et Esprit* 51.3 (1999) 265–83.

———. "Les 'sacrifices' d'Abraham et d'Anne: Regards Croisés Sur l'offrande du Fils." *Études Théologiques et Religieuses* 76.4 (2001) 513–27.

Wente, Edward F., Jr. "The Tale of the Doomed Prince." In *The Literature of Ancient Egypt: An Anthology of Stories, Instructions, Stelae, Autobiographies, and Poetry*, edited by William Kelly Simpson, 3rd ed., 75–79. New Haven, CT: Yale University Press, 2003.

Werline, Rodney A. "Prayer, Politics, and Power in the Hebrew Bible." *Interpretation* 68.1 (2014) 5–16.

West, Gerald O., et al. "From Homosexuality to Hospitality; From Exclusion to Inclusion; From Genesis 19 to Genesis 18." *Journal of Theology for Southern Africa* 168 (2021) 5–23.

Westbrook, Raymond. *Old Babylonian Marriage Law*. Archiv für Orientforschung 23. Horn, Austria: F. Berger, 1988.

———. *Property and the Family in Biblical Law*. JSOT Supplement Series 113. Sheffield: JSOT, 1991.

Westenholz, Joan Goodnick. "Tamar, Qĕdēšā, Qadištu, and Sacred Prostitution in Mesopotamia." *Harvard Theological Review* 82.3 (1989) 245–65.

Westermann, Claus. *Genesis 12–36: A Commentary*. Translated by John J. Scullion. Minneapolis: Augsburg, 1985.

———. "Structure and Intention of the Book of Ruth." *Word and World* 19.3 (1999) 285–302.
Wharton, James A. "The Secret of Yahweh: Story and Affirmation in Judges 13–16." *Interpretation* 27.1 (1973) 48–66.
White, Kayla A. "Deconstructing Barrenness in the Texts of the Ancient Near East: A Re-Reading of the Sarah-Hagar Narrative." MA thesis, Denver Seminary, 2014.
Wilcox, John T. *The Bitterness of Job: A Philosophical Reading*. Ann Arbor: University of Michigan Press, 1989.
Wildavsky, Aaron. "Survival Must Not Be Gained Through Sin: The Moral of the Joseph Stories Prefigured Through Judah and Tamar." *JSOT* 19.62 (1994) 37–48.
Wiley, Henrietta L. "They Save Themselves Alone: Faith and Loss in the Stories of Abraham and Job." *JSOT* 34.2 (2009) 115–29.
Williams, James G. "The Beautiful and the Barren: Conventions in Biblical Type-Scenes." *JSOT* 5.17 (1980) 107–19.
Williams, Jennifer Johnson. "Contracts and Care of Oneself in the Book of Ruth." *Horizons in Biblical Theology* 42 (2020) 14–46.
Willis, John T. "Cultic Elements in the Story of Samuel's Birth and Dedication." *Studia Theologica—Nordic Journal of Theology* 26.1 (1972) 33–61.
Willis, Timothy. "Barren, Barrenness." In *The New Interpreter's Dictionary of the Bible*, edited by Katharine Doob Sakenfeld, 1:400–401. Nashville: Abingdon, 2006.
Wilson, Eleanor Amico. *Women of Canaan: The Status of Women at Ugarit*. Whitewater, WI: Heartwell, 2013.
Wilson, Lindsay. *Job*. Two Horizons Old Testament Commentary. Grand Rapids, MI: Eerdmans, 2015.
Winitzer, Abraham. "Etana." In *Encyclopedia of the Bible and Its Reception*, 8:57–59. Berlin: De Gruyter, 2014.
———. "Etana in Eden: New Light on the Mesopotamian and Biblical Tales in Their Semitic Context." *Journal of the American Oriental Society* 133.3 (2013) 441–65.
Winslow, Karen Strand. *1 and 2 Kings: A Commentary in the Wesleyan Tradition*. New Beacon Bible Commentary. Kansas City, MO: Beacon Hill, 2017.
Winter, Urs. *Frau und Göttin: Exegetische und Ikonographische Studien zum Weiblichen Gottesbild im Alten Israel und in Dessen Umwelt*. Göttingen: Vandenhoeck & Ruprecht, 1983.
Wolowelsky, Joel B. "Rachel, a Mother of Israel." *Jewish Bible Quarterly* 43.1 (2015) 7–16.
Wray Beal, Lissa M. *1 and 2 Kings*. Apollos Old Testament Commentary 9. Downers Grove, IL: InterVarsity, 2014.
Wright, David P. *Ritual in Narrative: The Dynamics of Feasting, Mourning, and Retaliation Rites in the Ugaritic Tale of Aqhat*. Winona Lake, IN: Eisenbrauns, 2001.
Wright, G. R. H. "The Positioning of Genesis 38." *ZAW* 94.4 (1982) 523–29.
Würthwein, Ernst. *Die Bücher der Könige*. Vol. 2. Das Alte Testament Deutsch: Neues Göttinger Bibelwerk 11.2. Göttingen: Vandenhoeck & Ruprecht, 1984.
———. *Die Fünf Megilloth: Ruth, das Hohelied, Esther*. 2nd ed. Handbuch zum Alten Testament 18. Tübingen: J.C.B. Mohr, 1969.
Wyatt, N. "Epic in Ugaritic Literature." In *A Companion to Ancient Epic*, edited by John Miles Foley, 246–54. Malden, MA: Blackwell, 2005.
———. *Religious Texts from Ugarit*. 2nd edition. Biblical Seminar 53. Sheffield: Sheffield Academic, 2002.

———, ed. "The Story of Aqhat." In *Religious Texts from Ugarit*, 2nd ed., 246–312. Sheffield: Sheffield Academic, 2002.

———, ed. "The Story of King Keret." In *Religious Texts from Ugarit*, 2nd ed., 176–241. Sheffield: Sheffield Academic, 2002.

———. "Word of Tree and Whisper of Stone: El's Oracle to King Keret (Kirta), and the Problem of the Mechanics of Its Utterance." *VT* 57.4 (2007) 483–510.

Xella, Paolo. "L'episode de Dnil et Kothar (KTU 1. 17 [= CTA 17] V 1–31) et Gen. XVIII 1–16." *VT* 28.4 (1978) 483–88.

Yafeh-Deigh, Alice. "Children, Motherhood, and the Social Death of Childless Women: The Social and Theological Construction of Infertility in the Hebrew Bible and in Cameroon." *BibInt* 28.5 (2020) 608–34.

Yannai, Yigal. "Elisha and the Shunammite (II Kings 4:8–37): A Case of Homoeoteleuton, or a Text Emendation by Ancient Masoretes?" In *Estudios Masoréticos: V Congreso de La IOMS: Dedicados a Harry M. Orlinsky*, edited by Emilia Fernández Tejero, 123–35. Textos y Estudios "Cardenal Cisneros" 33. Madrid: Arias Montano, 1983.

Yaron, Reuven. *The Laws of Eshnunna*. 2nd ed. Jerusalem: Magnes, 1988.

Yee, Gale A. "Ruth." In *Fortress Commentary on the Bible: The Old Testament and Apocrypha*, edited by Gale A. Yee et al., 351–60. Minneapolis: Fortress, 2014.

Yon, Marguerite. "Women's Daily Lives in Late Bronze Age Ugarit (2nd Millennium BCE)." In *Women in Antiquity: Real Women Across the Ancient World*, edited by Stephanie Lynn Budin and Jean MacIntosh Turfa, 453–64. New York: Routledge, 2016.

You, Cheryl. "The Historian's Heroines: Examining the Characterization of Female Role Models in the Early Israelite Monarchy." *Journal of Biblical Perspectives in Leadership* 9.1 (2019) 178–200.

Zakovitch, Yair. *Das Buch Rut: Ein Jüdischer Kommentar*. Stuttgarter Bibelstudien 177. Stuttgart: Verlag Katholisches Bibelwerk, 1999.

———. *The Life of Samson (Judges 13–16): A Critical-Literary Analysis*/חיי שמשון (שופטים יג-טז) : ניתוח ספרותי-ביקורתי). Jerusalem: Magnes, 1982.

———. "The Strange Biography of Samson." *Scandinavian Jewish Studies* 24.1–2 (2003) 19–36.

———. "The Woman in Biblical Narrative: An Outline." *Beit Mikra* 32 (1987) 14–32.

Zenger, Erich. "Das Buch Rut." In *Einleitung in das Alte Testament*, edited by Erich Zenger, 7th ed., 222–29. Studienbücher Theologie 1.1. Stuttgart: W. Kohlhammer, 2008.

———. *Das Buch Ruth*. Zürcher Bibelkommentare: Altes Testament 8. Zürich: Theologischer Verlag, 1986.

Zevit, Ziony. "Dating Ruth: Legal, Linguistic and Historical Observations." *ZAW* 117.4 (2005) 574–600.

———. *The Religions of Ancient Israel: A Synthesis of Parallactic Approaches*. London: Continuum, 2001.

Zhakevich, Iosif J. "An Apparent Contradiction in Targum Pseudo-Jonathan Genesis 25:20–26: Was Rebekah Barren for Twenty or Twenty-Two Years?" *Aramaic Studies* 16.1 (2018) 42–63.

———. "Converse Translation in Targum Pseudo-Jonathan Genesis 19.33: Did Lot Really Not Know That His Older Daughter Lay with Him?" *Aramaic Studies* 14.2 (2016) 184–211.

Zorn, Jeffrey R. "Estimating the Population Size of Ancient Settlements: Methods, Problems, Solutions, and a Case Study." *Bulletin of the American Schools of Oriental Research* 295 (1994) 31–48.

Zornberg, Avivah Gottlieb. *The Murmuring Deep: Reflections on the Biblical Unconscious.* New York: Schocken, 2009.

Zucker, David J. "Isaac: A Life of Bitter Laughter." *Jewish Bible Quarterly* 40.2 (2012) 105–10.

———. "Romanticizing Samson's Mother." *Women in Judaism* 15.2 (2018) 1–19.

Zucker, David J., and Moshe Reiss. "Righting and Rewriting Genesis 38: Tamar and Judah in the Pseudepigrapha." *Biblical Theology Bulletin* 45.4 (2015) 195–201.

SCRIPTURE INDEX

Genesis

	8
2–3	109n19
2	6
2:24	64n40, 72
4	118n57
7:7	137
12–50	142n35
12:1–3	88n132
13:1–13	137
15–21	105
15–17	108–9
16	143
16:2	98n13, 147
16:15	116
17:16	85
17:17	108
17:18–20	2
18	4, 7, 11, 15, 38, 104, 105n4, 107, 162, 121n70, 133
18:1–15	105n3, 112
18:9–15	109
18:12	108
18:13	111n27
18:14	121n70
19	11, 15, 36
19:12–15	38
19:14	107n9
19:17	38
19:20–23	40
19:26	38
19:30–31	40
19:30	38, 108n13
19:31	37
19:33	37
19:35	37
19:37–38	37
20:17–18	2
20:18	98n13
21	108, 112
21:1–7	137
21:1	108
21:3	116
21:10	147
21:21	137
22	125n85
24	7
24:28	62n34
24:60	85, 141
24:67	112
25	7, 11, 15, 104, 133
25:20–21	113
25:21–24	112
25:21	2, 128n96
25:23	115
25:25–26	116
25:26	113
25:28	114
27	114
27:46	137
28	5–6
29	6
29:23–24	117
29:30	118n55
29:31–30:22	5
29:31–35	116n47
29:31	2, 116–17, 119, 120n68
29:32–35	116
29:32–33	118

Genesis (continued)

29:32–33	39
29:35	118–19
30	4, 7, 11, 15, 104, 118, 120n66, 125, 133, 143
30:1–24	115
30:1–2	116, 147
30:1	2
30:2	98n13, 117
30:6	117–18, 120
30:8	39, 115n46, 117, 120
30:17–18	118
30:18	39
30:20	118
30:22–24	118
30:22–23	7
30:22	116, 119–20, 120n68
30:23	117, 120
31	72n78
31:1–55	137
35:18	39
38	11, 15, 36, 55n8
38:7	42–43
38:9	44
38:10	42–43
38:11	42–43
38:12–13	44
38:14–15	42
38:17	44
38:24–26	43
38:26	45
46:12	43
48	90
48:12	89

Exodus

20:5–6	2
22	138n12
22:28	94n6
23:26	2
34:10–17	137n9

Leviticus

18–20	41n24
18:15	46n52
20:11	45n48
20:12	46n52
24:15	94n6
25	81n104
25:25	82
26:9	2

Numbers

16:27	48
16:32	48
27	11, 15, 36, 48–49, 51n70, 89
27:3	47, 52
27:4	3n11, 49
27:7–8	49
27:7	3n11, 52
27:8	50
27:9–10	49
36	3, 47, 51n70, 67, 138
36:5–9	50
36:6	49
36:11–12	51

Deuteronomy

4:40	2
5:29	2
7:1–5	137n9
7:14	2, 143
21:15–17	82
22	138n12
23:4–5	72n78
25:5–10	3n11, 43n36, 82
27:20–23	41n24
28:11	2
28:65	75

Joshua

17	51n70
18	126n88
19	126n88
23:12	137n9

Judges

	55n8, 59n16
6	121n70
13–16	121n70
13	4, 11, 15, 104, 125, 133

13:2–7	124n82	1:12–14	128
13:2–3	2, 122	1:14	129
13:2	121	1:17	129
13:3	123	1:19–20	126
13:7	123	1:19	7, 127, 129
13:8–9	123	1:20	129
13:9	122n74	2:5	2
13:13–14	123		
13:18	121n70		
13:22–23	124	## 2 Samuel	
13:24	123–24		8
14	137	7	126n88
21	137n9	12:11–18	2
		12:23	149n61
		18:18	65n44

Ruth

1	148n59
1:6	148n59
1:20–21	149n61
2	148n59
2:20	149n61
3	148n59
4	43n36
4:1–12	148n59
4:3	49
4:11–12	138
4:12	41–42
4:13	148n59
4:15	22n23
4:27	149n61

1 Kings

	162n42
6	126n88
13:6	149n61

2 Kings

	157n12
4:8–17	155
4:8	157
4:14–16	156
4:14	157
4:17	158
4:18–37	156
4:28	157
8	89
8:1–6	156
17:9–11	151

1 Samuel

	8
1	4, 7, 11, 15, 104, 116n47, 125, 127, 133, 143, 143n37, 143n40, 147
1:2	157
1:3	150
1:5–6	126
1:5	126n89, 157
1:6	127
1:6–8	125
1:8	127, 150
1:9	150
1:10–12	128
1:10–11	126
1:11	7, 126–27, 128n98, 129

Ezra-Nehemiah

53, 53n1, 55, 66n50

Ezra

9:2	137n9

Job

11–13, 15–16, 18, 29–30, 34, 36, 49, 52, 61, 69n63, 135–36, 148, 149n61, 149n62, 159n22

Job (continued)

1:1	26
1:4–5	151
1:8	26
19:25	149n61
42:8	151
42:15	49

Psalms

41:10[9]	72n78
45:10	78n98
113:9	2
115:14	2
127:3–5	2

Proverbs

2:16	71
5:20	71n74
6:24	71n74
6:26	71n74
7:5	71n74
31	59

Song of Songs

	59

Isaiah

34:14	75

Jeremiah

1:6	115n44

Lamentations

1:3	75

Hosea

9:11	98n13

Amos

8:10	65n44

SUBJECT INDEX

Abraham, 8, 38n8, 55n6, 72n76, 88n132, 105–6, 106n6, 106n7, 107–8, 109–10, 110n23, 111, 111n28, 111n29, 112, 114, 114n42, 116, 121n70, 125n85, 141n27, 142–43, 147, 160–61, 160n30, 163, 163n45
Anat, 8, 24–26, 27n46
Angel, 4, 6, 31, 36–38, 40, 105–7, 106n7, 114, 121–24, 121n70, 121n71, 122n73, 122n74, 122n75, 123n80, 125n85, 158
Athirat, 21

Bilhah, 104n1, 116, 119–20, 120n66, 120n67, 143

Chilion, 55n8, 60, 60n25, 61n28, 65n44, 83n111
Cult(ic), 16, 20n16, 23, 27, 31n63, 42n30, 46n51, 52, 131, 149–53, 151n65, 151n68, 152n69, 152n71, 153n75

Danatay, 29, 30n57
Danel, 3–4, 23–25, 23n30, 24n32, 24n35, 27–29, 29n56, 30n57, 163n45
Daughter(s), 2–3, 3n11, 9, 11–12, 15, 19, 22, 25, 27–30, 32, 36–37, 37n3, 37n4, 38–41, 39n12, 40n18, 40n19, 41n24, 43–44, 43n35, 45–47, 46n53, 48–49, 48n61, 48n62, 50–52, 51n70, 53–54, 55n6, 57–58, 59, 62–65, 62n34, 63n36, 64n42, 67–68, 71, 74–75, 78, 78n98, 84n115, 88–89, 91n143, 92, 93n2, 94, 102, 102n26, 117n54, 135, 138–40, 138n10, 140n22, 141n29, 164
Descendants, 83–84, 86, 87, 87n128, 88n132, 94, 96, 100–2, 137
Dream, 4, 15, 20n16, 104, 132, 133, 135–36, 146

Eagle, 130, 130n107, 130n109, 131–32, 131n112
El, 4, 8, 14, 18–26, 20n13, 151
Eli, 126, 126n88, 128–29, 128n97, 128n100
Elimelech, 49, 53–54, 55n6, 59–60, 59n16, 61n26, 62, 63n36, 69–70, 74n83, 77n95, 78, 80, 81–82, 81n108, 83, 83n111, 85, 87, 87n127, 88–90, 90n140
Elite, 142n35, 143n37, 152n69
Elkanah, 125–29, 125n87, 127n91, 127n93, 127n95, 128n96, 128n100, 129n103, 143, 147, 150

Father(s), 3, 3n11, 5, 9, 25, 27, 28–30, 31, 37, 37n3, 37n4, 38–41, 39n12, 41n24, 42n28, 43, 45n48, 46, 47, 49–52, 50n65, 54, 55n6, 57–58, 59, 62, 62n34, 63n36, 67, 71, 73, 75, 79, 89, 94, 96–97, 101, 103, 111n25, 121, 136–41, 137n8, 138n10, 139n20, 149, 152n73, 158n17

227

SUBJECT INDEX

Fertility/Infertility, 2n8, 4, 8, 10–12, 16, 17–18, 24n33, 38–39, 41, 45–47, 50–51, 52, 53–54, 56–57, 56n10, 59, 60n25, 62n29, 64–65, 64n42, 65n43, 80–91, 97–98, 102, 102n26, 108, 112, 116, 116n50, 117, 117n54, 118n56, 119–120, 119n60, 119n61, 120n66, 122–23, 124, 127, 127n94, 130, 131, 132, 132n118, 141, 141n27, 142n34, 143, 143n36, 143n37, 144n41, 146–47, 146n56, 152–53, 153n74, 153n75, 154, 155, 160–61, 160n31, 162, 164

Foreign(er/ness), 12, 53–54, 58, 61n27, 61n28, 66n50, 69n65, 71–72, 71n73, 73n79, 74n85, 78, 88, 91–92, 164

Gender, 16, 18, 24n33, 29n56, 63n35, 67, 72n78, 85n117, 135, 138n10, 149–50

Genealogy, 42, 55n8, 81, 90, 90n140, 130n110, 137, 137n9

Generation, 3n11, 4, 47–51, 51n70, 74n83, 87, 89–90, 96, 102, 116–17, 136–37

Genre, 10, 12–14, 15, 17, 30n60, 35

Hagar, 7–8, 8n28, 104n1, 108, 142n30, 143, 147

House(hold), 1, 3–4, 5, 11, 15, 17, 20–22, 23n27, 27–29, 33–34, 36, 41–43, 42n28, 45–47, 50–52, 53–54, 55n8, 56–65, 59n16, 61n26, 62n31, 62n34, 63n36, 66–82, 69n64, 70n67, 74n83, 77n97, 84–92, 87n128, 93–103, 98n13, 99n18, 104, 106n6, 108, 110n23, 119n63, 126n88, 127–28, 136–42, 136n5, 138n11, 139n19, 142n35, 143n37, 145, 147–49, 151, 153, 153n75, 155, 161–62, 163n45

Hurriy, 18–19, 22, 30n57

Husband(s), 3n11, 5, 8–9, 15–16, 29, 30n57, 40, 45–46, 48, 50–51, 55n6, 57–58, 59–65, 61n26, 62n29, 63n36, 64n39, 64n42, 67–70, 74–76, 74n83, 74n86, 80–82, 83n111, 84, 88, 92, 104, 108, 111, 116n47, 116n50, 119, 122, 122n73, 128n96, 128n100, 129n103, 132n114, 133, 136, 138–41, 138n13, 140n24, 141n27, 141n28, 142–43, 143n36, 143n39, 144–45, 144n43, 144n44, 147, 149–50, 152n73, 153–54, 156–58, 157n12, 158n17

Ilimilku, 18n2, 23n27

Incubation, 18, 18n5, 23–24, 24n32, 152

Isaac, 5–6, 7–8, 105, 105n3, 106n6, 112–13, 112n33, 114, 114n40, 114n42, 115, 116, 125n85, 128n96, 156n3, 160–61

Jacob, 5–6, 8, 42n28, 72n78, 89–90, 112–13, 115n46, 115–16, 116n47, 116n50, 117–18, 117n54, 118n55, 118n56, 119–20, 119n60, 119n62, 143, 146–47

King(ship), 5, 9, 14, 18–19, 19n7, 20n13, 21, 22n23, 22n26, 27–28, 28n49, 30, 33–34, 56n8, 59n16, 85, 91, 94n4, 114–15, 130, 130n110, 131n111, 147, 158n19, 161–62, 161n37, 163–64

Kothar, 24, 26, 29, 30n57

Levirate, 3n11, 12, 42–43, 43n36, 46, 46n52, 48, 53, 55n6, 63n36, 75n91, 80–81, 81n104, 81n107, 82–84, 87, 90n104

Mahlon, 55n6, 55n8, 60, 60n22, 60n25, 61n28, 69–70, 79–80, 81n108, 83n111, 84–85, 87n127, 87n128

Marriage, 2–3, 3n11, 5, 12, 16, 18, 19, 22, 38–40, 42–43, 43n36, 45–46, 47–48, 49–51, 51n70, 53, 55n6, 55n8, 59–60, 60n21, 60n22, 61n27, 61n28, 62n34, 63, 63n36, 64–65, 64n39, 64n40,

SUBJECT INDEX 229

65n43, 66–67, 68, 70, 72, 74n84,
75–77, 75n91, 76n94, 77n95,
79–81, 19n100, 81n104, 82–85,
84n115, 86n121, 87–88, 87n126,
87n128, 91, 92, 108, 113, 117n54,
120n67, 127n91, 134, 136–41,
137n9, 138n11, 138n12, 138n13,
139n19, 139n20, 140n22,
140n24, 142n35, 143n39, 144–
45, 144n43, 145n46, 145n51,
145n53, 146–47, 146n55, 148,
153, 152n73, 160–62, 161n36
Matriarch, 9, 66n51, 87, 105n2, 142,
152n72
Matrilineage, 62n34
Meal, 72–73, 72n78, 73n79, 106n7,
111, 111n25, 125–26, 128
Moses, 47–52, 114–15, 138
Mother(s), 5, 6n24, 7, 12, 25, 29, 31,
38–40, 39n12, 41n24, 48, 58–59,
61n26, 62–63, 62n34, 65n45,
67–68, 71, 73, 75–76, 78–80,
83n111, 85, 87n126, 88–90,
90n139, 91n143, 92, 95, 116n50,
118, 118n55, 119n60, 120–21,
120n67, 124, 125n85, 129n103,
137, 139, 140–41, 142n35, 147,
149n61, 152n72, 153n75, 156,
158, 158n17

Name, 3, 3n11, 8, 18n2, 18n3, 21–22,
22n24, 23n27, 29n56, 30n57,
30n61, 37–39, 46, 46n51,
48–51, 50n65, 55n6, 59, 59n16,
60n25, 62, 64, 67–69, 69n63, 76,
79–81, 83–89, 87n127, 87n128,
89n133, 91n143, 92, 95–96, 100,
102n26, 103, 110–11, 110n23,
116, 116n47, 120–22, 120n67,
121n69, 121n70, 128n100, 130,
132, 137, 152, 155–58, 158n17,
159–60, 160n26, 160n28, 160n30
Nazirite, 121–22, 122n72, 122n73,
129n103

Obed, 5, 54, 77n95, 80, 87,
88–89, 90n138, 90n139, 90n140,
91n141, 149n61

Pabil, 18, 19n6, 22
Patriarch, 3, 5, 8, 14n40, 28, 37, 40,
48, 48n61, 55n6, 61n26, 62n34,
64n39, 72n76, 84, 116, 137, 142,
142n35, 143n37, 148
Patrilineage, 51, 87, 137
Peninnah, 8, 125–27, 125n87, 127n91,
127n93, 143
Polycoity, 143n39, 145n46
Polygamy, 146n55
Polygyny, 143n36, 143n38, 143n39,
145n46
Priest, 23n27, 47, 126, 128n100, 140,
150, 152, 152n71
Priestess, 46n51, 139n19, 150, 152n71
Progeny, 1–4, 1n3, 16, 22n22, 42,
42n30, 45, 50–51, 53, 59,
59n19, 64, 75, 84–85, 87n128,
90, 90n140, 91, 94–95, 96, 98,
101–3, 109, 112
Promise, 7, 14, 22, 23–24, 24n33,
44–45, 47–48, 51n70, 65–68,
69n65, 73, 84, 88n132, 90n140,
92, 105–10, 106n6, 106n7, 112,
121n70, 124, 128, 131, 132–33,
152n72, 156–57
Prophecy/Prophetic, 12n33, 114n42,
115n44, 132–33, 135–36, 146,
152, 158
Prophet, 114–15, 125n85, 152, 157,
158n19
Pughat, 25, 27n46, 28–29, 29n56

Rabbi/Rabbinics, 84, 109n17, 109n18,
111n27, 118n55, 122n73
Religion/Religious, 19, 68, 72, 134,
150–53, 151n65, 152n69,
152n71, 152n73, 153n74, 153n75
Royalty, 8, 14, 14n40, 24n34, 27,
34–35, 56n8, 59n17, 142n35,
143n37, 163n45

Sacrifice, 3, 18, 84, 94, 94n5, 94n6,
122, 122n74, 127–28, 128n100,
131, 151, 151n68, 153, 156n3,
159–60
Samuel, 7, 91n141, 125n85, 126, 129,
129n102, 129n103

SUBJECT INDEX

Samson, 91n141, 121–22, 121n70, 122n73, 124, 124n82, 125n85
Shamash, 8, 33, 131–32, 133
Shame, 81n104, 147
Snake, 130n107, 130n109, 131, 163
Son(s), 3–4, 3n12, 6n24, 8, 11, 18–19, 22, 22n23, 23–25, 24n32, 27–29, 27n46, 32–34, 38–39, 38n8, 42–46, 42n28, 48–49, 51, 51n70, 54, 55n6, 55n8, 56–58, 59–64, 59n19, 60n21, 60n22, 60n25, 61n26, 64n39, 64n42, 67–69, 69n63, 74n83, 74n86, 75, 80, 81n108, 83n111, 84–91, 87n126, 88n130, 89n133, 89n137, 90n139, 90n140, 91n141, 91n142, 91n143, 92, 93n2, 94, 96–97, 102, 106–110, 106n7, 107n9, 112, 115–18, 117n53, 120, 120n67, 121–24, 121n70, 125n85, 126, 127–29, 127n91, 128n96, 130–31, 130n110, 132n114, 137–39, 137n8, 141n29, 142, 144n43, 146–47, 150, 156–58, 158n17, 160, 160n28, 163–64
Stranger, 71n73, 72n76, 73n79, 79n101, 107, 110, 110n23
Sun God, 159–61, 160n26

Targum, 37n3, 61n27, 109n18, 109n19, 113
Temple, 7, 23n27, 125–26, 126n88, 126n90, 128n100, 129n102, 149–51, 160n26
Trauma/Traumatic, 40, 40n20, 116n50

Trinity, 105, 106n6
Type-scene, 4–9, 10, 34–35, 36, 73n79, 115n46, 117n53, 121n70, 125n86, 156–57, 157n9, 157n12

Usufruct, 82, 83n111

Vow, 20n16, 21, 55n8, 121–22, 122n73, 128–29, 129n102, 129n103, 138

Widow, 3n11, 42, 44, 46, 49, 54, 55n6, 60n23, 68, 81–84, 81n104, 83n111, 86, 87n127, 88–89
Wife/Wives, 4, 5–6, 6n22, 6n23, 7n25, 8–9, 8n28, 11, 14–15, 19–20, 20n13, 22, 29, 30n57, 31, 37–38, 42, 48, 61n26, 61n27, 62, 74n83, 75, 77n97, 82–83, 81n108, 84, 87n128, 104, 107–8, 110–11, 110n22, 110n23, 112, 115n46, 116, 116n47, 116n50, 118, 118n56, 119n62, 121n70, 122, 123, 123n80, 124n82, 125, 125n86, 125n87, 126, 127n95, 129, 132, 132n114, 132n116, 133, 135–36, 137–38, 137n8, 140–41, 142–43, 142n34, 142n35, 143n36, 143n37, 143n39, 144–46, 144n43, 144n44, 145n46, 146–47, 145n53, 148–49, 150, 152, 154, 158, 159–61, 160n31, 160n33, 162n40, 163
Yasib, 11, 19, 21, 21n20
Yatipan, 25, 28

Zilpah, 104n1, 120n67, 143

www.ingramcontent.com/pod-product-compliance
Lightning Source LLC
Chambersburg PA
CBHW062017220426
43662CB00010B/1373